An Introduction to
International Investment Law

David Collins
City University London

CAMBRIDGE
UNIVERSITY PRESS

CAMBRIDGE
UNIVERSITY PRESS

One Liberty Plaza, 20th Floor, New York, NY 10006, USA

Cambridge University Press is part of the University of Cambridge.

It furthers the University's mission by disseminating knowledge in the pursuit of education, learning, and research at the highest international levels of excellence.

www.cambridge.org
Information on this title: www.cambridge.org/9781107160453

© David Collins 2017

First published 2017

Printed in the United States of America by Sheridan Books, Inc.

A catalogue record for this publication is available from the British Library.

ISBN 978-1-107-16045-3 Hardback
ISBN 978-1-316-61357-3 Paperback

An Introduction to
International Investment Law

This insightful and accessible introduction provides students and
practitioners with a comprehensive overview of the increasingly
important discipline of international investment law. Focusing
primarily on the legal principles contained in the growing body of
international investment agreements, this book covers the core
concepts of the discipline, with attention given to their relation to
each other and to the manner in which they have been developed
through arbitration case law. The context of each legal principle is
explored, along with a consideration of some of the major debates
and emerging criticisms. Avoiding extensive case extracts, this book
adopts an engaging and succinct narrative style which allows readers
to advance their understanding of the topic while examining the
legal principles with academic rigour and discerning commentary.

David Collins is a Professor of International Economic Law at City
University London where he teaches and researches in the fields of
world trade and international investment law. He has authored
numerous books and articles and his research has attracted funding
from sources such as the British Academy and the Society of Legal
Scholars. David has lectured around the world and has been a
visiting fellow at several institutions including Georgetown
University, Columbia University and the Max Planck Institute in
Heidelberg. David is a Solicitor (England and Wales) and is admitted
to the Bars of Ontario, Canada and New York State.

Contents

Table of Cases

International Courts and Tribunals

Ad hoc tribunals

American Arbitration Association (AAA)

Arbitration Institute of the Stockholm Chamber of Commerce (SCC)

The International Centre for the Settlement of Investment Disputes (ICSID)

(Award unless otherwise stated.)

International Court of Justice (ICJ)

Iran–United States Claims Tribunal

London Court of International Arbitration (LCIA)

North American Free Trade Agreement (NAFTA)

Permanent Court of Arbitration (PCA)

Permanent Court of International Justice (PCIJ)

Southern African Development Community (SADC)

United Nations Commission on International Trade Law (UNCITRAL)

National Courts

Australia

Canada

United Kingdom

United States of America

Abbreviations

ACIA	ASEAN Comprehensive Investment Agreement
AIIB	Asian Infrastructure Investment Bank
ASEAN	Association of South East Asian Nations
BIT	Bilateral Investment Treaty
BOT	Build Operate and Transfer
BRIC	Brazil, Russia, India, China
BRICS	Brazil, Russia, India, China, South Africa
CAFTA	Central American Free Trade Agreement
CETA	Comprehensive Economic and Trade Agreement
CFIUS	Committee on Foreign Investment in the United States
COMESA	Common Market for Eastern and Southern Africa
CSR	Corporate Social Responsibility
ECOWAS	Economic Community of West African States
ECT	Energy Charter Treaty
GATS	General Agreement on Trade in Services
GATT	General Agreement on Tariffs and Trade
FCN	Friendship, Commerce and Navigation
FDA	Food and Drug Administration
FDI	Foreign Direct Investment
FET	Fair and Equitable Treatment
FPS	Full Protection and Security Standard
FTA	Free Trade Agreement
NGO	Non-Governmental Organization
ICC	International Chamber of Commerce
ICJ	International Court of Justice
ICSID	International Centre for the Settlement of Investment Disputes
IFC	International Finance Corporation
IFSWF	International Forum of Sovereign Wealth Funds
IIA	International Investment Agreements
IMF	International Monetary Fund

IP	Intellectual Property
LCIA	London Court of International Arbitration
MAI	Multilateral Agreement on Investment
MFN	Most Favoured Nation
MIGA	Multilateral Investment Guarantee Agency
NAFTA	North American Free Trade Agreement
NATO	North Atlantic Treaty Organization
NDB	New Development Bank
NIEO	New International Economic Order
OECD	Organization for Economic Cooperation and Development
OPIC	Overseas Private Investment Corporation
PCA	Permanent Court of Arbitration
PCIJ	Permanent Court of International Justice
PRI	Political Risk Insurance
PSNR	Permanent Sovereignty over Natural Resources
RTA	Regional Trade Agreements
SOEs	State-Owned Enterprises
TiSA	Trade in Services Agreement
TPP	Trans Pacific Partnership
TRIMS	Trade-Related Investment Measures
TRIPS	Trade-Related Aspects of Intellectual Property
TTIP	Transatlantic Trade and Investment Partnership
UN	United Nations
UNCITRAL	United Nations Commission on International Trade Law
UNCTAD	United Nations Conference on Trade and Development
UNESCO	United Nations Educational, Scientific and Cultural Organization
VCLT	Vienna Convention on the Law of Treaties
WTO	World Trade Organization

Introduction to Foreign Direct Investment: 1
History, Trends and Rationales

....

1.1 International Investment Law

International investment law is best described as a field of public international law which deals with the laws governing the commercial activities of multinational enterprises that are undertaken in foreign states. This occurs when a business or firm decides to open a branch of operations overseas, such as a factory or a mine, and in so doing it may come into conflict with that host state's laws. These may control the nature or extent of the economic activities the firm is allowed to pursue, such as licensing requirements, labour or environmental standards. While this situation may appear to be a matter for resolution by application of domestic laws of the host state through its courts, increasingly recourse is given to international law and international tribunals for answers. International investment law is a species of public international law in the sense that it comprises legal commitments made by sovereign states at the international level as captured by the international investment agreements. While often overlooked, it also has private law elements because the rights (and to a lesser extent obligations) of firms are in some cases formulated by investment contracts between firms and the states in which they operate. In this latter sense, international investment law can be viewed as a field of transnational contract law, governed both by domestic legal systems and the rules of international law.

The law of foreign investment is one of the oldest branches of international law. But it remained relatively undeveloped until the latter part of the twentieth century, growing in-step with globalization, meaning the intense interrelation of markets as well as the mobility of people and capital around the world. Prior to the 1990s there were few treaties governing international investment and the resolution of disputes between investors and host states was mostly informal, consisting for the most part of diplomatic pressure, often backed up by the threat of force. Yet within a relatively short period of time this area of law witnessed a phenomenal growth to become one of the most dynamic and intensively studied spheres of international law. It now comprises many thousands of treaties and highly formalized dispute settlement procedures which have resulted in hundreds of cases brought by expert practitioners and a growing body of specialized jurisprudence. Investor–state arbitration itself has acquired a new status in international law – it has transformed from its origins as a rather obscure, private dispute settlement mechanism to a high-profile forum for the resolution of complex claims. It often has a significant public dimension because of the legal consequences of regulations pursued in the interest of society at large. International investment law has far-reaching implications with respect to both international commerce as well as fundamental issues of sovereignty and by extension the constitutional role of states – essentially the way in which a country governs itself.

The remarkable growth of international investment law as a semi-autonomous discipline within international law is largely the consequence of foreign investment's importance both to the highly mobile firms which engage in it and the growth-focused states which seek to attract it. Just as many companies rely on an international presence in order to sustain and enlarge profits, so many countries depend on foreign capital in order to develop and achieve economic prosperity. Yet there is now widespread concern that the rapid pace of change in the global economy, including the fervid ascendance of the emerging markets, the role of State-Owned Enterprises (SOEs) pursuing non-traditional strategies, highly interconnected financial markets and the dominance of supply chain manufacturing has transformed the way governments interact with foreign investors. There is justifiable concern that the encroachment of states on the commercial activities of multinational enterprises has not been properly managed, in that it is at times excessive and undisciplined while at other times it is merely the manifestation of government's right to regulate its own economic affairs. Likewise, it is often suggested that many of the decisions of international tribunals have gone too far in interpreting the protective provisions of treaties in favour of investors, undermining the legitimate sovereign rights of host states, for example by construing environmental regulations as a form of expropriation, effectively taking private property that does not belong to it.[1] On the other hand, some feel that strong

---

[1] See e.g. D. Schneiderman, *Constitutionalizing Economic Globalization* (Cambridge University Press, 2008).

protection for the foreign firms which have risked exposing their assets to the whims of unstable governments is essential to stimulate the flow of badly needed capital to poorer nations. These issues will be explored in greater detail throughout this book.

1.2 Foreign Direct Investment

International investment law primarily covers the international laws which control Foreign Direct Investment (FDI). The phrase 'direct' investment is important because this is meant to exclude investment activities for which the extra-territorial component of the enterprise is too small for it to genuinely be considered foreign, although such forms of investment may also be contemplated by some treaties in this field. Put another way, direct investment means that the foreign firm has a sufficient stake in the firm that it exercises meaningful management or control. This is normally thought to be at least 10 per cent of the voting shares in the firm.[2] Below 10 per cent ownership would normally qualify the investment as 'portfolio investment'. Portfolio investment refers to investments that lack direct personal management, such as when ordinary people purchase stocks and shares in large public corporations. The inclusion of portfolio investment into the understanding of 'investment' for the purposes of international investment law has the potential to bring various entities within the ambit of protection available under an investment treaty that may not necessarily deserve special protection under international law, because such individuals are not exposed to the same level of risk as genuine managers of foreign firms. Moreover, such entities do not provide the same advantages of foreign capital to host states that are associated with the truly multinational firm. Still, as will be explained in Chapter 3, a number of investment treaties have extended their coverage to indirect forms of investment.

While the direct component of FDI is reasonably straightforward, the definition of 'investment' itself remains controversial. It is undefined in some treaties, or expressed in a purposefully open manner, leaving arbitration tribunals the task of interpreting the concept on a case-by-case

---

[2] *IMF Glossary of Selected Financial Terms and Definitions*, 31 Oct 2006, www.imf.org/ external/np/exr/glossary/showTerm.asp#117.

basis. Perhaps more controversially, this affords tribunals the latitude to consider various commercial ventures as deserving of protection where this is arguably unjustified for the reasons noted above. Establishing a definition for 'investment' and 'investor' will be explored more fully in Chapter 3, but for now it is useful to observe that most investment treaties define the term 'investor' to include all sorts of commercial entities including SOEs, foreign nationals or a private enterprise of a foreign state that has engaged in commercial activity in the territory of another state.

For now it should be noted that the trend in modern investment treaties is to define the terms 'investor' and 'investment' broadly, with indicative rather than definitive lists of investors and investment. In order to encompass as many forms of commercial activity as possible, many treaties provide that the term 'investment' includes 'every kind of asset' and supply a non-exhaustive list of specific forms of investment, such as the equally expansive 'property, rights and interests of every nature'. For example, the US Model Investment Treaty of 2012 states that investment means: 'every asset that has the characteristic of an investment, including such characteristics as the commitment of capital or other resources, the expectation of gain or profit, or the assumption of risk', followed by a non-exhaustive enumerated list of various types of investment.[3] This is obviously very wide, covering effectively all varieties of commercial activity by foreigners in host states. Clearly this wide definition is of value to a capital-exporting state such as the USA because it protects as many varieties of businesses as possible.

Still, not every kind of commercial venture will amount to an investment and therefore attract the protections of international investment law, including most importantly, the protections enshrined in treaties. One of the ways in which 'investment' has been established by arbitration tribunals, at least for the purposes of establishing jurisdiction under the International Centre for the Settlement of Investment Disputes (ICSID) Convention, is known as the *Salini* Test, taken from the *Salini* v. *Morocco*[4] dispute. There remains a lively debate as to whether the *Salini* Test should be followed even in the context of ICSID disputes because it is seen by some to expand ICSID's jurisdiction beyond what is granted in that organization's founding documents, and in so doing introduces

---

[3] Art 1.   [4] Decision on Jurisdiction, ICSID Case No. ARB/00/4 (23 July 2001).

a significant degree of uncertainty into international investment.[5] Some of these issues will be explored later in Chapter 3. For the time being it is important to mention that the *Salini* Test states that to be an investment, the activity in question must: (1) involve the transfer of funds or the contribution of money or assets; (2) be of a certain duration; (3) have the participation of the individual transferring the funds in the management and risks associated with the project; and finally (4) bring economic contribution to the host state. Of these, the requirement of certain duration is perhaps the hardest criterion to satisfy. To be an investor, one must have a lasting relationship with the host state, although whether that means a few months or a few years is unclear. More certainly this means that a single transaction, such as a one-off contract, does not count.[6] The final component of the test, the obligation to contribute to the host state's development, has been rejected by some tribunals in part because it is simply too ambiguous to constitute an enforceable legal obligation.[7] The lack of this final component is problematic however, given the obligations of investment treaties are placed uniformly on host states rather than investors who enjoy all of the benefits.

While it has less legal relevance, economists often split FDI into two additional categories that help clarify the nature of foreign firms' involvement in the domestic economies of other states: mergers and acquisitions (meaning a foreign company purchasing all or a portion of an existing local company) and greenfield. Greenfield investment means creating an entirely new project or company from nothing – such as an oil field, a mine or a new factory. Host states often have a preference for the second category because it represents an entirely new source of capital, rather than the reorganization of an existing one. Mergers and acquisitions are often associated with the loss of employment as old companies are restructured by foreign managers to become more competitive, sometimes referred to euphemistically as 'synergies' in management speak. The concept of 'investment' will be revisited again throughout this book. The precise definition is often challenged in the context of establishing jurisdiction for the purposes of arbitration.

[5] See e.g. A. Grabowski, 'The Definition of Investment Under the ICSID Convention: A Defense of *Salini*' 15:1 *Chicago Journal of International Law* 287 (2014).
[6] E.g. *Burimi SRL and Eagle Games SH.A v. Republic of Albania*, ICSID Case No. ARB/11/18, Decision on Jurisdiction (29 May 2013).
[7] E.g. *Quiborax v. Bolivia*, ICSID Case No. ARB/06/2, Decision on Jurisdiction (27 Sept 2012).

1.3 Historical Context – Beginnings of Foreign Direct Investment (FDI)

In order to appreciate the content of international investment law as a living discipline and an area of legal practice, it is useful to have an understanding of the origins of foreign investment itself. While FDI levels have reached unprecedented levels in recent years, the presence of commercial entities from one state in the territory of another is not a phenomenon exclusive to the twenty-first or even twentieth century. Foreign investment has occurred throughout history and across the world for many hundreds of years. Indeed, the establishment of foreign investment was one of the chief motivations behind the expansion of the European empires to the four corners of the world in the early pre-modern period. Conscious of a certain historic irony, the forays of modern multinational enterprises into developing states is depicted by some critics as a kind of neo-colonialism, reasserting the historic power imbalances between capital-importing and capital-exporting countries.

One of the earliest known examples of foreign investment in its purest form is that of the Phoenicians, a civilization that flourished from 1500 BC in what is now Israel and Palestine. The Phoenicians traded by ship with the Greeks and established outposts around the Eastern Mediterranean from which they could sell goods from their homeland, such as wood and textiles. It is important to recognize that this type of activity was not simply international trade (an item from one place being sold somewhere else) – the Phoenician outposts are correctly described as a lasting commercial presence in a foreign state. Interestingly, the act of establishing commercial settlements in foreign states on the shores of the Mediterranean Sea also led to the diffusion of the Phoenician alphabet, which is the ancestor of all modern Western alphabets. While this may not have been an intended benefit at the time, this eventuality helps fulfil the requirement of contribution to the economic development of the host state. As will be shown later, the transfer of knowledge is often seen as one of the 'spillover' advantages of FDI.

A few centuries after the Phoenicians, the Silk Road land-based trading routes were established between Europe (then controlled by the Roman Empire), the Middle East and the Pacific Ocean, extending over 6000 km through the deserts, plains and mountains of Asia. This early conduit allowed for the exchange of goods such as fabrics, spices and jewels.

Importantly, these commercial relationships also involved the transfer of language and culture, primarily through trading agents who often established themselves in foreign states for extended periods of time. These were the settlements which became some of the early cities of regions like the Persian Empire such as Samarkand. Recall that a key feature of investment as distinct from trade or other forms of commercial activity is the creation of a long-term relationship – the commitment of resources to an enterprise for the pursuit of profit over a period of time, rather than linked to one particular transaction. Help in the creation of lasting outposts may further be seen as key contributions to the development of foreign lands.

The Silk Road remained a key link between Europe and Asia until the Middle Ages when sea travel came to dominate international investment, as well as international trade. Beginning in the fifteenth century there was extensive trans-oceanic commerce between Europe and China, as well as India, involving exotic commodities like spices and tea. Port cities became the major focus of commercial activity and money was increasingly channelled into the building and maintenance of the ships themselves. The operation of commercial shipping can be viewed as an early form of foreign investment – the sailing vessels were constructed and operated at great expense, and successful missions abroad were fraught with risk both for the crew as well as the owners. The rise of commercial shipping during this period was in tandem with the expansion of ports in the destination countries. As then, the creation of infrastructure in host states remains one of the chief benefits associated with FDI.

1.4 The Colonial Period

During the early modern period (the fifteenth century and onwards) Western European states began to establish permanent colonies in the locations where they had previously visited on trade missions, buildings ports such as Hong Kong and New Amsterdam (later New York). The Dutch East India Company was formed in 1602 in order to carry out commercial activities in Indonesia, particularly in relation to the transportation of spices like pepper. It is quite rightly described as the world's first multinational corporation. Likewise, the Portuguese began establishing colonies in India and Africa, as did the British and French. The latter two states also set up colonies in North America where fur trapping was a lucrative enterprise. Spain and Portugal had also begun settling South and Central America by the mid-seventeenth century, driven in part by the pursuit of gold.

The practice of colonialism as employed by the European powers of the time was rooted in the economic objective of exploiting the abundant resources and in some cases cheap labour available in lesser developed countries through a military and administrative presence. Wealth generated from foreign investment, and trading activities overseas was itself tied to the political goal of land acquisition and expansion of territorial sovereignty of the major European powers as wealth from the colonies, especially gold and silver, enriched the home country which in turn funded greater armies and navies. Much like a good portion of modern FDI is predicated on the application of technology and infrastructure from the industrial world to resource-rich developing states, colonialism was made possible by an imbalance in technology. The European states had expertise in tools like cartography, shipbuilding, navigation and weaponry which translated into extractive capabilities that native peoples in Africa and the Americas did not possess. This paradigm is worth keeping in mind when considering the relationship between signatory parties and modern international investment treaties.

Perhaps more than any other power, the British Empire exemplified the colonialism that contained the seeds of modern international investment. It reached its peak in the nineteenth century and was the largest empire in the history of the world, covering a quarter of the land area of the planet. Multinational enterprises, often enjoying government-granted monopolies, played a significant role in its expansion and dominance, including the British East India Tea Company and Hudson's Bay Company. These organizations were focused on exploiting particular resources in the then-developing world by building and enlarging permanent outposts and infrastructure such as housing, roads and ports. These commercial activities were closely tied to the home state's drive for territorial and geopolitical dominion, and while the legacy of these ventures and their effects on indigenous peoples remains highly dubious, the role that the early multinationals played in the spread of European civilization cannot be denied.

In the very early days of international travel for the purposes of business when Europeans began to go to Asia, Africa and the Americas to set up trading posts with local communities, it was understood that local law, such as it was, could not be applied to these people because they were already subject to the law of their more powerful and more civilized (as they saw it) home country. Viewed by many as the first international jurist, the Dutchman Hugo Grotius supported this position in his seminal writings on international law in the seventeenth century.[8] This concept went on to be enshrined in treaties concluded between the many European states and their colonies, collectively known as Friendship Commerce and Navigation treaties. These early treaties, extensively used by the USA in particular, addressed a wide range of issues including not just investment and trade, but also immigration, taxation and issues which today we now understand as human rights.[9] The idea that early investors carried their own law with them wherever they went normally meant that the foreigner was entitled to better treatment by the local community than a native person would be, where punishments for petty crimes could end in execution, a reflection of the need to maintain order in an environment lacking a permanent military presence. Over time this superior treatment came to be defined by reference to an international minimum standard of protection with which all aliens should be treated, which survives today as a principle of customary international law as a check on the arbitrariness of a state's exercise of its power over individuals. This baseline of legal entitlement grew largely out of the nineteenth-century US experience in Latin America where there had initially been much resistance to the notion that the rights of individuals could come from anywhere other than domestic law.[10] Clearly the presumption behind the international minimum standard of treatment was the often inaccurate view that some countries' legal systems were simply inadequate, at least from the standpoint of the European power.

Since, as suggested above, much early foreign investment was done in the context of colonial expansion by the European powers, these forms of investment did not need protection from interference by troublesome locals through a specialized regime for foreigners because the colonial

---

[8] E.g. H. Grotius, *The Freedom of the Seas* (1608), Carnegie Endowment For International Peace, J. B. Scott (ed.) (Oxford University Press, 1916).

[9] J. F. Coyle, 'The Treaty of Friendship, Commerce and Navigation in the Modern Era' 51 *Columbia Journal of Transnational Law* 302 (2013).

[10] E. Borchard, 'Minimum Standard of Treatment of Aliens' 38:4 *Michigan Law Review* 445 (1940).

systems were well integrated within the imperial system. In this sense the colonies were effectively within the jurisdiction of the home state. This gave sufficient protection for the investment against the risk of seizure of the investor's assets by the colonial authorities, or at least the risk was no greater than that which would be faced by domestic investors who had stayed at home.

1.5 Post-colonialism and Gunboat Diplomacy

Often by force but in many instances through peaceful settlement, colonialism began to unravel in the late nineteenth century. The Spanish Empire was among the first to dissolve, followed by the German, Ottoman and Russian Empires after World War I, then those of the other European powers like the British and French after World War II. When colonies gained independence they began to challenge the concept that foreigners who continued to reside and do business in those countries were not governed by the laws enacted by the local population. The international minimum standard of protection of aliens did not sit well with these new nation states eager to assert their own autonomy. Indeed, the ability of the newly independent states to impose their own laws on residents, including aliens, was a key aspect of nascent sovereignty. Uncertain as to the nature of their rights, this unsurprisingly left foreign investors apprehensive about the security of their commercial endeavours abroad. During this time a mixture of diplomacy and force (so-called 'gunboat diplomacy') was used by the former imperial powers to ensure that those new states did not encroach on foreign investors' use of their property adversely, for example by seizing it outright or applying onerous taxes or other fees. If this type of interference did happen, then instead of relying on international or domestic law, capital-exporting states would retaliate by sending a fleet of warships to moor off the coast of the host state until it relented, reminding the former colonies of the might of their former masters even if there was notional autonomy. In one example of this practice, in 1850 the British navy blockaded the Greek port of Piraeus as retaliation for the harming of a British subject without compensation. Half a century later Great Britain and Italy sent ships to the Venezuelan coast to demand reparation for Venezuela defaulting on its sovereign debt. The implication was clear: just as former colonies were expected to safeguard the interest of foreigners on their soil, they were also expected to honour their obligations.

Gunboat diplomacy, effectively negotiation backed by the conspicuous threat of force, was in many respects the antecedent of what we now understand as diplomatic protection. Diplomatic protection means that the state itself has the discretion to intervene on behalf of its citizens abroad, and demand protection and compensation from the host states directly, rather than expecting the citizen to act for himself. This concept can be found as early as the mid-eighteenth century in the writings of Swiss diplomat and philosopher Emmerich de Vattel.[11] It was eventually enshrined in a ruling of the Permanent Court of International Justice (PCIJ) (forerunner of the United Nation's International Court of Justice (ICJ))[12] as a basic principle of international law and later established by the ICJ[13] itself. Although diplomatic protection remains a cornerstone of public international law, it will be shown later in this book that modern international investment law has relegated the notion of diplomatic protection in favour of a direct right of action by citizens against foreign governments through investor–state arbitration.

Power remained the final arbiter of foreign investment treatment during the period before the era of the bilateral investment treaty (BIT), which will be explored further in the next chapter. Even after the Convention on the Peaceful Resolution of International Disputes, a multilateral treaty which effectively precluded military intervention into economic matters that was brought about during The Second Hague Peace Conference in 1907, the use of force for the purposes of protecting investments continued after World War II. The invasion of Egypt by Israel, the UK and France following Egypt's nationalization of the Suez Canal in 1957 was probably the last incident where the protection of private property belonging to an alien was used as a justification for armed attack by a government. It is interesting that the Suez crisis was ended in part by the peaceful intervention of the USA, which threatened to inflict damage on the UK's financial system by selling off its UK bonds to devalue the British pound.

---

[11] B. Kapossy and R. Whitmore (eds.), *The Law of Nations or the Principles of Natural Law* (Indianapolis Liberty Fund, 2008), at 1883.

[12] *The Mavrommatis Palestine Concessions* (1924) PCIJ Ser A No. 2.

[13] *Barcelona Traction (Belgium v. Spain)*, Merits [1970] ICJ Rep 3.

The colonial age was followed by the beginnings of nationalism and more importantly, the yearning for genuine economic independence. Newly autonomous states, such as India and Canada, like Brazil and the USA before them, were eager to escape reliance on their former colonial rulers for the advancement of their citizens through debt. More specifically, they sought to stimulate economic growth through international trade (with shorter shipping routes thanks to the Suez and Panama Canals as well as faster ships) and more importantly, through access to foreign capital. This was becoming more readily available in global markets in part because of improvements in technology (including the first undersea telecommunications cables crossing the Atlantic Ocean).

The movement towards full autonomy of the former colonies was later formally supported by the United Nations (UN), an international organization which had formed in the aftermath of World War II for the purposes of fostering international cooperation and peace, where developing states including the many former colonies had numeric dominance in representation in the General Assembly. This allowed these countries to assert policies through the UN that were favourable to their interests as autonomous states eager to engage in international trade and to import capital as a means of growth. Chief of these was the Declaration of Permanent Sovereignty over Natural Resources (PSNR) of 1962[14] which granted nation states both jurisdictional rights as well as rights of ownership over natural resources found in their territories. PSNR, which did not receive unanimous support in the General Assembly, was linked then as now to maintaining control over FDI in these states, as foreign investors primarily entered these countries (as they do today) in order to access raw materials at low cost. This doctrine sought to ensure that the international minimum standard of protection was not used to undermine the self-regulatory capacity of newly independent countries struggling to achieve economic stability. In many ways this policy should be viewed as the backbone of international investment law because it embodies the default principle of a state's right to regulate, which is surrendered in part through its obligations contained in investment treaties, a tension which will be explored throughout this book.

---

[14] Declaration of Permanent Sovereignty over Natural Resources, United Nations General Assembly Resolution 1803 (XVII) of 14 December 1962.

Several resolutions contributing to the modern understanding of international investment law and in particular the state's right to administer its economy were enacted at the UN in the 1970s, creating what was known as a New International Economic Order (NIEO).[15] NIEO, which did not receive support from the developed states including the USA, established that developing countries were entitled to regulate and control the activities of multinational enterprises operating within their territories which included the right to expropriate foreign property when necessary, subject to the requirement to pay compensation. Again, these concepts remain active sources of conflict between investors and host states to this day and will be revisited throughout this book. It should be mentioned that while the status of UN resolutions as sources of international law remains contested, it is clear that UN support for these initiatives has intensified the debate over the extent to which such rights can be abrogated by international investment treaties, which UN agencies such as the United Nations Conference on Trade and Development (UNCTAD) has vocally supported as tools of economic development.

1.6 The Late Twentieth Century

During the energy crisis that gripped the West in the mid-1970s the price of oil rose drastically when the Member States of the Overseas Private Investment Corporation (OPIC) cartel proclaimed an oil embargo. This event not only propelled many oil-reliant developed economies like the USA into sudden recession, it demonstrated how vulnerable the West was to whims of governments in resource-rich developing states. This also captured a shift in power towards the former colonies. Strengthened by the UN's support of PSNR and NIEO, and aware that they had not always achieved the best deals in concession arrangements with Western oil companies, a number of expropriations of oil projects were instigated by developing states during this period, especially in Arab countries and in Latin America. Libya expropriated assets of a number of firms, starting with British Petroleum in 1971. Much as today, Venezuela had been nationalizing

---

[15] Declaration for the Establishment of a New International Economic Order, United Nations General Assembly document A/RES/S-6/3201 of 1 May 1974.

oil supplies for some time and intensified this practice after the energy crisis, also raising taxes on foreign oil companies to punishing levels. These events naturally generated much consternation not simply in the energy sector but across the developed world, which began to view the security of all types of FDI in former colonies with much apprehension. One way to assuage this nervousness was the increased demand for access to neutral dispute settlement in order to achieve full compensation for nationalizations and ultimately the enshrinement of investors' rights in more investment-specific treaties, notably the right to compensation for expropriation. While both of these had been prominent features of investor-state relations since the 1960s when the modern bilateral investment treaty first appeared (of which more will be mentioned in the next chapter), investor–state dispute settlement and other treaty-based rights for foreign investors did not rise to their full prominence until the beginning of the twenty-first century.

There were ideological shifts underway by the 1980s that further contributed to the creation of international law on foreign investment as a system of insulating foreign firms from an uncertain legal environment abroad. The rise of free market economics associated perhaps most closely with President Reagan of the USA and Prime Minister Margaret Thatcher of the UK, themselves influenced by economists like Milton Friedman,[16] bolstered a movement to liberalize foreign investment regimes in their respective countries. This made it easier for foreign firms to locate within states where previously there had been restrictions on foreign ownership of assets such as natural resources. Lifting barriers to entry for investors from overseas was seen, much as it is today, as one of the best ways of injecting capital into stagnant economies. Firms meanwhile began to recognize that the expansion into foreign states could translate to greater profits through the lowering of production costs and by accessing new markets where sales at home had flatlined. The rapid success of small city-states like Hong Kong and Singapore, which lacked natural resources but were able quickly to develop large financial services economies in part because of progressive attitudes towards FDI, prompted other developing states to follow the same route. Later, the entrenchment of 'open door' policies in newly industrializing countries like China also met with success which continues at a fervid pace to this day. The UN, which had launched

---

[16] E.g. M. Friedman, *Capitalism and Freedom* (University of Chicago Press, 1962).

the PSNR and NIEO doctrines, even began to encourage developing states to be more welcoming to FDI as a tool of economic development. Wedded to the philosophy of open markets which commentators now often decry as 'neo-liberalism', the International Monetary Fund (IMF) (which promotes currency exchange and provides debt relief to countries in the form of repayable loans) and the World Bank (which funds long-term development projects in poor countries) along with the newly formed World Trade Organization (WTO) (which reduces regulatory barriers to international trade) also began to urge their Members to welcome international competition in the form of FDI as a means of achieving economic stability. Together these so-called Bretton Woods institutions, named after the conference resort where they were conceived after World War II, strongly advocated the global interrelatedness of economies both as a bulwark against further armed hostility but also as a key route to prosperity for all. Whether these organizations have actually achieved that goal, particularly with respect to their impact on developing countries, remains a matter of some debate.

The explosion of FDI in the latter part of the twentieth century and the ensuing need to enshrine protections for foreign investors through international treaties was closely tied to the collapse of communism as a form of government and the resulting shift towards market economies among the former Soviet bloc countries. The ensuing privatization of what had been government-run monopolies in many sectors throughout Eastern Europe was heavily dependent upon Western capital. As multinational enterprises began to extend their influence much as the old colonial monopolies had done centuries earlier, these countries began to compete with each other for mobile capital, as they continue to do today. The signing of investment treaties was one such way of signalling a willingness to entertain foreign guests.

By the early years of the twenty-first century several large developing states began to witness the positive results of their endorsement of free market practices, including the reduction of trade barriers like import tariffs through organizations like the WTO, and most importantly for the purposes of this book, an unrestricted regime of inward FDI. This was (and to an extent still is) the era of the rise of the so-called BRIC states (Brazil, Russia, India and China) which until only recently had witnessed yearly growth on average of more than 6 per cent of GDP for more than a decade. Largely unfazed by the global financial crisis of 2008–09, FDI continued to explode during this period. While the astronomical growth rates of the emerging markets associated with the mid-2000s may have levelled off recently, there is little sign of global FDI abating any time soon.

1.7 Concepts of Property

Developments in the approach of nation states towards international investment law, including the modern treaty regime which will be examined in the next chapter and throughout this book, were heavily influenced by more fundamental ideas relating to property itself. The philosophical understanding of the ownership of property by the individual, and indeed the concept of what property is, is the very foundation of the law which is designed to protect it and which is echoed in international investment law.

At the risk of overgeneralization in particular with respect to the philosophy of non-Western cultures, prior to the twentieth century it is safe to say that it was widely accepted that a government that took a person's property (including that belonging to an alien) was obliged to compensate the owner. This principle rested on the deeply held belief that part of what it means to be a free individual is the ability to own possessions, meaning to have exclusive control over things, including the right to buy and to sell them as well as use them. These concepts may themselves be traced back to ancient Greece, but in modern times they are associated with the Enlightenment movement of the seventeenth and eighteenth centuries, found in such works as those of English philosopher John Locke.[17] Linked to this principle of property ownership was the belief in the need to control excesses of governments, mostly in relation to freedom of the person, a concept which found voice in instruments like the American Declaration of Independence of 1776. This document, and other constitutional instruments like it around the world which dictate the extent of a government's powers, have ideological roots as far back as the Magna Carta of 1215, which guaranteed what we now understand as due process for citizens, just as it set limits on the authority of kings.

---

[17] J. Locke, *Two Treaties of Government* (1690) (Yale University Press, 2003).

However two major events occurred after the onset of World War I which fundamentally shook the primacy of the belief in private property, paving the way for much of the state interference with foreign investment that called for the protections later embedded in international investment law. First, in October 1917 the Communist party of Russia, headed by the revolutionary Vladimir Lenin, took control of the government and over the next few years consolidated its control over what became the Soviet Union. By decree of 26 October 1917, all private ownership in land was eliminated with no provision for compensation. Within the next few years, the state seized all farms, banks, mines and eventually all forms of industry. This was the actualization of Karl Marx's theory of communism borne from the previous century – the total sharing of ownership of all productive elements within a society.

Second and also in 1917, a new constitution was established in Mexico as part of that country's revolution which had begun in 1910 and lasted until 1920. The new constitution stated that ownership of all lands and materials within the boundaries of the national territory belonged to the government of Mexico, which had the right to impose on private property any terms that were in the public interest. In other words, above the rights of individuals to own property there were superior rights of society represented by the state. This remarkable change in outlook was in many respects a reaction to the previous government's embrace of industry and openness to foreign investment, an approach which today is practised by most countries around the world. The interplay of social and private rights captured by these events remains an active source of tension in modern international investment law.

Partially as a consequence of these political events, as well as the UN's pivotal support for PSNR and NIEO enshrining colonial independence and economic self-determination, in the decades following World War II states around the world began to seize the private property of private parties, typically justified by reference to greater public needs. Such takings occurred particularly in Eastern Europe, China and Cuba, the countries which had embraced the radical tenets of communism. This trend was exacerbated by downturns such as the energy crisis discussed above. Economic strife can make the commodities upon which much FDI is based more valuable to host states than the revenue streams they derive from concession arrangements or simple taxation.

It is in large part because of these developments in the twentieth century that government taking of private assets, including those of aliens in the form of FDI, became widely accepted as a legitimate tool of economic governance, and indeed as a normal feature of business risk. To this day, the taking of private property for a public purpose (along with the payment of suitable compensation) remains lawful under international law. As will be examined in Chapter 6 when the concepts of expropriation and compensation are explored in more detail, instances of outright expropriation of foreign assets have become rare, but the understanding of expropriation itself (what it means to take property) has expanded enormously. It now covers a wide range of government action that has the indirect effect of deprivation of ownership. One of the key controversies in international investment law is the degree to which normal regulatory activities can be construed as compensable takings.

It should be acknowledged that the symbolic importance of the ownership of property to individuals as a fundamental manifestation of a person's relationship to the state is for the most part a Western concept. Notions of private property, effectively what it means to own something, and the types of things that can be owned, including physical as well as intangible things like songs or inventions, are quite different in other cultures in the world. The tension between these culturally constructed notions of property is central to the international law governing foreign investment, which must grapple with these types of claims on a regular basis, since what we now know as intellectual property (IP) (including elements such as patents and trademarks) are among the most valuable assets which a firm can possess. These types of property can be expropriated just as easily as traditional assets like natural resources.

1.8 Current Trends in FDI

FDI is conducted essentially by multinational enterprises, meaning commercial organizations which own or control production or service facilities in more than one country. As mentioned above, overseas productive facilities may be acquired by taking over existing locally owned capacity, or by investing directly in new plant or equipment. The former tends to be associated with FDI into developed countries where companies are normally acquired once they have reached a certain degree of maturity, whereas the latter is often the vehicle of choice for FDI into developing states that lack well-established businesses that can be bought by foreign firms but where natural resources are abundant.

Today there are more than 80,000 multinational enterprises collectively controlling almost a million foreign affiliates. Ranked by GDP or annual turnover, half of the world's largest economic units are multinationals rather than countries. Indeed, many of the largest foreign investors have a larger capitalization than the states in which they operate. This imbalance may be perceived as a cause for concern when considering the consequence of a host state enacting laws in its own interest which threaten the profitability of the commercial enterprise in its territory. Still, it is important to recognize that not all multinationals are large. Increasingly, small and medium-sized enterprises are able to maintain an international presence and to make use of international investment law to achieve redress for governmental interference. Contrary to the historic picture painted earlier in which developed states engaged in FDI in their former colonies, today roughly half of all FDI activity remains concentrated in the developed world (i.e. between two developed countries) and increasing activity takes place between two developing countries, many of which have reasonably equal bargaining power. While we tend to associate the multinational enterprise with private companies which may be publicly traded on stock markets, there are now more than 500 SOEs engaging in FDI with more than 15,000 affiliates. This form of business organization remains quite common in Asia. State-owned or partially state-owned enterprises account for approximately 11 per cent of global FDI flows. FDI by Sovereign Wealth Funds, essentially governments themselves investing their own capital, remains low but continues to expand as a portion of overall FDI.[18] This latter trend raises pressing questions of the relationship between host and home states, and whether this is adequately served by existing international legal frameworks.

In 2014, global FDI flows (both inward and outward) were US $1.2 trillion per year, a 16 per cent decline from 2013, although at the time of writing expectations are that 2015 data will show a full recovery. While the USA and other major industrialized countries like the UK, Germany and Japan remain the dominant sources of FDI, the modern era is characterized by a significant shift in FDI flows both to and from the developing

---

[18] World Investment Report 2015, UNCTAD (New York and Geneva, 2015), Chapter 1.

world. FDI flows to developing countries comprised 56 per cent of all FDI in 2014, the highest at any point in recorded history, although the growth rate in these flows declined somewhat compared to previous years. Perhaps more tellingly in terms of shifts in global economic patterns, FDI from developing countries has also peaked in recent years, constituting 35 per cent of all FDI outflows (up from only 12 per cent in the early 2000s). The USA and Europe saw their combined share of global FDI decline in 2014 to less than 30 per cent, well down from their peak of 50 per cent some ten years ago. While retaining its status as the largest home country for outward FDI, the USA lost its position as top host country for FDI in 2014, where it has been since the middle of the twentieth century, with China now in first place as the largest recipient of FDI in the world. Future global FDI flows are expected to rise at a somewhat more modest pace than originally envisioned, reaching $1.4 trillion in 2015 and $1.5 trillion in 2016. Perhaps most encouraging, today FDI accounts for more than 40 per cent of external finance for development among developing and transition economies.[19] FDI may indeed be a better catalyst for development than aid.

Generally speaking it can be concluded that the states which proceeded with market reform and privatization initiatives have attracted the majority of FDI, both by creating international confidence in their future economic and political stability, and by providing opportunities for foreign companies to buy local production and distribution facilities. It will be interesting to see how the approaching equilibrium in global flows of FDI between developed and developing countries will impact international investment law, which was arguably conceived as a tool to protect Western firms engaging in risky but lucrative forays into poor countries. As will be explored throughout this book, some changes to international investment law as a result of these shifts may have already taken place.

1.9 Economic Rationales for FDI – Cost and Profit

While multinational investors come in many sizes and forms, there is broad agreement among economists as to the primary motivation for

[19] Ibid.

locating in foreign states. Simply put, this is to seek higher or more secure profits in the long term. Locating abroad, also known as internationalizing, is essentially driven either by the firm's desire to cut costs, or increase revenues (or ideally, but less commonly, both). Cost-orientated multinationals aim to achieve the former goal. Market-orientated multinationals strive for the latter.

The chief strategy of cost reduction of the foreign investor is often one based on taxation – multinational firms often seek to arrange their production and distribution networks to minimize their exposure to taxation by host states. International taxation tends to be seen as outside the sphere of international investment law, however, and does not appear in the text of bilateral investment treaties. Examples of conventional cost-orientated multinationals include oil companies such as Exxon, Shell and BP. In order to secure control of strategic raw materials in natural oil fields around the world, they established overseas extraction operations in the early years of the twentieth century, largely in the Middle East. The same phenomenon has happened in manufacturing where cheap labour has allowed the mass production of goods, especially in factories in Asia, to be shipped back to the multinationals' home state. Low labour costs represent perhaps the most important determinant of production location in manufacturing.[20]

In contrast, market-orientated multinationals seek to expand markets and achieve greater sales abroad. Such companies gradually switch from engaging in international trade (exporting their goods abroad) to licensing foreign firms to produce on their behalf, to establishing a sales outlet and finally full production facilities overseas to be consumed in the host country, the latter two of which are properly seen as examples of FDI. Such companies consist of restaurants like McDonald's where customers are served directly on site, or even car manufacturers such as Toyota where local sales offices can augment market penetration. These companies typically established affiliates in states that possessed the largest markets, such as the USA, the UK, Germany and Japan. Market-orientated multinationals have been and will be increasingly drawn to China and India which, with growing middle-class populations, will most likely become the world's largest markets in coming decades.

---

[20] See generally, A. Griffiths and S. Wall, *Applied Economics*, 11 edn (Prentice Hall, 2007), Chapter 7.

It is interesting to note that cost-orientated multinationals often evolve into market-orientated multinationals as the economic condition of the host country improves. Citizens become more affluent, allowing them to consume rather than simply produce. This is occurring now in countries such as India and China. People that were once paid low wages to manufacture car parts being shipped back to the USA are now the very people buying those cars themselves. It is also theorized that firms internationalize and invest abroad in order to extend the 'life cycle' of their products. This is based on the fact that most products have a finite economic life, consisting of four phases: introduction into the market, growth, maturity and decline. But a product may be at different stages of its life cycle in different geographic markets. This leads to changing configurations of supply and demand which variously favour local production, export and importing from cheap overseas suppliers. A product that is obsolete in the UK might be popular in Japan – or more likely vice versa. A product life cycle drives production out of the innovating country to lower cost producers or more eager consumers overseas.[21]

It was suggested above that companies are able to engage in FDI in part because of advances in enabling technologies which have reduced the costs of doing business across national frontiers. These technologies include improved communications and advances in containerization and shipping (the automation of ports like Amsterdam and Hong Kong). Consumer markets themselves have globalized, to some extent because of technologies like the Internet which has made it cheaper for established producers to get a foothold in new markets in developing countries. Lastly, new organizational patterns have evolved, embracing a divisional corporate structure based on product or geographic specialities, which has made managing global companies more feasible.[22]

Noting the key trend of growth in FDI from emerging markets, it is now believed that some companies may choose to internationalize at a very early stage in their development in order to escape difficult regulatory conditions at home, such as excessive bureaucracy or corruption. Such companies may also be well-resourced by their home state governments as selected champions intended to dominate international markets. This so-called 'Born Global' phenomenon is believed to be one of the key motivators for outward FDI from emerging markets like India, China and

---

[21] Ibid.   [22] Ibid., Chapter 25.

Brazil, in contrast to traditional patterns of internationalization in the twentieth century which happened more gradually and incrementally.[23]

1.10 Foreign Direct Investment and Host States

1.10.1 Advantages

FDI is a contentious phenomenon because, as a key manifestation of globalization, the presence of a foreign firm along with their personnel can represent a significant intrusion into society, especially in the eyes of ordinary citizens who may perceive foreign firms as usurping local jobs and driving out local businesses. This tension colours some of the controversy underpinning international investment law. Foreign companies are sometimes treated with suspicion by governments and citizens alike because of the concern that they may undermine national security by controlling vital infrastructure or natural resources. Yet economists tend to agree that FDI on balance offers more advantages to host economies than drawbacks, and for this reason governments should do their best, within reasonable limits, to court foreign firms. There are many public benefits associated with FDI other than simply increasing the private profits of the multinational enterprise in question, which may itself represent enhanced tax revenue to the host and home state. These issues, including how some are accommodated into the text of investment treaties, will be discussed again later in this book, but for now it is instructive to illustrate some examples of the main advantages and disadvantages associated with FDI.

One of the major benefits associated with FDI is the spillover or indirect effect of technology transfer. Studies in the UK have shown that productivity in firms taken over by foreign multinationals was much higher after the takeover than comparative firms that were run domestically. Foreign managers brought in to orchestrate takeovers were able to provide instruction to workers in the local firm on how to improve their yields both in quantity and quality. Moreover, the presence of this improved global firm with its superior outputs placed pressure on local firms to 'up their game' in order to remain viable. This improvement through competition, when

---

[23] Y. Aharoni, 'Reflections on Multinational Enterprises in a Globally Interdependent World Economy' in K. Sauvant et al. (eds.), *Foreign Direct Investment from Emerging Markets* (Palgrave MacMillan, 2010).

it does not eradicate local firms, can actually benefit the whole sector. For example, the establishment of a Nissan car plant with higher technical standards than domestic car companies led to an overall improvement in the standards of vehicles in the UK.[24]

Another obvious advantage from FDI is that of employment. Multinational enterprises reorganizing existing firms or setting up new facilities can create local employment opportunities, which can be a vital form of stimulus for the local economy. Employment would be in the form of direct job creation, for example at a new or expanded factory as well as indirect job creation in industries locating close to the plant. This could include suppliers of inputs as well as restaurants and other services for workers. The increase in employment is linked to improvements in skills and training, such as literacy and IT skills, another manifestation of the technology transfer benefit associated with FDI that was discussed above. Work of this kind should not only be more financially remunerative, but also more rewarding, leading to overall increases in job satisfaction. Taken together, it is no surprise that politicians celebrate the arrival of a new production facility from an overseas company.

FDI promotes the host state's balance-of-payments equilibrium through the contribution of foreign capital. Balance of payments is the difference between the flow of money into and out of a host state, including its exports and imports but also its flow of direct investment. It indicates whether the state is spending or earning more money, essentially disclosing the health of its overall economy, which will in turn be reflected in the value of its currency. The IMF encourages its member countries to maintain a balance-of-payments equilibrium, which is one of the reasons why the IMF tends to favour policies which promote FDI, such as the elimination of restrictions on foreign ownership of firms or assets in various sectors. Of course, FDI does not always improve a host state's balance-of-payments status however, because capital is often repatriated back to the home country.

Lastly, FDI is thought to encourage infrastructure development, especially in developing states that tend to be deficient in this regard. Classic forms of infrastructure associated with FDI include the creation of dams for electricity, and roads and railroads in order to facilitate transportation of raw materials. Indirect infrastructure such as schools and hospitals may

---

[24] Griffiths and Wall, *Applied Economics*, Chapter 7.

also be constructed by foreign firms in order to service the employees of their factories or mines. Taken together, such additions can act as a critical component of development, often displacing the need for formal aid packages which are sometimes misdirected and underused. China has engaged in this type of infrastructure creation extensively as part of its FDI initiatives into Africa.

1.10.2 Disadvantages

As noted earlier, FDI can be harmful to host states in some instances. An important but often overlooked disadvantage of FDI is the cultural dissonance associated with the presence of foreign firms. This phenomenon is often associated with American 'cultural imperialism' which in the context of FDI can take the form of fast food restaurants appearing next to medieval churches on the streets of European cities. More gravely, FDI projects can act as a disruption to sensitive archaeological sites. For example, the building of a modern Western hotel near the Giza Plateau in Egypt was the source of an investor–state dispute in the early 2000s.[25] Somewhat less invasively, cultural dissonance between the foreign firm and the host state can result from different managerial styles. Japanese car companies reported difficulty in establishing Japanese-style hierarchical work practices at British and American companies where there was less emphasis on group culture. Wal-Mart famously had trouble getting a foothold in Germany because Germans did not like the American practice of greeting customers as they entered stores.

FDI is sometimes associated with human rights and labour transgressions against workers in host states, especially in the developing world. It is often alleged that multinational enterprises underpay local workers, provide below-acceptable working conditions and prevent unionization, the so-called 'sweatshop' model. Recall that cheap labour is one of the main motivations for internationalization. This is sometimes linked to complicity with oppressive political regimes which are eager to profit from foreign investment but not to share it with citizens. The collapse of a garment factory in Bangladesh that was partially foreign-owned and the ensuing death of more than 1000 workers is regularly cited as an example of foreign-owned firms cutting costs to the detriment of the local

---

[25] *SPP* v. *Egypt*, ICSID Case No. ARB/84/3 (20 May 1992).

population. Employees were ordered to continue working even as cracks appeared in the masonry. Studies have shown that this criticism of FDI is largely inaccurate, as foreign firms tend to pay more and provide better working conditions than equivalent local firms. The reason for this is simple: firms from developed countries tend to have greater resources with which to pay their employees, and well-paid employees tend to be more productive in the long run.[26]

Relatedly, FDI is sometimes accused of causing environmental damage in host states. Much as foreign firms theoretically seek to cut costs by underpaying workers, they may also do so by failing to ensure that costly environmental standards are upheld. It is often suggested that multinational enterprises, especially in the extractive sector, violate established environmental norms relating to emissions or waste disposal, or that they exploit natural resources in an unsustainable manner. This can take the form of either failing to observe local standards or operating in states where the environmental standards are low or unenforced, sometimes described as the 'pollution haven' theory. For example, Coca-Cola was heavily criticized for its draining of drinking water resources in central Africa, much as the oil company Chevron became engaged in litigation over allegedly dumping toxic waste in the Ecuadorean Amazon. The idea that foreign firms contribute to greater environmental degradation than local firms has been largely dispelled,[27] but the perception remains.

While FDI is normally associated with improvements to a host state's economy, some economists suggest that FDI can actually prevent economic development in some countries, rather than stimulate it.[28] For example, even if a foreign firm is able to offer employment to locals (rather than eliminate it through downsizing for efficiency gains), these positions are often low-skilled and low-paying, with little prospect of advancement and poor job satisfaction. This suppression of the entrepreneurial class is said to trap people in unrewarding work where they might have started

---

[26] D. Brown et al., 'The Effects of Multinational Production on Wages and Working Conditions in Developing Countries' *National Bureau of Economic Research*, Working Paper No. 9669 (May 2003).

[27] A. Harrison, 'Do Polluters Head Overseas? Testing the Pollution Haven Hypothesis', *ARE Update* (University of California Giannini Foundation of Agricultural Economics, 1 Dec 2002).

[28] S. Beugelsdijk et al., *International Economics and Business*, 2nd edn (Cambridge University Press, 2013), Chapter 14.

their own business or become managers, undermining the transition to meaningful careers by providing a more immediately attractive alternative. This situation may be exacerbated when the investor leaves after a particular project is completed. While firms are internationally mobile, workers tend not to be, and these people may find themselves unemployed and unskilled when the foreign firm moves on.

Tied to this dilemma is the often-asserted link between FDI and the loss of the host state's economic sovereignty, which we saw above has been a key aspect of a country's independence. In some instances the market size of multinational enterprises may result in the displacement of smaller, less efficient domestic producers, the driving out of local equivalents that cannot compete with more sophisticated firms from abroad. As local firms disappear, the host state becomes more dependent on FDI to sustain growth and maintain employment. In extreme cases this can amount to a loss of economic sovereignty of the host state because the government must be responsive to the needs of the firm rather than to its citizens in case the firm decides to leave. In theory this should not be problematic because a profitable firm should be beneficial to all parties, but as noted above, a highly mobile firm may choose to depart the jurisdiction when its profits diminish, leaving the host state vulnerable to economic collapse. Furthermore, over-dependence on FDI for sectors critical to the economy, like banking and telecommunications, can represent a national security concern.

1.11 Sources of International Law on Foreign Investment

Before this book embarks on its detailed examination of the international law which governs FDI, it is essential to conclude this chapter with a brief overview of international law itself, a concept which lacks clear definition in part because of its disparate sources. International law is accurately described as the rules that govern the relations between nation states, which are effectively organized communities under one government presiding over a defined territory. International law is a sphere of law that exists apart from the national law of any one nation state, although national laws can influence the development of international law if they are practised with sufficient regularity around the world. National law itself is relevant to the study of international investment law as it is the national laws, or domestic courts' interpretation and application of them, which are challenged by investors for unduly interfering with their commercial activities. International law in turn tells us whether these national laws are acceptable or not.

The recognized sources of international law are enumerated in Art 38(1) Statute of the ICJ, which obtains its jurisdiction by the consent of all Member States of the UN. This provision is the most widely cited point of authority for the definition of international law. Respectively these sources consist of treaties, custom, general principles of law and judicial decisions. International investment law draws upon each of these sources of law to varying degrees.

Treaties and conventions are by far the most important source of international law relating to foreign investment, and will be the principal focus of this book. Simply put, treaties are agreements concluded between two or more governments. Only states that are parties to a treaty are bound by it, although a number of states voluntarily adhere to many treaties and accept them as binding without ever becoming party to them. There are many thousands of treaties in existence, covering a wide range of topics. This book will examine the contents of international investment treaties, most of which have been concluded bilaterally (between two states). While there are now several thousand of these bilateral investment treaties, they tend to contain the same or largely similar provisions, which is one of the reasons that international investment law can be studied as a reasonably coherent field of law. There are a handful of important regional and multilateral (global) treaties, including those of the WTO, which have been concluded and touch on international investment. These will also be considered in more detail in the next chapter. One of the most important treaties of general subject matter is the Vienna Convention on the Law of Treaties (VCLT),[29] which among other things instructs how the provisions of all other treaties should be interpreted. As such, this treaty is regularly referred to by international investment tribunals.

Custom, or customary international law, has played a relatively small role in the development of international investment law. Customary international law consists of rules based on a widespread pattern of behaviour by states based on the belief that the principle involved is obligatory. In other words, states behave that way because they feel that they are

---

[29] 1155 UNTS 331, opened for signature 23 May 1969.

required to do so. The mere fact that a custom is followed widely does not mean that it is legally binding as a rule of international law. One leading principle of customary international law relevant to FDI is one that has already been alluded to above: when private property is taken by the state, there must be payment of compensation. It should be noted that the UN General Assembly has enacted a handful of resolutions in the area of foreign investment, including PSNR and NIEO, but the extent to which these can be said to create customary international law is uncertain, particularly since their adoption was non-unanimous. The resolutions of the UN, while formally non-binding, have legal character and have contributed significantly to the development of international law as it is understood and practised. Much of this is 'soft law' which means that it is not really authoritative, just instructive. The existence of thousands of investment treaties containing similar principles and legal obligations may itself contribute to the development of customary international law. One of the chief criticisms of customary international law is that it is subjective and inconsistent because states vary enormously in their opinion of what behaviour is legally binding.

General principles of law are a subsidiary source of international law that may be relevant in some limited circumstances to foreign investment, although the authority accorded to them is not as high as treaty or custom. General principles may be used by international courts, like the ICJ, to fill in gaps that exist in international treaties or custom, although the relevance of general principles may be decreasing because of the vast number of treaties now in existence covering so many topics. General principles refer to rules drawn from national legal systems around the world, as long as they are common to a sufficient degree. An example of a general principle relevant to international investment law is the concept of full compensation for the expropriation of foreign property, closely related to the principle of customary international law described in the previous paragraph. Other important general principles of law include due process, essentially access to justice and fair procedure when rights are challenged by governments; good faith (openness and honesty in dealings); and legitimate expectations (the requirement to fulfil an obligation that one has induced someone else to believe in). There is a significant level of subjectivity regarding the use of general principles.

Lastly, the Statute of the ICJ instructs that judicial decisions may be used as 'a subsidiary means for the determination of rules of law', which is strictly speaking different to a true subsidiary source of law. Judicial decisions can be used to recognize the law established by other sources. In other words, they may be seen as evidence of international law rather than a direct manifestation of it. There is no doctrine of precedent (courts bound by previous decisions) in international law. The decisions of international tribunals, including the ICJ itself, are only binding on the parties in that particular case. Still, the role of judicial decisions in international investment law is considerable. The most important judicial decisions in international investment law are those of the investor–state arbitration tribunals of which there are many, including both institutional (such as those constituted under ICSID) and ad hoc. Decisions of these tribunals are now widely accessible. Although again there is no formal doctrine of precedent in international arbitration, there remains a high degree of respect accorded to this growing body of jurisprudence. The process of investor–state dispute settlement will be explored further in Chapter 8, and many of the cases will be considered directly throughout this book. The decisions of the ICJ and its predecessor the PCIJ have had some influence in international investment law, although the ICJ's role in this regard is marginal today because of the dominance of investor–state arbitration. To the extent that the laws of the WTO have some impact on FDI, rulings of the WTO's dispute settlement system should not be neglected.

Some mention should also be made of the 'teachings of the most highly qualified publicists' which is also referred to in Art 38(1) Statute of the ICJ as a subsidiary means for the determination of rules of international law. As noted at the beginning of this chapter, in recent years international investment law has expanded enormously as a field of legal practice and also of legal academic writing and teaching in law schools. There are a number of well-regarded experts in the field who have produced textbooks and treatises on the law, as well as commentary and criticism appearing in specialist academic and practitioner journals. Investor–state arbitration tribunals have been known to refer to these in rendering their awards. Much of this commentary may accurately be described as *lex ferenda* (future law); in other words, it sometimes consists of advice about the way the law should be rather than the way it truly is. It should be noted that a number of international organizations, such as UNCTAD and the Organisation for Economic Cooperation and Development (OECD), also produce regular research reports on developments in international investment law. These writings should probably be regarded with the same status as the teachings of the most highly qualified publicists.

1.12 Conclusion

Foreign investment has been practised for some time and has played a significant role in history, including the expansion of European civilization and the toppling of communism. Today FDI is one of the centrepieces of economic globalization, responsible for the rise of many of the emerging markets. Firms pursue a strategy of internationalization in order to enhance their profits, just as host states seek FDI for economic advancement. While it is hoped that in most cases both parties will benefit from the exchange, in many instances harms can be suffered by states and in others states can enact laws which interfere with the investor's profits. The ensuing tension between host states, many of which were initially former colonies, and home states who espouse the interests of their firms forms the basis of the ongoing tensions in the international investment law, which has arisen in order to resolve disputes and provide a degree of security in what is otherwise a high-risk venture. International investment law, as a species of public international law, is drawn from various sources, with treaties being by far the most important.

This book will proceed very much as an anatomy of the treaties which govern foreign investment. Chapter 2 will provide an overview of bilateral investment treaties, along with the key regional and multinational ones. Chapter 3 will take a closer look at the notion of investment, establishing the subject matter jurisdiction for international tribunals and the scope of protection under investment treaties. The principle of non-discrimination, embodied by the standards of National Treatment and Most Favoured Nation (MFN) found in treaties, will be explored in Chapter 4. A range of additional protective standards contained in investment treaties will be examined in Chapter 5, the most crucial of which is Fair and Equitable Treatment (FET). Chapter 6 is devoted to the consideration of expropriation, the most severe form of interference with foreign firms at the hands of host states, with Chapter 7 looking over the related concept of compensation, which though associated most closely with expropriation is also available for other treaty breaches. Investor–state dispute settlement will be examined closely in Chapter 8, with some discussion of state-to-state dispute resolution as well as informal mechanisms. The controversies associated with public interest-based exceptions to investment treaty protections will be canvassed in Chapter 9, which will also look at various Corporate Social Responsibility (CSR) guidelines. Two special varieties of exception, national security and economic emergency, will be discussed in Chapter 10. Finally, Chapter 11 will explore some of the alternatives to international investment law, most notably Political Risk Insurance (PRI), concluding with some final thoughts on central criticisms of international investment law.

Bilateral, Regional and Multilateral Investment   2
Agreements and Investment Contracts

2.1 Introduction

Today treaties are the primary means through which investors seek to
protect their rights with respect to foreign investment against host states.
The use of treaties to protect foreign investment represents a seismic shift
away from the use of customary international law which had historically
been the chief means of protecting aliens who engaged in commerce.
More concrete than customary international law and the other sources of
international law like general principles, international investment agreements (IIAs) provide reasonably clear standards of protection for foreign
investors which can be interpreted and applied by international tribunals.
Perhaps most importantly, treaties can be tailored to suit the individual
needs of the states concerned, according useful flexibility to the pursuit
of economic growth.

This chapter will outline the nature of the chief treaty-based means
of regulating foreign investment under international law – the bilateral
investment treaty – explaining its purpose in offsetting the risks associated with FDI and perhaps more fundamentally, its stated aim to achieve
mutual economic advancement between treaty parties. Recognizing that
much treaty negotiation is now done at the regional level, this chapter will
then consider some of the most important multi-party or regional treaties
with investment disciplines, which tend to offer protection and in some
cases liberalization, for foreign investment in conjunction with other types
of economic activity, most notably trade. This will involve a discussion of
the North American Free Trade Agreement (NAFTA), the Energy Charter
Treaty (ECT), the Association of South East Asian Nations (ASEAN) as well
as modern instruments such as the Transatlantic Trade and Investment
Partnership (TTIP) and the Trans Pacific Partnership (TPP). This chapter
will proceed to discuss the key global treaties (and associated institutions)
that are relevant to international investment, including the World Bank
agreements (specifically the Multilateral Investment Guarantee Agency

(MIGA), the International Finance Corporation (IFC) and ICSID, and relevant WTO Agreements: the General Agreement on Trade in Services (GATS), the Trade-Related Investment Measures (TRIMS) and the Agreement on Trade-Related Aspects of Intellectual Property (TRIPS). Shifting the focus away from binding rules to guidelines, some of the most important regimes of guidance for states and firms covering international investment that have been promulgated by international organizations such as the OECD, notably its liberalization codes as well as various aspirational 'soft law' instruments of the UN, will be discussed. Finally, the often neglected role played by private investment contracts between investors and host states in protecting foreign investors will be considered.

The purpose of this chapter is to sketch an outline of the global regulatory framework governing international investment. The substantive content of these instruments, including explanations of their foundational legal principles, will be examined throughout the rest of the book.

2.2 Bilateral Investment Treaties

As discussed in the previous chapter, bilateral investment treaties (BITs) have been in existence for centuries although they initially contained substantially less in the way of formal rules than those in existence today. The forerunners of the modern BITs were the historic so-called Friendship, Commerce and Navigation (FCN) agreements that were concluded from the eighteenth century onward by the major colonial powers as well as the USA. The USA was perhaps the most active user of these treaties, establishing a large number during the nineteenth century. As noted earlier, these treaties were not confined to commerce; they extended to military matters involving matters such as access to ports and navigation through internal waters. In that sense they are quite removed from what we now understand modern BITs to be, although the historic parallels are compelling. The most critical contextual difference between the FCN treaties and modern BITs is that the FCN instruments were designed at a time when international commerce largely consisted of trading in goods by merchants. They did not contemplate direct investment by multinational corporations; they did not capture instances where consortiums set up permanent operations in host countries. At a very general level the

FCN treaties emphasized the protection that should be accorded to individual foreigners, as trading was largely done by individuals establishing themselves overseas for the purposes of trade – effectively the point at which trade becomes investment. Granting a minimum level of protection that was embodied in customary international law, FCNs were intended to ensure that travellers were not subjected to weak or unfair laws that existed in host states.[1]

What we now understand to be the modern era of BITs began in 1959 when Germany and Pakistan adopted a bilateral agreement, entered into force in 1962. This BIT and the many concluded by Germany in the coming decades represented its desire to attract foreign capital to help finance its regeneration following World War II. Other European powers followed Germany's lead, engaging in a programme of BITs throughout the remainder of the twentieth century. The USA, by contrast, was a latecomer to the world of BITs, preferring instead to concentrate on regional trade arrangements with investment chapters, most notably NAFTA, which will be explored further below.

As treaties, BITs are legally binding agreements between two sovereign nations which comprise various protections for international investment for the stated purpose of advancing the economic linkages of the signatory parties, with an ultimate objective of development or economic advancement. This goal tends to be found in the preamble of the average instrument. For instance, the Germany–Hong Kong BIT of 1996 states in its preamble:

> Desiring to create favourable conditions for greater investment by investors of one Contracting Party in the area of the other; Recognising that the encouragement and reciprocal protection of such investments will be conducive to the stimulation of individual business initiative and will increase prosperity in both areas;[2]

While the treaties are ostensibly for the benefits of the state parties, it is the national investors of one party investing in the territory of the other party who gain the direct benefits contained in the treaty, although in theory a state party itself could bring a claim against the other party under international law for failure to uphold the treaty's obligations. As with all

---

[1] M. Sornarajah, *The International Law on Foreign Investment* (Cambridge University Press, 2010).

[2] 19 Feb 1998 (entry into force).

treaties, BITs are concluded between the executive branches of the state's government. In many instances they must be ratified through internal legislative procedures, a process explored further in the next chapter.

In the past, BITs tended to be concluded between capital-exporting states (developed countries such as the former colonial powers) and capital-importing states (developing countries or former colonies), as indeed this was the manner in which FDI initially unfolded historically through its linkages to imperialism. Much as today, developed countries tend to be stable democracies governed by the rule of law where property rights are recognized and the judges are independent. Risk of unfair treatment in these environments accordingly tends to be negligible, which is one of the reasons that most of the world's largest corporations call these countries home. In contrast, developing countries, while often resource-abundant and attractively possessing cheap labour, tend to be associated with unstable regimes and unreliable legal systems, or at least are perceived that way by cautious firms. BITs are therefore correctly understood as commercial risk-mitigation strategies.

The capital-exporting/capital-importing BIT paradigm has changed dramatically in recent years, with FDI flows across the global moving towards equilibrium.[3] Developing states are accordingly negotiating these treaties between themselves. Given this momentous change, it is difficult to maintain that BITs should be viewed as instruments of Western colonial power (as they once may have been).[4] The use of bilateral investment agreements by developing states in part reflects the growth of FDI from these countries, particularly the large emerging markets. As mentioned previously, outward FDI from the developing world is at its highest level in history, comprising more than a third of global outward investment flows.[5] In some respects these global trends are necessitating a recasting of the old capital-importing/capital-exporting labels as many countries now share characteristics of both. What this means in terms of the contents of IIAs and in particular their adoption of somewhat more balanced features (pro-investor and pro-state) is very much a matter of ongoing debate.[6]

---

[3] D. Collins, *The BRIC States and Outward Foreign Direct Investment* (Oxford University Press, 2013).

[4] Sornarajah, *International Law*, generally.

[5] UNCTAD World Investment Report, 2015, unctad.org/en/PublicationsLibrary/wir2015_en .pdf.

[6] Collins, *The BRIC States*.

Perhaps most curiously, developed countries continue to conclude BITs and regional trade agreements (RTAs) with investment chapters with each other. While many of these instruments are understandable in that they contain provisions aimed at liberalizing investment flows (enlarging market access to foreign firms for more spheres of economic activity), many of these instruments consist of traditional BIT-style protections such as guarantees against expropriation and access to neutral international arbitration. Such legal entitlements are presumptively available in advanced democracies committed to the rule of law. This phenomenon somewhat belies the theory that IIAs are aimed at reassuring investors nervous about the exposure to political risk in unstable countries.

While there are now almost 3000 IIAs in existence, comprising thousands of BITs as well as investment chapters of RTAs, thankfully for scholars and practitioners of international investment law, these treaties tend to contain very similar language. This is why there is a reasonably cohesive discipline of 'international investment law', and why textbooks providing broad overviews such as this one can provide effective guidance. In fact, BITs in particular have become standardized to the point that they arguably contribute to customary international law. The irony of this statement should not be missed – the protections enshrined in BITs are now so well entrenched in our understanding that the treaties in which they are situated have in a sense become obsolete. In other words, many or at least some of the protections these instruments afford would now exist anyway even in the absence of the BIT itself. BITs are now even popular in Latin America, a region which had initially challenged the application of international law to foreign investment. Socialist countries have demonstrated a willingness to conclude them, notably China which now has 129 BITs (second only to Germany with 135) as well as Russia with 74 BITs, both of which have also embraced many of the investment-orientated features of the WTO Agreements, as will be explored further below. BITs have been instrumental in the privatization programmes in developing and transition economies countries, particularly in Eastern Europe.

As will be explored in detail throughout this book, BITs essentially provide safeguards against non-commercial risks, meaning risks outside the ordinary course of business. These risks are in turn the main issues which preoccupy international investment law. In addressing these risks, BITs have acted as an incentive to potential investors to establish business operations in high-risk countries. It would naturally be expected, then, that BIT signage should increase FDI inflows into the territory of the signatory state: the conclusion of the BIT sends a message to potential investors that the country is a reasonably safe place in which to do business. Yet there remains a very significant debate as to whether the many thousands of IIAs actually contribute to an increase in FDI flows. A number of studies applying varying methodologies has revealed varied responses to this question.[7] It would seem as though the most marked increase in FDI is associated with IIAs between states of similar levels of economic development.[8] Most surveys of investors appear to suggest that the existence of an IIA in a target host state plays at best a minor role in the decision-making process for foreign firms.[9] Even in the absence of clear linkage to greater FDI flows, other benefits from investment treaties such as improved governance in developing states should be kept in mind, although again, these claims are harder to justify in the case of IIAs among advanced economies with robust legal institutions.

Most BITs and investment chapters of RTAs follow a certain pattern and contain similar provisions, which may be generally divided into three categories: scope, substantive protection and dispute settlement. After the preamble, which tends to explain the overarching purpose of the BIT, the treaty will establish a definition for investment and investor in order to clarify the nature of the commercial activity which it is intended to cover, followed by conditions on the admission of foreign investors. The BIT then establishes guarantees against discrimination through two distinct yet relative standards, National Treatment and MFN. Most BITs then offer guarantees of FET and, somewhat less importantly, Full Protection and Security (FPS) along with other miscellaneous protections relating to currency transfer and the hiring of personnel. A guarantee against expropriation without compensation is found in almost all instruments. Dispute settlement features of a BIT, covering both state-to-state and more

---

[7] See generally K. Sauvant and L. Sachs, *The Effect of Treaties on Foreign Direct Investment: Bilateral Investment Treaties, Double Taxation Treaties and Investment Flows* (Oxford University Press, 2009).

[8] E. Neumayer and L. Spess, 'Do Bilateral Investment Treaties Increase Foreign Direct Investment to Developing Countries?' in Sauvant and Sachs, ibid.

[9] A. Berger, *Developing Countries and the Future of the International Investment Regime* (German Federal Ministry of Economic Cooperation and Development, December 2015), at 11–12.

significantly, investor–state dispute settlement, are normally saved until the end.

As mentioned in Chapter 1, the text of treaties is normally interpreted by tribunals constituted under all IIAs (RTAs and BITs) according to the VCLT, which states that the conditions under which a treaty was negotiated may be used as a supplementary aid to the interpretation of its provisions.[10] This guidance appears to suggest that the negotiation of all IIAs is done by governments purposefully and with full understanding of the nature of the obligations incurred, which may not always be an accurate depiction of reality. Studies have shown that particularly in the case of developing countries, some governments had little appreciation of the implication of what they were committing themselves to when signing IIAs.[11]

A number of traditionally capital-exporting and some capital-importing countries have adopted Model BITs, which are essentially blueprints of the types of provisions which these countries seek to place in their negotiated BITs. In that sense they are kind of a template or starting point from which negotiations of actual treaties with suitable refinements can follow. The US Model BIT is particularly instructive in this regard as it gives potential negotiating parties a sense of the types of obligations they will be asked to make when pursuing investment treaties with this country. Among developed country template agreements, Norway's 2007 Model BIT is also noteworthy because it expressly mentions sustainability goals and the need to incorporate principles of CSR as interpretive guides to its text. Among developing states, few of which opted to issue Model agreements, possibly because they perceive their bargaining power to be too weak to insist on any terms as a starting point, Colombia's Model BIT of 2007 contains a number of provisions which afford the host states somewhat broader latitude to enact regulatory measures in the public interest than in most treaties. Model BITs are often updated every few years to reflect changes in approach to foreign investment, informed by developments in case law as well as trends in the domestic and global economy.

---

[10] Art 32.

[11] L. Poulsen, *Bounded Rationality and Economic Diplomacy: The Politics of Investment Treaties in Developing Countries* (Cambridge University Press, 2015).

2.3 Regional Trade Agreements

An RTA is the term often used to collectively cover trade or investment agreements between three or more countries, or trade-based agreements between two countries, also known as Free Trade Agreements (FTAs) which contain an investment chapter. The investment chapters in these treaties tend to be longer than BITs and often contain more innovative provisions. Today, RTAs are now being pursued at a more rapid pace than BITs, possibly reflecting the desire for deeper economic integration across a range of matters including trade, IP and competition as well as investment. It is not the purpose of this chapter to list all or even most of the regional agreements which contain investment chapters – this would be impossible even in the most comprehensive textbook. However it is apposite to present a brief outline of some of the most important regional agreements which embrace foreign investment.

2.3.1 Energy Charter Treaty (ECT)

The ECT of 1994 essentially grew out of the desire of European states to cooperate closely with Russia and the new states of Eastern Europe and Central Asia in exploring and developing the energy sector after the end of the Cold War. Membership was open to all states committed to cooperation in the regulation of the energy sector. It entered into force in April 1998 and has been ratified by fifty-one states, some of which are nowhere near Europe geographically (for example, Australia). Having never actually ratified the agreement, Russia indicated its intention to withdraw from the ECT in 2009, a decision based on a number of costly and in some cases successful claims brought against it by energy companies, notably Yukos. In 2014 Yukos was awarded $50 billion in compensation in a claim it brought against Russia based on provisions of the ECT.[12]

The ECT protects foreign investment in the energy sector based on non-discrimination as to the source of the investment and protection against non-commercial risks, such as expropriation and currency restrictions, much as the BITs concluded by the Member States of the EU. The ECT also offers a mechanism through which disputes may be resolved between

---

[12] *Hulley Enterprises Ltd.* v. *Russian Federation* (PCA Case No. AA 226), Final Award (18 July 2014).

signatory parties, and in the case of investments, between investors and host states. At a general level, the ECT is based on the idea that international flows of investments and technologies in the energy sector are mutually beneficial, but national sovereignty over energy resources remains a core principle of the Treaty. Each member country is free to decide whether and how its national energy resources are developed, and also the extent to which its energy sector is open to foreign investors.

2.3.2 North American Free Trade Agreement (NAFTA)

The NAFTA is a treaty between Canada, the United States and Mexico that was entered into in 1994, as a follow-up to the Canada–US FTA of the late 1980s. The three Member States formed the largest trading bloc in the world in terms of the GDP of its constituent members. Unlike the ECT, which only deals with the energy sector, NAFTA addresses trade and investment generally. It aims to achieve free movement of goods, services, people and foreign investment. NAFTA's investment chapter seeks to establish a secure investment environment through the establishment of reasonably clear rules of fair treatment of foreign investment, to remove barriers to investment by eliminating or liberalizing existing restrictions, and to provide an effective means for the resolution of disputes between an investor and the host government. The substantive investment features of NAFTA are those that feature in many North American BITs, covering principles such as non-discrimination as well as guarantees against expropriation without compensation. Indeed NAFTA represents somewhat of a blueprint for both Canadian and American Model BITs, with these countries embracing a regime of IIAs later than many other developing countries, such as those in Europe. The USA now has forty-six BITs to Canada's thirty-seven and Mexico's thirty-one. As will be discussed in Chapters 3 and 4, like NAFTA itself a number of Canadian and American BITs guarantee National Treatment-based non-discrimination at the pre-establishment stage, which is uncommon to most of the world's many thousands of BITs which tend only to grant this protection after the investment has already been admitted. NAFTA also contains an investor-state dispute settlement mechanism which has led to extensive litigation between the state parties, and is responsible for a significant body of jurisprudence that has been highly influential in the development of the discipline international investment law.

2.3.3 Association of South East Asian Nations Comprehensive Investment Agreement (ACIA)

The ASEAN is a geopolitical economic organization of ten states of South East Asia formed in 1967. It consists of Indonesia, Malaysia, the Philippines, Singapore, Thailand, Brunei, Burma, Cambodia, Laos and Vietnam, the so-called ASEAN Community. Its objective is economic growth, social progress, cultural development and peace. ASEAN itself has some FTAs with various states in the region. First drafted in 1987, revised in 1998 then finalized in 2009 into its modern expanded form, the ASEAN Comprehensive Investment Agreement (ACIA) has the objective of liberalizing the movement of investment within the ASEAN region. With its enlarged mandate of liberalization and promotion as well as traditional protection, the ACIA is thought to have incorporated best practices in international investment treaty law from around the world.[13] The main principles of the ACIA are that all industries in the region are to be opened up for foreign investment, with exclusions to be phased out over time through schedules; that foreign investments are to be treated the same as domestic ones; that regulatory impediments to investment generally will be eliminated; and that investment procedures will be streamlined with enhanced transparency. There are also traditional protections including guarantees against expropriation without compensation, as well as provisions ensuring the ability of investors to repatriate their capital. ACIA contains provisions on investor–state dispute settlement, specifying a variety of procedures including ICSID, the United Nations Commission on International Trade Law (UNCITRAL) as well as the Kuala Lumpur Regional Arbitration Centre. The first arbitral decision under the original ASEAN investment treaty was issued in 2003[14] and there is a growing body of jurisprudence under its disciplines.

2.3.4 The Trans Pacific Partnership (TPP)

The TPP is an economic integration agreement covering trade and investment as well as matters such as IP and agriculture that was concluded in late 2015 among twelve Pacific Rim countries: Brunei, Chile, New Zealand,

---

[13] J. Salacuse, *The Law of Investment Treaties* (Oxford University Press, 2015), at 110.

[14] *Chi Oo Trading Pte Ltd* v. *Government of the Union of Myanmar*, ASEAN Case No. ARB/01/1, Award (31 March 2003).

Singapore, Australia, Canada, Japan, Malaysia, Mexico, Peru, the USA and Vietnam. Together these countries comprise almost 40 per cent of the world's GDP, making the TPP the largest economic integration agreement in the world. China and various other countries may join the TPP at a later date. It has been suggested by some commentators that the USA's push to conclude TPP negotiations with provisions that China would be unable to accept (for example, strong protections for organized labour) was part of a strategic effort to contain or marginalize China's role in the global economy.[15] In addition to its deep commitments in relation to trade, the TPP contains comprehensive investment protections such as guarantees of non-discrimination and against expropriation without compensation. There are also very progressive provisions on labour and the environment, issues which will be revisited in Chapter 9. The TPP grants investors access to investor–state dispute settlement, a feature which, though well established in international investment law, caused much consternation among citizens and commentators during the Treaty's protracted negotiations. One of the curious features of the TPP's investment chapter is its carve-out for the tobacco industry. Disputes in this sector of the economy may not be subjected to the agreement's investor–state dispute settlement rules. This concession was initiated at the behest of Australia which until recently faced a claim by the tobacco company Philip Morris based on Australia's plain-packaging laws which the investor had been presented as a form of expropriation,[16] an argument which had failed in the Australian courts. It is interesting that Philip Morris's claim ultimately failed, with the tribunal unanimously refusing to take jurisdiction over the matter. This outcome raises doubts as to whether the onslaught of tobacco-based lawsuits under IIAs would have actually materialized, as many had feared.

2.3.5 Transatlantic Trade and Investment Partnership (TTIP)

While strictly speaking a bilateral rather than a regional agreement given the EU bloc's competence over foreign investment, of all the RTAs with investment chapters none has attracted the level of attention and

---

[15] E.g. D. Pilling, 'The "Anyone but China" Club Needs a Gatecrasher' *The Financial Times* (London) 7 Oct 2015.

[16] *Philip Morris Asia Ltd* v. *The Commonwealth of Australia*, UNCITRAL, PCA Case No. 2012–12 (brought under the Hong Kong–Australia BIT).

controversy of the notorious TTIP, an economic integration agreement under negotiation at the time of writing between the USA and the EU, two of the three largest economies in the world. The EU launched a public consultation into the TTIP in 2014 mostly because of the highly controversial investor–state dispute settlement mechanism contained in its investment chapter. The response to the consultation was so overwhelming that the TTIP quickly became a hot button issue in EU political machinations as well as in the US presidential elections. Putting aside the discussion of the TTIP's original and somewhat creative investor–state dispute settlement mechanism for the time being (which will be evaluated in more detail in Chapter 7), the TTIP's investment chapter contains a number of innovative provisions designed to respond to some of the key controversies in international investment law. Generally speaking, the TTIP's investment chapter was designed to redress some of the perceived imbalances between investors and host states, with the former typically enjoying all of the rights and the latter incurring all of the average agreement's obligations. Some of these provisions will be referred to throughout this book, including its key establishment of the highly anticipated 'right to regulate' in areas of significant public interest. Whether or not the TTIP will ever be ratified by the EU or the USA in its current form (at the time of writing this seems unlikely) is unclear. Still, one clear lesson has already been learned from the TTIP which represents a vital contribution to international law: when fully presented to citizens in a timely manner, international investment law is a source of incredible public engagement, which in one sense should be quite heartening from a democratic standpoint. The TTIP perhaps also represents the point at which international investment law truly came of age – it catalysed a moment in which the discipline went from an obscure subject of interest for a handful of lawyers to one which galvanized the attention of millions of people.

2.3.6 Economic Community of West African States (ECOWAS)

While the Economic Community of West African States (ECOWAS) has only marginal importance in terms of the GDP of its constituent members, it is worth including here because it is an example of a RTA with an investment chapter that has been concluded among a bloc of developing states, many of which may be regarded as least developing. ECOWAS is made of up fifteen Member States in West Africa, of which Nigeria is by far the most economically powerful and is poised to become one of the world's key emerging markets in the coming decades. The ECOWAS Treaty,[17] signed in 1975, contains protections on investments in the Member States by nationals of other Member States. It includes material on compensation for expropriation, guarantees of free transfer of currency as well as commitments to promote investment between Member States. Many of the standards found in conventional IIAs are missing from the ECOWAS treaty, including FET and FPS. While the ECOWAS treaty has a mechanism for state-to-state dispute settlement among members, it does not contain any reference to investor–state dispute settlement.

There are many other RTAs with investment disciplines, many of which will be referred to throughout this book. Following the entry into force of the Lisbon Treaty in 2009, the EU itself now has competence over the entry into treaties covering foreign investment, meaning that individual Member States will no longer be concluding IIAs on their own. New IIAs concluded by the EU, including the TTIP and before it the Comprehensive Economic and Trade Agreement (CETA) with Canada constitute much-anticipated embodiments of a European approach to investment treaties. Some commentators have depicted this development as representative of a new era of IIAs with significant changes to substance and procedure which help to achieve a more even balance between the obligations on states and the rights of investors.[18]

2.4 The World Bank

The World Bank (the International Bank for Reconstruction and Development) is an international financial institution that provides loans to poor countries for the purposes of undertaking large-scale projects, such as hydroelectric dams, roads and recovery from war or famine. It was created in 1944 as a means of preventing the outbreak of war (along with the IMF and the forerunner of the WTO) and today consists of 188 member countries. Several of the World Bank's constituent agencies are important for the purposes of international investment. In addition to the work of

---

[17] 28 May 1975.
[18] C. Titi, 'International Investment Law and the European Union: Towards a New Generation of International Investment Agreements' 26:3 *European Journal of International Law* (2015).

some of its constituent branches, noted below, the World Bank engages in important information-gathering and sharing about a broad range of international (as well as national) economic matters. Chief among these in terms of influence may be the annual Doing Business project which assesses the extent to which each of its member countries is amenable to commercial activity. A country's World Bank Doing Business Ranking[19] is one of the most important indicators of a country's capacity to attract FDI. This metric, and others like it, will be considered in Chapter 11.

Before turning to the role of the World Bank's constituent agencies in facilitating FDI, it should be noted that there are a number of regional development banks which serve a similar purpose, such as the Asian Development Bank and the African Development Bank. Given that these entities have for the most part played a subordinate role to the World Bank, they will not be examined here, although they will be considered briefly in Chapter 11.

2.4.1 The Multilateral Investment Guarantee Agency (MIGA)

The MIGA is a key instrument for the purposes of facilitating international investment that was achieved through the World Bank. It is quasi-legal and in some sense norm-generating as borrowers seeking to use MIGA are bound by its rules. MIGA is based on the premise that in addition to seeking legal certainty, potential foreign investors wish to have additional financial assurance when they invest in countries with a deficient legal infrastructure and where non-commercial risks are accordingly severe (just as economic opportunities in these places may be considerable). It reflects the practical reality that winning an arbitration claim against a host state that is insolvent may be of little use to a foreign investor.

Created in 1988, today MIGA consists of 181 Member States and has the purpose of providing guarantees against non-commercial risks faced by investors operating in developing states as a way of augmenting investment in the world's poorest countries.[20] This is known as PRI, which will be examined further in the final chapter and consists of four main categories: host country restrictions of currency transfers; expropriation; breach or

---

[19] www.doingbusiness.org.

[20] The Convention Establishing the Multilateral Investment Guarantee Agency came into effect 12 April 1988 (MIGA Convention).

repudiation of contract by the host government where no effective judicial processes are available; and lastly, war or civil disturbance.[21] Coverages for these eventualities may be purchased individually or in combination. Given that MIGA is part of the World Bank, an organization with a clear developmental objective, only investments that contribute to the host country's development and conform to its national laws are eligible for MIGA coverage, as determined by MIGA itself. In addition to normal commercial risks (such as the sudden drop in the value of a given commodity), certain risks are not covered by the guarantee, such as losses as a consequence of devaluation or depreciation and acts of the host government which have been consented to.[22] The eligible host country (which must be a developing country) must consent to the guarantee against particular risks designated in any particular guarantee. In the contract between the investor and the MIGA, the investor promises to operate on a commercial basis and the investor is required to pay premiums for the benefit of the guarantee. In addition to providing insurance for investments against this specified set of non-commercial risks, MIGA engages in investment promotion activities which involve cooperation with investment-related national agencies, private insurers and generally the promotion of investment conditions in developing member countries. As will be discussed in Chapter 11, uptake of PRI by investors has been uneven. Still, MIGA issued US $2.8 billion in new investment guarantees for forty individual projects in 2015.[23] MIGA implements a policy on Environmental and Social Sustainability, which aims to safeguard and promote culture, the environment, community health and safety and indigenous rights as well as employment and training in host states.[24] These rules are mandatory for all investors using MIGA – the organization will not offer assistance to investors who do not address these objectives when designing their projects.

2.4.2 International Finance Corporation (IFC)

The IFC is a branch of the World Bank which promotes private sector investment in developing countries to reduce poverty and improve the

---

[21] Ibid., Art 11.   [22] Ibid., Art 12.

[23] MIGA Annual Report, Fiscal Year 2015, www.miga.org/Documents/Annual-Report-2015 .pdf.

[24] MIGA Policy on Environmental and Social Sustainability (1 Oct 2013), www.miga.org/ documents/Policy_Environmental_Social_Sustainability.pdf.

standard of living. Unlike the World Bank proper, the IFC funds the foreign investors themselves. It finances private enterprises at market rates, either through loans, equity investment or the facilitating of financing through the mobilization of loans from private sources. It was established in 1956 and is composed of 184 member countries. The main idea behind the IFC is that it provides support for foreign investment projects that would be otherwise unfeasible because private investors would be unwilling to take the risk when the relevant host state is simply too unstable.[25] The IFC Articles of Agreement state that its purpose is to further economic development through the encouragement of productivity of private enterprises in member countries, and thereby supplement the efforts of the main branch of the World Bank.[26] These goals will be achieved through: financing with private investors, the establishment and growth of productive private enterprises without guarantee of repayment by the member government concerned, where sufficient private capital is not available on reasonable terms; bringing together investment opportunities, domestic and foreign private capital, and experienced management; and creating conditions for the flow of investment in member countries. The IFC Articles establish various criteria for its investments which are similar to those of MIGA. First, the investment must be in productive private enterprises.[27] The financing must be undertaken on sound commercial grounds, which is understood to mean that the IFC will be able to recoup its capital.[28] Reflecting the World Bank's developmental aims, the investment must benefit the host state's economy and should satisfy environmental considerations.[29] As noted above, the financing must be for activities which do not have available sufficient private capital on reasonable terms – like a lender of last resort.[30] Other conditions include the requirement that the financing of an enterprise in a member country must be with the consent of that member country and the IFC cannot dictate where the proceeds of the investment are to be further invested, and that there should be no attempt by the IFC to become involved in the management of the enterprise.[31]

In addition to investing in private enterprise with a development purpose, the IFC engages in investment promotional activities. It provides technical assistance, particularly in matters relating to privatization. It also advises on foreign investment laws in developing host states as a way

---

[25] IFC Articles of Agreement, Art 1(i) (as amended 28 April 1993).   [26] Art 1.
[27] Art 3.   [28] Art 1.   [29] Art 1.   [30] Art 1.   [31] Art 1.

of reducing barriers to capital movement. The IFC has published its Performance Standards, which are rules for borrowing firms and which embrace the IFC's commitment to sustainable development, including safeguarding the environment and ensuring that there are no adverse social impacts from funded investment projects. The IFC's standards incorporate principles on resource efficiency, climate change, and business and human rights.[32] These policies are mandatory conditions on borrowing investors which compel them to use the resources of the IFC in a manner that acknowledges the non-economic needs of the host state.

2.4.3 The International Centre for the Settlement of Investment Disputes (ICSID)

The World Bank established the ICSID in 1965.[33] Emerging from a position of relative obscurity, ICSID is now one of the main systems of arbitration for the resolution of disputes between foreign investors and host states, and represents perhaps the single greatest achievement in the multilateralism of international investment law. Today 150 states are party to the ICSID Convention. Its rules will be explored in more detail in Chapter 7. For now it is important to establish that ICSID grants a level of security to investors located in regions lacking in political or legal stability by providing a means of legal redress for commercial losses caused by the excessive or undue regulatory and administrative actions of host state governments.[34] ICSID is advantageous because it provides a recognized, neutral procedure for the resolution of disputes between investors and host state governments. Tied to the consent of the parties, the dispute settlement process is self-contained, meaning that it is independent of the influence of outside bodies such as courts and crucially that other forms of dispute settlement are foreclosed. Awards of the ICSID tribunals are final and binding, except in very narrow circumstances, and are enforceable automatically in all party states, precluding the need for additional

---

[32] International Finance Corporation's Policy on Environmental and Social Sustainability, 1 Jan 2012, www.ifc.org/wps/wcm/connect/7540778049a792dcb87efaa8c6a8312a/SP_English_2012.pdf?MOD=AJPERES.

[33] Established by the Convention on the Settlement of Investment Disputes between States and Nationals of Other States, also known as the Washington Convention or the ICSID Convention 575 UNTS 159, 4 ILM 524 (1965).

[34] R. Dolzer and C. Schreuer, *Principles of International Investment Law* (Oxford University Press, 2012), at 222.

procedures through domestic courts. Moreover, as an agency of the World Bank, ICSID can potentially use the denial of World Bank assistance as a sanction against the refusal to enforce its awards. Criticisms of ICSID are its poor transparency,[35] its lack of an appeal mechanism[36] and the observed inconsistency of its decisions.[37] Many of these issues will be revisited in Chapter 7.

2.5 The World Trade Organization (WTO)

The WTO is an international organization created in 1995 and composed of 162 Member States as of 2015. It has the primary objective of reducing or eliminating barriers to the trade in goods and services across international borders. At least with respect to goods, the WTO and its predecessor, the General Agreement on Tariffs and Trade (GATT), has been remarkably successful. Its dispute settlement system in particular has been celebrated as one of the greatest achievements in international law.[38] The WTO has played a minor role in the regulation or liberalization of international investment, but it had been hoped that the WTO would embrace investment (along with a number of other issues) as part of its enlarged mandate during the early stages of the Doha Round of trade negotiations (the so-called Singapore Issues). However this was never achieved and appears unlikely in the near future – indeed the future of multilateralism in economic matters appears today to be on very shaky ground. The WTO operates on a consensus basis requiring the consent of all of its Members when new disciplines are created. This one-nation-one-vote system has become increasingly unwieldly as membership has grown just as divergences between developed and developing countries have intensified around issues such as agricultural subsidies. As of late 2015 with the Doha Round of negotiations collapsing during the Nairobi Ministerial Council meeting, the WTO has sensibly indicated a willingness to pursue

---

[35] E.g. Collins, *The BRIC States.*

[36] E.g. S. Subedi, *International Investment Law: Reconciling Policy and Principle* (Hart, 2008), at 205.

[37] E.g. S. Montt, *State Liability in Investment Treaty Arbitration* (Hart, 2009), at 139–141.

[38] P. Van den Bossche and W. Zdouc, *The Law and Policy of the World Trade Organization* (Cambridge University Press, 2013).

trade liberalization on a plurilateral (optional) basis as it has done with government procurement, for example. It may be that this more incremental style of negotiation may pave the way for progress on matters such as foreign investment in the future. In the meantime, negotiation of bilateral and regional trade agreements, such as the TTIP and the TPP, seems to be progressing enthusiastically.

Regardless of the success or lack thereof of the WTO's efforts in creating and enforcing international investment law, it is important to recognize that most foreign investors are also traders. For example, a multinational may obtain raw goods from outside the jurisdiction in which they have located, just as they may sell their finished products abroad. Firms may choose to internationalize in order to circumvent trade barriers, and the reduction of such barriers through WTO membership may preclude this strategy. In this sense many WTO rules have an indirect impact on foreign investors.

A number of WTO agreements deal more directly with investment, and these will be discussed briefly in turn.

2.5.1 General Agreement on Trade in Services (GATS)

The most significant WTO agreement covering international investment is the GATS. This treaty regulates foreign investment in the services sector on the basis of the provision of services through the commercial presence of an enterprise within a foreign state, the third 'mode' of service supply. This mode of service is often the only practical way in which some services can be provided, such as energy distribution. The widely acknowledged benefits of FDI have led many WTO Members to make foreign access to certain services industries contingent on the local presence of providers.

GATS consists of general obligations, applying to all measures affecting trade in services, and specific obligations, which require commitments by Members in specific sectors. GATS's specific commitments relate to market access and National Treatment (non-discrimination on the basis of foreignness) in certain services sectors for which Members were prepared to make commitments.[39] Market access commitments prevent Members

---

[39] Art XVII.

from placing limitations such as the number and size of services or service suppliers in listed service sectors operating within its territory, whether they are domestic or foreign.[40] Specific commitments are set out as a 'positive list' in each Member's service schedule.

This flexibility allows Members to exclude whichever sectors they want, which was key to GATS's existence as a multilateral agreement covering an intensively regulated sector of economic activity.

Unfortunately, Members chose to exclude many sectors from their GATS commitments, such as financial services, telecommunications and transportation. Still, of the four designated modes of supply of services in GATS, most specific commitments have been through the commercial presence, or FDI, mode. This may reflect the desire of host countries to be able to regulate multinational enterprises that are located within their territory rather than doing business within their borders from a remote location under another jurisdiction's control.[41] GATS also contains exceptions to its obligations, including national security and general exceptions covering public interest issues such as health and public order.[42] It is important to clarify that GATS does not, however, provide a complete set of investment protection rules, such as guarantees against expropriation or nationalization by host states as would be found in BITs, for example.

GATS has been praised for creating a more secure environment for trade in services through the progressive removal of barriers to trade, in part because of the availability, through the WTO framework, of recourse to its dispute settlement mechanism instead of unilateral pressure.[43] Moreover, whereas most BITs tend only to protect established investments, GATS actually liberalizes FDI flows by removing barriers to entry, setting in place conditions for the entry of new investment; this distinction will be explored further in later chapters. Nevertheless, some commentators have criticized the GATS for failing to liberalize more fully trade in services as a consequence of its specific commitment list format.[44] With many

[40] Art XVI.
[41] A. B. Zampetti and P. Sauve, 'International Investment' in A. Guzman and A. Sykes (eds.), *Research Handbook in International Economic Law* (Edward Elgar, 2007), at 255.
[42] Arts XII–XIV.
[43] P. Delimatsis, *International Trade in Services and Domestic Regulations* (Oxford University Press, 2007), at 19.
[44] See e.g. R. Adlung and M. Roy, 'Turning Hills Into Mountains? Current Commitments Under the General Agreement on Trade in Services and Prospects for Change' 39:6 *Journal of World Trade* 1161 (2005).

Members still maintaining significant barriers to FDI in services, such as high percentages of domestic ownership, further progress in commercial presence liberalization may take place in the context of the new Trade in Services Agreement (TiSA), currently being negotiated outside the WTO but involving a number of key WTO Members.

2.5.2 Agreement on Trade-Related Investment Measures (TRIMS)

The TRIMS is the only one of the WTO's agreements that deals expressly with foreign investment, and in a sense it represents the only issues that the WTO's Members were able to agree upon in place of comprehensive investment protections such as those found in IIAs. The TRIMS essentially prohibits a narrow range of trade-orientated laws which interfere with foreign investment. WTO Members are forbidden from applying restriction on foreign investors that are inconsistent with the central commitments of the WTO's GATT: the TRIMS imposes National Treatment for imported goods and prohibits quantitative restrictions on imports and exports as a condition of entry of foreign firms.

Trade-related investment measures are themselves left undefined; instead there is an Annex containing an illustrative list of investment measures that are inconsistent with these GATT commitments. The list includes prohibitions against local content requirements, which are measures requiring the purchase or use by an enterprise of domestic products, whether specified in terms of particular products, in terms of volume or value of products, or in terms of a proportion of volume or value of its local production; trade balancing requirements which are measures requiring that an enterprise's purchases or use of imported products be limited to an amount related to the volume or value of local products that it exports or measures restricting the importation by an enterprise of products used in or related to its local production, generally or to an amount related to the volume or value of local production that it exports; foreign exchange requirements which are measures restricting the importation by an enterprise of products used in or related to its local production by restricting its access to foreign exchange to an amount related to the foreign exchange inflows attributable to the enterprise; and lastly export restrictions, which are measures restricting the exportation or sale for export by an enterprise of products, whether specified in terms of particular products, in terms of volume or value of products, or in terms of a proportion of volume or value of its local production. These prohibitions have serious implications for a Member State's industrial policies, which may be designed to support the development of domestic capacity, secure benefits from foreign investment or limit the effects of foreign competition.[45] The TRIMS covers investment-related measures that apply to goods only; it does not apply to services.[46] As such it is more closely associated with FDI in manufacturing.

2.5.3 Agreement on Trade-Related Aspects of Intellectual Property (TRIPS)

The TRIPS deals with standards of protection of IP. While the TRIPS was drafted largely with the purpose of addressing piracy, it is crucial to keep in mind that IP frequently falls within definitions of investment in IIAs, and as such this type of asset is perceived as being at risk from undue interventions by host states. In this regard, the TRIPS usefully mandates standards of protection for IP that should be transposed into national law. Failure to address violations of IP rights through the domestic legal system would therefore represent a violation of this agreement. The TRIPS contains minimum protections for copyright, trademarks, patents, industrial designs and various other IP rights. Members are free to provide greater protection, but the process of obtaining and enforcing IP rights must not be unduly onerous. As with many WTO provisions, transparency in the regulation of IP at the national level is also mandated.

The importance of ensuring that WTO Member States provide adequate protection for IP can be seen in the case of compulsory licensing of IP in emergency situations, such as epidemics. Under such circumstances, patent rights holders, such as pharmaceutical companies, can be compelled to allow the cheap or free reproduction of their drugs. This could be viewed as an illegal taking of an investment which would be prohibited under most IIAs as a form of expropriation.[47] With the capacity to enact compulsory licensing intact, developing host states are able to safeguard this important public policy concern without fear of reprisal in the form of arbitration claims. Despite suggestions that FDI in IP-based industries

---

[45] D. Collins, *Performance Requirements and Investment Incentives under International Economic Law* (Edward Elgar, 2015).

[46] Art I.   [47] Art 31.

may lead to valuable knowledge transfer, there remains sparse evidence that the TRIPS has actually resulted in significant increases in technology transfer or the flow of FDI to or from WTO Members. Some developing countries claim that the TRIPS has actually harmed their economies.[48]

2.6 The International Monetary Fund (IMF)

While not strictly speaking an administrating organization of international law because of the largely unenforceable nature of its obligations, the IMF has placed regulatory oversight over some key aspects of international investment. Created in the aftermath of World War II during a period of reorganization in governance over the global economy, the IMF has a membership of 187 countries. Unlike the one-nation-one-vote system of the WTO, the IMF has a quota-based voting rights system linked to economic size, with the USA having by far the largest power. The IMF is charged with maintaining free transfer of currencies, ensuring that international commercial transactions can take place and most crucially, that foreign investors can have access to domestic capital in host states to fund their operations. The IMF also seeks to prevent its Member States from suffering balance-of-payment imbalances, with the provision of short-term loans on condition that they implement certain economic reforms with a view to eventual repayment. This aspect of the IMF's purview has come under recent scrutiny in international investment law as a consequence of various states' sovereign debt restructuring regimes which in some cases have questionably interfered with investor's operations. The IMF requirement under its Articles of Agreement that Members must liberalize currency transfers[49] in order to promote capital movement is a central component of many states' profile as attractive destinations for foreign capital. Investors concerned that their profits cannot be fully repatriated will be comforted by a host state's dedication to IMF principles in this regard. The issue of unrestrained currency transfer, as well as the link between sovereign debt restructuring and the treatment of foreign investors, will be discussed later in this book. Following the global financial crisis, the

---

[48] E. Graham, 'Will Emerging Markets Change Their Attitude Toward an International Investment Regime?' in K. Sauvant (ed.), *The Rise of Transnational Corporations from Emerging Markets* (Edward Elgar, 2008), at 311.

[49] Art IV.

IMF indicated that in some cases it may be appropriate for states to impose capital restrictions as this may be viewed as a necessary response to economic emergency. This issue will be revisited in Chapter 10.

2.7 The Organisation for Economic Cooperation and Development (OECD)

The OECD is an international organization created in 1961, composed of thirty-four member countries generally comprising the most economically advanced nations in the world. It is essentially a forum through which its member countries can develop policies with the objective of promoting economic development among themselves and in developing countries. The OECD evaluates a wide range of economic data and constructs policies on that basis, including a number of instruments aimed at augmenting the global flows of FDI. The OECD's publications do not constitute international law by any means, but some of them have been highly influential in establishing various countries' approaches to the regulation of foreign investment.

The OECD's Code of Liberalization of Capital Movements is perhaps one of the organization's most important legal policy documents with regards to the manner in which international investment is regulated.[50] Drafted over a period of several decades but revised in 2013, this Code provides highly generalized rules for countries in order for them to remove barriers to capital as a means of attracting foreign investment in order to strengthen their domestic economy. The Code encourages OECD Members to avoid any exchange restrictions, with exceptions available for maintaining order in times of economic crisis or for national security interests. Members who choose to adopt the Code must also commit to notifying the OECD of any barriers placed on FDI and to state reasons for so doing. The Code specifies that transfers for the purpose of facilitating FDI among OECD Members should be free, meaning that there should be no discriminatory regulatory barriers imposed such as special conditions or authorizations that are not also placed upon domestic investors.[51] The OECD's Investment Committee meets on a regular basis to administer the

---

[50] www.oecd.org/daf/inv/investment-policy/CapitalMovements_WebEnglish.pdf.
[51] Annex A List A 1.

Code. Non-OECD Members are able to participate in these meetings with a view to adopting the Code in terms of their own foreign investment law practices.

The OECD Guidelines for Multinational Enterprises are an influential set of non-binding guidelines which may be adopted by governments and then placed upon international firms which are incorporated in those states.[52] The Guidelines are voluntary recommendations, relating essentially to business ethics and including commitments on labour relations, human rights, accountability and disclosure as well as environmental protection. Aimed at helping redress the imbalance of IIAs which place obligations on the state parties but not on the investors, many of which operate in highly sensitive extractive industries, they also specify that signatory states will maintain national contact points, meaning that dedicated government offices to disseminate information about the Guidelines have been put into practice among their corporate citizens. Updated most recently in 2011, the Guidelines are adhered to by all government members of the OECD which in turn encourage their enterprises to observe the Guidelines wherever they operate. The OECD publishes annual reports indicating what each adhering government has done to fulfil their commitments under the Guidelines. As they are non-binding, the OECD Guidelines are not traditional international law but are perhaps among the strongest (meaning in this case the best recognized) examples of 'soft law' in the sphere of international investment. The Guidelines will be revisited again in Chapter 9.

Some mention should be made of the OECD's attempt to create a Multilateral Agreement on Investment (MAI) in the late 1990s. The reasons for the collapse of the MAI tend to concentrate on the lack of participation in the negotiation process by the developing world as well as pressure from Non-Governmental Organizations (NGOs) to include provisions on environmental and labour protections, which proved unpopular in industrialized countries such as the UK.[53] Perhaps more fundamentally, the OECD's efforts in investment multilateralism may have been unsuccessful because of ideological conflicts concerning the function of the state in relation to the economy which were well entrenched in the late 1990s. Traditional capital-exporting countries were most concerned

[52] www.oecd.org/dataoecd/43/29/48004323.pdf.
[53] E.g. M. Sornarajah, *International Law*, at 2–3.

with constraining a state's power, guided instead by the primacy of markets. Capital-importing states stressed the sovereignty of the government in organizing the economy, a view which appears to hold less sway in many of today's emerging markets. After the collapse of communism, many newly independent nations were more interested in safeguarding their economic independence than facilitating the capital accumulation of private citizens.[54] In the MAI negotiations the positions of most of the wealthy OECD countries reflected their status as FDI exporters, whereas developing states (many later to become known as emerging markets) viewed themselves as importers or host states. It may be that as the economic position of developed and developing countries continues to rebalance towards equilibrium between inward as well as outward FDI, negotiating positions should lean towards equality, making the achievement of a multilateral investment treaty along the lines of the OECD's MAI more feasible.

2.8 Other Multilateral Initiatives

Some further discussion should be offered regarding other multinational quasi-legal frameworks that are relevant to international investment. First, the Convention on the Recognition and Enforcement of Foreign Arbitral Awards (the New York Convention)[55] is a multilateral instrument that facilitates investor–state dispute settlement, which is the focus of Chapter 9. With 156 signatory states, the New York Convention requires courts of signatory states to give effect to private agreements to arbitrate and to recognize and enforce arbitration awards made in other contracting states as if they were judgments of domestic courts. Arbitration awards may still be challenged in national courts if there were procedural irregularities in the composition of the arbitral tribunal, or if the tribunal exceeded its jurisdiction. Awards that violate the public policy of the enforcing state may also be disregarded, and in that sense the Convention provides an additional layer of sovereign control that is absent from the self-enforcing ICSID regime. It must be recognized that the New York Convention tends not to be necessary in the context of arbitration

---

[54] S. Schill, *The Multilateralization of International Investment Law* (Cambridge University Press, 2014), at 370.

[55] 330 UNTS 38, signed on 10 June 1958, entered into force 7 June 1959.

based on IIAs because these agreements usually require that signatory states guarantee that their courts will recognize and enforce arbitral decisions, obviating the need of the Convention. In the absence of such provisions in IIAs, the New York Convention is essential – its rules allow for procedural systems of international arbitration other than the automatically self-enforcing ICSID to be used, including those of UNCITRAL Arbitration Rules[56] and ad hoc fora such as the London Court of International Arbitration (LCIA) and the International Chamber of Commerce (ICC). These tribunals tend to be frequently engaged for investment contract-based arbitrations rather than those rooted in treaties.

UNCITRAL, which is a branch of the UN dealing with international economic matters, may itself be said to be among the most influential multinational governance initiatives in the sphere of international investment. In addition to its system of rules for investor–state arbitration which will be examined later, UNCITRAL also promulgates model rules of domestic arbitration which have been adopted by a number of developing countries. Implementing this recognized system of rules in domestic arbitrations is somewhat of a badge of respectability, and acts as a signal to foreign investors (and local investors) that the relevant country recognizes the rule of law and is committed to binding, neutral and effective resolution of commercial disputes.

One of the UNCITRAL's most significant recent contributions to international investment law, or at least the soft version of it, are the Rules on Transparency in Investor–State Dispute Settlement which were adopted by a UN Resolution in 2013.[57] Created in response to accusations that investor–state dispute settlement is insufficiently transparent given its public dimension, these Rules mandate certain levels of openness in proceedings. They recognize the public interest in having access to what transpires in an arbitration hearing as well as the effective resolution of the matter. They include provisions on the timely publication of all information on the hearing itself as well as related documentation. They also include commitments on efforts to increase the participation by third parties. Together these may be seen as a vital step towards achieving the legitimacy that investor–state arbitration is often thought to lack, because it

---

[56] UNCITRAL Arbitration Rules (revised 12 July 2010), www.uncitral.org/pdf/english/texts/arbitration/arb-rules-revised/pre-arb-rules-revised.pdf.

[57] UN Resolution 68/109 (16 Dec 2013).

is not available for close scrutiny by the parties who are affected by it – namely citizens and other stakeholders who are not directly participating in the process. The UNCITRAL Transparency Rules apply to all investor-state arbitrations taking place under UNCITRAL Arbitration Rules, unless the parties agree otherwise.

Lastly, UNCITRAL must be praised for its unparalleled information-gathering and dissemination in the field of international investment and international investment law. Its Investment Policy Hub[58] is a comprehensive and free online database of all IIAs and many investor–state dispute settlement cases, organized with an interactive map. For example, each year UNCITRAL publishes its detailed World Investment Report which outlines trends in global FDI and provides in-depth analysis into trends in investment treaty practice. These reports are among the most highly anticipated and probably most widely read annual reviews of the discipline.

International economic governance has undergone a major change in recent years with the creation of a new international development organization, formerly known as the BRICS Development Bank but now officially named the New Development Bank (NDB). A potentially game-changing organization aimed at extending development loans as well as foreign investment insurance and financing, the NDB is the first institution of global governance created in the post-Bretton Woods era and is intended to reflect the growing role of emerging markets in contributing to the smooth running of the global economy. Created in 2014 by the BRICS consortium, the NDB is a multilateral development agency with a similar mandate to that of the World Bank and the IMF combined. While BRICS-initiated, membership of the NDB is open to all Members of the UN. The objective of the NDB is to channel global capital reserves into infrastructure and development projects with a view to helping advance the world's poorer countries. This could help stimulate significant levels of FDI into developing countries where non-commercial risks are high, as the World Bank itself, and to a lesser extent the IMF, have done. To achieve these goals, the NDB will provide financial support in the form of loans, equity or insurance to public and private projects.[59]

The NDB was established with a view to avoiding some of the controversies associated with the lending policies of the World Bank and the

[58] http://investmentpolicyhub.unctad.org/IIA.
[59] New Development Bank Articles of Agreement, Art 1 (15 July 2014).

IMF, some of which are thought to have worsened economic crises in borrowing states by focusing too closely on repayment rather than the actual effects of reforms on society.[60] Precisely how the NDB will achieve this remains unclear. The so-called Delhi Declaration (a meeting among the BRICS states in 2012) announced that an alternative, more democratic, global financial architecture was needed in light of the global financial crisis which had resulted from excessive reliance on market fundamentalism. The NDB may assist projects that the World Bank would not, such as nuclear power plants. It may also impose fewer conditions on its beneficiaries, both possibly with higher rates of interest. It is likely that the NDB will be less closely wedded to market-orientated reforms than its Bretton Woods counterparts, likely advocating more centralized planning along the lines of China itself.[61] Whether or not the NDB's approach will actually work to achieve its aims, such as enhanced FDI, remains to be seen. Along with the NDB is the Asian Infrastructure Investment Bank (AIIB) which is an institution proposed by China to support infrastructure projects in the Asia-Pacific region and which also aims to act as a counterpoint to the approach taken by the World Bank and the IMF. The AIIB quickly received wide support among the international community, attracting membership from a number of developed countries including Japan, Canada and the UK.

2.9 Investment Contracts

A vital point to note is that in addition to bringing claims through IIAs, international investors may also use commercial contracts to protect their assets from undue interference by host states. As a discipline of academic study, international investment law tends to focus more on IIA-based rights and disputes, but contract-based ones are equally important and are the basis of many investment claims. Host states dealing directly with foreign firms will often choose to govern their legal relations through concession agreements or other types of contracts such as Build Operate and Transfer (BOT) agreements. Such contracts are used frequently where

---

[60] A. Dreher and M. Gassebner, 'Do IMF and World Bank Programs Induce Government Crises? An Empirical Analysis' 66:2 *International Organization* 329 (2012).

[61] L. Brahm, 'A New Global Financial Architecture Emerges' *Institutional Investor* (22 Dec 2015).

host states seek foreign firms' expertise for the exploitation of natural resources or to build and manage large-scale infrastructure projects such as airports, bridges and hydroelectric dams. Since these arrangements are highly individualized, in many cases long-term and idiosyncratic, specialized contracts delineating the precise nature of the investor's legal relationship to the host state are required. Many of these instruments contain standalone rights or obligations in addition to those which are available under IIAs or under customary international law. One good example of a contract-based right often granted to foreign investors that is absent from IIAs is that of the stabilization clause. Stabilization clauses promise that host states will not change their legal regimes to disadvantage the investor over the duration of the investment project. Somewhat similar to FET and in some respect FPS clauses (to be examined further in Chapter 5), such provisions ensure that the law of the receiving jurisdiction will remain the same, allowing investors to plan ahead without fear of being subjected to a sudden reversal in policy that could have severe consequences on their business activities. The breach of a stabilization clause could itself amount to a violation of the FET Clause in an IIA, leading to a situation where the investor could bring claims under both the investment contract and the investment treaty, potentially raising jurisdictional issues especially where a domestic court is willing to hear one aspect of the claim and not the other. Such overlap can occur because breach of contractual terms may undermine the investor's legitimate expectations.[62]

Although strictly speaking private in nature because they are essentially commercial contracts between two parties, by definition any contract must be governed by a system of national law. This is often specified in the contract's choice of law provision, typically by reference to the host state's laws or in some cases the investor's home state's laws where these are perceived as being more sophisticated. Choice of forum clauses in such contracts enable international arbitration tribunals to take their jurisdiction over associated disputes. Such arrangements also have a clear public dimension because one of the parties is a government or a government agency funded by tax and accountable to its citizens, at least in theory. The distinction between actions undertaken by sovereign states in their capacity as sovereign states rather than as private commercial actors is a blurred one that can cause much confusion when claims are brought

---

[62] *AGIP* v. *Congo*, 21 ILM 735 (1982).

by investors against states in international arbitration tribunals on the basis of treaties and contracts.[63] While the focus of this book is primarily on international investment law as derived from treaties and investment treaty arbitration, some of these issues will be dealt with again in other chapters out of necessity.

2.10 Conclusion

Treaties remain the chief source of law governing the activities of international investing firms, and while there are now more than 3000 of these instruments in operation around the world, they tend to contain the same or very similar concepts, which form the basis of international investment law. The dominant form of international investment treaty remains the BIT, but there are an increasing number of RTAs with investment chapters, including the mega-regional TTIP and TPP. Multilateral instruments governing international investment have had a much less pronounced impact, but there are a number of critical initiatives that have been undertaken at the global level, notably those of the WTO (especially the GATS and to a lesser extent the TRIMS and the TRIPS) and those of the World Bank in its capacity as an agency which offsets some of the risks associated with engaging in FDI in the developing world. Non-binding instruments such as the Guidelines of the OECD and UNCTAD have played a minimal role in regulating foreign investment but their capacity to mitigate some of the one-sidedness normally attributed to the IIA regime should not be ignored. Such instruments may reflect the direction that international investment law will take in the future. Finally, a significant number of foreign investment projects are undertaken on the basis of rights contained in commercial contracts between the investor and the host state. These instruments can contain standalone rights or in some cases bolster parallel claims under treaties.

While ensuring a degree of protection for foreign investors, IIAs and other treaty-based sources of international investment law limit signatory states' capacity to regulate their economic affairs. In that sense, although these regimes are rooted in consent (namely that of the government of

---

[63] See e.g. I. Alvik, *Contracting With Sovereignty: State Contracts and International Arbitration* (Hart, 2011).

the state party) they may be still be viewed as an undue encroachment on national sovereignty of economic affairs. Likewise, the relative clarity of treaty-based obligations (as opposed to the somewhat less tangible rights that are drawn from customary international law) must be seen as the bedrock of international law's attempt to strengthen the protections available in this high-risk, high-value commercial activity. Given their unquestionable importance to FDI, the content of IIAs will be explored in this book, commencing in the next chapter with a closer examination of the definition of investment, and followed by further illustration of the role played by the national laws of admitting states.

3.1 Introduction

When advising clients on how to invest in certain countries, it is of course essential to be familiar with the commitments which that country has made regarding foreign investment at the international level. But there is more to the legal landscape than IIAs. To have an understanding of the legal regime facing a foreign firm, one must also come to terms with national laws on investment, including most importantly any conditions which may be placed on foreign firms by host states. Just as they must ascertain where they stand in relation to domestic rules on running a business, firms which are contemplating internationalization must be certain that they will meet the definition of investors to secure the protection of IIAs. These concerns engage several crucial elements of international investment law.

This chapter begins the closer analysis of the substantive content of IIAs that will form the basis of this book. It will explore the controversy associated with the definitions of investment and investor found in many instruments, considering some of the key arbitration case law which has contributed to the modern understanding of this concept and its recognized limits, including so-called 'mailbox companies' and other refinements which generally embrace the necessity of a close connection to the host state. The status of SOEs and entities such as Sovereign Wealth Funds as potential investors deserving of treaty protection will be discussed. This chapter then delves into the various conditions placed on foreign firms by host states before they are admitted into the jurisdiction, such as the important requirement that the investor conforms to the law of the host state, necessitating a consideration of domestic laws, as well as modern developments including carve-outs for various forms of economic activity through Denial of Benefits clauses. Before proceeding to the analysis of the requirements placed on investors before they are entitled to the protections afforded by IIAs, it is essential to establish that states themselves can incur legal liability for breaches of international law.

3.2 State Responsibility

One of the primary functions of IIAs is to clarify and expand upon the protections which are already available to aliens through customary international law, as actualized through diplomatic protection and the law of state responsibility. When an act of a state, meaning an organized sovereign entity, interferes with the rights of aliens either under customary international law or more importantly under an IIA, this gives rise to state responsibility. This means that the state must account for its actions which have transgressed international law. The key principles associated with state responsibility are to an extent codified in the International Law Commission's Articles on State Responsibility, which will be referred to several times throughout this book. Article 1 of the Articles reads: 'Every international wrongful act of a State entails the international responsibility of that State.'[1] Following from this, a state may incur legal liability and therefore faces the obligation to compensate an injured party. The nature of compensation will be considered in detail in Chapter 7, but for now it is enough to establish that the existence of meaningful legal consequences denotes the practical significance of international investment law. Clearly the obligations contained in IIAs create a situation where a wide range of domestic regulations may become unlawful under international law. This may engender severe impacts on host states seeking to pursue many social as well as economic policies. A number of commentators critical of international investment law, especially its dispute settlement features, have observed that virtually any kind of regulation can potentially be challenged by investors under broadly construed provisions of IIAs.[2]

This restriction on host state sovereignty must be viewed in light of the sometimes complicated relationship between international law and

---

[1] United Nations, International Law Commission, Report on the work of its fifty-third session (23 April–1 June and 2 July–10 August 2001), General Assembly, Official Records, Fifty-fifth Session, Supplement No. 10 (A/56/10).

[2] E.g. J. W. Yackee, 'Bilateral Investment Treaties, Credible Commitment, and the Rule of (International) Law: Do BITs Promote Foreign Direct Investment?' 42:4 *Law and Society Review* 805 (2008).

domestic law that colours much of the discipline of international invest-ment law. Indeed, the constitutions of many countries establish that they are the paramount source of law within their territories. For example, the Constitution of the Federal Republic of Nigeria states that the 'Constitution is supreme and its provisions shall have binding force on all authorities and persons throughout the Federal Republic of Nigeria'.[3] The Nigerian Constitution goes on to explain that a treaty ratified by the government of Nigeria will not have the force of law except to the extent that it is enacted into law by the legislature (a process known as domestication). Such an assertion becomes problematic where the constitution conflicts with the country's international legal commitments, particularly when considering the statement in the VCLT which specifies that a state may not invoke the provisions of its internal law as justification for its failure to perform a treaty.[4]

Unlike customary international law, which most countries regard as enforceable in domestic courts and of equal force as domestic laws, inter-national treaties like IIAs do not automatically have a legally binding effect until they have been enacted as statutes locally, even after the treaty has been ratified. Like Nigeria, Canada maintains this so-called dualist approach to international treaty law requiring an extra step to legitimize the treaty's rules[5] although, in Canada as in many countries, even without this procedure international law is still persuasive and also used by judges as an interpretive aid.[6] In dualist countries domestic law is supreme, and for domestic judges to be competent to apply international treaties these must be specifically adopted or transposed into domestic law by an act of the legislature or parliament. This system allows the country to make com-mitments under treaties and even to ratify them without actually being bound by their obligations. In some countries, such as the USA, many (but not all) varieties of international treaties become part of domestic law upon ratification, at which point the US Constitution regards them as part of the supreme law of the land.[7] In this 'monist' approach, treaties are considered to be self-enforcing once they have been ratified, precluding the need for a separate step of authentication. In other countries, such as

---

[3] S 1(1) (1999).   [4] Art 27.

[5] *Canada (AG)* v. *Ontario (AG)* [1937] UKPC 6 (UKPC).

[6] J. Brunnee and J. Toope, 'A Hesitant Embrace: The Application of International Law by Canadian Courts' *Canadian Yearbook of International Law* (Volume 40) (2002), at 5.

[7] Art VI.

Germany, international treaties are given constitutional status and actually take precedence over national legislation.[8]

But the distinction between domestic and international law, and the unenforceability of the latter because of the hierarchy of the former, at least in dualist systems, is largely irrelevant in the case of IIAs because these instruments create their own system of enforcement. It does not matter how domestic courts or the constitution view these rules. While the rights contained in IIAs do not have direct effect in domestic courts (claims for treaty breaches cannot be heard by domestic courts), they do not need to. This is because there is a dedicated system of dispute settlement in most IIAs where decisions of international arbitrators are enforceable as if they were final decisions of courts.[9] In this sense, IIAs do not require a process of domestication for them to entail legal consequences for the state parties which sign them. This is one of the reasons that investor-state dispute settlement is so powerful as well as controversial, as will be examined further in Chapter 7.

The irrelevancy of the requirement of ratification reveals the vital need for states to ensure that the obligations which it incurs in an IIA are extended only to the extent that it wishes. Otherwise, liability and with it the obligation to pay compensation can ensue. More pointedly, the host state needs to be certain that it only extends the protections of the treaty to the types of commercial activity that serve its purpose. This is controlled through provisions in IIAs governing the admission of investment.

3.3 National Investment Laws

Although any protection provided for in an investment treaty is always under the law of the host country, this law has to conform to the commitments undertaken by the state concerned under the treaty. So, as suggested above, when advising clients about the legal environment of host states, lawyers must be familiar with the national legislation governing foreign investments as well as with any IIAs. This is more accurately described as the comparative law of international investment, rather than

---

[8] Art 25 of the Basic Law of the Federal Republic of Germany.

[9] Pursuant to the New York Convention on the Recognition and Enforcement of Foreign Arbitral Awards or through the self-enforcing system of ICSID for signatories of the Washington Convention.

international investment law, because although these laws affect the operations of multinational enterprises, they are laws which are themselves not truly international. For this reason, as well as the obvious difficulties in considering the national legal systems of hundreds of countries, this aspect of international investment law tends to receive less scrutiny by international legal scholars and commentators. This is not to say that national investment regimes are not considered by arbitration tribunals – indeed many claims by foreign investors brought through international investment tribunals are based in part on breaches of the national legislation of host states.[10] Tribunals have held that investors may submit any legal dispute to arbitration whether or not it is based upon a treaty, the domestic law of the host state or other applicable legal norms.[11]

The link between national investment laws and those contained in international law, namely IIAs, is the phrase found in most IIAs indicating that the protections contained in the treaty are available to those investments which are in conformity with the laws of the host state. Such a provision is typically found under the heading 'Admission and Protection of Investments', and a good example may be seen in Art 2(1) of the German Model BIT of 2008:

> Each Contracting State shall in its territory promote as far as possible investments by investors of the other Contracting State and admit such investments in accordance with its legislation.

The phrase 'in accordance with its legislation' is telling. It effectively incorporates by reference all of the domestic laws which have an effect on the foreign investor. In other words, if the foreign investor breaches the relevant national laws, the investor is not entitled to be admitted into that state's territory and the protections of the IIA do not operate.

Some very open countries, such as the UK, place almost no restrictions on foreign investment whatsoever and as a consequence there is no specific domestic legislation governing foreign investment. In such jurisdictions, foreigners or foreign-controlled firms operating in all spheres (with the exception of national defence, and some transport and energy activities) are treated virtually identically to domestically owned ones. Many countries which maintain a somewhat tighter control of foreign investment, such as the USA, do not have one dedicated piece of

---

[10] E.g. *Tokios Tokeles* v. *Ukraine*, ICSID Arbitration (No. ARB/02/18) (29 June 2004).

[11] *Wena Hotels Ltd.* v. *Arab Republic of Egypt*, ICSID Case No. ARB/98/4 (8 Dec 2000).

legislation for dealing with any restrictions or conditions on foreign firms. Rather, investment by foreign entities is regulated by various provisions contained in a wide range of statutes covering different sectors of economic activity, meaning that foreign firms seeking entry into the USA often require quite complex legal advice. Given the economic importance of attracting foreign investment, as well as the recognition that regulation through many different laws rather than a single regime can itself operate as a barrier to foreign investment because of confusion and complexity, it is becoming increasingly commonplace for countries to consolidate all of their foreign investment laws into one simplified regime.

As a consequence of the importance of FDI to national economies of both capital-importing and capital-exporting states, as well as the risks involved for investors and the states which receive them, some countries' governments operate dedicated agencies for the assessment of incoming foreign investment projects. In Australia, for example, the Foreign Investment Review Board examines foreign investment proposals and advises on the national interest implications. Such specialization is also required because of the increasing complexity of Australia's rules relating to foreign firms, which are contained in several legal instruments and include various categories and multiple thresholds for investments in different sectors.[12] Such processes will be explored further in Chapter 10 in relation to national security.

One of the best examples of a consolidated piece of national legislation governing foreign investment intended for the purposes of streamlining the administration of FDI is the Investment Canada Act. This federal statute, enacted in 1985 and regularly updated, establishes the procedures in place for assessment of large-scale FDI projects (both acquisition-based as well as greenfield) including the famous (or infamous, depending on one's view of economic globalization) review for the purposes of determining whether the investment is of 'net benefit' to Canada. This is found in Art 16(1):

> A non-Canadian shall not implement an investment reviewable under this Part unless the investment has been reviewed under this Part and the Minister is satisfied or is deemed to be satisfied that the investment is likely to be of net benefit to Canada.

---

[12] Media Release, 'Government strengthens the foreign investment framework' (2 May 2015), http://jbh.ministers.treasury.gov.au/media-release/034-2015.

'Net benefit' is a controversial concept in Canada because failure to fulfil this requirement means that the investment cannot proceed, potentially resulting in a significant loss of business opportunity to the investor and to the Canadian economy. In determining whether an investment satisfies the net benefit test, the relevant department of the Canadian government will consider several factors including: the effect of the foreign investment on the level of economic activity in Canada; its effect on employment and on the use of Canadian goods and services; the degree of participation by Canadians in the business; the effect on the investment of productivity and industrial efficiency as well as technological development; the effect on competition within any industry in Canada; and its compatibility with Canada's industrial and cultural policies.[13] A number of these considerations appear to transgress at least the spirit of the WTO TRIMS Agreement, which prohibits performance requirements and other preferential industrial policies which could affect foreign investments.

As of 2017, the net benefit test applies to investments greater than C $800 million in enterprise value, and which are from WTO Member countries and are not SOEs. The review threshold will rise to C $1 billion in 2019. Reflecting the concern that SOEs may represent a greater risk to Canada because of their closer ties with foreign states which could therefore pose a greater risk to national security, the review threshold for SOEs from WTO Member countries is substantially less, currently under $400 million.[14] Investments from non-WTO Member countries into Canada are subject to even lower thresholds, with direct investments of value greater than only $5 million required to satisfy the net benefit test.[15] This lower threshold also applies to all foreign investors seeking to invest in a 'cultural business' in Canada, for which a list of designated national heritage or cultural identity-orientated activities is provided.[16] It is noteworthy that much higher thresholds of review have been offered to investments originating from other signatories of the new TPP. A separate review procedure which does not specify any relevant factors to be taken into consideration is in place in the Act for foreign investments where there are national security concerns.[17] A number of high-profile applications from foreign investors seeking entry into Canada have been rejected on the basis of national security concerns, namely the concern that it is unwise to surrender significant valuable natural resources to companies

---

[13] Art 20 (a)–(f).   [14] Ss 14.1(1) and 14.1(2).   [15] Ss 14(3) and 14(4).   [16] S 14(6).
[17] Ss 25.1, 25.2.

that are effectively branches of their home state's national governments.[18] It would seem as though in the future, SOEs will be permitted to invest in Canada's natural resources on an exceptional basis only.

The national investment laws of many countries are structured according to the percentage of foreign ownership in the investment project seeking entry. In other words, the more foreign the investment actually is, the stricter the conditions of entry. For example, the Law on Foreign Investment in Vietnam[19] reads:

Article 15
Foreign investors may establish in Vietnam an enterprise with one hundred (100) per cent foreign owned capital. An enterprise with one hundred (100) per cent foreign owned capital shall be established in the form of a limited liability company and shall be a legal entity in accordance with the law of Vietnam. An enterprise with one hundred (100) per cent foreign owned capital may co-operate with a Vietnamese enterprise to establish a joint venture enterprise. With respect to important economic establishments as determined by the Government, Vietnamese enterprises shall, on the basis of agreements with the owner of the enterprise, be permitted to purchase a part of the capital of the enterprise to convert such enterprise into a joint venture enterprise.

Article 16
The legal capital of an enterprise with foreign owned capital must be at least thirty (30) per cent of its invested capital. In special cases and subject to approval of the body in charge of State management of foreign investment, this proportion may be lower than thirty (30) per cent. During the course of its operation, an enterprise with foreign owned capital must not reduce its legal capital.

Article 17
The duration of an enterprise with foreign owned capital and the duration of a business co-operation contract shall be stated in the investment licence for each project in accordance with regulations of the Government, but shall not exceed fifty (50) years. Pursuant to regulations made by the Standing Committee of the National Assembly, the Government may, on a

---

[18] J. Grey, 'Ottawa's National Security Review a Warning to Foreign Investors' *The Globe and Mail* (Canada) (2 July 2015).

[19] 12 Nov 1996, as amended 9 June 2000.

> project by project basis, grant a longer duration but the maximum duration shall not exceed seventy (70) years.

Many countries issue lists outlining the spheres of economic activity in which foreign investment is either prohibited or restricted, typically via a percentage of foreign ownership. For example, the Philippines provides a negative list of the sectors on which restrictions are imposed based again on degree of foreign ownership, starting from the most severely restricted to the most liberalized:

> List A: Foreign ownership is limited by mandate of the constitution and specific laws:
> No Foreign Equity: 1. Mass media, except recording... 2. Practice of all professions, 3. Retail trade enterprises with paid-up capital of less than US$2.5 million... 4. Cooperatives, 5. Private security agencies... 6. Small-scale mining... Up 20% Foreign Equity: 12. Private radio communications network... Up 25% Foreign Equity: 13. Private recruitment, whether for local or overseas employment... 14. Contracts for the construction and repair of locally funded public works... except: a) infrastructure/development projects... and b) projects which are foreign funded or assisted and required to undergo international competitive bidding... Contracts for the construction of defense-related structure... Up to 30% Foreign Equity: 16. Advertising... Up to 40% Foreign Equity: 17. Exploration, development, and utilization of natural resources... 18. Ownership of private lands... 19. Operation and management of public utilities... 20. Ownership/establishment and administration of educational institutions... Up to 49% Foreign Equity: 27. Lending companies... Up to 60% Foreign Equity: 28. Financing companies regulated by the SEC... 29. Investment houses regulated by the SEC.[20]

The emphasis on local control of the financial sector is clear, evincing the concern that this sector should not be unduly controlled by foreign elements as this may represent a risk to national security.

There is a growing trend among emerging market countries to streamline their foreign investment legislation, making the administrative approval processes less burdensome, raising monetary thresholds for admission and lowering thresholds for percentage of domestic ownership. In some cases these instruments even grant incentives to foreign investors,

---

[20] Executive Order No. 98 Promulgating the Ninth Regular Foreign Investment Negative List (29 Oct 2012).

such as promises not to raise income tax over a certain period. The use of incentives to induce FDI will be considered further in Chapter 11. Some countries choose to regulate foreign investors under the same piece of legislation as domestic investors, typically applying a stricter set of criteria for the former in terms of capitalization as well as ownership restrictions.[21]

It is important to acknowledge that national legislation governing foreign investment tends not to be reviewable in domestic courts or other administrative procedures (or international tribunals, for that matter) as the decisions encapsulate the sovereign authority of the government over its economy. This should be contrasted with national legislation governing domestic investment where most administrative decisions regarding the legality of mergers and acquisitions as well as greenfield investments would be reviewable by domestic courts as per conventional administrative review under the principles of public law. In this way, a foreign investor whose project is denied entry, such as under Canada's net benefit test, would have no recourse for example to have their application re-examined, appealed or possibly even to receive reasons for the rejection.

3.4 Definitions of Investment and Investor

The principal method by which host states control the application of their commitments under IIAs and in so doing effectively structure the nature of the foreign investment operating in and in some cases entering their territory is through the definition of investment and investor. Clearly, wide definitions will afford protections and in some cases a right of entry (of which further will be discussed in the next chapter) whereas narrow ones will be restrictive, precluding the application of treaty rights to parties wishing to exercise them. Assigning definitions to these concepts is a delicate balance that must be approached with caution by parties to IIAs.

There remains no settled definition of either 'investment' or 'investor' in international law. States are left to assert their own definitions of these terms in their individual IIAs and in doing so they set the scope of the protections laid out in the rest of the instrument. Only those types of

---

[21] A good example of a recent national law on foreign investment is the Law of Mongolia on Investment (1 Nov 2013).

commercial activities which fall within the listed definition, as interpreted by an arbitration tribunal in the event of a dispute, will be entitled to enjoy the benefits of the treaty.

3.4.1 Investment

The definition of investment engages questions relating to the nature of the economic activity undertaken in the host state; that is, the state whose actions are being challenged under an IIA in investment arbitration. A clear example of definitions of 'investment' that is broadly representative of those found in many EU Member State IIAs can be found in Art 1(6) of the ECT. It begins with the commonly used and incredibly wide phrase, 'every kind of asset', which itself uses open-ended language:

> 'Investment' means every kind of asset, owned or controlled directly or indirectly by an Investor and includes:
>
> (a) tangible and intangible, and movable and immovable, property, and any property rights such as leases, mortgages, liens, and pledges;
> (b) a company or business enterprise, or shares, stock, or other forms of equity participation in a company or business enterprise, and bonds and other debt of a company or business enterprise;
> (c) claims to money and claims to performance pursuant to contract having an economic value and associated with an Investment;
> (d) Intellectual Property;
> (e) Returns; [which is defined under Art 7(9) as]: the amounts derived from or associated with an Investment, irrespective of the form in which they are paid, including profits, dividends, interest, capital gains, royalty payments, management, technical assistance or other fees and payments in kind.

Some IIAs, such as those of Canada, prefer instead to use a closed definition of investment, seen for example in Canada's 2009 BIT with Jordan which defines investment:

> (i) an enterprise, (ii) shares, stocks, and other forms of equity participation in an enterprise, (iii) bonds, debentures, and other debt instruments of an enterprise, (iv) a loan to an enterprise ... (vi) an interest in an enterprise that entitles the owner to a share in the income or profits of the enterprise, (vii) an interest in an enterprise that entitles the owner to a share in

> the assets of that enterprise on dissolution (viii) interests arising from the commitment of capital or other resources in the territory of a Party to economic activity in such territory, such as under a) contracts involving the presence of an investor's property in the territory of the Party, including turnkey or construction contracts, or concessions, or b) contracts where remuneration depends substantially on the production, revenues or profits of an enterprise, (ix) intellectual property rights, and (x) any other tangible or intangible, moveable or immovable, property and related property rights acquired in the expectation or used for the purpose of economic benefit or other business purpose.[22]

Such broad definitions, sometimes characterized as 'enterprise-based definitions', contemplate indirect control over the investment. This is in contrast to the understanding of investment as the subject of the field of international investment law which tends to focus on FDI as illustrated in Chapter 1. Naturally, firms seeking to protect as much of their commercial activities as possible have led capital-exporting states to expand traditional understanding of foreign investment in this manner. Indeed, many modern IIAs consider shareholdings or participation in a company as a form of investment. As noted in Chapter 1, the threshold for ownership is thought to be somewhere around 10 per cent of the voting shares of the firm.[23] As such, a local business under foreign control may be able to invoke the dispute settlement mechanism in the IIA, whereas under traditional international investment law a local incorporated affiliate of a foreign parent would not be entitled to claim diplomatic protection as a foreign investor. The ICSID Convention allows for the treatment of a local affiliate as a foreign investor where it is agreed by the parties to the dispute that it is under foreign control and that it is in fact under such control.[24]

The expansion of the scope of investment to include so-called portfolio investment where there is no ownership or control, and in so doing enlarging the traditional focus of international investment law, has the obvious effect of bringing a much wider range of commercial activities within the scope of protection of the IIA. This expansion could call into question some of the alleged benefits associated with conventional

---

[22] Art 1 (14 Dec 2009).

[23] IMF Glossary of Selected Financial Terms and Definitions, 31 Oct 2006, www.imf.org/external/np/exr/glossary/showTerm.asp#117.

[24] Art 25(2)(b).

FDI – can knowledge transfer and employment be expected where there is a simple sales presence in the host state, or even less, merely a promissory note? A simple sales presence by a US company was regarded as an investment in the NAFTA claim under *SD Myers* v. *Canada*.[25] According to one tribunal, a pre-shipment inspection agreement between a company and the government of Pakistan was enough to satisfy the very expansive definition of investment under the Swiss–Pakistan BIT which included the phrase 'every type of asset ... including claims to money and any performance having economic value'.[26] When interpreting the definition of investment in IIAs, tribunals tend to consider how the domestic laws of the host state have defined investment, often by reference to the investment codes discussed above. In some cases this will be wider than that which is contemplated by the text of the IIA itself.[27]

Given the exposure engendered by IIAs and the uncertain benefits which may be entailed by non-direct foreign investment, a number of countries expressly exclude portfolio investment from the definitions of investment contained in the treaty. For example, the above noted BIT between Canada and Jordan tightens the definition of investment considerably by going on to state explicitly what does not count as an investment:

> (xi) claims to money that arise solely from a) commercial contracts for the sale of goods or services by a national or enterprise in the territory of a Party to an enterprise in the territory of the other Party, or b) the extension of credit in connection with a commercial transaction, such as trade financing.[28]

Some countries exclude portfolio investment indirectly by specifying that only direct investment will be covered by the treaty's protections.[29]

As noted in Chapter 1, it is sometimes thought that in order to qualify as investment there should be some contribution by the foreign investor to the economic development of the host state, which is highly questionable in the context of simple portfolio investment or one-off contracts. To a degree this requirement is captured by the developing investment arbitration jurisprudence, including the so-called *Salini* Test discussed

---

[25] *SD Myers* v. *Canada*, UNCITRAL (21 Oct 2002).
[26] ICSID Case No. ARB/01/13 (8 Sept 2003).
[27] As in *Mihaly International* v. *Sri Lanka*, ICSID Case No. ARB/00/2 (15 March 2002).
[28] Art 1.   [29] As in the Australia–Thailand FTA, Art 901(c).

previously. As suggested earlier, the various components of the *Salini* Test are far from established requirements. This controversy was cogently alluded to by the one-person tribunal in *Pantechniki* v. *Albania*:[30]

> A number of tribunals have struggled with what has become known as the '*Salini* Test'... This appears to be a misnomer. It is not so much a test as a list of characteristics of investments. The *Salini* award identified five element as 'typical' of investment but made clear that the absence of one could be compensated by a stronger presence of another. The resulting margin of appreciation is unfortunate.[31]

Most questionable of the *Salini* requirements is no doubt that the investment must be of a certain duration and that it must contribute to the economic development of the host state – both of which suffer from vagueness and an associated impossibility of demonstration through evidence. To be sure, the preambles of many IIAs refer to the objective of achieving the economic development of party states,[32] something seen also in the preamble of the ICSID Convention.[33] Some commentators also suggest that there is a duty on the part of the foreign firm to contribute to the development of the host state.[34] Under this logic, the obligation to contribute to the host state's economic development is the corresponding duty to the assortment of rights enjoyed by the investor under the IIA. The existence of a right to development is reflected in comments made by arbitrators, some of whom appear to be willing to infer the contribution to development as part of the definition of investment.[35]

Still, it is highly uncertain that there is any kind of autonomous definition for investment outside that specified by the relevant IIA, particularly since the ICSID Convention, the leading set of rules for investor–state arbitration, is conspicuously silent on the matter. As the *Pantechniki* tribunal rightly observed:

---

[30] ICSID Case No. ARB/07/21 (30 July 2009).   [31] At 36.

[32] E.g. France–Ethiopia (25 June 2003).

[33] ICSID Convention (also known as the Washington Convention) preamble: 'Considering the need for international cooperation for economic development, and the role of private international investment therein.'

[34] E.g. D. Desierto, 'Development as an International Right: Investment in the New Trade-Based IIAs' 3:2 *Trade Law and Development* (2011).

[35] E.g. *Malaysia Historical Salvors Sdn Bhd* v. *Malaysia*, ICSID Case No. ARB/05/10, Decision on the Application for Annulment, 16 April 2009: '[t]he outer limits of an ICSID investment comprise a requirement for contribution to the development of the host state'. Dissenting Opinion of Judge Mohamed Shahabuddeen, sec. B, at [21].

[B]roadly acceptable descriptions [such as the *Salini* Test] cannot be elevated to jurisdictional requirements unless that is their explicit function. They may introduce elements of subjective judgment on the part of arbitral tribunals (such as sufficient duration or magnitude or contribution to economic development) which a) transforms arbitrators into policymakers and above all b) increase the unpredictability of ICSID to settle given disputes.[36]

That tribunal went on to conclude, somewhat desultorily, that an investment was indeed present in the host state given the commitment of resources and equipment that had been made by the claimant. Perhaps most tellingly, the tribunal appeared to suggest that the jurisdictional objection had to be rejected because the claimant's project lacked the quality of being too 'simple and instantaneous' which might have precluded it from being considered an investment.[37] These adjectives, while hardly amounting to a legally sophisticated 'test', go a long way to capturing the essence of what investment is understood to be. Though ephemeral, most would agree that an investment is the kind of thing that you know when you see.

This issue was addressed in the *Burimi* v. *Republic of Albania*[38] arbitration which concerned an Italian gaming company's use of certain products which had been allegedly interfered with by the government of Albania in violation of the Albania–Italy BIT. The state had revoked Burimi's gaming permit, which the company claimed constituted regulatory expropriation. Albania was able to defend itself on the basis that Burimi's activities did not constitute an investment because they were of insufficient duration and did not contribute meaningfully to the host state's economy. This was because the company's financing and pledge agreements relating to the gambling project were not long-term investments but simply 'freestanding contracts'. In other words, a series of private loan contracts for the purpose of securing financing do not reach the level of economic commitment required of an investment.

In another recent example of a tribunal identifying the limits of the concept of investment, in *Global Trading* v. *Ukraine*[39] an American company brought a claim against the Ukraine under the US–Ukraine BIT because of legislated restrictions to artificially reduce prices, as well as breach

---

[36] Ibid., at [43].   [37] Ibid., at [48].   [38] ICSID Case No. ARB/11/18 (29 May 2013).
[39] ICSID Case No. ARB/09/11 (1 Dec 2010).

of contract regarding export arrangements. The tribunal was required to make a determination under Rule 45(1) of the ICSID Convention, in which a claim can be dismissed at an early stage for being manifestly without merit – in this case because there was allegedly no investment. The tribunal decided that even when a BIT has a broad definition of investment it still must fit within the ICSID Convention's understanding of that term. As the claimant's position was based upon a series of individual contracts of limited duration, these were purely commercial transactions that were better described as those of trading suppliers, not investors. As such they were never intended to fall within ICSID's jurisdiction.

Postová banka v. *Hellenic Republic (Greece)*[40] was a dispute in which the tribunal dismissed a case arising out of Greece's sovereign debt exchange for lack of jurisdiction with respect to subject matter, namely the non-existence of an investment. This arbitration was initiated in 2013 by a Slovak bank and its former Cypriot shareholder under the Slovakia–Greece BIT and the Cyprus–Hellenic Republic (Greece) BIT. In deciding whether it had jurisdiction over the dispute, the tribunal noted that the BITs contained broad asset-based definitions rather than a closed list. Still, it determined that the careful drafting of various categories of protected investments in the subsections demonstrated that there were meant to be limits to the definition. The tribunal noted the fact that the BIT referred to 'shares in and stock and debentures of a company and any other form of participation in a company' but not to sovereign debt or bonds issued by the state parties. The tribunal also examined the special features of sovereign debt that distinguish it from private debt, including the reality that creditors' legal recourse against a sovereign debtor is much more limited and there is therefore greater than normal risk. There were also various practical realities associated with sovereign debt, including that it is subject to specific and strict regulations. This led it to the logical conclusion that neither of the relevant BITs was intended to cover sovereign debt in their definitions of investment.

Hassan Awdi v. *Romania*[41] involved a privatization project relating to a building in Bucharest being converted into a luxury hotel and restaurant. The tribunal rejected Romania's jurisdictional challenges which were based on the claimant's lack of a contribution to the host state's economy, a concept which did not appear in the text of the relevant IIA between the

---

[40] ICSID Case No. ARB/13/8 (9 April 2015).   [41] ICSID Case No. ARB/10/13 (2 March 2015).

home and host states. Nor did the tribunal accept Romania's contention that the *Salini* criteria, in particular the requirement of a contribution to the development of the host state, should be read into the term 'investment' under the ICSID Convention. Instead, the tribunal ruled that the meaning of 'investment' should be determined exclusively and strictly as set forth in the BIT. The tribunal went on to determine that the open-ended asset-based definition under the BIT made the mere existence of an economic linkage between the claimants and the investments sufficient for purpose of establishing jurisdiction.

To take another illustrative example, *Nova Scotia Power Incorporated* v. *Bolivarian Republic of Venezuela*,[42] which concerned a coal supply arrangement undertaken by an investor incorporated in Canada and Aruba, also explored the meaning of investment. The decision again deferred to the language of the relevant BIT. The tribunal declared that it lacked jurisdiction under the Canada–Venezuela BIT because the dispute arose out of an ordinary commercial contract. This commercial operation did not deserve the protection of the treaty as an investment because it was not sufficiently long term. Moreover, the eventualities of the commercial activity, namely the shipment of coal, were well within the parties' control and as such the element of risk was missing. This award is memorable for the tribunal's artful description of the limits of IIAs: 'neither the definition of investment, nor the BIT, should function as a Midas touch for every commercial operator doing business in a foreign state who finds himself in a dispute.' To be sure, it is not as easy as it might seem to satisfy the definition of investment in order to avail oneself of the protections of international investment law. Many types of commercial activity will be excluded, particularly in modern IIAs using narrower or closed-list definitions.

3.4.2 Investor

In contrast to the definition of investment, the definition of investor enquires as to the nature of the claimant's relationship with the home state. If the claimant is not sufficiently linked to that state then it will not be entitled to claim the benefits of that state's entitlements under the IIA. Arbitration tribunals will not be able to take jurisdiction over the dispute

---

[42] ICSID Case No. ARB(AF)/11/1 (30 April 2014).

if the definition of investor cannot be satisfied. In addition to specifying the types of business activities that will constitute investments for the purposes of engaging treaty protections, IIAs also typically include definitions for 'investor' to delineate the scope of the instrument's intended beneficiaries. For example, the ECT states:

(7) 'Investor' means:
   (a) with respect to a Contracting Party:
       (i) a natural person having the citizenship or nationality of or who is permanently residing in that Contracting Party in accordance with its applicable law;
       (ii) a company or other organization organized in accordance with the law applicable in that Contracting Party;
   (b) with respect to a 'third state', a natural person, company or other organization which fulfils, mutatis mutandis, the conditions specified in subparagraph (a) for a Contracting Party.

This provision discloses the authority of the signatory governments in deciding how nationality will be ascertained. Only nationals of signatory states can use the treaty. Questions of nationality can be quite complex given the various corporate structuring that is employed by investors in order to take advantage of various IIAs.

IIAs modelled on the European approach (as opposed to the US Model inspired in part by NAFTA) typically include very expansive definitions of investor, encompassing a broad spectrum of commercial activity and linkages to party states in order to maximize the protections afforded in the treaties. These wide definitions have the effect that national investors with substantial business activities in a home country are not the only ones to be protected by an IIA signed by their home country. In addition to what might be perceived as more genuine national investors (companies establishing a lasting presence in the host state with a view to contributing to that country's economic development), other perhaps somewhat less worthy investors can also rely on the protection of an IIA signed between a country they have invested in to bring a claim against a host country in international arbitration. Subsidiaries owned by foreign companies and in some cases shell or 'mailbox' companies with limited genuine linkages to the home state can rely on the protection of another home country's IIA with the host country. Arbitration tribunals have even allowed national investors to bring claims against their own government through a foreign subsidiary, as in *Tokios Tokels* v. *Ukraine*.[43] This so-called 'treaty shopping' through technicalities is thought to be one of the features of international investment law that brings the system into disrepute.

The jurisdictional stage of the dispute *Tokios* offers a good illustration of a situation where a foreign investor's status as an investor has been challenged by the host state. In this dispute, brought under the Lithuania–Ukraine BIT, the respondent contended that the claimant's business was owned and controlled predominately by Ukrainian nationals by whom 99 per cent of the voting shares were owned and who comprised two-thirds of the company's management. Even the company's headquarters were maintained in Ukraine – a situation which effectively amounted to a state being sued by its own nationals. This appeared to be outside the parameters of the ICSID Convention, particularly since there was a corresponding lack of business activity in Lithuania. The tribunal responded to this allegation by pointing out that the ICSID Convention itself does not specify the manner in which the nationality of an investor is to be determined – this is to be decided by the national laws of the parties as outlined in the relevant IIA. It quoted an academic source to add that Contracting Parties to the ICSID Convention enjoy broad discretion to define corporate nationality as they wish.[44] Since the Lithuania–Ukraine BIT used the highly inclusive phrase 'any entity' to define investor, the tribunal felt that it was inappropriate to require more substantial connections to Lithuania, including ownership or management requirements. The tribunal was motivated also by the fact that this treaty also did not include a 'Denial of Benefits' clause, of which more will be discussed below, which would prohibit investors without sufficient ties to the home state from asserting its nationality for the purposes of accessing the treaty's protections. The tribunal stated:

> In our view, it is not for tribunals to impose limits on the scope of BITs not found in the text, much less limits nowhere evident from the negotiating history. An international tribunal of defined jurisdiction should not reach out to exercise a jurisdiction beyond the borders of the definition. But equally an international tribunal should exercise, and indeed is bound to exercise, the measure of jurisdiction with which it is endowed...Rather,

---

[43] *Tokios Tokeles* v. *Ukraine*, ICSID Case No. ARB/02/18 (29 April 2004).
[44] C. Schreuer, *The ICSID Convention: A Commentary* (Cambridge University Press, 2001), at 286.

> under the terms of the Ukraine-Lithuania BIT, interpreted according to their
> ordinary meaning, in their context, and in light of the object and purpose
> of the Treaty, the only relevant consideration is whether the Claimant is
> established under the laws of Lithuania.[45]

Thus the appropriate course of action for a tribunal evaluating whether or
not the specific business structure of the alleged 'investor' should be able
to benefit from the protections afforded in the IIA is simply to look at the
definition contained in that instrument, not to transpose understandings
from other contexts of what an investment or an investor should be.

In *Renée Rose Levy and Gremcitel S.A.* v. *Republic of Peru*[46] the tribunal dismissed the dispute on jurisdictional grounds, ruling that there
was no investor capable of triggering the France–Peru BIT's protections.
The tribunal instead found an abuse of process in the corporate reorganization carried out by the claimants (a real estate company), whose
sole purpose in this action was to gain access to arbitration against Peru
under the BIT. After the relevant land (a historic site) had been transferred
to the claimants, a resolution had been issued protecting the site from
development. This frustrated the claimant's attempts to proceed with the
development project. Peru argued that the claimants were not investors
and therefore did not deserve protection of the BIT. The tribunal ruled that
corporate reorganization (transferring control of the company to a parent
of French nationality) to take advantage of a treaty was not illegitimate
in itself, but doing so for the purposes of litigation with a specific foresee-
able future dispute has the appearance of an abuse of process. Although
this test has a high threshold, it was satisfied in this case because of the
very high probability that a dispute would arise given the land's historic
status. The fact that the corporate reorganization was instigated in a rush
demonstrated the strategic purpose of accessing the BIT to resolve the
land controversy which had already begun to crystallize into a formal
dispute.

In *Saluka* v. *Czech Republic*, the claimant was incorporated in the
Netherlands but the host state alleged that the investor was a shell company that was in fact controlled by its Japanese parent. The tribunal considered the definition of investor in the Czech–Netherlands BIT which

---

[45] At [36] and [38].   [46] ICSID Case No. ARB/11/17 (9 Jan 2015).

referred to a legal person constituted under the laws of the Netherlands, concluding that there is:

> some sympathy for the argument that a company which has no real connection with a State party to a BIT, and which is reality a mere shell company controlled by another company which is not constituted under the laws of that State, should not be entitled to invoke the provisions of that treaty.[47]

Yet the tribunal still found in favour of the claimant, holding that it satisfied the agreed definition under the treaty. In other words, the wording of the IIA with respect to the definition will govern.

Some IIAs specify that a controlling interest of nationals over a company is all that is required to satisfy the definition of investor and thereby reap the treaty's protections. Such a provision is found, for example, in the BIT between the Netherlands and Venezuela.[48] This provision was contested in *Mobil* v. *Venezuela*,[49] where the investment had been made by a Dutch holding company through its 100-per-cent-owned subsidiaries in the USA and the Bahamas. Having nationalized the oil project owned by the claimant, Venezuela argued that the protections of the BIT could not be exercised under the circumstances because the Dutch company did not in fact exercise genuine control over the company. This was rejected by the tribunal which held that the issue of whether or not control was in fact exercised by the company was irrelevant when contemplating the definition of investor which specified the percentage of capital needed for control. It was sufficient that the share structure was such that it was capable of exercising control over the subsidiaries. The tribunal stated that the restructuring of the investment through a holding company was entirely valid, as far as it contemplated future, rather than already existing, disputes. The situation would have been different had the dispute with Venezuela already crystallized, in which case the restructuring to obtain the benefits of the BIT would have appeared to be an abuse of the system of international investment protection.[50] Put more clearly, prospective restructuring in order to treaty shop is acceptable, but retrospectively doing so will not be permitted.

---

[47] Partial Award (17 March 2006), at para 240.   [48] Art 1(b).
[49] Decision on Jurisdiction, 10 June 2010.   [50] Ibid., at [205].

In a similar vein, *Fraport AG Frankfurt Airport Services Worldwide* v. *Republic of the Philippines*[51] concerned a dispute arising out of a contract to build and operate a new terminal at Manila's international airport. The Philippines objected to ICSID's jurisdiction under the Germany–Philippines BIT on the basis that the Fraport venture had not been accepted in accordance with domestic law and consequently did not qualify as an investment under the BIT. Establishing a legality requirement for investments to be covered under the BIT, the tribunal stated that there is a well-established principle in international law which makes treaty-based remedies unavailable where the investment is illegal under domestic law. The relevant domestic law in this case was the Philippines' 'Anti-Dummy Law' which prohibits foreign intervention in the management, operation, administration or control of a public utility. Fraport had attempted to circumvent this requirement through its share structure, a strategy that was not accepted by the tribunal which viewed this activity as one undertaken for the sole purpose of accessing the BIT's protections.

These cases provide a flavour of the nature of the legal analysis conducted by tribunals when responding to allegations that the commercial activity does not satisfy the definition of investment or investor. Generally speaking it is clear that tribunals are guided foremost by the wording of the relevant IIA.

One of the obvious missing elements in most definitions of investor is that of SOEs which reflects the twentieth century and Western origins of most IIAs, in which there was no tradition of governments owning a significant stake in firms which would be engaged in international activity. It also demonstrates the apprehension associated with companies that have a very close relationship with their home state as the endeavour may represent geopolitical strategizing rather than commercial enterprise. The number of IIAs which refer SOEs in the definition of investor is clearly rising,[52] in no small part due to the rise of FDI from emerging market states such as the BRIC nations. For example, the Mexico–India BIT of 2007 defines investor as a natural person or an enterprise of a Contracting Party and then separately defines an enterprise as 'any entity...whether

---

[51] ICSID Case No. ARB/11/12 (10 Dec 2014).

[52] Y. Shima (2015), 'The Policy Landscape for International Investment by Government-controlled Investors: A Fact Finding Survey', *OECD Working Papers on International Investment* (OECD Publishing, 2015/01), http://dx.doi.org/10.1787/5js7svp0jkns-en, at 12.

privately or governmentally owned'.[53] SOEs often raise national security concerns and are regularly screened for that purpose, as will be examined in Chapter 10.

Presumably definitions referencing governmentally owned entities would also capture Sovereign Wealth Funds. These are state-owned investment funds rather than companies pursuing commercial activities. Among the largest in the world are the funds belonging to Saudi Arabia and Norway. Sovereign Wealth Funds are controversial in part because, as they are directly controlled by governments, they may be perceived as instruments of foreign policy, meaning that they may pursue motives other than making profits. Perhaps more problematically, they are also largely unregulated under international law. The role of Sovereign Wealth Funds in foreign investment has grown in recent years, raising significant questions about their status as investments entitled to protection under IIAs.[54] The first investment claim brought by a Sovereign Wealth Fund was initiated by the Saudi Arabia-based IPIC (in conjunction with a Dutch investor) against Korea in 2015.[55]

3.4.3 Denial of Benefits

One of the ways that states can ensure that the protections contained in IIAs are only available to those companies who actually deserve them, meaning that they have a sufficient economic linkage to the home state, is through Denial of Benefits provisions. In that sense Denial of Benefits clauses tend to control the definitions of investor rather than investment. In their most conventional form, these statements in treaties allow states to reserve the right to deny the protection of the IIA to a company incorporated in a party state but with no meaningful economic ties to that state. They essentially require that the claimant seeking to rely on the IIA must have a substantial business activity in the home state. For example, the Australia–Czech Republic BIT states:

---

[53] 21 May 2007.

[54] M. Burgstaller, 'Sovereign Wealth Funds and International Investment Law' in C. Brown and K. Miles (eds.), *Evolution in Investment Treaty Law and Arbitration* (Cambridge University Press, 2011).

[55] *Hanocal Holding B.V. and IPIC International B.V.* v. *Republic of Korea*, ICSID Case No. ARB/15/17 (20 May 2015).

> Subject to prior notification and consultation, a Party may deny the ben-
> efits of this Chapter to an investor of the other Party and to investments
> of that investor if the investor is an enterprise:
>
> (a) owned or controlled either by persons of a non-Party or of the denying
>   Party; and
> (b) has no substantive business operations in the territory of the other
>   Party.[56]

This can be a very effective method for shaping the contours of the definition of investor based on holistic rather than scientific (voting shares
and place of incorporation) ones. This approach may be more effective
than using multiple grounds to prove nationality, such as place of incorporation, organization or place of real business activities. Some Denial of
Benefits provisions include the requirement that there are diplomatic relations between the two states, allowing parties to deny protections under
the treaty if the relationship between the two countries has soured. Such
a Denial of Benefits term may be found in the US–Ukraine BIT.[57] The lack
of diplomatic relations between Cyprus and Turkey enabled a tribunal to
find that an investor was ineligible for the protections of the ECT as a
consequence of this variety of provision.[58] Denial of Benefits provisions,
which may quite accurately be viewed as a tool to control treaty shopping,
have been given effect by a number of tribunals.[59]

It should be noted that modern IIAs have used Denial of Benefits provisions more expansively in order to permit state parties to enact a range of
measures that may be in the public interest, meaning that parties which
transgress these norms are not entitled to assert their rights laid out elsewhere in the treaty. The TPP has a lengthy Denial of Benefits provision
which could effectively enable parties to escape their obligations under the
treaty in a number of circumstances, including when regulations are pursued for environmental or health reasons.[60] These issues, which are quite
distinct from those affecting the definitions of investment and investor,
will be explored further in Chapter 9.

---

[56] Art 10.13.   [57] Art 1.2.

[58] *Libananco Holdings Co. Limited* v. *Republic of Turkey*, ICSID Case No. ARB/06/8 (2 Sept
2011).

[59] E.g. *Plama* v. *Bulgaria*, Decision on Jurisdiction, ICSID Case No. ARB/03/24 (8 Feb
2005).

[60] Art 9.15.

3.5 Performance Requirements

In addition to prescribing precisely the nature of the business activity that will be considered as an investment and the identity of the entity doing it for the purposes of attracting the substantive and procedural protections of the IIA, host states may impose certain conditions on foreign investors in order for them to be allowed entry into the host state. The protections afforded by their foreign investment laws and their IIAs are only engaged when the foreign firm satisfies these conditions. Such conditions are sometimes referred to as performance requirements – the firm must perform in a designated manner in order for it to access the legal protections available under treaty or legislation.

Performance requirements may take the form of a specific business structure, such as a mandatory joint venture with a local partner. More commonly, performance requirements may specify that the foreign investor must use a given percentage of local products, hire local workers or engage in knowledge exchange with local firms. These kinds of rules are imposed by the host state because of its desire to maximize the economic benefits from FDI which are far from certain. Conditions are often associated with particular industries which most need assistance, meaning the least able to withstand foreign competition from larger, well-resourced multinationals. This is the logic behind the so-called infant industry protections, which ensure that a state has the right to nurture its nascent local industries to the point at which they can more effectively survive in a more globalized market, enhancing the overall health of the economy in the longer term. Many developed states implemented this strategy during the process of industrialization in the twentieth century. Performance requirements imposed on foreign firms as a condition of entry may also be seen more generally as a way for the host state to control the nature of the FDI which it receives, allowing it to retain some autonomy over what might otherwise be viewed as a dangerously unchecked influence on domestic markets, particularly when one considers issues such as the loss of economic sovereignty, dependency and the risk of capital flight.

However, performance requirements are heavily regulated under international economic law.[61] To begin with, the WTO TRIMS Agreement

---

[61] See further D. Collins, *Performance Requirements and Investment Incentives under International Economic Law* (Edward Elgar, 2015), Chapters 3 and 4.

prohibits a range of performance requirements which a host state might otherwise attempt to impose on the admission of a foreign investor. As indicated in the previous chapter, the TRIMS more specifically controls a sub-set of performance requirements which it terms 'trade-related investment measures'. These are conditions that directly impact upon foreign firms by imposing direct or indirect quantitative restrictions on imports or exports. The TRIMS provides that no WTO Member may apply a trade-restrictive investment measure that is inconsistent with the GATT's prohibition on National Treatment (essentially discrimination based on foreign origin) or on quantitative restrictions.[62] For example, a requirement that a foreign manufacturer of machinery may be allowed to establish in a host state only if it uses raw materials that were mined in that country would be TRIMS-illegal. While trade-related investment measures themselves are not defined under the TRIMS, an illustrative list of trade-related investment measures is contained in an Annex to the TRIMS, which essentially covers the mandatory use of local materials. The TRIMS has been the subject of limited jurisprudence under the WTO Dispute Settlement System. Most of the WTO disputes citing TRIMS provisions have been related to the automotive industry, which is not surprising given the significant role that the automotive manufacturing sector plays in the economy of many developed countries. Foreign investment automotive industry is also often subjected to conditions imposed by host states such as quantitative restrictions and local content rules. Many developing country WTO Members, such as those in Africa, had already adopted an approach to the admission of FDI that was consistent with the TRIMS by the time it was concluded.[63] The TRIPS also appears to restrict the use of performance requirements by WTO Members as host states through its provisions on patentable subject matter. Patents are to be made available without discrimination and whether products are imported or locally produced.[64] If this provision were not in place, a host state would be able to encourage foreign investors to use local products, effectively preventing them from entry were they not to do so.

---

[62] TRIMS Art 2(1) and (2).

[63] V. Mosoti, 'Bilateral Investment Treaties and the Possibility of a Multilateral Framework on Investment at the WTO' 26 *Northwestern Journal of International Law and Business* 95, at 201 (2005–06).

[64] Art 27.

Performance requirements are prohibited by many IIAs, precluding host states from imposing a range of conditions on foreign investors as a condition of entry or as a condition of enjoying the benefits of the IIA. Many treaties simply incorporate the TRIMS's rules to control this type of condition.[65] For example, the ACIA affirms the TRIMS in its provision on performance requirement prohibitions.[66] Wider performance requirement prohibitions in IIAs are sometimes referred to as TRIMS-plus obligations because they encompass more conditions than the trade-related investment measures specified in the TRIMS. Such broad prohibitions on admission qualifications for foreign investors are found in numerous RTAs containing investment chapters.[67] The most common method of dealing with performance requirements in IIAs is not to mention them at all, providing host states much more room to dictate the terms under which they receive FDI. Where IIAs are silent on the use of performance requirements, then the TRIMS will govern, at least for WTO Members. Generally speaking, modern IIAs between developing states (concluded within the last five years) tend not to include any reference to the use of performance requirements. Developed states are more likely to include performance requirement prohibitions in their IIAs, including those concluded by Asian states. For example, the Japan–Singapore Economic Partnership Agreement contains prohibitions on performance requirements including those which are based on labour and environmental standards.[68]

Prohibitions on performance requirements found in IIAs have evolved from broad, often hortatory phrases to more precise rules. An example of an early provision of this kind is contained in the Turkey–United States BIT of 1985 which states:

> Each party shall seek to avoid performance requirements as a condition of establishment, expansion or maintenance of investments, which require or enforce commitments to export goods produced, or which specify that goods or services must be purchased locally, or which impose any other similar requirements.[69]

NAFTA provides a definitive list of prohibited performance requirements which expands upon the trade-based approach reflected in TRIMS. In the first paragraph of NAFTA Art 1106, there is a list of seven specific types

---

[65] E.g. New Zealand–China FTA, Art 140 (7 April 2008).   [66] Art 7(2).
[67] E.g. Korea–Australia FTA, Art 11.9 (17 Feb 2014).
[68] 13 Jan 2002.   [69] Art II(7) (signed 3 Dec 1985).

of host state measures that the state cannot impose or enforce, including those regarding the use of local goods as well as mandatory technology transfer. Japan has included exacting performance requirement prohibitions in some of its new IIAs. A recent example, which is very similar to that of NAFTA, can be found in the Japan–Myanmar BIT of 2013.[70]

There have been a handful of investment arbitration cases which have dealt with the imposition of performance requirements on foreign firms as a condition of entry or as an ongoing requirement to continue operations, most of which related to claims brought under NAFTA.

In *Mobil Investments Canada Inc. and Murphy Oil Corporation* v. *Government of Canada*[71] the tribunal determined the provincial government's imposition of a requirement on foreign investors to spend several million dollars per year in research and development as well as education and training was a breach of NAFTA's prohibition on performance requirements. The tribunal in *CPI* v. *Mexico*[72] held that an excise tax that was imposed by Mexico on drinks using sweeteners that were not made from sugar cane effectively forced suppliers to switch from foreign corn syrup sugars to local cane-based ones. As such it violated NAFTA's prohibition on performance requirements. *Cargill* v. *Mexico*[73] was a dispute brought by a US sugar company because of alleged tax-based mistreatment at the hands of the Mexican government. Here the tribunal held that Mexico breached its obligations under NAFTA through the imposition of a production tax which amounted to a performance requirement. It determined that Mexico conditioned the tax advantage on the use of domestically produced cane sugar instead of corn syrup-based sugar for the very purpose of affecting the sale of local sugar. In *ADF* v. *United States*[74] a Canadian construction company argued that the US imposition of a domestic content requirement violated Art 1106(1)(b) of NAFTA. ADF was obliged to purchase only US steel and either to fabricate that steel in the USA itself, or to subcontract the fabrication to US steel fabricators rather than to its Canadian parent. The tribunal denied the claim, noting that the investor

---

[70] Art 6.   [71] ICSID Case No. ARB(AF)/07/4 (20 Feb 2015).

[72] *Corn Products International, Inc. (Claimant)* v. *United Mexican States (Respondent)*, ICSID Case No. ARB(AF)/04/1; Decision on Responsibility (15 Jan 2008).

[73] *Cargill, Incorporated (Claimant)* v. *United Mexican States (Respondent)*, ICSID Case No. ARB(AF)/05/2, Award (18 Sept 2009).

[74] *ADF Group Inc. (Claimant)* v. *United States of America (Respondent)*, ICSID Case No. ARB(AF)/00/1, Award (9 Jan 2003).

knew that the relevant state authority was not subject to NAFTA's prohibition on performance requirements (because it was an exempted procuring entity) and as such was permitted to enact local content requirements in government construction contracts.

One of the only non-NAFTA investment arbitrations which considered performance requirements was *Lemire* v. *Ukraine*.[75] In this dispute the claimant argued that the host state's requirement that the investor, a radio broadcaster, play 50 per cent songs that had Ukrainian content violated the prohibition of performance requirements found in the IIA between the USA and the Ukraine. The *Lemire* tribunal rejected the investor's claim, ruling that the Ukraine had the right to safeguard its national identity. The tribunal went on to explain that performance requirement prohibition in the US–Ukraine BIT should be interpreted according to its object and purpose, which was linked to the overall purpose of improving economic cooperation between the parties; this was not incompatible with protecting the Ukraine's cultural heritage.

3.6 Conclusion

The laws governing foreign investment activities are not exclusively international in character – indeed in order to fully appreciate the extent of the legal landscape affecting the multinational enterprise it is often necessary to consider the domestic laws of host states, many of which are contained in consolidated investment codes. Such instruments may overlap with the commitments contained in IIAs. In particular the typical IIA's application to investments which conform to host state laws requires an examination of these laws in order to ascertain whether or not the relevant project is indeed a covered investment. Part of this investigation necessitates the even more preliminary question as to whether the commercial activity of the multinational is indeed an investment at all. The definitions of investment and investor are among the most controversial features of this field of international law, and are regularly tackled by investment tribunals. In one sense the concepts of investments and investor are not as broad as is often perceived, but it is also often the case that firms may derive the benefits of treaties while maintaining only tenuous links with the home or

---

[75] ICSID Case No. ARB/06/18 (28 March 2011).

host state. The simple answer to this dilemma is that the definition is the one which the parties to the relevant treaty (or contract) have specified and no more, despite aspirational jurisprudence and associated commentary insisting upon an enlarged understanding, including in the case of investment criteria such as the right to development. What is clearer is that host states retain the right to admit investments on the terms that they specify, subject to their commitments as Members of the WTO as well as promises made in bilateral and regional investment-specific instruments. In this regard, host states seeking to place conditions on foreign firms, such as those mandating the use of local materials, must be careful to avoid transgressing prohibitions on performance requirements which are found in many IIAs as well as WTO instruments. While potentially serving worthwhile aims in terms of domestic economic policy, such conditions represent encroachments on the principle of liberalization upon which much of international investment law rests. One of the even more fundamental pillars of this regime, non-discrimination as to the origin of the foreign investment, itself linked to many conditions placed on admission by host states, will be probed further in the next chapter.

Guarantees Against Discrimination: National Treatment and Most Favoured Nation

4

4.1 Introduction

Operating a successful business in a foreign country can be challenging, not least because it is difficult to win over customers who may be uncomfortable purchasing goods or services from companies that are unfamiliar to them. Foreign firms operating without a local partner can have all sorts of problems finding the right suppliers and hiring talented workers as well as adapting to the regulatory environment of the host state, even where they receive expert legal advice. This is simply because it can take some time to develop an understanding of how things are done in other places on a more practical level. As demanding as internationalization can be on its own for these and many other reasons, it is infinitely more problematic if the host state places additional barriers on foreign firms or firms from certain countries than are placed on other ones operating in the same field. Surviving in an already competitive market can become near impossible if foreign firms suffer unfair regulatory treatment at the hands of the domestic government because this can give an advantage to other businesses, even unintentionally. Eliminating discrimination in the application of laws imposed on foreign investors is therefore one of the most important features of international investment law.

This chapter focuses on the two non-discrimination guarantees found in most IIAs: National Treatment and Most Favoured Nation (MFN), each of which will be considered in turn. It will look at several examples of how these vital standards of protection for foreign investors have been used in specific instances as well as the key exceptions to them, most notably the limit of post-establishment in the case of National Treatment and the arguable exclusion of procedural protections such as access to dispute settlement in the case of MFN. The crucial but unsettled concept of 'likeness' for the purposes of comparison between investors in order to ground a claim of discrimination under both of these standards will also be examined in part by distinguishing this from similar tests developed in the context of international trade law.

Before embarking on a consideration of the non-discrimination standards in IIAs, it is worth considering the backdrop to these protections, namely what exists in customary international law. Chief among the obligations regarding foreign investment in customary international law is the responsibility of states to provide the international minimum standard of protection to aliens. This concept was mentioned briefly in the previous chapter. The classic statement as to the content of the minimum standard of treatment was voiced by the arbitration tribunal in *Saluka Investments* v. *Czech Republic* when it said: 'the customary minimum standard of treatment is ... binding upon a State and provides a minimum standard guarantee to foreign investors, even where the State follows a policy that is in principle opposed to foreign investment.'[1] This statement quite simply means that there is a baseline standard of decent treatment of aliens that exists whether or not the state has pursued a policy of openness to foreign investment, even if the country is a closed-door xenophobe. This should be somewhat reassuring to multinational enterprises, but the precise content of the international minimum standard is a matter of intense debate in investment jurisprudence and academic commentary. Commercial parties, ever sensitive to the need for certainty in their high cost ventures overseas, understandably sought assurances as to what type of treatment they were entitled to receive from host states under the customary international law. Fearful that it would not grant enough, IIAs have been drafted with a view to solidifying the meaning and scope of this obligation. In particular, IIAs have sought to address one of the international minimum standard's chief misgivings – that it is an absolute standard not a relative one. In other words, no matter how good the treatment at the hands of the host state, it is not much help if competitors get something better. This is precisely why non-discrimination standards were inserted into IIAs.

4.2 National Treatment

4.2.1 Overview

National Treatment has been described as the 'single most important standard of treatment enshrined in international investment agreements.'[2] At a

---

[1] *Saluka Investments (BV the Netherlands)* v. *The Czech Republic*, UNCITRAL (17 March 2006) at [292].

[2] UNCTAD, 'National Treatment', *UNCTAD Series on Issues in International Investment Agreements* (New York and Geneva, United Nations, 1999), at 1.

basic level, it ensures that the host state makes no negative differentiation between foreign and national investors through its laws. Foreign investors are therefore able to compete on an equal footing to local investors, which in turn should encourage a healthy economy overall because it emphasizes quality and price of goods and services rather than regulatory favouritism. While it eliminates discrimination against foreign investors on the basis of the nationality of ownership of an investment and in theory should promote FDI, National Treatment can also significantly interfere with a nation's capacity of self-government on a wide range of issues, some of which may be of a more general, public policy nature or which may actually serve legitimate economic aims. Seeking to achieve a degree of competitive equality between foreign and domestic firms, National Treatment in international investment law effectively protects individual investors from targeted attacks by host states. It assures the multinational enterprise that its substantial resource commitments in other countries are relatively safe from arbitrary governmental action, mitigating the chilling effect of inconsistent and unpredictable state interference that would otherwise act as an impediment to FDI.

To be sure, some degree of differentiation between foreign and domestic firms may be necessary for the very purpose of attaining some level of operative equality, particularly when host states are developing countries. Clearly there are still considerable inequalities in economic and technological power among nations, and this often means that an investor from a foreign state will have an unfair advantage in the absence of regulatory measures which seek to level the playing field, as it were. Larger firms may deserve higher taxes or licensing fees because they place a greater strain on infrastructure, for example. The only way to ensure genuine equality of competitive conditions may be to treat the foreign investor, which happens to be larger, worse than the local one. Furthermore, discriminating against foreign firms, for example by imposing special taxes or licensing requirements, is often the only way for non-industrialized host states to promote their domestic industries either at home or abroad in order to achieve a healthy competitive marketplace leading to more full economic development.[3] This is precisely why there are a number of IIAs which do not contain a National Treatment provision. Indonesia[4] and

---

[3] S. Subedi, *International Investment Law: Reconciling Policy and Principle* (Hart, 2012), at 71–2.
[4] E.g. BITs with Thailand (17 Feb 1998) and Sweden (17 Sept 1992).

Singapore[5] typically do not grant National Treatment at all in their IIAs. National Treatment is also lacking entirely from some Philippine[6] and earlier Chinese[7] IIAs. This leaves the host state free to apply different laws to firms on the basis of their nationality (either directly or indirectly), granting advantages to domestic firms as required.

Another interesting paradox in the application of the National Treatment standard of non-discrimination is the reality that in countries with a tradition of expropriation and other interferences with private property, the application of national law could actually be less protective of foreign investors than the general rules of international law, specifically the historic international minimum standard of treatment of aliens noted above. The poor regulatory environment of some host states vis-à-vis their local firms is reflected in the commonly used words 'no less favourable' found in many IIAs National Treatment clauses, leaving open the potential for greater treatment than local competitors based on customary international law prohibiting egregious harm to aliens or their property. The practical effect of applying the international minimum standard as a kind of enhanced National Treatment is that foreign investors are effectively placed in a position superior to that of their domestic equivalents, which can of course lead to market distortions, including those resulting from the eradication of indigenous competition. Better treatment of foreign investors is highly controversial and has been a source of much consternation in many countries, in no small part because it is often associated with corruption and bribery. Investment incentives tend to treat foreign investors better than local ones. Denial of the entitlement to so-called 'better than national treatment' has been a central component of the Calvo Doctrine, a principle of international law named after an Argentine jurist which gained widespread support in Latin America. This principle, which will be revisited in Chapter 8, theorized that foreigners should receive formally identical treatment to nationals in all respects. In particular the foreign firm must use the host state's internal dispute settlement mechanisms rather than potentially advantageous international ones, just as any domestic investor would do.[8]

---

[5] E.g. BITs with Mongolia (24 July 1995) and Peru (27 Feb 2003).
[6] E.g. Philippines–UK (3 Dec 1980).   [7] E.g. China–Cambodia (19 July 1996).
[8] K. Lipstein, 'The Place of the Calvo Clause in International Law' 25 *British Yearbook of International Law* 130 (1945).

National Treatment clauses are very common in IIAs. The language expressing the standard has been described as 'minimalist' in its style.[9] While some RTAs use more expansive language, the National Treatment standard in most IIAs in particular BITs tends to be stated in one short sentence. Here is a specimen, taken from the UK BIT with Mexico:

> Neither Contracting Party shall in its territory subject investments or returns of investors of the other Contracting Party to treatment less favourable than that which it accords, in like circumstances, to investments or returns of its own investors.[10]

A somewhat more elaborate version of the standard can be found in the ECT:

> Each Contracting Party shall accord to Investments in its Area of Investors of Contracting Parties, and their related activities including management, maintenance, use, enjoyment or disposal, treatment no less favourable than that which it accords to Investments of its own investors.[11]

National Treatment clauses tend to appear near the beginning of IIAs and are often presented in conjunction with the other non-discrimination standard, MFN (see below).

The high degree of consistency with respect to National Treatment standards in IIAs is one of the reasons that it is often seen as an easier standard to apply than some of the other chief protections contained in IIAs, such as FET or expropriation. Indeed, the relative homogeneity of National Treatment in IIA practice around the world could indicate that it has itself become part of customary international investment law, precluding the need for it to be expressly granted in the text of a treaty.

4.2.2 Exceptions

Although National Treatment clauses may appear more or less the same in the text of the treaties, as a practical matter the implications differ enormously from case to case because of wide-ranging exceptions that

---

[9] J. Kurtz, 'The Merits and Limits of Comparativism: National Treatment in International Investment Law and the WTO' in S. Schill, *International Investment Law and Comparative Public Law* (Oxford University Press, 2010), at 249.
[10] Art 4(1).   [11] Art 10(7).

many nations maintain for certain business sectors and for the type of investment.[12]

Perhaps the most crucial limitation on National Treatment found in most IIAs relates to its application only to investments which have already been admitted under the laws of the host state. All National Treatment clauses apply to post-entry investment. The promise of non-discrimination based on the foreign nature of the investment applies once a business is established in the host state. Most developing countries tend to apply National Treatment in their treaties only to post-entry treatment. For example, South Africa's BIT with Turkey grants National Treatment only to investments 'once established'.[13] With this qualifying language in place, the host state is free to discriminate against the foreign investor on whatever grounds it wishes as long as this is done prior to the firm's entry into its territory. The power to act in a discriminatory manner against foreign firms prior to entry is reflected in the provisions on admission found in most IIAs which were discussed in the previous chapter. As noted earlier, most IIAs state something to the effect that the state 'shall admit such investments in accordance with its laws and regulations'.[14]

Accordingly, if the relevant investment legislation of the host state is itself discriminatory, meaning it places certain requirements on foreign investors which are not placed on equivalent local ones, for example by compelling them to satisfy a 'net benefit' test, then there is little that the foreign investor can do. The fact that most IIAs confine National Treatment only to the pre-establishment stage, allowing a wide range of pre-establishment discriminatory regulation, may be one of the reasons that the link between IIA signage and FDI flows remains tenuous. Since few IIAs open markets to new FDI by granting National Treatment to the pre-establishment stage (they merely make it safer for investments that have already occurred) then there is less chance that an investor will even be legally able to enter a foreign market, let alone be unafraid to do so. Of course, the assurance of non-discrimination after entry is itself very attractive to firms which have been able to locate in high-risk states, as discussed earlier. Lacking a pre-establishment guarantee, investors which

---

[12] D. Collins, 'National Treatment in Emerging Market Investment Treaties' in A. Kamperman Sanders (ed.), *The National Treatment Principle in a EU and International Context* (Edward Elgar, 2014).

[13] Art II 3 (23 June 2000).   [14] As in Art 2(1) of the UK–Mexico BIT.

have not yet been admitted have no legal recourse under international investment law. So for example in the dispute *GEA Group Aktiengesellschaft* v. *Ukraine*, brought under the German–Ukraine BIT, the tribunal held that an additional administrative burden placed on foreign investors by the government that did not apply to local firms was not discriminatory because the investor had not yet been admitted.[15]

Some IIAs, most notably those concluded by the USA and Canada such as NAFTA as well as the US and Canada Model BITs, also include provisions on pre-entry National Treatment, which means that they are genuine instruments of investment liberalization. The first paragraph of NAFTA's National Treatment paragraph provides:

> Each Party shall accord to investors of another Party treatment no less favourable than that it accords, in like circumstances, to its own investors with respect to the establishment, acquisition, expansion, management, conduct, operation, and sale or other disposition of investments.[16]

Singapore's RTA with India contains a pre-establishment National Treatment guarantee, although it has sectoral restrictions.[17] Vietnam's BIT with Japan also extends National Treatment to the pre-establishment stage, specifically including the word 'establishment and acquisition' in the treaty's relevant clause.[18] The ACIA contains a National Treatment provision that embraces the pre-establishment stage for investors from Member States.[19] In order to limit the risks of unbridled foreign competition in vulnerable sectors, this Agreement allows Members to submit reservation lists, excluding certain industries from the benefit of this provision.[20]

Such provisions effectively grant foreign investors a right of entry into the host state as if they were domestic businesses. As such, these agreements tend to lack statements to the effect that investments will be admitted in accordance with the laws of the host state. Discarding the capacity to screen aliens to suit a country's general economic needs, pre-establishment National Treatment is a profound commitment to economic integration for which many countries are unprepared. This may be because they do not feel that their industries are sufficiently mature to withstand the entry of multinational enterprises without restrictions, for

---

[15] ICSID Case No. ARB/08/16 (31 March 2011) at [344].   [16] Art 1102(1).
[17] Art 6.3(1).   [18] Art 2.1 (14 Nov 2003).   [19] Art 5 (6 Feb 2009).   [20] Art 9.

example as to percentage of foreign ownership or sector of operation. Such nationality-based requirements are clearly discriminatory and as such represent severe barriers to FDI. The expanded pre-establishment notion of National Treatment is becoming more popular as IIAs, especially RTAs with investment chapters, are designed as instruments of liberalization of FDI rather than simply shields against egregious mistreatment of foreign firms such as expropriation. Pre-establishment National Treatment guarantees have even been the subject of investor–state dispute claims. In 2016 Canada brought a claim against the USA for its failure to fulfil NAFTA's pre-establishment National Treatment promise by its alleged inconsistent and discriminatory implementation of its own domestic admission process for the Keystone Pipeline oil project.[21] Claims based on the denial of pre-establishment National Treatment are sure to be controversial because of the inherently speculative nature of allegations of lost profits for investments that never occurred.

Normal post-establishment National Treatment, by far the more common variety in IIAs, can itself be subjected to sectoral limitations. This means that the state reserves the right to discriminate against the foreign firm when applying laws, regulations or judicial proceedings in those specified spheres of economic activity. For example, Singapore's BIT with Jordan states that parties may maintain limitations to National Treatment in relation to any sectors or matters to be covered by later annexes.[22] Similarly, Vietnam's BIT with Japan includes an Annex that specifies forms of economic activity that are excluded from National Treatment, with each country listing its own exclusions.[23] Such limitations can be an effective means through which host states can preserve their capacity to shield domestic firms from foreign competition or to ensure that certain vital assets are kept within national control.

Since the guarantee of National Treatment under international law raises the potential that a wide range of regulatory actions may be subjected to the scrutiny of international tribunals (through IIA's dispute settlement mechanisms), it goes without saying that this standard heavily encroaches on a state's economic sovereignty as well as its capacity to enact laws that may serve social purposes. Although most investment

---

[21] http://keystone-xl.com/wp-content/uploads/2016/01/TransCanada-Notice-of-Intent-January-6-2016.pdf (6 Jan 2016).

[22] Art 5(2) (16 May 2004).   [23] Annex II (13 Nov 2003).

treaties do not expressly say so, it is widely accepted that differentiations in treatment between foreign and local investors are justifiable if rational grounds are shown, meaning there is a reason for the less advantageous treatment accorded to the foreign firm that transcends the economic value of an internationally competitive marketplace. Guarantees of National Treatment may therefore be further circumscribed by various exceptions contained in the text of the treaty. Some IIAs contain lists of the types of matters that are excluded from the coverage of the treaty's protection (including National Treatment along with other clauses), allowing the host country to enact discriminatory laws because of justifications linked to health, national security, public order or the environment.[24] The idea behind such clauses is that there may be situations in which domestic investors and only domestic investors are capable of providing the good or service because of the particular quality or expertise which they possess and which an equivalent foreign firm does not or cannot. In such circumstances, tribunals assessing breach of the National Treatment standard should take into account circumstances that would justify governmental regulations that treat them differently in order to protect the public interest.

As will be explored in Chapter 9, public interest is a notoriously difficult concept to define, which means that it is a concept that can be abused by host states seeking to undermine the capacity of foreign firms to out-compete domestic equivalents. These issues intensely intrude on the sovereignty of host states and require a cautious balancing that can be assisted through careful drafting in the text of the IIA. Modern IIAs have facilitated the evaluation of justifications for discrimination by providing more exhaustive language. When assessing the policy-based justification for the unequal treatment, investment tribunals will consider whether the host state could have achieved its goal with alternative measures that would have had a less restrictive impact on the foreign investor. Most IIAs provide lists of the types of matters that are excluded from the coverage of the instrument's protection, including its National Treatment (and MFN clauses, of which more below), allowing the host country to enact discriminatory laws on the basis of issues such as health, public order or

---

[24] Many IIAs, notably RTAs, specifically adopt the language of the General Exceptions contained in the GATS Art XIV and GATT Art. XX, e.g. NAFTA (Art 2101) and ASEAN Chapter 15 Art 1.

the environment.[25] For example, Russia's BIT with Germany permits discrimination against foreign investors taken on the grounds of 'law, order and security, morality or public health'.[26]

Some countries have governmental policies that grant preferential treatment to specific ethnic groups in an attempt to redress historic discrimination inflicted upon indigenous minorities. Such ethnic groups are often assured a certain percentage of ownership of various investment projects, most notably those in the natural resources sector.[27] Malaysian and South African IIAs do not make explicit reference to these policies in their IIAs, but such forms of positive discrimination, which have been implemented in the past by these countries, could be contemplated by the general public policy exceptions to National Treatment in these treaties such as those referring to public order. Some of these issues will be revisited in Chapter 10.

4.2.3 The Application of the Standard

A high level of standardization of National Treatment provisions in IIAs has resulted in a generally straightforward application of the concept in arbitration practice, certainly with respect to other more ambiguous standards of protection such as FET. There is relatively limited arbitral practice on National Treatment, which is somewhat curious given the comparative depth of inquiry associated with other IIA standards, again such as that associated with FET. Very few investment disputes have dealt with National Treatment provisions in IIAs, possibly because it can be difficult to identify a violation of National Treatment for the simple reason that there tend to be very few laws that discriminate against foreigners in an outright way. Furthermore, the coverage of National Treatment in most IIAs to the post-establishment stage means that complaints based on a lack of access to a given foreign market are often framed as trade disputes and brought under WTO dispute settlement rules.[28] Finally, the

---

[25] Many IIAs specifically adopt the language of the General Exceptions contained in the GATS Art XIV, e.g. Jordan–Singapore Art 18 (16 May 2004).

[26] Protocol Art (2)(c).

[27] M. Sornarajah, *The International Law on Foreign Investment* (Cambridge University Press, 2010), at 344.

[28] E.g. United States – Investigation of the International Trade Commission in Softwood Lumber from Canada, WT/DS277/AB/R (13 April 2006).

dearth of National Treatment jurisprudence in investment arbitration may also be because the much broader and more commonly used FET standard includes a non-discrimination component.[29] Likewise, claims of illegal expropriation are often founded upon discriminatory treatment of foreign property.

Among the most contentious aspects of applying National Treatment in practice relates to the comparison at the standard's heart. Other than its implicit accommodation of the international minimum standard as a baseline, National Treatment is a relative standard, not an absolute one. It grants foreign investors treatment that is defined by reference to treatment granted to local ones. A comparison is therefore necessary. As with most standards within IIAs, the application of the National Treatment clause is determined by the precise factual context as well as the wording of the clause in the treaty.

When an investor alleges that the National Treatment standard has been violated, it must also establish that there has been different treatment between itself and a similarly placed domestic investor. In other words, for the National Treatment standard to apply to a foreign investment, it must first be determined whether the foreign investor and the domestic investor are placed in a comparable setting. This is what is meant by discrimination – someone is treated worse than someone else in a similar position. To answer this question, tribunals addressing a complaint brought by the investor must ascertain if the investors are in a like 'situation' or in a like 'circumstance' to each other. This analysis effectively calls for a comparison between the two firms themselves and the nature of their business activities. The concept of 'like investment' or 'like investor' is a relative one that will involve a close assessment of what has taken place, essentially meaning what regulatory burdens have been placed on the foreign firm and crucially, whether the firms are engaged in the same kind of commercial activity.

This determination will not always be an easy one. In order to satisfy the requirement of like circumstances, is it necessary to point to a domestic investor who is in exactly the same business? Or is it enough to find an investor who is not in the same line of business but in the same economic

---

[29] This similarity was noted recently by the tribunal in *Tulip Real Estate and Development Netherlands B.V.* v. *Republic of Turkey*, ICSID Case No. ARB/11/28 (10 March 2014) at [445].

sector? This then raises questions of how concepts such as 'business' and 'sector' are to be defined. The precise method of comparison between the activities of national investors and foreign investors is a difficult one, having attracted attention from investment tribunals. Generally speaking, investment tribunals have been reluctant to construe the basis of comparison for the purposes of applying National Treatment too narrowly out of concern that to do otherwise would restrict the protection offered by the standard to the point of uselessness.[30] In order to achieve the purpose of the rule, which may be seen as one of equality of competitive conditions, like situations and like conditions should be construed broadly.

In *Pope & Talbot* v. *Canada*,[31] a dispute brought under NAFTA, the tribunal explained that by their nature, 'circumstances' are context-dependent and have no invariable meaning outside the particular facts. Circumstances will be understood to refer to investors that are within the same business or economic sector.[32] The *Feldman* v. *Mexico* dispute (also brought under NAFTA) held that like circumstances would be established if investors were in the same business,[33] whereas the *Occidental Exploration* v. *Ecuador* tribunal (under the US–Ecuador BIT) ruled that like circumstances could apply to local producers in general, regardless of the type of commercial activity.[34] This reasoning has been supported on the basis that non-discrimination in the investment context has historically been linked to the notion of diplomatic protection of aliens, which says nothing about competing businesses.[35] In *Occidental* the tribunal debated whether the market-based concept of directly competitive or substitutable firms was relevant to the analysis of the likeness comparator for the purposes of investment law.

The *Methanex Corporation* v. *USA*[36] tribunal was unwilling to apply the concept of direct competition to the companies themselves in order to develop an understanding of the concept of like circumstances because of the lack of use of the phrase 'direct competition' in the text of NAFTA.[37]

---

[30] R. Dolzer and C. Schreuer, *Principles of International Investment Law* (Oxford University Press, 2012), at 200.
[31] Award on the Merits, UNCITRAL (10 April 2001).   [32] At [78].
[33] ICSID Case No. ARB(AF)/99/1, Award (16 Dec 2002).
[34] *Occidental* v. *Ecuador*, ICSID Case No. ARB/06/11, Award (1 July 2004).
[35] R. Howse and E. Chalamish, 'The Use and Abuse of WTO Law in Investor-State Arbitration: A Reply to Jürgen Kurtz' 20:4 *European Journal of International Law* 1087 (2010), at 1092.
[36] UNCITRAL (3 Aug 2005).   [37] Ibid., at [33].

Methanex involved an allegation of discriminatory treatment based on a ban by the US state of California on the substance methanol (but not on ethanol) for environmental purposes. The foreign firm, a producer of methanol, argued that the ban discriminated against them because the two chemicals were similar. The tribunal concluded that the foreign firm did not receive less favourable treatment because in fact the law did not treat domestic methanol producers better. The Californian law did not discriminate between methanol producers themselves even if it did discriminate between ethanol and methanol producers – evidently a narrow understanding of National Treatment. In evaluating like circumstances of investors rather than competition between the products they produce, the tribunal emphasized that if an identical or at least more similar comparator is available, as it was in *Methanex* because there were local producers of the same fuel additive, then this is the comparison through which the meaning of like circumstances should be derived.[38] Like circumstances, in this case methanol producers, should be interpreted as restrictively as possible given the class of available local investors that may have been affected by the measure in question, not through a strained approximation to an arguably inappropriate one.[39]

The *Occidental* and *Methanex* tribunals' effective rejection of an equality of competitive opportunities test for likeness have been criticized for their lack of economic rigour relative to the WTO-based assessment of National Treatment, which also necessitates a likeness comparator.[40] Others have praised them for their judicious integration of a shared standard (competing products under GATT) into the diffused system of multi-tribunal arbitration.[41]

The difficulty in applying 'like circumstances' or 'like situations' to find discriminatory treatment against foreign investors was considered by the tribunal in *Loewen* v. *United States*.[42] Here the tribunal found that there was no violation of NAFTA's guarantee of National Treatment because the circumstances of the two litigants at the trial (the Canadian and the American companies) were not sufficiently similar to be caught by the treaty's National Treatment clause. In a narrow application of the

---

[38] Ibid., at [17].   [39] Ibid., at [19].
[40] Kurtz, 'The Merits and Limits of Comparativism', at 257–60.
[41] Howse and Chalamish, 'The Use and Abuse of WTO Law', at 1094.
[42] ICSID Case No. ARB(AF)/98/3, Award (26 June 2003).

'likeness' test, the *Loewen* tribunal ruled that there was no comparator in like circumstances which could be used in order to identify discrimination.[43]

The comparison test for National Treatment was considered by the tribunal in *Sergei Paushok* v. *The Government of Mongolia*,[44] a dispute brought under the Russia–Mongolia BIT. In ruling that there was no evidence of nationality-based discrimination against the Russian investor, the tribunal claimed that the test for discrimination involved an assessment of the sectors in which the relevant investors (foreign and local) operated, in this case the Mongolian gold sector. The concept of sector was itself linked to competitive and substitutable products as developed in WTO jurisprudence.[45]

In addition to satisfying the likeness test, when bringing a claim based upon a National Treatment clause in an IIA, an investor must show prima facie evidence that it has been treated in a different and less favourable manner than an equivalent domestic investor. The burden then shifts to the respondent state to disprove this allegation.[46] The precise procedure for evaluating such a claim will depend upon the specific wording of the relevant IIA. NAFTA jurisprudence, which remains the richest source of law on the application of the National Treatment standard, has shown that it is sufficient for the investor to show that there was less favourable treatment accorded to it than to domestic investors in like circumstances. The investor does not have to show that the discrimination is motivated by nationality.[47] In other words, there does not need to be a reference to the nationality of the investor in the text of the regulation, or even in any official record related to the measure, in order for it to be a violation of National Treatment. The mere fact of the less favourable treatment is enough. Both *de jure* and de facto discriminatory treatment are equally violations of the National Treatment standard. Surely this extension of the concept is essential otherwise only blatantly discriminatory laws would be caught.

The relevant test for the breach of the National Treatment standard is whether the alleged discrimination is effectively based upon nationality

---

[43] Ibid., at [140].   [44] UNCITRAL, Award (28 April 2011).   [45] Ibid., at [315].

[46] *Felman* v. *Mexico*, ICSID Case No. ARB(AF)/99/1, Award (16 Dec 2002).

[47] Ibid., at [181].

rather than some other policy reason.[48] Indeed it appears as though the practical focus of the relevant regulatory measure is what matters, not the intent. Tribunal decisions have shown that there is no need to find a discriminatory intent in order for a regulation to violate a National Treatment commitment, although such an intention can be indicative of a violation.[49] One of the reasons for precluding the need to find intent is that it is often very difficult to prove the legislative aim behind a particular measure. Few countries, particularly non-democratic ones, keep accurate, publicly accessible records of what their governmental officials say. Concentrating instead on the impact of the law, tribunals will typically inquire whether the foreign investor's competitive position was compromised by the less favourable treatment.

4.3 Most Favoured Nation (MFN)

4.3.1 Overview

MFN is one of the oldest and most important standards of protection in international law, having appeared in treaties for hundreds of years. Yet, as with National Treatment, it is not a feature of customary international law, with beneficiaries depending entirely on treaties to base related claims. The purpose of MFN clauses in IIAs (as in trade treaties such as those of the WTO where MFN appears in GATT[50] and GATS[51]) is to ensure that states treat each other in a manner that is at least as good as they treat third parties. Parties making MFN commitments in treaties must treat all other states with whom they have made commitments the same as each other. In international investment law, this means that parties to IIAs cannot discriminate between similarly placed foreign investors. So like National Treatment, MFN concerns equality of competitive opportunities among investors, but in this instance the comparison is treatment between investors from two different countries, not between domestic and foreign investors. Accordingly, one of the ancillary purposes of the MFN

---

[48] N. DiMascio and J. Pauwelyn, 'Nondiscrimination in Trade and Investment Treaties: Worlds Apart or Two Sides of the Same Coin?' 102 *American Journal of International Law* 48 (2008), at 76.

[49] E.g. *Siemens* v. *Argentina*, ICSID Case No. ARB/02/8 (6 Feb 2008) at [320].

[50] Art I.   [51] Art II.

clause, in addition to levelling the field of competition among investors from different states, is to promote harmony among nations on a global scale by preventing favouritism on the grounds of nationality.

MFN is a dangerous commitment to make in an IIA because of its deceptively all-embracing potential across many types of commitments found in many hundreds of other treaties made by the party which offers it. The standard allows the investor, arguably disingenuously, to capture benefits granted to other investors in other treaties, often in a manner that was not intended by the host state. When evaluated by tribunals, MFN obligations require an analysis of two treaties – the one containing the MFN provision and the one containing the better treatment sought by the investor.

It is often thought that MFN provisions in IIAs (as in other types of treaties) guard against incompetent treaty draftsmanship. If the negotiator of the treaty forgets to include something important – or perhaps does not have the skill or bargaining power to achieve a certain concession – an MFN clause can come to the rescue by simply incorporating better provisions and stronger commitments found in treaties with third countries who may have enjoyed the fruits of more shrewd (or possibly better paid or more powerful) negotiators. While this aspect of MFN may be laudable, UNCTAD has drawn attention to the associated 'free-rider' situation created by MFN clauses. It can compel a country to extend a benefit to a treaty partner for which that party did not genuinely negotiate or offer a suitable compromise, a kind of unearned benefit that defeats the objective of negotiating through reciprocal concessions. UNCTAD also referenced the problem of identifying the nation that actually benefits from an MFN clause because the globalization of investment activities renders the concept of corporate nationality more elusive.[52] This is linked to problems in the definition of investor discussed in the previous chapter.

As a relative standard like National Treatment, the extent of the MFN clause depends on the other treaties of the particular granting state – meaning the treatment that it has been prepared to accord any country. In this sense, an MFN clause in an investment treaty will have no practical significance if the state which has made this obligation does not grant any relevant benefit to a third party. However, as soon as the state does confer a relevant benefit, it is automatically extended to the state to which the

---

[52] UNCTAD, *Most Favoured Nation Treatment*, UNCTAD Series on Issues in International Investment Agreements (New York and Geneva, United Nations, 1999), at 1.

MFN clause was extended. The scope will of course depend on the wording of the clause, and the precise benefit conferred will depend upon the right granted to the third state.

As with other standards in international investment law, different types and versions of MFN clauses have been adopted in treaty practice. A classic example, in which MFN is promised alongside National Treatment, can be found in Art 3 of the German Model Treaty:

> Neither Contracting State shall subject investors of the other Contracting State, as regards their activity in connection with investments in its territory, to treatment less favourable than it accords to its own investors or to investors of any third State.

This provision implicitly allows the foreign investor to choose which regime of treatment it wishes to be subjected to: that enjoyed by local investors, or that by investors of any other country should they enjoy better treatment than the locals. For example, in *CME* v. *Czech Republic* the arbitral tribunal held that the MFN provision in the Netherlands–Czech Republic BIT would allow the investor to invoke a particular standard of compensation (full market value) found in the BIT between the Czech Republic and the USA.[53]

The MFN standard's capacity to incorporate provisions from one treaty into another one has provided a basis for the suggestion that the MFN clause itself has created a kind of de facto multilateralism in international investment law.[54] With the MFN clauses virtually ubiquitous in IIAs, by definition all protections in all treaties are available to all investors who are from countries which have ever signed an IIA. The extent to which this model of multilateralism is credible depends on the precise scope that is accorded to the MFN clause in a given treaty, including any exceptions.

4.3.2 Exceptions

Given the potential breadth of the MFN clause and its capacity to control the manner in which host states apply laws to foreign investors coming from different home states, the MFN clause is also regularly subject to a

---

[53] Final Award (14 March 2003).
[54] See e.g. S. Schill, *The Multilateralization of International Investment Law* (Cambridge University Press, 2014).

range of exceptions. As with National Treatment, MFN also tends only to be extended after the establishment of the investment, allowing states to discriminate against investors from whatever country they wish before they have agreed to let them set up their business in their territory. For example, the ECT contains the following MFN provision appearing again in conjunction with National Treatment. As it lacks a reference to establishment, this clause confines its reach to investments that have already passed scrutiny under the host state's admission laws:

> Each Contracting Party shall accord to Investments in its Area of Investors of other Contracting Parties and their related activities including management, maintenance, use, enjoyment or disposal, treatment no less favourable than that which it accords to Investments of its own Investors or of the Investors of any other Contracting Party or any third state and their related activities including management, maintenance, use, enjoyment or disposal, whichever is most favourable.[55]

Some IIAs do extend MFN to the pre-establishment stage. For example, in its standalone MFN provision, NAFTA states:

> Each party shall accord to investors of another Party treatment no less favourable than that it accords, in like circumstances, to investors of any other Party or of a non-Party with respect to the establishment, acquisition, expansion, management, conduct, operation and sale or other disposition of investments.[56]

Accordingly, NAFTA-based investors receive as least as good regulatory treatment as investors from any country with which the NAFTA states have made previous commitments.

Under conventional principles of treaty interpretation, in the absence of express limitation in the text of the treaty, the scope of MFN treatment is unconditional. Many states wish to preserve the special arrangements they have made with various countries with which they have closer economic ties, as in RTAs or customs unions. MFN is therefore often specifically excluded in relation to certain third countries, meaning countries which retain the entitlement to receive better treatment accorded to their investors.

For example, Brazil's IIAs tend to subject their MFN promises to an exemption for regional integration agreements, such as free trade areas

---

[55] Art 10(7).   [56] Art 1103(1).

or customs unions.[57] This exemption is normally available provided that either Contracting Party is a party to the regional arrangement.[58] The regional integration exception is often further refined by a clause which states that nothing in the treaty should derogate from favourable treatment received by a Contracting Party's investors because of other international agreements, provided that both Contracting Parties are a party to them.[59] For example, Russia's BIT with China requires that in order for regional economic integration agreements to operate as a justification for the violation of MFN guarantees, the relevant regional agreement must conform with its WTO obligations.[60] Exceptions to National Treatment and MFN for customs unions and regional economic integration agreements are often specified to include any such agreement that either Contracting Party is or will become a party to at some point in the future.[61] International taxation treaties are also typically exempt from a state's MFN obligations.[62] As mentioned at the beginning of this book, taxation treaties are not normally seen as part of international investment law, and IIAs treat them accordingly by carving them out of their non-discrimination obligations.

In addition to exempting preferential regional arrangements for which the best treatment is granted, many IIAs specify that MFN will not apply to various types of protections granted elsewhere in the relevant treaty, such as dispute settlement procedures. Alternatively, some recent IIAs refer in their MFN clauses to specific articles in the treaty in order to clearly designate the areas to which the clause is meant to apply. For example, the UK has specifically clarified the scope of its MFN clauses in some treaties by reference to certain articles of the treaty, omitting the articles covering the extension of the time period of the treaty – twenty years for existing investments after the date of termination.[63]

It is not clear whether the MFN principle in the WTO GATS, which covers the commercial presence delivery of services and is binding on 162 countries around the world, could be used to subsume the advantages that are available to investors in BITs or RTAs. It has not yet been interpreted by a tribunal in this manner. If the GATS MFN clause were to have this

---

[57] Brazil–Chile Art III.5 (22 March 1994).
[58] Brazil–Finland Art 4(1)(a) (28 March 1995).   [59] Brazil–Korea Art 10 (1 Sept 1995).
[60] Art 3.4, meaning that they do not violate GATT Art XXIV.
[61] E.g. India–Czech Republic Art 3(3)(a) (8 July 2010).
[62] E.g. Brazil–Cuba Art III.6 (26 June 1997).   [63] UK–Barbados Art 3(3) (7 April 1993).

effect, then powerful benefits such as the investor–state dispute settlement provisions in IIAs could be accessed through the GATS. This may explain why exemptions to GATS MFN obligation for certain sectors and for RTAs were so popular among WTO Members.

One of the chief restrictions on MFN clauses is in relation to their applicability to procedural rather than substantive benefits found in other treaties. Chief among these is the entitlement to investor–state dispute settlement. In this regard, some countries expressly forbid the incorporation of such benefits through MFN. For example, the 2009 India BIT with Colombia states that the MFN guarantee does not extend to dispute settlement mechanisms contained in the Agreement.[64] This clear statement is the best way to resolve some potential controversy in this area, as will be explored further below.

4.3.3 The Application of the Standard

As MFN is also a relative standard granting a guarantee against discrimination as to the origin of the investor, it also calls for a 'likeness' comparison between two investors. Following the typical wording found in IIAs, the relevant investors from two foreign states must be in 'like circumstances' for the standard to have any meaning in terms of its assurance of equal competitive opportunities. Jurisprudence regarding this test is mostly derived from that covering National Treatment, described above, and will not be explored further here.

The more controversial feature of MFN relates to the fact that as a source of investor's protection, the MFN provision enables the investor to grasp an advantage offered in another treaty. Most disputes involving the MFN rule accordingly concerned situations in which benefits granted in treaties with third states were invoked. This requires the tribunal to assess two treaties – the treaty between the investor's state and the host state which contains the MFN clause, and the treaty between the host state and the state of the other investor from somewhere else that received that better treatment. When assessing whether or not a given treaty's protections should be applicable via an MFN clause, the tribunal will need to assess the precise wording of the MFN clause and any exceptions related to it. So in *MTD* v. *Chile*, the arbitration tribunal was able to use the MFN

---

[64] Art 4.3.

guarantee in the Chile–Malaysia BIT to bring in an obligation to award permits to the investor, which was itself construed as an extension of the FET standard found in Chile's BIT with Denmark.[65]

As with any treaty provision, the application of the MFN clause in an IIA will depend upon its interpretation in accordance with accepted methods of treaty interpretation. The rules of interpretation found in the VCLT will apply when assessing the meaning of an MFN clause. Therefore the first step is to identify the ordinary meaning of the clause in the context of the purpose of the IIA in which it appears. It is normally understood that the MFN standard only operates in relation to the subject matter of the IIA, namely foreign investment. This means that the scope of the standard cannot be extended by implication to matters covered by other treaties, such as for example, conventions on the protection of IP.

It is not clear if MFN must be expressly extended to cover issues such as procedural benefits, or if it must be expressly confined to preclude such things in favour of a more traditional application to substantive matters. Some tribunals appear to be willing to extend MFN to cover all kinds of areas unless a particular area is excluded, whereas others have MFN to cover issues like dispute settlement if they are clearly mentioned in the treaty's text.

This is seen most readily in the issue of dispute settlement, mentioned above. The application of MFN to dispute settlement procedures has been a source of much aggravation for countries such as Russia, which maintains different types of dispute settlement in different BITs, reflecting different stages of its approach to FDI. By pointing to the more generous class of treaties from a certain era, a modern investor may gain a procedural advantage which was not truly intended by the government of the host state, frustrating the notion of a state's consent to its international treaty obligations. This is one reason why it is important to distinguish between the application of an MFN clause to substantive treaty guarantees, which tend to be more consistently applied across a given country's IIAs, and to matters of procedure, such as dispute settlement which may be less evenly extended and which are also inherently more controversial, as we will explore closely in Chapter 7. Indeed there is very little case law on the application of substantive treaty standards from another treaty through an MFN clause. This is because most IIAs

---

[65] ICSID Case No. ARB/01/7, Award (25 May 2004).

offer similar standards of substantive protection to investors and their investments.

There is a large body of arbitration decisions which examine the applicability of MFN clauses to dispute settlement, and it remains an unsettled area within international investment law. Perhaps the most widely cited decision in this regard is that of *Maffezini* v. *Spain* where the tribunal ruled that the broad definition of MFN contained in the Argentina–Spain BIT embraced not only substantive rights but also dispute settlement procedures.[66] This allowed the foreign investors resort to investor–state dispute settlement that had not been expressly provided by the relevant treaty but which had been granted in another IIA to which the host state was a party. The *Maffezini* tribunal stated:

> Unless it appears clearly that the state parties to a BIT or the parties to a particular investment agreement settled on a different method for resolution of disputes that may arise, most-favoured nation provisions in BITs should be understood to be applicable to dispute settlement.[67]

The tribunal went on to illustrate that there are some important limits to this default extension of the MFN provision's reach which it classified as matters of public policy:

> As a matter of principle, the beneficiary of the clause should not be able to override public policy considerations that the contracting parties might have envisaged as fundamental conditions for their acceptance of the agreement in question, particularly if the beneficiary is [a] private investor, as will often be the case. The scope of the clause might thus be narrower than it appears at first sight.[68]

The phrase 'public policy' perhaps unhelpfully clouded the analysis even further because of the highly subjective nature of that term. Still, the *Maffezini* tribunal listed a few more concrete qualifications to the automatic expansion of MFN, which essentially captured specialized conditions under which submission to investor–state arbitration was granted in the treaty text, such as the requirement of exhaustion of local remedies. This rationale (that MFN should be extended to dispute settlement unless there are clear grounds not to, evident in the third treaty's dispute settlement clause) has been followed by other tribunals, including that of

---

[66] ICSID Case No. ARB/97/7 (25 Jan 2000).   [67] At [49].   [68] At [62].

Siemens v. *Argentina.*[69] In that case the claimants were allowed to use the MFN provision in the relevant treaty to invoke the investor–state dispute settlement mechanism in another instrument because there was no compelling reason not to do so. The *Siemens* tribunal also alluded to the *Maffezini* list of what it termed 'public policy considerations' which could limit the enlargement of the MFN provision, again tied to any express conditions on the submission to this type of dispute settlement, ultimately holding that none were applicable.

The decidedly pro-investor decision in *Maffezini* is often contrasted with that of *Plama Consortium* v. *Bulgaria*, brought under the Cyprus–Bulgaria BIT where the extension was denied. The *Plama* tribunal held that when the IIA is silent on the issue of the scope of the MFN standard with respect to the coverage of procedural matters contained in other treaties, then the tribunal should not deem such an extension to be incorporated. Instead, for MFN to cover procedural protections then this must be clearly stated in the text of the IIA. In other words, the default position should be that the MFN clause is a substance-only guarantee. In addition to some of the conditions identified by the *Maffezini* tribunal itself relating to qualified consent to arbitrate, the *Plama* tribunal cautioned against the use of 'disruptive treaty shopping' that could be engendered by an over-zealous interpretation of MFN.[70] So for example, where a treaty states that MFN will apply to 'all matters' then this can empower tribunals to expand the clause to cover dispute settlement provisions in another treaty.[71]

The tension between these two approaches (the expansive, inclusionary reading of *Maffezini* and the narrow, strict reading of *Plama*) in many ways represents one of the central conflicts of international investment law as captured in investor–state arbitration jurisprudence which may variously appear to support the interests of investors or states depending on the composition of the given tribunal. Since there is no strict doctrine of *stare decisis* in international arbitration, investment tribunals are not bound by the decisions of previous ones so they are free to make their own rulings. The precise text of the relevant IIA will ultimately govern the outcome of an assessment of MFN's scope, and the IIA as the source law of the dispute will tend to change each time.

---

[69] At [109].   [70] ICSID Case No. ARB/03/24 (8 Feb 2005) at [223].
[71] As in *Gas Natural SDG* v. *Argentine Republic*, ICSID Case No. ARB/03/10 (17 June 2005) decided under the Argentina–Spain BIT.

For example, in *HOCHTIEF Aktiengesellschaft* v. *Argentine Republic*[72] the state alleged that the claimant had not allowed the mandatory waiting period specified in the BIT between Germany and Argentina to elapse before bringing its claim. The claimant attempted to argue that it was entitled to instigate the arbitration on the basis of a shorter period allowed in Argentina's BIT with Chile, via the MFN clause in the Argentina–Germany treaty. The tribunal concluded in favour of the claimant – it could take jurisdiction over the dispute because the concept of 'treatment' for the purposes of applying MFN protections included actions which may superficially appear to have occurred outside the state's own jurisdiction but which may still be embraced by its scope. This included bringing an objection based on the time limitation in a BIT before an international arbitration tribunal. The tribunal held that the relevant place of the treatment guaranteed under MFN is not the location of the enactment of treatment, but where the effects of it are felt, a rather inventive means by which the tribunal has extended the scope of the MFN guarantee to dispute settlement.

The application of the MFN provision was examined in *Berschader* v. *Russia*[73] in which a construction services tender was issued by the Russian government and executed by a Belgian company. The government failed to make payments on time following completion of the project, leading to claims of expropriation on the basis of the Belgium–Russia BIT. Importantly for the purposes of MFN analysis, the treaty in question did not contain an arbitration clause that was applicable to the question of whether an expropriation had occurred or not. Holding that the essential test with respect to the scope of MFN is one of the intention of the parties, the tribunal held that it was incapable of taking jurisdiction over this issue through the MFN provision in the treaty. The *Berschader* tribunal instead expressly followed the reasoning of *Plama* to hold that for an MFN clause to cover procedural matters such as dispute settlement, it must clearly and unambiguously do so in the text of the IIA.[74] Taking a particularly narrow view of MFN clauses, the *Berschader* tribunal said that not even the phrase 'all matters' would be enough to encompass dispute settlement provisions. Investor–state dispute settlement would need to be referred to expressly.[75]

---

[72] ICSID Case No. ARB/07/31 (24 Oct 2011).
[73] SCC Case No. 080/2004 (21 April 2006).   [74] At [181].   [75] At [184].

In *White Industries* v. *India*,[76] India was held liable for breaching its BIT with Australia because of the excessive delay of the Indian courts in enforcing a judgment in favour of the claimant investor that had been issued by a domestic arbitration tribunal. The tribunal found, on the basis of the treaty's MFN provision, that India had breached its obligation to provide an effective means for enforcing the treaty rights,[77] having failed to enforce the arbitration award for more than nine years. The tribunal clarified that this use of the MFN clause was not strictly speaking an attempt to access procedural rights in another regime, but rather a more traditional use of MFN as a means of bringing in another substantive right, namely the resort to international law as governing law rather than the domestic law of India (international arbitration rather than domestic arbitration).[78] This is a somewhat creative attempt to sidestep the controversy of MFN's extension over procedural matters. The tribunal appears merely to label a procedural matter as a substantive one. Perhaps more instructively, the *White Industries* tribunal clarified that limits to the MFN clause in a treaty should not be artificially read in to the text of the IIA. In this instance India had attempted to argue that MFN should be limited simply by pointing to the IIA's reference to domestic law and its narrower understanding of MFN.[79]

The application of MFN was examined in *Şirketi* v. *Turkmenistan*[80] when a claim was brought by a Turkish construction company against the state of Turkmenistan under the Turkmenistan–Turkey BIT. The BIT required that disputes had to be submitted to the national courts before arbitration proceedings could be brought but the investor had argued that it could circumvent the local courts on the basis of the BIT's MFN clause. It attempted to seize upon the Turkey–Switzerland BIT which lacked an equivalent exhaustion of local remedies requirement, thereby overriding the need to use the local courts; this is precisely the type of situation that was identified by *Maffezini* as representing a risk to the extension of MFN. Denying this strategy, the tribunal held that the MFN clause did not encompass the Turkey–Turkmenistan BIT's dispute resolution provisions. The tribunal reasoned simply that an MFN clause in an investment

---

[76] *White Industries Australia Limited* v. *Republic of India*, Final Award (30 Nov 2011) (London, UK).

[77] Art 4(2) of the India–Australia BIT contains an MFN clause which was used to incorporate Art 4(5) of the India–Kuwait BIT.

[78] At 11.2.3.   [79] At 11.2.9.   [80] ICSID Case No. ARB/10/1 (2 July 2013).

treaty does not incorporate by reference, either in whole or in part, provisions relating to the jurisdiction of the arbitral tribunal unless there is an unequivocal provision to that effect in the main treaty.[81]

Impregilo v. Argentine Republic[82] also considered the scope of MFN during the annulment stage of the dispute (an aspect of ICSID procedure that will be explored in Chapter 7). In this dispute Argentina argued that the earlier tribunal had manifestly exceeded its powers in part by allowing international arbitration through an MFN clause in the BIT to the exclusion of a local remedies requirement. The committee pointed out that the scope of an MFN clause over dispute settlement remains contentious, and the respondent could not expect the original tribunal to reach definitive general conclusions in that respect as it is a highly contextual matter which requires a case-by-case analysis. It found that the original tribunal's assessment of the law on the scope of an MFN provision had been cogently explained. The annulment committee noted that the original tribunal had adequately explained that there is near-unanimity among investment tribunals that IIAs using MFN wording to cover 'all matters' or 'any matter' would be enough to engage another instrument's dispute settlement facility.[83]

The fact that some tribunals have been willing to extend MFN to dispute settlement might be depicted as a general trend in international investment law towards enhancing investor protection through IIAs. It also acknowledges the importance placed by investors on recourse to international arbitration rather than submission to domestic courts by investors. Still, tribunals have remained cautious to do so, cognizant of the risks of taking an overbroad approach to the MFN clause in relation to dispute settlement. There are important public policy implications for this kind of an extension, particularly if there is no requirement to exhaust local remedies before seeking international arbitration as it can expose a state to international litigation in a manner that was wholly unexpected.

When contemplating the scope of an MFN clause, it is also important to make a distinction between the legitimate extension of rights and benefits as the clause was likely intended, and what some may view as harmful or overtly strategic 'treaty shopping'. It is often viewed as inappropriate for

---

[81] At 7.8.10.   [82] ICSID Case No. ARB/07/17 (21 June 2011).
[83] At [144] quoting [108] of the Award.

an investor to canvass all sorts of treaties until it finds exactly the one that it wants in terms of the suite of protections it provides, even if there is a tenuous connection between the investor and the treaty, such as through an MFN clause. It is not entirely clear that such strategic behaviour on the part of multinational enterprises is wrong, but it tends to be met with derision because it may seem to exploit a host state's good faith in concluding treaties with MFN provisions in them. So far, no investment tribunal has permitted the use of an MFN clause in a manner that would have led to a full-on 'regime change' with respect to the basic treaty containing the clause. In other words, MFN has never allowed an investor to fundamentally extend the first treaty's obligations beyond that which was conceived by the treaty itself, such as bringing in other spheres such as competition law or IP, or non-economic matters such as environmental or human rights treaties. This suggests that an MFN clause will operate only to the extent that the provision in the other treaty is compatible in principle with the overall scheme negotiated by the parties in the basic treaty, and departs from it only in a manner that is consistent with that broader scheme.

4.4 Conclusion

The assurance by host governments that they will not discriminate against foreign firms on the basis of their foreign character is a major feature of international investment law as captured by IIAs. National Treatment and MFN have existed for some time yet they have no life in the absence of a commitment in a treaty. This is why virtually all of the many thousands of IIAs contain these protections in one form or another. With the promise that the host state will not make an adverse differentiation against or between foreign firms when enacting its laws and regulations, and even when engaging in judicial or administrative review of the application of these rules, the multinational firm has the confidence that it will be able to operate on an even footing in the domestic market, allowing it to compete based on the quality of the services and products that it offers. Foreign investors have recourse to these protections when they are subjected to targeted attacks by governments as a consequence of their national origin. In this sense, the guarantees of non-discrimination are an essential guard against the market distortions that would undermine the value of FDI in the first place, just as they make the host state more attractive as a safe place to do business.

Still, many countries have been unwilling to make across-the-board commitments for either National Treatment or MFN, reflecting their developmental status or more simply because there are certain spheres of economic activity which host governments feel should be conducted by firms which have a domestic character or which originate from countries with which closer economic ties are maintained. The chief limitation to National Treatment found in IIAs is that of establishment – very few countries are willing to promise non-discriminatory treatment for firms before they have entered their territory and without screening based on their particular economic needs. This omission in IIAs discloses their non-status as genuine tools of economic liberalization but rather as protective assurances for firms which have already made the decision to locate in a foreign country and which have satisfied any conditions of admission. For MFN, most IIA parties tend to preclude the application of this standard to regional arrangements with strategic economic partners, such as those with whom they have formed customs unions or RTAs. The lack of application of MFN to these regional groupings should not necessarily be viewed as a failure of the host state to make a stronger commitment to non-discrimination based on an investor's nationality, but rather as an incentive for countries to join such regional groupings, a trend that appears to be occurring with the advent of the mega-regionals.

In terms of legal debates surrounding National Treatment and MFN as applied by investment tribunals, two key issues stand out. For National Treatment, there has been extensive debate in investment tribunals regarding the likeness comparator between foreign and local firms, much of which has been generated by disputes brought under NAFTA. A reasonably clear picture has emerged in which tribunals understand that the concept of like circumstances is a highly contextual one which will depend heavily on the facts, and that proof of intent to discriminate by the host state is non-essential. The greatest source of controversy for MFN meanwhile remains the scope of its application to other features of the IIA in which it appears. In particular, there is much debate regarding whether it can be applied to procedural benefits such as access to investor–state dispute settlement. While there is conflicting jurisprudence on this point, as with National Treatment the answer appears to lie in the wording of the relevant IIA and the particular context in which it was drafted. Clear words extending the MFN standard in this regard would go a long way to ensuring that investors could avail themselves of this particular procedural advantage.

While guarantees of non-discrimination based on the nationality of the investor are an unquestionably powerful feature of international investment law, at their foundation these standards remain purely relative, meaning that strictly speaking the host state can still engage in a wide variety of harmful behaviour without it being discriminatory. To guard against these unfortunate happenings, international investment law has established other standards of protection which have also become essential features of IIAs.

5 Fair and Equitable Treatment, Full Protection and Security, and Umbrella Clauses

5.1 Introduction

In the decades since IIAs have emerged as the key component of international investment law having been accepted by most countries around the world, a number of forms of protection within them have become standardized features. These specific safeguards reflect the reality that customary international law was an inadequate defence of the interests of foreign firms, just as it appeared to be insufficient to augment flows of capital to the states where it was sought. Ever seeking to ensure that the climate into which they were directing their business activities was a secure and by extension at least potentially profitable one, IIAs came to include guarantees against a range of behaviours, which, unlike those discussed in the previous chapter, were unrelated to discrimination on the grounds of nationality. Rather, absolute standards of protection were sought and developed. Whether or not these standards have achieved the degree of coherence desired by foreign firms in practice is another question.

Continuing with this book's focus on the content of IIAs, this chapter will outline several of the other key forms of protection for foreign investors contained in these instruments. It will begin by examining the powerful but highly indeterminate Fair and Equitable Treatment (FET) standard, which in its essence guarantees fairness in dealings with the host state government and in so doing controls the manner in which laws and regulations are applied to foreign firms. It will go on to the somewhat related guarantee of FPS, which promises that foreign investors receive adequate protection by the host state against civil unrest. Next, umbrella clauses will be presented as deceptively powerful features of IIAs, allowing investors to assert ordinary breaches of contract as treaty violations. This chapter will also consider the promise of free transfer of currency found in most IIAs, which allows investors to repatriate their profits without undue restrictions. Perhaps the most important of all substantive protections, that of guaranteeing that there will be no expropriation of foreign property without full compensation, will be left to the next chapter.

5.2 Fair and Equitable Treatment (FET)

5.2.1 Scope and Application

Most IIAs including both BITs and RTAs with investment chapters provide for FET of foreign investments, which is the standard that is most frequently claimed in investment disputes. It probably also has the greatest practical importance in that most successful claims pursued in international investment arbitration are based at least in part on a breach of the FET standard. The FET standard is also regarded as the most difficult of the standards commonly found in IIAs to define. Whole books have been written attempting to trace its contours,[1] and it regularly forms the focus of much deliberation by arbitration tribunals. Still, it is only really in the last fifteen years or so that investment tribunals have begun to give some substantive content to the meaning of the standard.

At the risk of over-simplifying, FET essentially refers to the *manner* in which the host state's laws are applied and less so the content of the laws themselves. In this sense it can be related to what is more commonly known in some jurisdictions as 'due process', which suggests that it is somewhat procedural in nature. It is also linked to openness and transparency in the way in which laws are applied to foreign investors, acknowledging the reality that having near full and timely information about the nature of the laws to which one is expected to conform helps diminish the severity of their impact. FET has existed for quite some time, and it bears a substantial resemblance to the international minimum standard of treatment of aliens that has already been looked at and which can be found in customary international law.

There is a high degree of commonality among the wording used in FET clauses in IIAs. Still, it is difficult to make generalizations about the FET standard because no single version exists. A simple example can be found in Spain's BIT with Albania:

> Investments made by investors of one Party in the territory of the other Party shall be accorded fair and equitable treatment.[2]

FET is merely granted without any attempt to delineate its scope or content. Lacking further articulation, such a provision clearly grants a

---

[1] E.g. M. Paparinskis, *The International Minimum Standard of Fair and Equitable Treatment* (Oxford University Press, 2013).

[2] Art 3(1).

tribunal called upon to apply it to various forms of governmental action quite a wide latitude.

A somewhat more expansive version of FET can be found in ACIA, which, in addition to granting FET, also offers a very useful definition of the term:

> [F]air and equitable treatment requires each Member State not to deny justice in any legal or administrative proceedings in accordance with the principle of due process.[3]

This suggests that FET will be engaged once some kind of legal procedure has commenced, meaning one in which the government renders a decision which affects a particular investor's rights. The US Model BIT of 2012 provides even more clarity with this definition:

> '[F]air and equitable treatment' includes the obligation not to deny justice in criminal, civil, or administrative adjudicatory proceedings in accordance with the principle of due process embodied in the principal legal systems of the world.[4]

It is noteworthy that this definition does not reference legislative proceedings, meaning that FET cannot be asserted in response to the content of a law itself, but rather in relation to the way in which that law is applied by a governmental authority such as a court or administrative tribunal. Interestingly, due process itself appears to be defined by reference to national law.

Among the most comprehensive definitions of FET in any IIA is that contained in the negotiated text of the TTIP. It provides a list of the actions which will constitute an FET violation:

(a) denial of justice in criminal, civil or administrative proceedings; or
(b) fundamental breach of due process, including a fundamental breach of transparency and obstacles to effective access to justice, in judicial and administrative proceedings; or
(c) manifest arbitrariness; or
(d) targeted discrimination on manifestly wrongful grounds, such as gender, race or religious belief; or

---

[3] Art 11(2)(1a).   [4] Art 5(2)a.

(e) harassment, coercion, abuse of power or similar bad faith conduct; or

(f) a breach of any further elements of the fair and equitable treatment obligation adopted by the Parties in accordance with paragraph 3 of this Article.[5]

While substantially more specific than earlier iterations of the standard, the last sentence leaves room for inclusion of a range of other actions, preserving FET's status as a 'catch-all' provision.

FET can address a wide variety of government actions that affect investments where more specific rules might be unsuitable. The flexibility inherent in the highly abstract concepts of 'equity' and 'fairness' are therefore desirable means of protection for foreign investors. Indeed the breadth of the FET clause regularly features in the criticisms levied against investor-state dispute settlement, in particular the excessive discretion of arbitrators in applying it.[6] To be sure FET has been applied to an incredibly wide range of circumstances, almost to the point that it would seem that investors argue that there has been a breach of a treaty's FET standard as a matter of course in their pleadings. Indeed any time the investor interacts with the government there appears to be the potential for a claim of FET violation to be raised, calling into question all sorts of governmental behaviour in a manner that could be seen as fundamentally hostile to the notion of sovereignty.

The essential purpose of the FET clause as used in an investment treaty may indeed be to fill in the gaps that have been left by the more specific standards. Such residual protection may be the only way to actually achieve the degree of investor security intended by the treaties. It may be linked to a more fundamental goal of legal stability generally or as an embodiment of an overarching principle of good faith that informs the interpretation of other clauses. The idea behind good faith is that the parties are not hiding anything: they are being open and honest with their intentions as reflected in the text of the document. Moreover, it may appear as though FET actually encompasses two standards, 'fair' and 'equitable' with independent meanings for each concept, but there is no evidence that the clause has ever been intended this way. It is generally thought that it is one standard and in fact there is no difference between

---

[5] Chapter II Art 3.

[6] E.g. I. Tudor, *The Fair and Equitable Treatment Standard in the International Law of Foreign Investment* (Oxford University Press, 2008), Chapters 3–4.

the two concepts, with the inference being that the two-part phrase is structured that way simply for emphasis.[7]

As a rule of international law, the FET obligation is independent of National Treatment which means that it can be violated even if the foreign investor is treated the same as investors from the host state.[8] Likewise, there may also be a violation of the FET standard even if a foreign investor is not able to benefit from an MFN clause by showing that investors of other nationalities have received better treatment. The expansiveness of the FET standard has also led to its use as an alternative means of providing investment protection in cases where there are no clear grounds for expropriation,[9] although conversely a finding of expropriation quite often results in a finding of FET breach.[10] As a way of transcending these more specific forms of protection, the inclusion of an FET in an IIA is indicative of host states' willingness to deal with foreign investors on standards set by the international community. Some IIAs clarify that the mere existence of a breach of another provision of an IIA should not be understood to automatically indicate that there has also been a breach of FET.[11] Still, it appears as though the breach of another provision of a treaty may strengthen a claim of FET violation, as in *Loewen* v. *United States*,[12] where prejudice on account of nationality violating National Treatment helped establish a gross violation of due process, breaching FET. The general sense of vagueness in the FET obligation is advantageous to foreign investors in that it grants maximum flexibility to apply the requirement of due process to their particular factual situation. It may also be said to acknowledge that states are free to establish legal procedures as long as they do not fall below a minimum threshold.[13]

Despite the evident breadth of FET and its ensuing popularity among claimant investors, succeeding in such a claim will not be easy. This is why common allegations that international investment law is a powerful weapon against governmental interference do not always ring true in

---

[7] R. Dolzer and C. Schreuer, *Principles of International Investment Law* (Oxford University Press, 2012), at 133.

[8] *SD Myers* v. *Canada*, UNCITRAL (21 Oct 2002).

[9] *Hassan Awdi* v. *Romania*, ICSID Case No. ARB/10/13 (2 March 2015).

[10] *OI European Group B.V.* v. *Bolivarian Republic of Venezuela*, ICSID Case No. ARB/11/25 (2 March 2015).

[11] E.g. Japan–Peru BIT, Art 5(3) (22 Nov 2008).

[12] ICSID Case No. ARB(AF)/98/3 (26 June 2003).

[13] Dolzer and Schreuer, *Principles*, at 148.

practice. Indeed, FET appears to contemplate very poor behaviour on the part of the host state. It is not the kind of treatment that a company comes across every day when dealing with the government, such as tax collection or day-to-day bureaucracy. The difficult test for establishing a breach of FET has been developed over many decades of investment arbitration jurisprudence, the language of which generally demonstrates a decidedly egregious treatment at the hands of governmental officials.

Setting a high threshold for breach, the ICJ stated in *Elettronica Sicula* that a FET violation involves a 'wilful disregard for due process of law, an act which shocks or at least surprises a sense of judicial propriety'.[14] Shock and surprise clearly contemplates something well beyond minor irritation, as many foreign investors would no doubt wish to believe. The *Tecmed* tribunal (an ICSID case brought against Mexico) offered one of the most widely cited definitions of FET:

> The foreign investor expects the host state to act in a consistent manner, free from ambiguity, and totally transparently in its relations with the foreign investor, so that it may know beforehand any and all rules and regulations that will govern its investments as well as the goals and administrative policies, the investor expects the state will not arbitrarily revoke any pre-existing decisions... the investor expects the state to use the legal instruments that govern the actions of the investor in conformity with the functions usually assigned to such instruments.

Key elements noted here include consistency, non-ambiguity, transparency and non-arbitrariness. Another decision under NAFTA against Mexico by the corporation *Waste Management* stated that the FET standard involved:

> conduct that is arbitrary, grossly unfair, unjust or idiosyncratic, is discriminatory and exposes the claimant to sectional or racial prejudice or involves a lack of due process leading to an outcome which offends judicial propriety – as may be the case with a manifest failure of natural justice in judicial proceedings or a complete lack of candour in administrative process.[15]

The language of gross unfairness and offensiveness is quite extreme, representing an incredibly poor standard of governmental conduct. Somewhat less sensationally, the tribunal in *Saluka Investments* held that FET

---

[14] *Elettronica Sicula SpA (ELSI) (United States* v. *Italy)*, 1989 ICJ Reports, 15 at [128].
[15] ICSID Case No. ARB(AF)/00/3 (30 April 2004).

aimed to ensure that the host state 'will not act in a way that is manifestly inconsistent, non-transparent, unreasonable or discriminatory'.[16] Taken together, these statements suggests that under FET investors will be entitled to have at least the opportunity to be heard and to receive basic explanations for decisions in which their rights are affected. The decisions must be reasonable and unbiased at a fundamental level as would be required by what is commonly understood as natural justice, a concept that transgresses any culturally specific preconceptions about judicial procedures.

In some cases, assessment of the FET standard will involve enquiring as to the adequacy of domestic legal procedures in terms of their satisfying the understanding of due process. For example, in *Apotex* v. *USA*[17] the tribunal considered the challenge procedures available under the US Food and Drug Administration Act. The tribunal ultimately denied the claim of FET breach based on the inadequacy of these procedures because the claimants chose to seek all available legal remedies for the Food and Drug Administration (FDA) decisions under established domestic procedures in the USA, which were seen as being entirely fair and reasonable. Given the options available under US law, the respondent's conduct did not cross the 'threshold of severity and gravity' required for there to be a breach of NAFTA's FET provision.

Despite some tribunals' indications that by definition FET is a general standard which 'cannot be reduced to precise statements or rules',[18] there are a number of more specific types of conduct on the part of the host state that may be indicative of a violation of this provision. Perhaps most notably, tribunals have found that FET covers the protection of investors' legitimate expectations. Such expectations are derived from the legal framework of the host state, including written or even oral representations by government officials as well as contractual undertakings which have been made by the government. The denial or breach of such statements would be considered to be a breach of FET. Put simply, the investor was led to believe that one set of circumstances existed and took action on that basis and then the state let them down. This category of FET breach is elaborated in the text of the TTIP:

[16] *Saluka Investments* v. *Czech Republic*, UNCITRAL, Partial Award (17 March 2006) at [309].
[17] ICSID Case No. ARB(AF)/12/1 (25 Aug 2014).   [18] *Saluka.*

> When applying the above fair and equitable treatment obligation, a tribunal may take into account whether a Party made a specific representation to an investor to induce a covered investment, that created a legitimate expectation, and upon which the investor relied in deciding to make or maintain the covered investment, but that the Party subsequently frustrated.[19]

For example in the *Tecmed* v. *Mexico* case, the revocation of a licence that had been granted to the investor was considered as unfair and inequitable because it was a breach of the investor's legitimate expectations.[20] Likewise, in *David Minnotte & Robert Lewis* v. *Poland*[21] the investor claimed it had suffered detrimental effects as a consequence of the revocation of a business permit to operate within the host state. It argued that this was a violation of the US–Poland BIT's FET. Deciding in favour of Poland, the tribunal ruled that the investor had not been given formal assurances that there would be an extension of their permission to operate within a special economic zone. While there had been some long delays in responding to the investor's letters, this was not sufficient to constitute a denial of fundamental justice as contemplated by FET.

In *Rumeli Telekom and Teslim Mobil* v. *Kazakhstan*[22] the investor brought a claim partly on the basis of an FET breach because of the removal of tax concessions, which had been offered to induce the investor to locate in the host state. The tribunal ruled that the respondent's wrongful termination of the investment contract without offering the possibility of renegotiation amounted to a breach of the FET standard. It said that the host state had a duty to act in a manner which conformed to the investor's reasonable and legitimate expectations, which included the fulfilment of the host state's contractual promises. The government's decision to terminate the contract, particularly given that there had been no prior notification that such termination was pending, was seen as arbitrary, unfair, unjust and lacking in due process.[23] This decision suggests that the removal of the concession might have been lawful under the IIA had it been done in a timely and open manner.

---

[19] Art 3(4).   [20] ICSID Case No. ARB(AF)/00/2 (29 May 2003).
[21] ICSID Case No. ARB(AF)/10/1 (16 May 2014).
[22] *Rumeli Telekom A.S., Telsim Mobil* v. *Kazakhstan*, ICSID Case No. ARB/05/16, Award (28 July 2008).
[23] At [615].

In a similar vein, the *Micula* v. *Romania*[24] tribunal upheld the investor's claim based on breach of the FET standard resulting from the state's revocation of a fiscal incentive programme, which breached the investor's legitimate expectations that the incentives would continue. The revocation of the incentives led to increased costs of materials, causing the company, a soft drink manufacturer, to lose significant market share. In reaching this conclusion, the tribunal focused again on the manner in which the host state withdrew the incentives which it held to be arbitrary and discriminatory. Romania failed to inform the investor of the premature termination of its incentive regime in a timely fashion, exacerbating the resulting injury. Moreover it terminated the incentives entirely at once, rather than phase them out incrementally, which would have been less harmful.[25]

Still, breach of contract alone and by extension the undermining of legitimate expectations, will not necessarily indicate that there has been a FET violation. The tribunal in *Malicorp Limited* v. *Arab Republic of Egypt*[26] ruled that breach of the FET standard could not be inferred from a breach of contract between the investor and the host state. According to that tribunal, some further evidence of unfair conduct was needed.

It is clear that FET can also incorporate transparency in the host state's dealings with the foreign investor. This aspect of the standard focuses on the investor's need to know all of the requirements in place for its business operations so that it can plan its investments accordingly in advance, rather than be forced to act in haste as a consequence of delay, lack of clarity or the withholding of information. Clearly the lack of information about the laws to which they are subject can place investors in a difficult position in terms of their forward planning. This aspect of FET was established in the *Metalclad* case when the Mexican government failed to respond to queries regarding the investor's application for a building permit which was eventually denied but only after the investor had already begun its operations.[27] While the investor also has a duty to inform itself about the host state's laws and any changes which may have occurred, the state remains obliged to act consistently in terms of the application of its various policies, and to do otherwise can violate FET.[28]

---

[24] ICSID Case No. ARB/05/20 at [672]–[679].   [25] Ibid., at [1019].
[26] ICSID Case No. ARB/08/18 (7 Feb 2011).
[27] ICSID Case No. ARB(AF)/97/1 (30 Aug 2000).
[28] *MDT* v. *Chile*, ICSID Case No. ARB/01/7, Award (25 May 2004).

Somewhat confusingly because of the seeming overlap with the FPS standard discussed below, FET may also apply in situations where there has been coercion or harassment of the investor. Pressure and/or threats from the government towards the investment may therefore be seen as a breach of FET. An illustration of this facet of FET can be seen in *Rompetrol Group N.V.* v. *Romania*.[29] This dispute concerned the allegation of a FET breach linked to the arrest, detention, criminal investigations and wire-tapping of the investing company's directors. The claimant asserted that this constituted state-sponsored, politically and commercially motivated harassment. In deciding in favour of the investor, the tribunal held that the state conduct directed against the company officers amounted to a pattern of disregard for the rights of Rompetrol's employees, constituting a breach of FET. There had been consistent arbitrary treatment of the procedural rights of Rompetrol's directors. Linking this aspect of FET to one discussed earlier, the tribunal held that the legitimate expectations of an investor include the expectation that state authorities will attempt to minimize the adverse effects on an investment if the investor's interests become caught up in the criminal process, either directly or indirectly.

As with National Treatment and MFN, if not all laws, the precise meaning of the FET standard depends on the circumstances of the case. This understanding was expressed by the tribunal in the *Mondev* v. *United States* dispute: '[a] judgment of what is fair and equitable cannot be reached in abstract; it must depend on the facts of the particular case.'[30] Accordingly, the meaning of 'fair and equitable' may expand and contract from place to place, tied to the idiosyncrasies of various legal systems, not to mention cultural practices. Some governments in developing countries do not have the same capability to grant investors in their territory a stable and secure environment in which to operate, as would likely be the case in a country with an independent and effective judicial system. This is why it would be unreasonable for investors setting up in developing countries to have expectations of treatment by the local government that is equivalent to that anticipated in the most advanced countries. In that sense FET may be perceived as a relative rather than an absolute standard. The variable nature of FET is reflected for example in the Common Market for Eastern and Southern Africa (COMESA) Agreement on Investment:

---

[29] ICSID Case No. ARB/06/3 (6 May 2013).
[30] *Mondev* v. *USA*, ICSID Case No. ARB(AF)/99/2 (11 Oct 2002) at [118].

> For greater certainty, Member States understand that different Member States have different forms of administrative, legislative and judicial systems and that Member States at different levels of development may not achieve the same standards at the same time. Paragraphs 1 and 2 of this Article do not establish a single international standard in this context.[31]

This provision explicitly requires that tribunals take into account particularities of local governance practices in each member country when interpreting FET. It means different things in different places.

Such qualification of FET necessitates flexibility in interpretation of the standard by investment tribunals. Different types of language used in treaties (as well as context as per the VCLT) may point to an enlarged or diminished responsibility on the part of the state under FET. Despite the lack of globally consistent language on the standard in treaty or arbitral practice, tribunals tend to justify their findings by reference to earlier awards; a kind of de facto doctrine of precedent can lead a tribunal to finding an infringement because an infringement was found in a similar case. Indeed the absence of a global investment treaty coupled with a weak doctrine of precedent in international investment law may be one of the reasons that a clear understanding of FET has failed to develop.

5.2.2 FET and Customary International Law

In light of the above controversy, there is extensive debate as to whether the FET standard merely reflects the international minimum standard of treatment as contained in customary international law or whether it offers an autonomous standard that is additional to customary international law that requires iteration through a treaty. Given FET's deep roots in customary international law, it is not surprising that this provision featured prominently in many of the bilateral and multilateral investment treaties that states began to conclude in the aftermath of World War II.[32]

The debate over the standard's link to customary international law's minimum standard of treatment has led some countries to clarify the matter in their IIAs. For example, the US Model BIT of 2012 states:

---

[31] Art 14.

[32] S. Subedi, *International Investment Law: Reconciling Policy and Principle* (Hart, 2012), at 62–3.

> The concept of 'fair and equitable treatment'... do[es] not require treat-
> ment in addition to or beyond that which is required by that standard [the
> minimum standard of treatment], and do[es] not create additional substan-
> tive rights.[33]

In its FET clause, Spain's BIT with Albania notes: '[I]n no case shall a Party
accord to such investments treatment less favourable than that required
by international law.'[34] This sets a lower limit rather than an upper one,
potentially allowing for the inclusion of many types of treatment. Of
course these statements call into question the purpose of including FET in
a treaty at all.

Some tribunals have found that the FET clause can be equated with
the minimum standard of treatment of foreign investment required under
customary international law.[35] Others tribunals have viewed it as autonomous, ruling that the standard should be taken in its plain meaning, and
in light of the object and purpose of the treaty.[36] This approach captures
that of the general principles of treaty interpretation outlined in the VCLT.
The flexibility inherent in the FET standard cannot exist, however, where
the standard is equated with the minimum standard of treatment of aliens
which is best seen as 'a floor, an absolute bottom, below which conduct
is not accepted by the international community' and which 'is not meant
to vary from state to state'.[37]

Where an IIA links the FET obligation to the minimum standard of
treatment, the threshold of liability as applied by arbitral tribunals has
been generally higher. In contrast, a simple unqualified use of the term
may result in a low liability threshold. Although many tribunals, including those applying the unqualified FET clauses, tend not to find violations lightly, the varying threshold that results from a different wording
of the FET clause has the potential to create a problem of uneven treatment across the globe. The threshold for qualifying governmental conduct

---

[33] Art 5(2).   [34] Art 3(1).

[35] E.g. *M.C.I. Power Group L.C. and New Turbine, Inc.* v. *Ecuador*, ICSID Case No. ARB/03/6,
Award (31 July 2007), at [369]; *Siemens AG* v. *Argentina*, ICSID Case No. ARB/02/8, Award
(6 Feb 2007), at [291].

[36] See, for example, *Compañía de Aguas del Aconquija S.A. and Vivendi Universal S.A.* v.
Argentina, ICSID Case No. ARB/97/3, Award (20 Aug 2007) and *Tecmed* v. *Mexico*, ICSID
Case No. ARB(AF)/00/2, Award (29 May 2003).

[37] *Glamis Gold Ltd.* v. *United States*, UNCITRAL (NAFTA), Award (8 June 2009), at [615].

towards one investor, protected by one type of standard, can be different from the finding of a violation with respect to another investor of a different nationality. The result is not only unpredictable but also contrary to the purpose of investment treaties to guarantee non-discrimination. As suggested above, the lack of coherence regarding standards such as FET is also one of the reasons that commentators have queried the legitimacy of investor–state arbitration.[38]

When there is an explicit link between the FET obligation and the minimum standard of treatment in an IIA, this may prevent over-expansive interpretations of the standard by tribunals. It may also guide them by referring to an example of egregious misconduct that would violate the minimum standard of treatment. However this strategy presupposes the existence of a general consensus as to what constitutes the minimum standard of treatment, whereas in reality the minimum standard of treatment is itself ambiguous.[39]

It is clear from the jurisprudence that there is a significant overlap between the substantive contents of the two approaches as well as a possibility of convergence. This begs the question as to whether there is truly a difference between the two standards at all. The *Azure* tribunal commented that the difference may be more apparent than real:

> the question whether or not fair and equitable treatment is or is not additional to the minimum treatment requirement under international law is a question about the substantive content of fair and equitable treatment and whichever side of the argument one takes, the answer to the question may in substance be the same.[40]

The possibility that there is no genuine difference between the international minimum standard of protection of customary international law and the treaty-based FET standard belies the standard's near ubiquity in IIAs. It may simply be that FET is a relic of past IIA practice, and as such its inclusion in modern treaties could be taken as evidence of so-called path-dependence or the unwillingness to change things to which one has

---

[38] S. Franck, 'The Legitimacy Crisis in Investment Treaty Arbitration: Privatizing Public International Law through Inconsistent Decisions' 73 *Fordham Law Review* (2004/05) at 1545.

[39] M. Porterfield, 'An International Common Law of Investor Rights?' 27 *University of Pennsylvania Journal of International Economic Law* 79 (2006) at 88.

[40] *Azurix* v. *Argentine Republic*, ICSID Case No. ARB/01/12, Award (14 July 2006), para 361.

become accustomed. Indeed, concluding an IIA which lacked a FET clause could signal danger to potential investors even if the standard is actually redundant.

The FET standard raises highly contentious issues as to the types of administrative and governmental action that can be reviewed under the standard and the degree of seriousness of breach that is required to succeed under such a claim. This approach increases the chances that a wide range of state regulations or measures can be found to infringe the standard, including those that arguably have a legitimate public purpose. The approach poses further special challenges for developing countries where the state may be required to intervene more intensively in the economy than would be the case in an industrialized country. There are also questions about how the FET standard has evolved, arising from the relationship between regulatory measures adversely affecting investors and the reasons underlying these measures. For example, the host country may be under an international obligation to achieve a specific regulatory outcome, such as that relating to the environment or human rights. Where a government undertakes a regulatory measure in furtherance of such a commitment and this results in a change to the legal or commercial environment and negatively affects investment, it is uncertain whether the tribunal will accept the nature of the measure as defeating a FET claim. Some of these issues will be evaluated further in Chapter 9.

5.3 Full Protection and Security (FPS) Standard

5.3.1 Scope and Application

The FPS standard, much like FET, is a form of protection that has developed a somewhat general understanding, although its primary focus on physical harm means that it tends to be applicable to a narrower set of facts. FPS requires the host state to grant physical protection and security to the foreign investor's property, meaning that it must deploy its police or military personnel to guard the assets of the investor that are at risk of damage. Physical damage to the investment could occur, for example if there is a political uprising which may result in civil disturbances. Most investment treaties contain clauses providing for 'full protection and security' or sometimes 'constant protection and security' often in conjunction with the guarantee of FET, although it is not clear that this slight difference in wording has any legal consequences. For example, the UK's BIT with Bosnia and Herzegovina states:

> Investments of nationals or companies of each Contracting Party shall at all times be accorded fair and equitable treatment and shall enjoy full protection and security in the territory of the other Contracting Party.[41]

Note that in this instrument a separate definition of FPS is not provided, allowing any tribunal called upon to interpret this provision to draw from jurisprudence to complete their understanding of the term. In ACIA, on the other hand, the FPS provision also appears in the same sentence as that of FET but receives its own definition:

> [F]ull protection and security requires each Member State to take such measures as may be reasonably necessary to ensure the protection and security of the covered investments.[42]

Again, this expression does not really attempt to define the content of the standard in a functional manner, but rather emphasizes that it is one that is tied to both reasonableness (possibly facilitating broad discretion to arbitration tribunals as well as flexibility based on circumstances) and necessary (appearing to somewhat tighten this discretion by suggesting that the state action must only be used when it is clearly important to do so).

The FPS clause in an IIA establishes the host state's obligation to take active measures to protect foreign investments from adverse effects (primarily physical harm) caused either by the actions of the host state itself, meaning the government or other authorities, or by third parties, meaning private citizens. This effectively creates a two-pronged liability: first, the investor's property must not be harmed by action of the host state's armed forces or police (the duty not to harm); and second, the investor's property must be protected against the actions of the unruly public (the affirmative duty to protect). Failure to fulfil either of these obligations will entail liability on the part of the state.

Unlike FET for which there is virtually boundless arbitral jurisprudence, the FPS standard has received fairly limited attention by investment arbitration tribunals, likely due to its much narrower focus, at least in its

---

[41] Art 2(2).   [42] Art 11(3)(b).

traditional iteration as a safeguard against damaged property. In what perhaps might be termed its pure form, the standard tends to be asserted by claimants in situations where host states have not provided protection against various types of physical violence, often in situations where there has been an invasion of the premises of the investment during an incident of civil unrest such as a protest or revolution. As such situations are relatively rare even in unstable countries, the FPS standard remains somewhat of an obscure feature of IIAs. Still, an evolving body of case law has developed and is likely poised to expand because of ongoing political instability around the world, and also given modern expansions of the concept to interference that is non-physical.

The FPS standard was examined in the *Wena Hotels* v. *Egypt*[43] dispute which was brought by a British company against Egypt for the state's failure to prevent the state-owned Egyptian Hotels Corporation's attacks against the hotel's properties. Guests of the hotel had been forcibly evicted and property damaged due to political unrest, in part relating to a foreign presence on a culturally sensitive site. Although the investor could not establish that the host state had actually participated in the attacks against the hotels, Egypt was held liable for breach of the FPS standard because it was aware of the hotel attacks by citizens yet did nothing to prevent them. This is an example of the state's duty to prevent harm from befalling foreign investors.

It would seem as though discrimination based on nationality is not required for a finding of FPS breach. In other words, an investor seeking to identify the level of protection it feels entitled to will not necessarily benefit from demonstrating that a local investor was protected when it was not. So in *AMT* v. *Zaire*[44] a dispute was initiated under the US–Zaire BIT, brought because of the alleged failure of Zaire to protect the US investor from property damage sustained as a result of activities of the Zairian armed forces in the capital city, Kinshasa. Zaire claimed that it had not violated the FPS standard because it had not treated AMT any less favourably than it treated other investors, including nationals and those from other countries. The tribunal disagreed, holding that Zaire had breached the FPS provision because it had taken no measures whatsoever to ensure the protection of AMT's property. The fact that the host state had also failed to protect other investors was irrelevant.

---

[43] ICSID Case No. ARB/98/4 (8 Dec 2000).   [44] ICSID Case No. ARB/93/1 (21 Feb 1997).

In *Asian Agricultural Products (AAPL)* v. *Sri Lanka*[45] the tribunal considered the FPS clause in the BIT between the UK and Sri Lanka in response to property damage suffered by the British Hong Kong shrimp farm during an armed Tamil uprising against the government. The tribunal held that the phrase 'full protection' in the BIT did not refer to any standards higher than the minimum standard of treatment required by general international law, echoing the debate noted above in relation to FET. In times of civil conflicts, the tribunal ruled, there was a duty on the part of the host state to confer adequate protection to foreign investment and that the failure to give such protection will engage the liability of the state, namely to compensate the investor for damage suffered. This obligation which existed independently of the express FPS, was violated by Sri Lanka. In this instance, however, the FPS provision itself was unhelpful to the investor because it was qualified with the exception that no compensation would be payable if the damage resulted from necessary combat action taken by the host state's military, which included the action taken against the Tamil rebels.

As with FET, there is some controversy regarding whether the FPS standard is autonomous or merely incorporates customary international law. The provision of protection to investors against physical harm has been viewed as an embodiment of customary international law standards relating to the protection of aliens.[46] Some suggest that the FPS standard was simply another way of referring to the traditional international minimum standard of protection provided in customary international law, comprising core responsibilities of maintaining public order.[47] Helping to resolve this tension, NAFTA states that FPS does not require treatment in addition to or beyond that which is required by the customary international law minimum standard of treatment of aliens.[48] Likewise, Canada's Model Treaty Art 5.2 and the US Model Treaty Art 2(b) state that the FPS standard is only that provided by customary international law. The Central American Free Trade Agreement (CAFTA) specifies that FPS requires each Party to provide the level of police protection required under customary

---

[45] (1992) 17 YCA 106.
[46] M. Sornarajah, *The International Law on Foreign Investment* (Cambridge University Press, 2010), at 237.
[47] S. Montt, *State Liability in Investment Treaty Arbitration* (Hart, 2009), at 70.
[48] Art 1105(1).

international law.[49] Following this trend, *Noble Ventures* v. *Romania*[50] established that an FPS clause should not be understood as being wider in scope than the general duty to provide protection and security to foreign nationals found in the customary international law of aliens. The tribunal stated that in order to claim FPS it was necessary to demonstrate that the measure implemented by the host state that caused the damage was directed specifically against a certain investor by reason of its nationality.[51] Thus if all investors are injured during a widespread attack against the country itself, then FPS may not be engaged. Some IIAs specify that the FPS expressly does not provide a standard of treatment that is better than that which is accorded to nationals, foreclosing the 'better than National Treatment' conundrum discussed in the previous chapter.[52] This suggests that a foreign investor would therefore have difficulty succeeding in a claim of FPS violation in situations where domestic investors suffered the same lack of protection by the host state.

If discrimination is not necessary for finding breach of FPS, then it would seem as though the standard may be an absolute one; however, this does not appear to be the case either. It is now widely accepted that the FPS standard of protection against physical damage is tied to the host state's failure to exercise a proper level of care under the circumstances, which might be termed due diligence.[53] Although FPS has been referred to as an absolute standard of treatment along the lines of the minimum standard of treatment of aliens,[54] the 'due diligence' approach suggests that the host state must only make its best efforts to protect foreign investors from physical harm rather than accord some base level of protection that is understood to apply around the world.[55] This view was embraced by the *Noble Ventures* tribunal.[56] Under this view, a violation of FPS depends on whether the state exercised a reasonable level of effort in affording protection to foreign investors, meaning one that is proportional to the situation at hand. This in turn should be tied to the state's available resources,

---

[49] Art 10.1(2).   [50] ICSID Case No. ARB/01/11, Award (12 Oct 2005).

[51] At 111.   [52] E.g. India–Columbia Art 3(4)(b) (10 Nov 2009).

[53] C. McLachlan, L. Shore, M. Weiniger, *International Investment Arbitration: Substantive Principles* (Oxford University Press, 2007), at 247.

[54] T. Grierson-Weiler and I. Laird, 'Standards of Treatment' in P. Muchlinski and F. Ortino (eds.), *Oxford Handbook of International Investment Law* (Oxford University Press, 2008), at 263.

[55] E.g. Montt, *State Liability*, at 70.   [56] ICSID Case No. ARB/01/11 (12 Oct 2005).

meaning its capacity to hire, train and equip police officers or soldiers. Liability will exist in the state if there is a capacity to exercise control or protection and there was a failure to do so.[57]

Under the understanding of FPS as a relative obligation, in response to an allegation of FPS violation the host state must demonstrate that it has taken all practical measures of precaution to protect the investment of the investor and its territory. In other words there is no strict liability imposed upon the state.[58] *Tulip Real Estate* v. *Turkey*[59] noted that the FPS obligation is not one of strict liability. Some have suggested that this characterizes a state's FPS duty as an 'obligation of means'. In other words, the extent to which a host state must provide security will be linked to its resources.[60] This characteristic of the standard seems fair. When investors have established themselves in a country with limited infrastructure, likely in order to reduce their costs because of the availability of raw materials or cheaper labour, they should not be entitled to the level of police or military protection that they would expect in a developed country where wages and taxes are probably much higher.

The relative nature of FPS is seen in *Pantechniki* v. *Albania*,[61] a dispute which concerned riots by citizens which damaged an investor's roadworks project. The tribunal in this case suggested that proportionality is required when assessing violations of the FPS standard. Proportionality is needed because a failure in providing protection and security is likely to arise in:

> an unpredictable instance of civil disorder which could have been readily controlled by a powerful state but which overwhelms the limited capacity of one which is poor and vulnerable ... [I]t seems difficult to maintain that a government incurs international responsibility for failure to plan for unprecedented trouble of unprecedented magnitude in unprecedented places.[62]

Following this reasoning a host state should not bear responsibility under an IIA for the failure to respond to a violent incident that is wholly

---

[57] *Wena Hotels Ltd* v. *Arab Republic of Egypt*, ICSID Case No. ARB/98/4 (8 Dec 2000) [84].
[58] ICSID Case No. ARB/01/11 (12 Oct 2005) at [164].
[59] ICSID Case No. ARB/11/28 (10 March 2014).
[60] C. Moss in A. Reinisch (ed.), *Standards of Investment Protection* (Oxford University Press, 2008).
[61] ICSID Case No. ARB/07/21 (30 July 2009).   [62] At [77].

unprecedented in nature and size. This logic hints at the defence of necessity, which will be revisited in Chapter 10.

Likewise, *OI European Group B.V.* v. *Venezuela*[63] was based on a claim brought by a glass bottle maker for nationalization of its investments including two plants by the government of Venezuela, during which time the National Guard was sent in to ensure that the seizure took place without incident. Denying the FPS claim, the tribunal agreed with Venezuela that by sending the National Guard to the plants in the first weeks after the expropriation, the country was actually ensuring compliance with the FPS standard. This reflects the 'best efforts' component of FPS – as long as the state tries to diminish the harm to a foreign investor, the actual consequences may be unimportant.

Given the changing nature of assets and the inclusion of IP in the definition of investment in many IIAs, it might also be possible to extend FPS to cover damage to intangible assets belonging to investors, such as websites or digital databases. The modern preoccupation with cyberattacks may indicate that a state's responsibility to provide protection in this sphere is poised to be enlarged in the future.[64]

5.3.2 FPS and Non-Physical Security

Clearly the main focus of the FPS standard is protection against damage to physical assets, such as vehicles or buildings.[65] But FPS also appears to include guarantees by the host state against infringements of the investor's rights by the operation of laws and regulations of the host state; in other words, the investor's *legal security*. As such it may be seen to encroach upon protections included in the FET standard, especially in relation to protection against the host state's laws. This may be why many treaties grant FET and FPS in the same section or even paragraph of an IIA, although the link between FPS and FET is more than simply the consequence of treaty drafting. Tribunals have held that treatment which is not fair and equitable automatically entails an absence of FPS.[66]

---

[63] ICSID Case No. ARB/11/25 (2 March 2015).

[64] D. Collins, 'Applying the Full Protection and Security Standard of International Investment Law to Digital Assets' 12:2 *Journal of World Investment and Trade* (2011) 225–43.

[65] E.g. *Asian Agricultural Products (AAPL)* v. *Sri Lanka*, ICSID Case No. ARB/87/3 (27 June 1990) (fishing vessel), *Wena Hotels* v. *Egypt*, ICSID Case No. ARB/98/4 (8 Dec 2000) (hotel).

[66] *Occidental* v. *Ecuador*, ICSID Case No. ARB/06/11 (5 Oct 2012).

The FPS standard is seen to extend beyond physical violence and physical intimidation to cover entitlements to legal rights. Following from this, the host state must ensure that there is a stable and effective legal environment. Some BITs actually use the phrase 'full protection and legal security'[67] in order to make this point clear. With this expansion of the standard in mind, FPS could be invoked to protect an investor from shortcomings in due process, such as excessive delays in court procedures. In this regard, effective access to the host state's judicial system including the enforceability of judgments may also be a component of the FPS standard.

This iteration of the standard was established in *Azurix* v. *Argentina*.[68] The tribunal in this case found a breach of the FPS standard in the host state's conduct in failing to complete work on critical public utilities, exacerbating the public's hostile response to the events. The tribunal noted that FPS did not simply concern physical protection but also contained a further requirement that host governments ensure the stability afforded by a secure investment environment. However in *Tulip Real Estate* v. *Turkey*[69] the tribunal dismissed an FPS claim which had been rooted in the police's inaction during the land seizure because of a lack of violence associated with the land seizure, emphasizing the importance of a physical element to an FPS claim rather than as a failing of criminal law enforcement. Furthermore, the tribunal in *Vannessa Ventures Ltd.* v. *Bolivarian Republic of Venezuela*[70] considered a breach of the FPS clause caused by the Venezuelan court system's failure to adequately respond to Vannessa's claims for breach of contract, primarily because of excessive delay. The tribunal dismissed claims that Venezuela had breached the BIT's FPS standard (as well as FET provision) because although the Venezuelan court system was slow, it was not excessively so. Moreover the government did not engage in delay for a discriminatory or strategic purpose. This award emphasizes the severity of state intervention required in order to succeed with an FPS (and FET) claim, and reiterates the need for third-party action coupled with the state's lack of intervention to succeed in an FPS claim, which was lacking here.

---

[67] Argentina–Chile IV(1): '*plena protección y seguridad jurídica*' (2 Aug 1991).
[68] ICSID Case No. ARB/01/12 (14 July 2006).
[69] ICSID Case No. ARB/11/28 (10 March 2014).
[70] ICSID Case No. ARB(AF)04/6 (16 Jan 2013).

Possibly in an attempt to foreclose claims based on the provision of an unstable legal environment and related denials of due process which are perhaps more in the spirit of FET, the negotiated draft of TTIP clarifies:

> For greater certainty, 'full protection and security' refers to the Party's obligations relating to physical security of investors and covered investments.[71]

This section lacks reference to legal security, suggesting that claims concerning the failure of the host state to provide a stable, functioning legal system would need to be grounded under FET.

5.4 Umbrella Clauses

Umbrella clauses are unquestionably among the most controversial components of IIAs and indeed of all international investment law. Empowering foreign investors to bring a wide range of seemingly marginal or unrelated matters through an IIA, they expand the scope of investor–state dispute settlement considerably, often beyond that which was expected by treaty parties. The importance of the umbrella clause is grounded in the reality that host states may incur many types of legal obligations to the foreign investor, many of which are arguably unsuitable to be brought before international tribunals. In particular, when engaging in commercial activities in foreign states, investors may enter into contracts with the domestic government. Clearly governments have the capacity to enter into contracts just like ordinary private citizens. Such contracts, for example concession agreements, or possibly ordinary contracts for services or goods, will inevitably contain binding contractual promises. They will often provide for dispute settlement in local courts, or if silent on the issue of forum, domestic law will dictate that claims for breach of contracts should be brought in domestic courts, as they are in most jurisdictions. However, as will be explored in Chapter 8, the foreign investor will often wish to avoid local courts, instead pursuing their claims through international investment arbitration. One way they can get international arbitration is by inserting an umbrella clause into an IIA.

---

[71] Chapter II Art 3(5).

Traditionally under international law, it is understood that a breach of a private contract by a state does not give rise to direct international responsibility on the part of that state.[72] Umbrella clauses change this by elevating an ordinary breach of contract to the level of a treaty violation. Umbrella clauses, now found in many if not most IIAs, are therefore seen to provide blanket protection for foreign investment, granting them international remedies even in relation to breach of contract. Given that they accord significant power to foreign investors, sometimes beyond that which may be intended by host states, developing countries in particular are often advised to think carefully about including umbrella clauses in their IIAs.

Umbrella clauses are usually very short and can easily be missed because of the bland nature of the wording which they tend to contain. They are also often hidden inside one large provision in which both FET and FPS are granted, as in this specimen from the Australia–Hong Kong BIT:

> Investments and returns of investors of each Contracting Party shall at all times be accorded fair and equitable treatment and shall enjoy full protection and security in the area of the other Contracting Party. Neither Contracting Party shall, without prejudice to its laws, in any way impair by unreasonable or discriminatory measures the management, maintenance, use, enjoyment or disposal of investments in its area of investors of the other Contracting Party. Each Contracting Party shall observe any obligation it may have entered into with regard to investments of investors of the other Contracting Party. This Agreement shall not prevent an investor of one Contracting Party from taking advantage of the provisions of any law or policy of the other Contracting Party which are more favourable than the provisions of this Agreement.[73]

The phrase 'shall observe any obligation it may have entered into' is classic umbrella clause language, and is seemingly so vague to the point of meaninglessness. However its very vagueness accords this provision its tremendous power. In addition to other sorts of obligations, this phrase means most importantly that any breach of contract can violate this section of the treaty. Once the activity is regarded as being covered by a BIT, then contractual undertakings are liable to be recast as international law obligations. Some umbrella clauses are less clearly phrased and a

---

[72] Subedi, *International Investment Law*, at 104.   [73] Art 2 (15 Sept 1993).

substantial controversy exists, particularly in some French IIAs,[74] as to whether or not the wording used can function to engage international legal obligation in the manner of an umbrella clause. The main effect, then, of an umbrella clause is that an international tribunal could be used to settle disputes regarding the breach rather than a domestic court, even if a domestic court would arguably be a more suitable forum. This blurs the distinction between private law and public law disputes by elevating private breach of contract to the level of treaty violation. This aspect of the clause was expressed by the tribunal in *Noble Ventures* v. *Romania* which stated that an umbrella clause is 'usually seen as transforming domestic law obligations into obligations directly cognizable in international law'.[75]

Whether or not umbrella clauses achieve the effect of engaging international legal remedies is debatable given inconsistent arbitral decisions on this matter. For example, the tribunal in *SGS* v. *Pakistan*[76] held that these provisions do not automatically establish that contract breaches are breaches of international treaty law. The tribunal could not find anything in the Swiss–Pakistan BIT that could be read as vesting the tribunal with jurisdiction over claims resting exclusively on contract. It added that the umbrella clause in the BIT:

> [d]id not purport to state that breaches of contract alleged by an investor in relation to a contract it has concluded with a State (widely considered to be a matter of municipal rather than international law) are automatically 'elevated' to the level of breaches of international treaty law.[77]

It would seem from this decision that only an express inclusion of contract breach would allow a tribunal to extend an umbrella clause in this manner. In other words, a tribunal will not 'read in' an enlargement of its jurisdiction unless there is clear intent for it to do so in the text of the relevant IIA. More recently, the tribunal in *Nova Scotia Power Incorporated* v. *Venezuela*[78] declined to take jurisdiction over a claim for breach of contract on the basis that the dispute arose out of an ordinary breach of contract, notwithstanding the existence of an umbrella clause. On the other hand, in *SGS* v. *Philippines*,[79] the tribunal considered that a very

---

[74] E.g. France–Bahrain BIT Art 10 (24 Feb 2004).
[75] ICSID Case No. ARB/01/11 (12 Oct 2005) at [53].
[76] ICSID Case No. ARB/01/13 (8 Sept 2003).   [77] At [361–3].
[78] ICSID Case No. ARB(AF)/11/1 (30 April 2014).
[79] ICSID Case No. ARB/02/6 (29 Jan 2004).

similar clause regarding the observation of 'any obligation' which was contained in the Swiss–Philippines BIT did encompass breach of contractual obligations. The tribunal held on the basis of this umbrella clause that the BIT had incorporated contractual commitments undertaken by the host state. This was despite the fact that the treaty's language did not specify that 'any obligation' included contract breach.

Use of umbrella clauses as a basis for claims grounded in breach of contract has become commonplace, often receiving little more than perfunctory analysis by tribunals.[80] In *Salini* v. *Jordan* the tribunal examined the umbrella clause in the BIT between Italy and Jordan which referred to the creation and maintenance of 'a legal framework...including compliance...of all undertakings assumed'.[81] The tribunal concluded that this provision required that the relevant legal framework must be 'such as to ensure compliance of all undertakings assumed under relevant contracts'.[82] In other words, the concepts of framework and undertakings were sufficiently broad to allow the tribunal to infer that obligations contained in contracts were included. The use of umbrella clauses to ground claims based on breach of contract has also been upheld by ICSID annulment committees.[83]

Tulip Real Estate and Development Netherlands B.V. v. *Republic of Turkey*[84] involved allegations of breach of a BIT's umbrella clause, as well as breaches of FET and FPS. The dispute concerned a series of assurances made by Turkey that were followed by land seizures. The tribunal concluded that the actions did not constitute violations of the BIT because the umbrella clause could not cover actions that were not contractual but merely expressions of support for the proposed investment that were contained in a legislative instrument. This ruling was based on the existence of the words 'entered into' in the Netherlands–Turkey BIT's umbrella clause. A legislative instrument is not something that is entered into, rather it is enacted by the sovereign and as such departure from its contents could not engage the umbrella provision. Relatedly, the breach of pre-contractual assurances could not amount to a violation of the FET because contractual rights had not crystallized. Lastly, noting that the FPS obligation is

---

[80] *OI European Group B.V.* v. *Venezuela*, ICSID Case No. ARB/11/25 (2 March 2015).

[81] Art 2(4).   [82] ICSID Case No. ARB/02/13 (31 Jan 2006).

[83] *SGS Société Générale de Surveillance S.A.* v. *Paraguay*, ICSID Case No. ARB/07/29 (6 Aug 2003).

[84] ICSID Case No. ARB/11/28 (10 March 2014).

not one of strict liability, the tribunal also dismissed the claim rooted in the police's inaction during the land seizure on the basis of a lack of violence associated with the land seizure.

One way of resolving the dispute as to whether umbrella clauses serve to elevate breach of contract to breach of international law is to conceptualize different categories of contractual actor. Put another way, there may be ordinary contractual parties and there may state-like contractual parties. This could be described through the distinction between Act of Merchant and Act of Sovereign. Where the state is merely acting as a merchant, meaning that it has entered into an ordinary commercial contract in the same way that any private individual could, then breach of a contract should not be viewed as a treaty violation. This distinction can be very difficult to establish in practice. Where the host state is acting in the capacity of a government, exercising powers that could only ever belong to a government, then a breach of contract can and should be conceived as a BIT violation, and accordingly deserves resolution through international arbitration.[85]

5.5   Other Protections in IIAs

There are a few other common provisions found in BITs that should be mentioned, even though they have generated relatively few disputes and as such lack refinement through investment arbitration jurisprudence.

5.5.1   Guarantees of Free Transfer of Capital and Returns

Most IIAs provide that the host state promises that investors will be able to transfer the profits that they make from their business abroad back to their home state. Without such guarantees in a treaty, there is not much point in pursuing an international investment project because the money which foreign investors generate from the activity may be tied up in a foreign bank account. Relaxing controls of currency transfer are therefore a key means by which states enhance their attractiveness to foreign investors seeking to return profits back to their shareholders in the home state or elsewhere. Clearly internationalization serves no strategic

---

[85] *El Paso* v. *Argentina*, ICSID Case No. ARB/03/15, Decision on Jurisdiction (14 April 2006).

commercial purpose if the capital that it generates cannot be effectively transferred across borders.

In many IIAs such clauses are included under the heading 'Repatriation of Investments and Returns', as in this specimen from the Sweden–India BIT:

1) Each Contracting Party shall permit all funds related to an investment of an investor of the other Contracting Party in its territory to be freely transferred, on an expeditious and non-discriminatory basis. Such funds may include:
   (a) Capital and additional capital amounts used to maintain and increase investments;
   (b) Net operating profits including dividends and interest in proportion to their share-holding;
   (c) Repayments of any loan, including interest thereon;
   (d) Payment of royalties and services fees;
   (e) Proceeds from sales of their shares;
   (f) Proceeds received by investors in case of sale or partial sale or liquidation;
   (g) Compensation received under Articles 5) and 6); and
   (h) The earnings of nationals of one Contracting Party or of a third state, who work: in connection with investment in the territory of the other Contracting Party.
2) Unless otherwise agreed between the parties, currency transfer under Paragraph 1) of this Article shall be permitted in the currency of the original investment or any other convertible currency. Such transfer shall be made at the prevailing market rate of exchange on the date of transfer.[86]

This provision not only explains the nature of the assets which are entitled to free transfer but also specifies the nature of the currency as well as timing, both of which are crucial to an investment's international mobility. In order to maximize the flow of FDI, foreign investors should not be required by host states to retain a specific quantity of capital in the domestic currency, nor should administrative burdens be placed upon foreign investors seeking to transfer capital in or out of the host state. These promises are often made subject to requirements relating to bankruptcy and other domestic civil liabilities such as unpaid civil or criminal judgments,

[86] Sweden–India BIT Art 7 (4 July 2000).

economic emergencies and maintaining balance-of-payments equilibrium. Such restrictions are seen in the Australia–Mexico BIT:

> a Contracting Party may prevent a transfer through the equitable, non-discriminatory and in good faith application of its laws relating to:
>
> (a) bankruptcy, insolvency or the protection of the rights of creditors;
> (b) issuing, trading or dealing in securities;
> (c) criminal offences; or
> (d) ensuring the satisfaction of judgements in adjudicatory proceedings.[87]

These conditions reflect instances where it is appropriate for the host state to keep a foreign investor's money in the jurisdiction and are broadly in keeping with commitments that are made regarding currency exchange among Members of the IMF.[88]

Very few disputes have been brought under investor–state arbitration involving the breach of transfer clauses. This may be because it is more likely that these types of claims would be framed as expropriations: in denying repatriation of its assets, the investor loses the enjoyment of its investment. Expropriation will be examined in the next chapter.

OI European Group v. *Venezuela*[89] was based on a number of provisions including the relevant BIT's freedom of transfer clause. The tribunal accepted Venezuela's argument, determining that the investor OI waived its right to free transfers under the treaty when it opted to transfer funds via the parallel exchange market. In parallel (dual) foreign exchange markets, which are extremely common in developing countries, the market-determined exchange rate coexists with one or more pegged exchange rates. Venezuela resorted to a dual system at the time of its debt crisis to smooth out the devaluation in the exchange rate, to achieve the needed depreciation of its currency. This helped it to maintain limited control over domestic inflation, also avoiding a sudden drop in real wages while safeguarding its balance of payments. The investor was deemed to have accepted this system and could therefore not later challenge it. Currency transfer provisions were also argued recently in

---

[87] Art 9 (23 Aug 2005).
[88] Articles of Agreement of the International Monetary Fund, Art VIII (adopted 22 July 1944, revised 28 April 2008), www.imf.org/external/pubs/ft/aa/index.htm.
[89] ICSID Case No. ARB/11/25 (2 March 2015).

PNG v. *Papua New Guinea*[90] but all claims were ultimately rejected for lack of jurisdiction.

5.5.2 Entry and Sojourn of Personnel

Most IIAs include a clause which allows for the 'Entry and Sojourn of Personnel', meaning the entrance of foreign citizens for the purpose of operating the business. Clearly the capacity to bring in foreign workers may be an essential component of the foreign firm's business strategy. A good example of such a provision may be seen in the China–India BIT:

> A Contracting Party shall, subject to its applicable laws and regulations relating to the entry and sojourn of non-citizens, permit natural persons of the other Contracting Party and personnel employed by companies of the other Contracting Party to enter and remain in its territory for the purpose of engaging in activities connected with investments.[91]

This provision, allowing alien individuals to enter the host state to work for the foreign investor, is made 'subject to its applicable laws' which means that the host state is free to transgress this clause if its national laws impose caps on numbers of migrant workers or other restrictions on employees. It also allows a country to prohibit the entry of a person who has a criminal record or is on a terrorist watch list, for example.

Some such provisions elaborate that states will permit investors to employ within its territory key technical and managerial personnel of their choice, regardless of citizenship. Some Chinese BITs specify that foreign investors are permitted to hire 'key technical and managerial personnel' of their choice regardless of citizenship.[92] Technical and managerial personnel will most likely not be locals if the host state is a developing state. This is why the host state will want these experts to enter their territory to bring knowledge, as it is understood that technology transfer is one of the advantages of FDI. It would be rare for an IIA to extend this provision to ordinary workers, because most hosts want their local citizens to gain employment from the foreign investor; indeed, offering employment is one of the major advantages of FDI. In this regard, the China–Guyana BIT of 2003 further elaborates that foreign investors will 'employ their

---

[90] ICSID Case No. ARB/13/33 (5 May 2015).   [91] Art 11 (21 Nov 2006).
[92] E.g. China–Australia BIT Art IV.2 (11 July 1988).

best efforts to facilitate the training of local personnel and the transfer of skills'.[93] Interestingly, these provisions are therefore one of the few features of IIAs that attempt to impose any obligations on investors, as unenforceable as they might be.

5.5.3 Transparency

Finally, many IIAs contain clauses in which states promise that they will ensure that their laws, as they pertain to foreign investors, are fully transparent and accessible. The rationale for such provisions is that the more readily available information on the laws which affect foreign investors, the easier it will be for foreign investors to comply with it. This will reduce costs and improve compliance. A reasonably elaborate transparency provision can be found in the US Model BIT of 2012,[94] which speaks of the duty to publish all relevant laws and to respond to queries. Transparency requirements are also found in the GATS.[95] There is evidently some overlap between transparency and the FET requirement, which also covers openness and good faith in the administration of laws. The FET requirement is more likely to be engaged with respect to adjudicatory processes, such as would be engaged during the removal of entitlements, rather than with clarity and disclosure of legislation relevant to FDI. This may be one reason why claims based on breach of transparency provisions are rarely found with investment arbitration.

5.6 Conclusion

It may not be enough for a multinational enterprise planning to expand into another jurisdiction to know that it will be treated as well as the equivalent domestic investors, because equal treatment can sometimes be harmful, particularly in countries which lack a strong tradition of rule of law. Similarly, the protections afforded by customary international law may simply be too vague and insubstantial for an investor to overcome its fear that its commitment of time and resources will not be unduly interfered with by governments which do not share the same view of fair dealing when it comes to interactions with the business community.

[93] Art 2.4 (27 March 2003).   [94] Art 11.   [95] Art V.

International investment law has responded to this dilemma through the establishment and development of additional standards of protections, which, although somewhat ambiguous, still serve to enhance a host state's responsibility with respect to its treatment of foreign investors.

FET is the most widely used standard of protection contained within IIAs given its capacity to encompass a wide range of behaviour. At its most basic level, the FET principle captures the essence of what we understand to be due process – governments should be open and consistent in terms of the way regulations and judicial and administrative decisions are applied. It is often thought to overlap with the international minimum standard of protection which is expected under customary international law to be accorded to foreign investors by host governments in situations not contemplated by the more specific treaty provisions. While breach of FET will be difficult to demonstrate because it sets a high threshold for harmful conduct, over the years arbitration tribunals have moved towards an expansive understanding of this term, leading many modern IIAs to provide tighter definitions. An assortment of specific forms of conduct through which it will often be engaged is widely recognized.

FPS is a somewhat narrower form of protection now well established in IIA practice which traditionally guarded against physical harm that befell investors' assets. Under this standard, host governments are required not to damage investors' property and, perhaps more crucially, are expected to prevent third parties from doing so by furnishing some reasonable level of police or military protection. The notion of a minimal level of protection is problematic under FPS, as it is widely held that the standard actually contemplates a principle of due diligence. Host states are to be held accountable under the standard only where their provision of protection against physical harm falls below the level that is achievable given their level of resources and development. Recent extensions of FPS have suggested that it captures not only security from physical harm, but also legal security. Seemingly overlapping with FET, the FPS standard calls upon host states to ensure that there is a stable legal environment, including functioning and accessible civil as well as criminal courts.

In addition to these rather far-reaching forms of protection, most IIAs contain highly specialized provisions which shield foreign investors from specific types of inappropriate conduct on the part of their host governments. The guarantee of free transfer of currency allows investors to repatriate the profits from their international projects back to the home state, actualizing the main profit-making purpose behind FDI. Entry and sojourn of personnel clauses facilitate multinational enterprises' ability to bring in foreign workers where certain skills may be lacking among the local population. Lastly, many IIAs contain transparency provisions which, echoing some of the responsibilities embraced by FET, press upon governments the need to be clear and open in their communication of the legal obligations placed on foreign firms.

The capacity of foreign investors to make good on any of these provisions – meaning to ensure that the commitment behaviour is in fact offered – depends of course on the procedural features of IIAs, namely their investor–state dispute settlement mechanisms, which will be explored in a later chapter. But first we will focus on the foreign investor's greatest source of protection under international investment law, the guarantee against expropriation without compensation.

6 Guarantees Against Expropriation

6.1 Introduction

Expropriation is the most serious interference that a host state can impose on a foreign investor. Beyond simply imposing barriers or denying access to legal processes, or establishing conditions which grant an unfair advantage to competitors, expropriation results in the transfer of an asset owned by the investor into the hands of the host government. Representing in many respects a fundamental transgression of the right of individuals to own and make use of their property, the various forms of expropriation consist of the host government taking possession of the investment itself, either directly through official decree, or through a series of measures that have the effect of taking because cumulatively they become so burdensome that the commercial operation in the hands of the foreign investor is drained of its practical value.

Since the understanding of the host state's actions that can constitute expropriation has become so expansive, and since many types of regulations serve a legitimate public purpose even where the effects on foreign investment are damaging, tribunals enquiring into allegations of expropriation must cautiously balance the investor's entitlement to enjoy the fruits of its labour and the government's sovereign right to enact laws to serve its citizens. The compromise of monetary compensation for takings, which will be examined in its own chapter, has been developed to address these tensions. For now this chapter will explore the concept of expropriation in international investment law, focusing closely on its much more controversial modern iteration, that of indirect expropriation.

6.2 Scope and Definitions

6.2.1 The Right to Expropriate

The starting point of the analysis of international investment law's doctrine of expropriation and the guarantees against this action without compensation enshrined in IIAs is the understanding that the state has a right to control property and economic resources within its territory in order to enhance its economic, political and other objectives. This right was explored earlier in relation to the UN's NIEO philosophy and is correctly viewed as one of the elements of statehood. Given this right, it is conceded that the taking of property by a state within its territory is fundamentally lawful. It is further generally accepted, however, that a lawful taking creates an obligation to pay compensation to the owner of the property that was seized. An unlawful taking, on the other hand, creates an obligation to pay damages. The precise nature of these two concepts, or at least the way tribunals and commentators have attempted to define it, will be explored further in Chapter 7.

One of the central functions of IIAs is to protect foreign investment against interference with property rights by the host states, meaning preserving the foreign investor's entitlement to own and make productive use of their assets. But the principle of sovereignty preserves the power of states over their internal affairs and includes the power to take title and possession of property when it is in the public interest (sometimes referred to as 'eminent domain') as well as the power to regulate for the health and safety of the people. States also retain the power to tax, as well as the right to manage their own natural resources pursuant to their own environmental and development policies, which may impair the value of an investment severely. For some time expropriation was the most important issue of investment protection. Indeed there was a time when foreign investor protection was virtually synonymous with protection against uncompensated expropriation. This was particularly so during the era of oil company nationalizations in the 1970s.

While it is arguably an aspect of customary international law, most IIAs tend to acknowledge the right of expropriation belonging to states. This is why, contrary to popular belief, IIAs do not make expropriation illegal outright, they simply guarantee that certain conditions are required for it to be viewed as legal, one of which is that when it does occur compensation will be paid. In that sense IIAs typically only address the conditions and consequences of an expropriation with the state's right to expropriate left essentially unaffected. Furthermore, it is important to recognize from the outset that intangible property, including rights arising from a contract as well as IP such as patents, is susceptible to a claim for expropriation in the same way as real property. This is reflected in the definition of the term 'investment' in many IIAs.

Investors are protected from expropriation in most IIAs by guarantees against expropriation without compensation. For example, the Germany–China BIT of 2003 states:

> investment by investors of either Contracting Party shall not directly or indirectly be expropriated, nationalized or be subjected to any measure the effect of which would be tantamount to expropriation or nationalization in the territory of the other Contracting Party except for the public benefit and against compensation.[1]

This provision encompasses all forms of expropriation and also specifies the requirements for its legality, both of which will be discussed below. One of the crucial points to take from this provision is that for purposes of ascribing state responsibility and the obligation to make adequate reparation, international law does not distinguish indirect from direct expropriations.[2] This issue will be discussed further in the next chapter. For now, the two varieties of expropriation will be examined.

6.2.2 Direct Expropriation

In international investment law, direct expropriation is defined as the formal or official withdrawal of property rights for the benefit of the state or for private persons designated by the state either on an individual investment basis or as part of a large-scale nationalization programme.[3] This definition captures what is often referred to more commonly as nationalization, which occurs when governments take productive private property and put it into public ownership, usually because this is viewed as more efficient or more egalitarian as the public is able to share in the profits. From a legal perspective, direct expropriation is the outright and overt taking of property achieved by means of transfer of title to the state. In international investment law it provides clear grounds for the deprived investors to seek compensation from the state.

---

[1] Art 4(2) (1 Dec 2003).

[2] See generally Articles on the Responsibility of States for Internationally Wrongful Acts, arts. I,31, in *Report of the International Law Commission on the Work of its Fifty-third Session*, UN GAOR, 56th Sess., Supp. No. 10, at 43, UN Doc. A56/10 (2001).

[3] *Sempra Energy International* v. *Argentina*, ICSID Case No. ARB/02/13, Award (28 September 2007) at [280]; *Enron Corporation and Ponderosa Assets, L.P.* v. *Argentina*, ICSID Case No. ARB/01/3, Award (22 May 2007) at [243].

Direct expropriations are uncommon today if for no other reason than they give the state involved a bad reputation which can affect its capacity to attract FDI. Argentina expropriated a significant portion of the Spanish-owned energy company YPF in 2014, leading to a claim for compensation. The dispute surrounding this expropriation of a formerly Argentinean state-owned company eventually settled with Argentina paying $5 billion to the investor. As noted above, direct expropriation as part of a governmental economic or social programme which is ostensibly in the public interest is often described as 'nationalization'. This term has a somewhat more benign connotation than that of expropriation and is a strategy that is pursued from time to time by governments around the world. Clearly there may be many situations where privately owned assets may be more effectively used, in terms of their role in addressing public welfare, in the hands of the government. In what circumstances this is true represents possibly the most fundamental debate in modern politics and captures the dichotomy between 'right wing' and 'left wing' governments. For example, in the UK there remains an ongoing debate about the nationalization (or re-nationalization) of the rail network and whether or not this is in the best interest of citizens. Nationalization may occur with much less controversy in situations where privately held land is taken over by the government for a public infrastructure project. To use another recent example from the UK, broad swathes of valuable commercial (and some residential) property in Central London were expropriated by the government for the Crossrail underground railway project. As required by national law (and IIAs, as will be mentioned below), affected citizens were compensated for this deprivation. There are perhaps somewhat more questionable circumstances where nationalization has occurred because of the race or ethnicity of the investors concerned. Known sometimes as 'indigenization measures', such takings were instigated by some African and Asian states in the post-colonial period. Venezuela and South Africa have also done this recently.

The most egregious form of direct expropriation is known as confiscation and describes the process of taking property for the personal gain of the governmental authority without the justification of a public purpose or without the payment of any compensation. Thankfully this heinous practice is exceedingly rare in modern times and is usually associated with the actions of dictators during particularly tumultuous periods of history such as wars or revolutions. Confiscations of private property, including both real property as well as movables such as artwork, took place during the Nazi period. More recently, the Ceausescu regime in Romania and that of Saddam Hussein in Iraq have engaged in confiscations. Such actions are illegal under international law and carry with them obligations that exist irrespective of IIAs. Reparations for such wrongs will be considered in Chapter 8.

Guarantees against direct expropriation without compensation can be found in most IIAs, but guarantees against direct expropriation *only*, meaning not including indirect expropriation, are relatively uncommon today because most expropriations are indirect. An example of the former clause can be seen in the Morocco–Serbia BIT of 2013, Art 4.1:

> Investments of investors of either Contracting Party in the territory of the other Contracting Party shall not be expropriated, nationalized or subjected to any other measures of dispossession (hereinafter referred to as 'expropriation') except for a public purpose, in accordance with due process of law, on a non-discriminatory basis and against prompt, adequate and effective compensation.[4]

Note that the phrase 'direct expropriation' is not used, meaning that the default understanding of 'expropriation' is one in which there is a removal of legal title to the asset, as captured by the phrase 'any other measures of dispossession'. Under a direct expropriation the investor no longer owns the investment because it is now in the hands of the state. 'Nationalization' appears here perhaps as somewhat of a euphemism for expropriation, although nationalism tends to convey the notion that the taking was done for a public purpose. 'Any other measures of dispossession' appears to be quite broad, but again it contemplates the taking of legal ownership and as such does not encompass indirect expropriation. The provision goes on to list the qualifications necessary for an expropriation to be lawful under the treaty, which will be explored further below.

Perhaps one of the best known disputes that arose in international investment arbitration as a consequence of a direct expropriation was *Amoco International Finance Corporation v. Iran*.[5] This dispute related to a series of nationalizations of foreign-owned oil companies in the early 1980s shortly after the Islamic Revolution. By official decree the Iranian government annulled all oil and gas industry contracts that included

---

[4] 6 June 2013.   [5] Iran–United States Claims Tribunal, The Hague (14 July 1987).

foreign companies. Iran did not dispute the fact that an expropriation had occurred, but it argued that it had acted lawfully in taking the property because it was in the public interest to do so. More specifically, it was in the best interests of citizens for productive natural resources to be in the hands of the government in order to achieve and sustain economic stability. The tribunal ultimately agreed with the host state in large part because the nationalization was of the entire petroleum industry, not simply one particular investor. The government was not selfishly appropriating this particular investor's assets for its own commercial gain, but as part of an overall plan for restructuring the country's economy.

Given the nature of direct expropriation, the fact of the expropriation itself will often be conceded by parties, leaving tribunals to assess the justification. With this issue in mind, a different view of the legitimacy of nationalization, meaning whether the taking served the public interest or not, was taken by the tribunal in *ADC Affiliate* v. *Hungary*.[6] Here the host state took over the operation of the foreign investor's project (the building and operating of an airport), claiming that this expropriation was in the strategic interests of the state, in particular the harmonization of their transportation strategy. The tribunal disagreed, finding that there was no legitimate purpose behind the nationalization which deprived the claimants of their airport project. In the absence of a more clearly articulated objective, the tribunal saw this action as the seizure of a particular commercial project without any linkage to a broader economic goal of interest to the public. The *ADC* tribunal also found that the takings lacked due process because the government did not notify the investors in a timely fashion about changes to the law which would have resulted in the deprivation of their asset.

6.2.3 Indirect Expropriation

Outright expropriations of foreign investments by host governments were essentially temporary phenomena of the 1960s and 1970s reflecting a particular historic context. This is why the importance of provisions regulating direct expropriation has declined while other provisions have become more important, most notably FET, but also the equally expansive concept of indirect expropriation. Put simply, an indirect expropriation is an

---

[6] ICSID Case No. ARB/03/16 (2 Oct 2006).

interference with an asset that, while damaging, falls short of resulting in an actual transfer of title.

This means that excessive regulation of a foreign investment can amount to a taking in terms of its effect on the value of the underlying asset, even though this was not originally what was envisioned by the concept of 'expropriation' which captures loss of ownership. In large part because of their ambiguous nature and the increasing spheres of activity in which governments engage in regulation, claims of indirect expropriation have increased dramatically. They have played a significant role in the explosion of investor–state dispute settlement in the late twentieth and early twenty-first centuries. This may further be explained by the fact that many existing IIAs do not provide a clear and comprehensive definition of the concept of expropriation, including its less formal iteration. Indirect expropriation is often referred to as de facto expropriation. This means that the state takes an action which has the practical effect of depriving the investor of the use of its assets, even though under law the investor retains ownership. Measures 'tantamount to expropriation' are also embodied in this principle.

At a general level, indirect expropriations are severe interferences with an investor's use of their property to the point that their capacity to make a profit is seriously undermined even though ownership remains. In modern arbitration practice, a wide range of regulatory interventions are regularly characterized (at least by claimant investors) as indirect expropriations where they might be more commonly viewed as a government acting like a government, simply regulating its economy for the benefit of its citizens. Of course, labelling normal types of regulatory behaviour as expropriation runs the risk of frightening governments against enacting all kinds of laws which may have an incidental effect on a foreign investor's business but which may have served a worthwhile purpose. Likewise, justifying an excessive intrusion into a company's operations on the basis that it serves some public need can lead to a dangerous situation where governments may selectively harm certain companies illegitimately, for example to assist uncompetitive local firms. Arbitration tribunals have taken various approaches to what precisely will constitute an indirect expropriation, with some giving weight to the extent of the investor's losses or its declining profitability, just as others focus on the degree of control that is retained. As with many issues in international investment law, the question of whether or not an indirect expropriation has occurred is highly dependent on the facts of the dispute.

The rules of international law governing the expropriation of foreign property have always been controversial, partly because of this expansion of the notion of what constitutes a governmental taking of private property. In a sense the doctrine of expropriation tests the limits of the degree of intervention that a state can be expected to exercise over an individual's property. This had led to much debate over the basic issue of the scope of permissible taking. It is often thought that tension surrounding the precise contours of expropriation has been exacerbated due to the irony that a concept initiated for the purposes of investment in the developing world has now been applied to the regulatory actions of states in the developed world. In other words, the expansion of the concept of indirect expropriation to serve the interests of Western multinational enterprises has been retracted as Western states are now having their own laws challenged as expropriations. States which had used the law of expropriation as a sword for their multinationals have come to regard it as a shield to safeguard their regulatory autonomy.[7]

The importance of indirect expropriation as a form of interference with foreign property has been identified by UNCTAD, which acknowledged:

> it is not the physical invasion of the property that characterises nationalisations or expropriations that has assumed importance, but the erosion of rights associated with ownership by State interference.[8]

An asset that is over-regulated, perhaps through excessive licensing, taxation or intrusive supervision by the government, is as good as worthless, even if the investor retains control. While harmful, such interventions are often harder to recognize than direct takings, requiring extensive analysis of the precise factual context.

A simple guarantee against indirect expropriation is seen in Art 4(2) of the Egypt–Germany BIT of 2005:

> Investments by investors of either Contracting State shall not directly or indirectly be expropriated, nationalized or subjected to any other measures the effects of which would be tantamount to expropriation or nationalization in the territory of the other Contracting State except for the public benefit and against compensation.[9]

---

[7] See generally, M. Sornarajah, *The International Law on Foreign Investment* (Cambridge University Press, 2010).

[8] UNCTAD, *Taking of Property*, Series on Issues in International Investment Agreements (United Nations, 2000) at [4].

[9] 16 June 2005.

The key phrase here is 'any other measure the effects of which would be tantamount to expropriation'. The state may not enact any measures which have the practical effect in terms of commercial utility of the investor losing the asset entirely. Put more forcibly, the legal burdens placed on the investor were so harsh that the state might as well have simply taken the investment from them. 'Tantamount to expropriation' has the same meaning as 'equivalent to expropriation',[10] an alternative phrase which is found in some treaties.

Many investment treaties establish wide definitions for indirect expropriation, including measures that have the equivalent effect to an expropriation.

The focus on the practical effect of the measure, rather than how it is labelled or the intention of the government, is grounded in the law of expropriation found in national legal systems. The most influential national system of law on international investment law, particularly as it has been expressed in the context of NAFTA, has been that of the USA. Most investment arbitration tribunals tend to embrace the effects rule of expropriation, finding in favour of the investor and awarding compensation for expropriation for effective deprivation suffered by the investor. Tribunals tend not to challenge the motivation of governmental authorities when rendering their decisions. As noted in Chapter 3, one of the reasons that intent generally does not matter is that evaluating the purpose behind a sovereign decision is notoriously difficult – the only way you can ascertain the motivation of a government is if accurate records are kept and there is no reason to expect that this is the case, or if it is, that such records will be available for scrutiny by foreign investors or arbitral tribunals. The distinction between intent and effects is in some respects the key factor underlying the difference between direct expropriation and indirect expropriation. As noted by the *Metalclad* tribunal brought under NAFTA, an expropriation can occur 'through actions or conduct, which do not explicitly express the purpose of depriving one of rights or assets, but actually have that effect'.[11] In this regard, tribunals will not normally enquire as to the legitimacy of the stated public purpose behind a measure in order to ascertain whether or not it should be construed as lawful. International investment tribunals will not normally substitute their own

---

[10] Art 6, Italy–Malaysia (12 Oct 1988).

[11] *Metalclad Corporation* v. *United Mexican States*, ICSID Case No. ARB(AF)/97/1 (30 Aug 2000).

judgment of what should constitute the public interest in various circumstances.

The first use of the standard of substantial and permanent interference as evidence of indirect expropriation in the context of international investment law was probably that implemented by the *Pope & Talbot* tribunal under NAFTA,[12] which borrowed from jurisprudence developed at the Iran–US Claims Tribunal, of which more will be mentioned in Chapter 8. The tribunal in *CMS* defined indirect takings as measures that do not involve an overt expropriation but that effectively neutralize the enjoyment of the property.[13] In the context of commercial property, enjoyment is understood to mean profitability. Following claims against it as a respondent under NAFTA, the USA changed the language in some of its IIAs in order to clarify the scope of its expropriation powers and to reduce claims of compensation as a result of regulatory actions of host states.[14] As will be examined below, these treaties, including the recent TTIP, establish that certain exercises of governmental authority in pursuit of the public interest should be viewed as legitimate takings and therefore not trigger an obligation to pay compensation.

When an investment tribunal assesses whether or not there has been an indirect expropriation by the host state, it is important to establish the effect of the measure upon the investment, as this will be the principal determinant of whether or not the action was equivalent to an actual taking. As noted above, this is normally evaluated in terms of changes in its value or, in most cases relatedly, in the ability of the investor to control it. Few treaties or arbitration decisions make reference to the intent to deprive the investor of the benefits of property. The intent of the expropriating government may however be relevant to establish whether the expropriation was lawful or unlawful. If there is a motivation of public purpose then it will more likely be held to be lawful, necessitating compensation rather than damages. If the measure is of a general regulatory nature that only incidentally affects the foreigner investor's property and the intent served the public interest, then there may be no expropriation at all and therefore no requirement of compensation. The state should be free to act in the broader public interest, possibly subject to the requirement of proportionality between the measure and the public interest aim.

---

[12] UNCITRAL (26 June 2000).   [13] At [261].
[14] E.g. Art 10.9(1) of the FTA with Chile (6 June 2003).

With respect to the effect, the investor may retain control over the business in the sense of being able to take decisions as to its operation, but the investment itself loses its financial viability. Even though the investment may actually survive, the key features that determine its profitability are no longer present. As the tribunal in *LG&E* v. *Argentina* established, it will not normally count as expropriation where the investor is still able to carry out the day-to-day operations of the business, even if the profits of the business are diminished.[15] Investment tribunals have refused to find an expropriation has occurred where the investor has kept a meaningful level of control over the business in terms of retaining managerial or decision-making authority.[16] So in that sense it is really a question of degree when assessing the state's behaviour and its consequences to the business operations. Control is therefore an important element, but it is not determinative if all that is left is a functionally useless company.

Additional manifestations of indirect expropriation appear to overlap with that of other standards, such as FET. As indicated by the *AMCO* tribunal, expropriation 'exists not only when a state takes over private property, but also when the expropriating state transfers ownership to another legal or natural person', meaning that another entity is able to take control. The *AMCO* tribunal went on to state that a taking 'also exists merely by the state withdrawing the protection of its courts from the owner expropriated and tacitly allowing a de facto possessor to remain in possession of the thing seized'.[17] These words recall matters covered by FET and FPS standards. The link to FET in particular appears evident, as there are a number of arbitration decisions where the facts do not quite support a finding of indirect expropriation but do support a breach of FET, suggesting that in some respects FET is a lesser version of an indirect expropriation.[18]

The precise nature of indirect expropriation is further convoluted because of the timeframe in which regulatory interferences amounting to a taking can occur. An expropriation need not arise in one single action.

---

[15] ICSID Case No. ARB/02/1 (3 Oct 2006).

[16] *Azurix* v. *Argentina*, ICSID Case No. ARB/01/12, Award (14 July 2007) and *LG&E* v. *Argentina*, ibid.

[17] *AMCO Asia Corporation* v. *The Republic of Indonesia*, ICSID Case No. ARB/81/1 (21 Nov 1984) at [244] and [248].

[18] S. Lopez Escarcena, *Indirect Expropriation in International Law* (Edward Elgar, 2014), at 209.

Indeed it may take place in stages over time in a manner sometimes referred to as 'creeping expropriation'. Creeping expropriation is difficult to identify because it is a form of indirect expropriation that takes place incrementally, meaning that each measure taken by the state may itself be insufficient to warrant a finding of expropriation but the cumulative effect is one that is equivalent to that of a de facto dispossession of property. A series of acts or measures committed by the state over a period of time in an incremental fashion can just as easily have the effect of depriving the investor of the benefit of their property as single devastating regulatory intrusion. Like the straw that broke the camel's back, eventually some threshold will be crossed at which it will be considered an expropriation. Tribunals have identified this gradual form of expropriation in a number of awards.[19] According to the tribunal in *Siemens* v. *Argentina*,[20] for creeping expropriation to have occurred, each step taken by the government must have had an adverse effect, meaning that none of them can be inconsequential. The tribunal in *Tradex* v. *Albania* focused on the cumulative effect of the measures when considering the concept of creeping expropriation – it was the 'combination of the decisions and events... in a long, step-by-step process'.[21] This ruling suggests that an individual measure may itself be insignificant.

It is also important to consider the timeframe within which a taking of property has occurred, for the purposes of assessing whether or not there has been an expropriation. This is rooted in the idea that an expropriation is understood as a lasting deprivation of property – it is not something that is a passing or temporary interference. Whether or not a taking, either direct or otherwise, is permanent will depend heavily on the circumstances and the nature of representations made to the investor. The deprivation could last a year or perhaps as little as six months, depending on the severity of the interference. In *LG&E* v. *Argentina* it was determined that generally speaking, only permanent deprivations will count as expropriations. It added: '[the expropriation] cannot have a temporary nature, unless the investment's successful development depends on the realization of certain activities at specific moments that may not endure variations.'[22] In other words, transitory takings may count as indirect (or direct for that matter)

---

[19] *Biloune* v. *Ghana*, Ad Hoc-Award of 27 October 1989 and 30 June 1990, *Tradex Hellas SA* v. *Republic of Albania*, ICSID Case No. ARB/94/2 (29 April 1999).
[20] ICSID Case No. ARB/02/8 (17 Jan 2007).   [21] *Tradex* v. *Albania*.   [22] At para [193].

expropriations where the interference occurs at a pivotal time where significant profits were lost as a consequence.

It must be said that in light of the potential for the concept of indirect expropriation to encompass a broad assortment of regulatory actions taken by host states, in recent years tribunals have shown a tendency to construe indirect expropriation narrowly. Tribunals often appear to be more willing to observe breaches of FET instead,[23] although it is far from evident that this standard will be an easy one to satisfy either. This approach could reflect the sense that the right of a state to regulate in the public interest should be preserved where possible, just as an investor's entitlement to due process should be seen as deserving of special attention because of its link to principles of fundamental justice.

6.3 The Legality of Expropriation

Having considered the two main varieties of expropriation, it is essential to further classify expropriation into the categories of lawful and unlawful, which apply equally to both the direct and indirect forms.

6.3.1 Lawful Expropriation

IIAs tend to treat the scope of both direct and indirect expropriation to be functionally equivalent, and as legally equivalent in terms of their consequences. Establishing when expropriation is lawful rather than unlawful is also a difficult exercise which regularly preoccupies investment tribunals, but its effect on consequences is more significant because the former triggers the obligation to pay compensation whereas the latter instils the obligation to pay damages. These concepts will be illustrated further in the next chapter. For now, requiring a state to pay a firm money of any amount for its own regulatory decisions represents a major encroachment on the sovereignty of states, subordinating national law to that of international law for the purposes of facilitating FDI. In order for such expropriation to be considered lawful, there are four commonly

---

[23] C. Dolzer and C. Schreuer, *Principles of International Investment Law* (Oxford University Press, 2012), at 101.

acknowledged requirements which regularly appear in the text of IIAs and which are also viewed as part of customary international law.

These are captured, for example, in the 2007 BIT between the UK and Mexico which specifies the following:

> Investments of investors of either Contracting Party shall not be nation-alised or expropriated, either directly or indirectly through measures having effect equivalent to nationalisation or expropriation ('expropriation') in the territory of the other Contracting Party except for a public purpose, on a non-discriminatory basis, in accordance with due process of law and against compensation.[24]

First, the measure taking alien property must serve a public purpose. As suggested earlier, the term 'public purpose' is very broad and notoriously difficult to define. It is difficult for a foreign investor to challenge this aspect of the taking, yet tribunals often find themselves evaluating this component of the four-stage test.

For example, in *SPP* v. *Egypt*,[25] a case which concerned a hotel development on the Giza Plateau in Egypt, the tribunal considered whether a series of decrees issued which resulted in the project's cancellation constituted lawful expropriation. The tribunal recognized that the host state's cancellation of the project in order to protect its archaeological and cultural heritage constituted a lawful exercise of the right of eminent domain, meaning that it was effectively in the public interest. Focusing on the effects of the measures imposed rather than the intent of the government which was clearly a noble one, the exercise of eminent domain still required that the state indemnify the investor for the harm it suffered. SPP was granted compensation for the cancellation based on the diminution of the value of the asset.

When considering public purpose, it is thought also that there must be a reasonable degree of proportionality between the means employed (the extent of the deprivation) and the aim sought to be realized, such as for example the taking of land for the purposes of building a highway. Some tribunals have emphasized the need to establish proportionality when assessing the public purpose behind a measure and whether this should engage the obligation to pay compensation as an indirect expropriation.

---

[24] Art 7 (12 May 2006).   [25] ICSID Case No. ARB/84/3 (20 May 1992).

The tribunal in *Tecmed* v. *Mexico*,[26] for example, considered the motives behind the host state's measure, not to ascertain whether it was lawfully imposed by the government but rather to establish if the BIT, which required that expropriation be undertaken for a public purpose, was breached. It concluded that there was no justification for the measure because it had been adopted on solely political grounds. In other words, it determined that the expropriation was unlawful. A proportionality-based assessment of intent or purpose and effects was also adopted by the tribunal in *Azurix*[27] and in *LG&E*. An interesting approach to the issue of intent behind an expropriation and therefore the critique of tribunals of the public purpose behind a measure can be seen in the recent *ADC* arbitration. That panel assessed the public purpose claimed by Hungary, reasoning that to fulfil this requirement there must be some proven genuine interest. It stated further that the mere reference to public purpose does not 'magically put such interest into existence and therefore satisfy the requirement'.[28] Put bluntly, it is not enough for a country to assert that there is a noble intent behind the taking – this must be demonstrated.

It is important to note that if these motives are sufficiently strong and reasonably connected, then there may be no expropriation at all and therefore no right to compensation. A legitimate public purpose underlying a regulatory measure does not necessarily exclude the existence of an expropriation for which compensation is payable. The distinction between normal regulatory action and a regulatory expropriation requiring compensation will depend on the extent, severity and duration of the deprivation. As noted earlier, the government's intention to expropriate is not relevant. In this way, despite IIAs, a state may still be required to compensate an investor for fulfilling its human rights, labour or environmental obligations. Such highly controversial issues will be revisited in greater detail in Chapter 9.

Second, the measure comprising the expropriation must not be arbitrary and discriminatory within the generally accepted meaning of those terms. The spirit of the National Treatment, and possibly also MFN, are echoed here. This means that the taking must not target property that belongs to a foreign investor or belongs to an investor from a particular

---

[26] ICSID Case No. ARB(AF)/00/2 (29 May 2003).
[27] *Azurix* v. *Argentina*, ICSID Case No. ARB/01/12 (14 July 2006).   [28] At [432].

country. Put more practically, there must be some reason for the taking of that particular property that is not related to the nationality of its owner. For example, in the *ADC* case noted above, the tribunal ascertained that the state had acted in a discriminatory fashion because it expropriated the only foreign company, leaving the equivalent domestic firm untouched.[29] When considering this aspect of the lawfulness test, in addition to the non-discrimination standards of international investment law discussed in Chapter 3, one must be cognizant of the general principle of non-discrimination within international law. This principle suggests that individuals should not be treated differently on the basis of their race or ethnicity. Expropriations based on race have tended to be viewed as unlawful (as in the case of Nazi expropriations of Jewish property) but there may be exceptions to this principle in situations where there is an arguable need to redistribute assets to a traditionally disadvantaged group. There have been instances where such forms of discriminatory expropriation (taking the property belonging to one group to give it to another) have been viewed as lawful acts of governments seeking to adapt to a post-colonial society.[30] Such expropriations would most likely also satisfy the requirement of public purpose.

Third, there is often a requirement in IIAs that the taking must follow the principles of due process, meaning the way in which the expropriation was carried out, apart from its substantive effect on the value of the asset. Due process is a minimum standard in customary international law and is also contemplated by the FET standard discussed in Chapter 5. It will likely involve observing practices such as reasonable notice before the expropriation takes place, an explanation of the purpose as well as a chance to object. The need for due process is perhaps somewhat less well established in customary international law than that of public purpose and non-discrimination as it tends to be a species of national legal systems, arguably falling under the category of general principles of law. It is unclear whether due process is an obligation of conduct or of result. If the former, then any defect, such as failure to provide notice, could amount to a breach of due process. If it is the latter then due process will be satisfied as long as there are local remedies which are available

---

[29] At [441]–[443].
[30] As in *Campbell* v. *The Republic of Zimbabwe*, Tribunal Windhoek, Namibia, SADC (T) Case No. 2/2007 (28 Nov 2008).

to correct problems in due process. If local courts are available to review unfair treatment by governments of investors, then due process should be satisfied.[31]

Finally and perhaps most importantly, as noted above the taking must be accompanied by some form of monetary compensation. As noted in Chapter 1, the notion that compensation must be paid in the event that a state asserts its ownership rights over its natural resources (under the PSNR doctrine) carried with it the obligation to compensate the individual from whom the assets were taken. Investors must receive the monetary value of the assets which they have lost, or an amount reflecting the extent to which the assets they still retain title to have declined in value as a consequence of the host state's actions. As will be illustrated in the next chapter, the standard method used to measure compensation is that it must be 'prompt, adequate and effective'. Of course many developing states are unable to provide compensation in the event of an expropriation because they do not always have the financial resources necessary to compensate investors. This may be the case in particular for countries experiencing severe financial crisis considering their intense need for legislative development of their economic policy, such as Argentina, which has faced a number of expropriation claims by foreign investors.

The four requirements must be fulfilled cumulatively, meaning that even if full compensation is paid, if the taking was discriminatory or it failed to follow due process, or if it lacked a public purpose, it will be deemed illegal.

6.3.2 Unlawful Expropriation

As noted above, confiscation is the most offensive form of unlawful expropriation. It contemplates situations where property is taken without a public purpose (meaning that it serves only the personal interest of the governing authority) and for which no compensation is paid. Only one component of the above four-stage test need not be fulfilled in order for the expropriation to be considered unlawful. The practical distinction between a lawful and an unlawful expropriation is in most instances meaningless because the same standard of compensation is generally

---

[31] A. Newcombe and L. Paradell, *The Law and Practice of Investment Treaties: Standards of Treatment* (Kluwer, 2009), at 375–6.

applicable to both kinds of takings. The often subtle differences in compensation for legal and illegal takings will be considered further in the next chapter. For now it is enough to mention that an unlawful expropriation (meaning one that does not observe all four of the criteria specified above) should be viewed as a treaty violation, in other words a breach of international law. Under customary international law, breaches of international law trigger a state's duty to engage in reparation for their wrongdoing. Such reparation, as will be examined further later on, is better described as damages rather than compensation because it connotes a misdeed, which is precisely what is envisioned by the failure to uphold the four conditions specified in most IIAs.

6.4 Legitimate Takings

Whether or not various types of interference with an investor's business amount to expropriation deserving compensation is clearly controversial, as states have the right to regulate themselves for the best interest of their citizens. Indeed this is a key component of sovereignty. There is therefore an important distinction to be made in international investment law (as in national law) between non-compensable regulatory governmental activity and measures amounting to indirect compensable expropriation. The category of legitimate takings (no compensation payable) must therefore be contrasted with that of lawful expropriation (compensation but not damages payable) above. To be clear, a 'legitimate taking' does not mean one in which all four conditions of lawful expropriation are fulfilled, although typically each of them will be. It encompasses situations where the taking of property was so important that to label it an expropriation would be to mischaracterize the state's behaviour.

There remains a vibrant debate in international law regarding the existence of the requirement to pay compensation for any kind of taking, regardless of whether there is a public interest component to the measure.[32] On one hand, the existence of a sufficiently strong public purpose may be regarded as a factor which removes the state's measure from the scope of indirect expropriation. On the other, public interest, even of the most important kind, does not preclude the state from paying

---

[32] Escarcena, *Indirect Expropriation*, at 198–9.

compensation to disaffected investors, and to hold otherwise would constitute an evisceration of international law.

As indicated above, a public purpose justification is one of the criteria for a taking to be deemed a lawful expropriation. But there may be circumstances where the public purpose behind a measure is so important that the taking does not constitute an expropriation at all. In such situations, where the public interest is of grave concern, no compensation may be payable at all. Part of the rationale for this view is that the adoption of an understanding of indirect expropriation and its consequences that is too broad, ascribing too much liability to states, may result in a situation where all state measures that harm an investor can be considered indirect expropriations necessitating expensive compensation claims, regardless of the reasons that underlie any such measure. This could result in the so-called 'chilling effect' in which governments are afraid to enact laws for fear that they will be categorized as expropriation by an international tribunal and required to make payments which they cannot afford.

It is at least arguable that under customary international law states have a right to regulate without engaging any duty to compensate in order to protect or promote the public interest. The uncertainty of this right has led to a number of countries asserting a 'right to regulate' in the text of their IIAs, an issue which will be explored further in Chapter 9. On the understanding that a state's right to regulate in the best interests of its people is at least a plausible component of customary international law, a foreign investment may be adversely affected by wholly legitimate state measures. Provided that such measures are non-discriminatory, meaning not targeted directly at the foreign investment, and they are not direct, meaning that they do not affect the investor's legal title to the investment, the state may be able to succeed in arguing that its regulation has been passed as part of its legitimate aims to serve the public welfare. It follows that the state may not be liable to compensate investors for any harm that may be caused unintentionally in fulfilling this duty.

The resolution to the issue of whether or not harmful regulatory actions can be taken by states without engaging the obligation to pay compensation (in other words, whether or not there can be legitimate takings) rests on the nature of the public interest that has allegedly been pursued. At the risk of encroaching on topics which will be explored in greater detail later in this book, the concept of public purpose is often aligned with the concept of 'police powers'. This theory captures situations in which the government acts as an agent for the protection society's interests and in so doing adopts measures that can harm an investor. Such actions may be regarded as indirect takings despite the evident reasons behind such measures in terms of their maintaining public order for the overall benefit of citizens. In such situations, the investor will claim that the investment has been expropriated indirectly while the host state will argue that the measure, which has adversely affected the value of the asset, has been passed out of a desire to serve public interest, and as a consequence the host state is not liable to compensate investors for any harm suffered. In what is an often highly sensitive analysis, tribunals will be called upon to ascertain if the government has acted within its accepted police powers when adopting its regulatory policy that has amounted to the taking of an investor's property. This will involve an inquiry into the legitimacy of the government's actions rather than its intent to expropriate.

Given that the boundary between indirect expropriation and legitimate general regulation pursued in the public interest is highly controversial, some IIAs have opted to establish limits to guarantee against regulatory takings. This often takes the form of a definition of indirect expropriation, as in the US Model BIT of 2004:

The Parties confirm their shared understanding that:

(a) The determination of whether an action or series of actions by a Party, in a specific fact situation, constitutes an indirect expropriation, requires a case-by-case, fact-based inquiry that considers, among other factors:
   (i) the economic impact of the government action, although the fact that an action or series of actions by a Party has an adverse effect on the economic value of an investment, standing alone, does not establish that an indirect expropriation has occurred;
   (ii) the extent to which the government action interferes with distinct, reasonable investment-backed expectations; and
   (iii) the character of the government action.[33]

The US Model BIT proceeds to state:

Except in rare circumstances, non-discriminatory regulatory actions by a Party that are designed and applied to protect legitimate public welfare objectives, such as public health, safety, and the environment, do not constitute indirect expropriations.[34]

---

[33] Annex B, Expropriation.   [34] Annex B, Expropriation, b).

These factors embrace US regulatory takings doctrine and its wide police powers exception. These are grounded in a number of domestic decisions, including those established by the US Supreme Court.[35] The Canadian Model BIT follows the same approach as does the investment chapter of the proposed TTIP. A similar carve-out for regulatory actions appears in the China–New Zealand FTA of 2008:

> Except in rare circumstances...such measures taken in the exercise of a state's regulatory powers as may be reasonably justified in the protection of the public welfare, including public health, safety and the environment, shall not constitute an indirect expropriation.[36]

Again, this provision appears to contemplate the notion of police powers, guiding tribunals to avoid a finding of expropriation in serious situations where the state has been compelled to act in a manner adverse to the investor for the best interests of its citizens. Generally speaking such provisions remain unusual in IIAs, and as such there remains a general principle of compensation for all forms of regulatory taking under international investment law.

Loss of property or the diminution of its economic value should not be seen as an expropriation where it results from bona fide general taxation or any other action that is commonly accepted as within the police power, provided such action is not discriminatory or designed to result in the effective abandonment of the property. The existence of generally recognized considerations of public health, safety, morals or welfare will normally lead to a conclusion that there has been no taking. Non-discriminatory measures related to competition law, consumer protection, environmental protection and land planning are often viewed as non-compensable takings since they are essential to the functioning of the state.[37]

It is very difficult to establish a clear demarcation between commonly accepted police powers or excessive regulation that unduly infringes on an investor's property rights without sufficient public interest. Furthermore, in some situations the interest of the host state may conflict with the interest of the foreign investor because of the host state's fulfilment of international legal commitments. For example, the host state may be

---

[35] *Penn Central Transportation Co.* v. *New York City*, 438 US 104 (1978) (USSC).

[36] Annex 13, Expropriation 5.

[37] G. Christie, 'What Constitutes a Taking of Property under International Law?' 38 *The British Year Book of International Law* 338 (1962).

compelled to regulate the cross-border transportation of hazardous waste, impose stricter recycling standards or cut back on chemical pollution. Given the importance of their international obligations, host states pursuing measures to achieve these aims cannot be pursued for compensation on the basis of expropriation.[38]

One of the major spheres of public policy in which regulations may be enacted that can potentially infringe on the business activities of foreign investors are those governing environmental protection. Placing undue environmental burdens on foreign investors would most evidently constitute expropriation, whereas those regulations that have a legitimate and proportionate environmental goal might be somewhat harder to challenge. Nevertheless, the tribunal in *Santa Elena* v. *Costa Rica* established that measures taken for the purposes of environmental protection do not escape categorization as indirect expropriation, regardless of their worth to society:

> Expropriatory environmental measures – no matter how laudable and beneficial to society as a whole – are in this respect, similar to any other expropriatory measures that a state may take in order to implement its policies: where property is expropriated, even for environmental purposes, whether domestic or international, the state's obligation to pay compensation remains.[39]

Whether or not states may be able to exclude environmental or other public interest type measures, such as those relating to public health, from the scope of the expropriation provision in IIAs through carve-outs will be considered in more detail later in this book.

Tribunals have acknowledged the 'police powers' of host states entitling them to take property without it amounting to an expropriation. The tribunal in the *Methanex Corp* v. *United States* dispute ruled:

> [N]on-discriminatory regulation for a public purpose, which is enacted in accordance with due process and, which affects, inter alia, a foreign investor or investment is not deemed expropriatory and compensable unless specific commitments had been given by the regulating government to the then putative foreign investor.[40]

---

[38] C. Henkels, 'Indirect Expropriation and the Right to Regulate' 15:1 *Journal of International Economic Law* 223 (2012).

[39] ICSID Case No. ARB/96/1 (17 Feb 2000) at [72].

[40] *Methanex Corp* v. *United States*, Final Award, UNCITRAL (3 Aug 2005), at [1456].

Expressly acknowledging that some kinds of takings are legitimate and therefore do not manifest liability on the part of the government, the tribunal in the *Saluka* dispute ruled:

> It is now established in international law that States are not liable to pay compensation to a foreign investor when, in the normal exercise of their regulatory powers, they adopt in a non-discriminatory manner bona fide regulations that are aimed at the general welfare.[41]

The tribunal went on to concede that the distinction between compensable and non-compensable expropriations is difficult to establish, stating that international law has yet to draw:

> a bright and easily distinguishable line between non-compensable regu-lations on the one hand and, on the other, measures that have the effect of depriving foreign investors of their investments and are thus unlawful and compensable in international law.[42]

Of course, this does not capture the reality that compensation is not merely the remedy for the breach of an international obligation (the expropria-tion provision of an IIA), it is also normally the requirement of a lawful taking. There therefore appears to be two categories of public interest: the normal one needed to make an expropriation lawful, and the very seri-ous one required to make an expropriation legitimate (non-compensable). Paradoxically, countries at the earliest stages of economic development or suffering severe financial crises are often those that require the most intensive regulation and the most frequent adjustments to economic pol-icy, which may unfortunately result in the loss of value to an investor's assets.

The acceptance of the right to expropriate IP in emergency situations under the compulsory licensing regime of the WTO's TRIPS demonstrates the willingness of most countries to allow some kinds of takings in times of crisis, notably pharmaceutical patents for generic reproduction to address epidemics.[43] Many IIAs specify that the expropriation of IP assets for the purposes of conforming to this provision of TRIPS shall not constitute expropriations.[44] The compulsory licensing provision of TRIPS does spec-ify that the right holder shall be paid 'adequate remuneration' for the IP which is seized.[45] This obligation to pay compensation suggests that

[41] At [255].   [42] At [263].   [43] Art [31].
[44] E.g. Israel Model BIT Art 5.   [45] Art 31 (h).

compulsory licensing is not truly a lawful taking precluding payment of compensation, but rather a legal expropriation.

Finally, it should be noted that the negotiated text of the TPP specifies that the removal of investment incentives or subsidies granted to investors will not constitute indirect expropriation unless a specific commitment to maintain these advantages was made by the state to the investor.[46] This provision was presumably included to deal with some of the tensions that have arisen in recent investment disputes regarding the potential action-ability of the removal of incentive packages granted to foreign investors by host states.[47] Thus no compensation will be payable for such actions.

6.5 Expropriation – Intangible Assets

Since IIAs mention direct and indirect expropriation but tend not to give definitions of them, this has left the development of the concepts to the practice of international arbitration tribunals. These tribunals tend to refer to each other's decisions, as well as decisions of the Iran–US Claims Tribunal and domestic courts, especially that of the European Court of Justice and the US Supreme Court (the latter especially in NAFTA arbitrations). International human rights tribunals have also featured in the awards of investment tribunals dealing with the subject of the deprivation of property.

Arbitration tribunals faced with a claim of expropriation must assess whether the measure imposed by the host state may be construed an indirect expropriation if it is not an outright expropriation, which again would be an unusual event today. They must then enquire whether the measure has been taken lawfully.[48] The case law on both of these issues is remarkable for its inconsistency.[49]

Clearly questions of indirect expropriation are going to be the most problematic because they are not clearly identified as expropriations. Tribunals will be required to investigate the factual consequences of any

---

[46] Art 9.7(6).

[47] See further D. Collins, *Performance Requirements and Investment Incentives under International Economic Law* (Edward Elgar, 2015).

[48] *Fireman's Fund Insurance Company* v. *Mexico*, ICSID Case No. ARB(AF)/02/1 (17 July 2006).

[49] See J. Salacuse, *The Law of Investment Treaties* (Oxford University Press, 2010), at 307–18.

regulations imposed on the foreign investor. As discussed above, tribunals have increasingly accepted that indirect expropriation must be analysed based on its effect rather than on superficial formalities, such as whether or not the state expressly proclaims its intent to expropriate through means such as legislation.[50] A measure imposed by a government may or may not constitute an expropriation because the asset which was adversely affected may not constitute an investment, depending of course on how investment is defined in the treaty, as outlined in Chapter 3. Clearly in order for a claim of expropriation to be valid there must be an investment in the first place. In other words, there must be an IIA-recognized asset for the guarantee against expropriation to be engaged. Following approaches of the ICJ, the European Court of Human Rights and the Iran–US Claims Tribunal, most tribunals have found expropriations to have occurred with respect to both tangible and intangible assets.[51]

In *CME* v. *Czech Republic*,[52] the undermining of contractual arrangements has been construed as a form of indirect expropriation. Similarly, the tribunal in *Azinan* v. *Mexico*[53] held that termination of contracts for irrelevant reasons may be seen as an indirect expropriation. The Iran–US Claims Tribunal held quite expansively in *Amoco* v. *Iran* that the guarantee against expropriation without compensation can cover any right that can be the subject of a commercial transaction.[54] Similarly, the tribunal in *Tokios Tokeles* confirmed that all forms of business operation that are associated with the physical property of the investors are covered by the term 'investment', including contractual rights.[55]

Divergent opinions regarding the concept of property have led to varied interpretations regarding whether or not an asset was capable of being expropriated by the state. Implementing a rather narrow view of the rights attached to property, the tribunal in *Lauder* v. *Czech Republic*[56] held that no taking had taken place, whereas the tribunal in *CME* v. *Czech*

---

[50] *Revere Copper* v. *Overseas Private Inv. Corp. (OPIC)*, Award of Aug 24 1978, (1980) 56 ILR 258, 271–2.

[51] Dolzer and Schreuer, *Principles*, at 126–9.

[52] UNCITRAL, Partial Award (13 Sept 2001).

[53] ICSID Case No. ARB(AF)/97/2 (1 Nov 1999).

[54] *Amoco International Finance Corp* v. *Iran*, Iran–US Claims Tribunal, Award (14 July 1987) at [108].

[55] *Tokios Tokeles* v. *Ukraine*, ICSID Case No. ARB/02/18, Decision on Jurisdiction (29 April 2004), paras [92]–[93].

[56] UNCITRAL, Final Award (3 Sept 2001).

Republic,[57] applying a broad understanding of investment to include the income-producing potential of property rights, held that an expropriation had occurred. Equating the destruction of the commercial value of the property to its deprivation, *CME*'s approach is the one that appears to have garnered the most favour by subsequent tribunals. The refusal to renew or the withdrawal of a licence was held to constitute indirect expropriation in *Tecmed S.A.* v. *Mexico*.[58] Similarly, in *Eureko* v. *Poland* the tribunal ruled that the right to acquire further shares constituted assets which would be capable of expropriation.[59] It would seem, then, that even contingent rights to property, i.e. rights which have not yet formally crystallized, are capable of being protected through guarantees against expropriation.

In this regard, it is worth mentioning the dispute *Emmis International Holding* v. *Hungary*[60] which was brought under the UK–Netherlands BIT in relation to an alleged expropriation of investment that included an FM radio broadcasting licence. The tribunal declined jurisdiction over the expropriation-based claim because the interference by the government with a tendering right (the right to bid on the licence) did not affect any proprietary rights capable of engaging the compensation for expropriation provision in the BIT. This was because tendering rights could not be bought or sold, nor did they have monetary value. They were merely non-exclusive contractual rights that had been acquired for consideration, and therefore the extinguishing of them did not constitute expropriation.

Returning to the focus on effects rather than intentions noted earlier, generally speaking every measure taken by a government which has the effect of a deprivation of ownership can be framed as a claim for indirect expropriation, regardless of the nature of the assets in question. Indirect takings of intangibles tend to be framed by tribunals through rather strict language: 'a severe deprivation' of rights with regards to an investment, or an 'almost complete deprivation of value'.[61] This will not always be an easy test to apply. As noted by the tribunal in *Biwater Gauff*, which concerned the termination of a lease in the water and sewage industry:

[57] UNCITRAL, Partial Award (13 Sept 2001).
[58] ICSID Case No. ARB(AF)/00/2, Award (29 May 2003).
[59] *Eureko* v. *Poland*, ad hoc, Partial Award (19 Aug 2005).
[60] ICSID Case No. ARB/12/2 (16 April 2014).
[61] *LG&E* v. *Argentina*, UNCITRAL (3 Oct 2006) at [200].

> A substantial interference with rights may well occur without actually causing any economic damage which can be quantified in terms of compensation... the absence of economic loss or damage is primarily a matter of causation and quantum – rather than a necessary ingredient in the cause of action of expropriation itself.[62]

Some tribunals tend to focus on the value of the investment, or more specifically, the extent to which the measure decreased the value of the investment.[63] As suggested above, a loss of control over the investment may be one effect of an expropriation, although this will tend not to be determinative where a substantial decrease of value has occurred.

When evaluating expropriation of assets such as contractual rights, some tribunals have been concerned with the investor's legitimate expectations of profit when it embarked on the investment. Whether or not an expectation may be perceived as legitimate rests on the link between the expectation and any express communications or assurances made by the host state to the investor. This is why many arbitration decisions spend quite a bit of time reviewing precisely what was said by governmental officials. This is often a question of admissibility of evidence. Tribunals have emphasized that an investor's legitimate expectations will be rooted in the host state's conduct and the corresponding reliance on that conduct by the investor,[64] a concept not dissimilar from that of the common law's doctrine of estoppel. An emphasis on the investor's legitimate expectations was seen, for example, in the *Methanex* v. *USA* decision under NAFTA. The tribunal there noted that lawful expropriations serving a public interest should not engage an obligation to pay compensation unless specific commitments have been made by the government regarding the investment.[65] In some circumstances lack of transparency in governmental procedures or the unreasonable application of laws, such as might be construed as breaches of due process or of the FET standard, could amount to an expropriation based on the denial of legitimate expectations. For example, in *RosInvest* v. *Russia*, the tribunal listed 'deprivation of legitimate investment-backed expectations' as one of the indicia of substantive or total deprivation, finding that there had been a pattern of

---

[62] *Biwater Gauff* v. *Tanzania*, ICSID Case No. ARB/05/22 (22 July 2008) at [464]–[465].
[63] E.g. *Tokios Tokeles* v. *Ukraine*.
[64] *Thunderbird* v. *Mexico*, UNCITRAL Award (26 Jan 2006) at 147.
[65] UNCITRAL (NAFTA) Final Award, Part IV Chapter D at 7–9 (3 Aug 2005).

unreasonable treatment against that particular investor at the hands of the government.[66] Clearly not every change in the legal system of the host state which has an adverse impact on the foreign investor's operations will constitute a violation of legitimate expectations – there will always be legitimate realignments in policy that have unfortunate consequences, indeed sensible investors should have strategies in place to cope with these eventualities. It is the uncertainty that is engendered by a country's regulatory environment that often makes it precisely the target of the most lucrative opportunities. With the greatest risk comes the greatest reward.

6.6 Conclusion

The international law of expropriation in many ways captures the essence of the central conflict within international investment law – namely the intersection of the rights of private entities versus those of states allegedly acting in the public interest. Guarantees against the taking of foreign investors' property without compensation are therefore among the most important and controversial features of IIAs. This is particularly true when they are framed as indirect takings, as they are in most modern IIAs, and as such cover a wide range of regulatory interferences that might not necessarily look like traditional expropriations. Without assurances that they will be adequately compensated in the event that their assets are taken (in one way or another) by the host state, foreign investors would be reluctant to invest abroad, especially in places that are politically unstable or have a history of excessive government intrusion into business. The potential for the guarantee against expropriation without compensation to encroach too deeply into a host state's capacity to regulate its economy has led to the creation of 'carve-outs' in many IIAs, preserving the right to regulate in certain vital sectors of public interest, such as health or the environment. These issues will be returned to later.

As with many aspects of international investment law, the jurisprudence on guarantees against expropriation is clouded, in no small part because of the complexity and expansiveness of the concept of indirect expropriation which can mean many things, including wresting control of

---

[66] Stockholm Chamber of Commerce (22 Dec 2010).

business from investors as well as decreases in value of all kinds of assets, both tangible and otherwise. Perhaps another major source of confusion in this sphere of investment law is the distinction between lawful expropriation and unlawful expropriation which hinges on, among other criteria, the existence of a public purpose. Satisfying this requirement, along with other ones, is normally taken to mean that the expropriation is lawful, but this does not preclude the host state from paying compensation. Indeed compensation must still be paid when an investment does not satisfy the criterion of lawfulness. Yet certain kinds of extreme public interest-based regulations, sometimes called 'police powers', are deemed to be so important that they can immunize the otherwise expropriatory activity from being so characterized. In such situations, no compensation is payable at all. These debates, while themselves fraught with uncertainty and highly discretionary interventions by tribunals, must be set alongside what is perhaps an even more fundamental conundrum, at least for practical purposes: how is compensation either for lawful or unlawful expropriation to be set? This requires an investigation into very basic concepts such as the meaning and purpose of compensation as well as the role of markets in ascribing value. These issues are the focus of the next chapter.

Compensation 7

7.1 Introduction

If the purpose of international investment law is to grant investors some degree of legal security in their commercial activities in foreign states, the ability to be compensated when their legal entitlements are undermined is surely among the most important facets of that security. The purpose of compensation is, in most systems of law, to make the injured party whole. To put this more bluntly, courts must facilitate the transferring to victims of an amount of money that is equivalent to the harm that has been suffered. If the compensation is properly calibrated the investor should be indifferent to whether they receive money or whether the injury had never occurred at all. The precise measure of the compensation is highly controversial, occupying a good portion of discussion in many arbitration decisions and the subject of a number of academic treatises.[1]

The nature and amount of compensation for aggrieved investors will be examined in this chapter, noting some of the persistent controversies in relation to different understandings of what is meant by full compensation: the Hull Formula favoured by developed states and the Calvo Doctrine which has traditionally found support in some developing states, particularly in Latin America where it originated. Compensation for lawful measures (such as expropriation that is in the public interest) will be contrasted with illegal measures, entitling investors to damages. These issues will be linked to technical problems in relation to asset valuation, as well as emerging debates concerning the capacity of tribunals to award moral damages as well as non-pecuniary remedies.

As observed in the previous chapter, it is widely accepted in international law that lawful expropriation by a host state must be accompanied by compensation to the disaffected owner. The centrality of this principle

---

[1] E.g. B. Sabahi, *Compensation and Restitution in Investor-State Arbitration: Principles and Practice* (Oxford University Press, 2011).

has unfortunately clouded our understanding of compensation in international investment law because host states incur many more obligations in IIAs than simply those concerning expropriation, violations of which also engage obligations to make reparations to injured investors. Moreover, if there is a requirement to pay compensation for a lawful expropriation, then what is a state's obligation with respect to an unlawful one? Surely it must be something more otherwise there is an uncomfortable moral equivalence[2] – but then going beyond mere compensation implies a punishment, which is not normally seen as a feature of international law. Even with a firm notion of the purpose of compensation as a means of restoring the investor to their position before they were injured, there remains a pressing problem of quantifying the value of the investment so that an appropriate amount of money can be set. Differing notions of compensation are linked to ideas about what constitutes an investor's assets in addition to and perhaps more profoundly, what it means to own something. Views on these matters are far from universally held. Ownership of private property is more entrenched in the West than in many Eastern systems of social organization, raising a spectre of further debates on these issues throughout the twenty-first century.

The amount of compensation awarded by investment tribunals tends to be a source of much controversy because such sums are often contrasted with those available through domestic courts for breach of contract, for example. Investment arbitration is often depicted as an exercise that is heavily weighted in favour of investors, especially well-financed ones, who are able to use it to secure vast transfers of wealth from governments.[3] The three Yukos petroleum expropriation cases brought against Russia[4] have played a significant role in creating an arguably distorted impression that investor–state arbitration is a massive windfall opportunity for multinationals (and their lawyers). In these disputes, which it must be acknowledged represent genuine outliers in terms of the magnitude of compensation, the tribunals awarded a combined US $50 billion to the investors, by far the highest sum ever awarded by an investment tribunal.

---

[2] See further, R. Higgins, *The Path to Law* (Oxford University Press, 1994), Chapter 9.

[3] See e.g. G. Van Harten and P. Malysheuski, 'Who Has Benefited Financially from Investment Treaty Arbitration? An Evaluation of the Size and Wealth of Claimants' *Osgoode Hall Law School Legal Studies Research Paper Series*, Research Paper No. 14, Vol 12:3 (2016).

[4] *Hulley* v. *Russia*, UNCITRAL, PCA Case No. AA 226 (4 Sept 2014); *Veteran Petroleum* v. *Russia*, PCA Case No. AA 228 (18 July 2014), *Yukos* v. *Russia*, PCA Case No. AA 227 (18 July 2014).

To be sure, awards in investment arbitration cases tend to be large, with tribunals regularly granting more than US $10 million in compensation for breaches of IIAs and investment contracts. Whether or not these levels of compensation should be viewed as excessive is in some respects a moral debate linked to issues of sovereignty which have been discussed earlier in this book, as well as the importance of public interest justifications, which will be examined in Chapter 9. More pragmatically and certainly as importantly, the appropriateness of compensation for breaches of international investment law raises highly technical issues relating to valuation of assets, timing and the denomination of currencies.

Before an investment tribunal turns to the analysis of how to assess the level of compensation for a breach of international investment law, it must obviously first verify that there has been some legal obligation that has been violated, such as those discussed in previous chapters. Second, the tribunal must establish that there is a link between the state's conduct and the investor's injury. This can be a difficult exercise, particularly in cases of non-expropriation violations where the effects of the state's measures on the value of assets are perhaps not as readily discernible. In other words, in order for compensation to be payable there must be an element of causation between the state's action and the harm suffered by the investor. The Articles on State Responsibility specify that states are obliged to make reparation for injuries which are *caused* by their wrongful acts, but does not elaborate on how this should be established.[5] Generally speaking there is very little in the way of guidance on how to establish causation in investment arbitration jurisprudence. The tribunal in *Biwater Gauff* v. *Tanzania* explained that the requirement of causation requires a sufficient link between the wrongful act and the damage in question, and a threshold beyond which damage is considered too indirect or remote.[6] These will normally raise questions of fact requiring a review of precisely what took place and what communications were made between the parties. This is one of the reasons that investment arbitration decisions resemble first instance trials – they are often heavily focused on factual context with often only brief legal analysis.

While cause and effect is unquestionably a critical aspect of the law of compensation in international investment law, by far the most pressing concerns relate to the assessment of compensation itself. This issue will be the focus of this chapter.

---

[5] Art 31(2).   [6] ICSID Case No. ARB/05/22 (22 Nov 2006) at [784].

7.2 Measure of Compensation

7.2.1 Prompt, Adequate and Effective

While it is now virtually standard in IIAs, 'prompt, adequate and effective' compensation (known as the Hull Formula after the US Secretary of State Cordell Hull who invented it) tends to be associated with developed countries seeking to empower their foreign investors by maximizing the extent of required compensation for expropriation and other interferences by foreign states. Rather than maximizing compensation, the purpose of the Hull Formula is one of consistency and clarity.

In many IIAs the language of 'prompt, adequate and effective' is linked expressly to expropriation, appearing under that heading, an embodiment of the law of compensation's focus on this particular breach of international law. Consequently it is not clear that it applies to other varieties of types of treaty breach, such as FET or FPS.[7] In other treaties, the phrase appears in a standalone provision on compensation, conveying its application to all varieties of treaty breach. This can be seen in the investment chapter of the Australia–Korea FTA:

> [the host state] shall provide the investor with restitution, compensation, or both as appropriate, for such loss. In the event of providing both restitution and compensation, their combined value shall not exceed the loss suffered. Any compensation shall be prompt, adequate, and effective.[8]

In this Agreement, the Hull Formula of prompt, adequate and effective appears again in the guarantee against expropriation provision, with elaboration as to its meaning:

(a) be paid without delay;
(b) be equivalent to the fair market value of the expropriated investment immediately before the expropriation took place (hereinafter referred to as the 'date of expropriation');
(c) not reflect any change in value occurring because the intended expropriation had become known earlier; and
(d) be fully realisable and freely transferable.[9]

---

[7] As in the Morocco–Serbia BIT Art 4.1 (2013).   [8] Art 11.6(2) (8 April 2014).
[9] Art 11.7(1)(c).

Putting aside for the moment that the use of this phrase in two different places in this treaty (as in many IIAs) appears to suggest that compensation for lawful expropriation will troublingly be the same for breaches of other parts of the treaty (presumably including unlawful expropriation), this provision provides some insight into precisely what prompt, adequate and effective means.

Taking each of the Hull Formula's three constituent elements in turn, 'prompt' means as soon as possible after the harmful action has occurred, and delays will cause an addition of accrued interest. This is important because inevitably there will be some delay between the moment at which the investor's interests in the host state are harmed and the moment at which its legal entitlement to compensation crystallizes. This is one reason why the Articles on State Responsibility, for example, specify that interest should be paid on any money that is awarded as a consequence of a state's wrongful act.[10] Most IIAs also provide that interest should be paid on compensation that is awarded for lawful expropriation. For example, the ECT states: 'Compensation shall also include interest at a commercial rate established on a market basis from the date of Expropriation until the date of payment.'[11] Interest will also be applicable to compensation awarded for other treaty breaches. Investment tribunals tend to spend time considering the rate of interest payable so clear provision with respect to this rate in the text of the IIA is obviously helpful.

'Adequate' is the most important and controversial element of the Hull Formula because it speaks of the amount of compensation rather than the time or format in which it is received. Adequacy is normally defined by reference to the market, which tends to be viewed by most people, at least in developed countries, as the only truly legitimate means of ascribing any monetary value to an asset. Something is worth what someone is willing to pay for it and no more or less. It is understood to mean full market value of the affected investor's assets at the time the damaging treaty violation(s) occurred, such as the moment just before the decree expropriating the assets was issued – obviously an expropriation decree will itself harm an asset's worth. Clearly markets change, sometimes rapidly, so in that sense the adequacy of remuneration is a highly variable concept. With respect to expropriation at least, the timing of when precisely the investment has moved from the investor's ownership or control, or

[10] Art 38.   [11] Art 13.1.

the point at which its value has been effectively diminished, is of major importance. In *Santa Elena* v. *Costa Rica*, the tribunal stated: 'the expropriated property is to be evaluated as of the date on which the governmental "interference" has deprived the owner of his rights or has made those rights practically useless.'[12] The calculation of compensation accordingly becomes more complicated in the case of creeping expropriations or other types of treaty breach that take place incrementally. Of course there are problems associated with market valuations, such as would exist in cases of a monopoly or assets which have unique value. To be clear, 'adequate' does not mean morally adequate in the sense that the investor receives compensation commensurate with what it deserves based on the quality of its goods or services, or their value to society. These are issues which are more accurately captured by the Calvo Doctrine, which will be discussed below. This is precisely one of the reasons that the Hull Formula has been viewed with circumspection by a number of developing or transitional economies with whom market-orientated valuations are less familiar or politically acceptable.

Finally, 'effective' expresses the condition that money paid to compensate the investor for the harms it has suffered must be in a recognized, usable currency that is transferable to the investor's own currency. This condition recognizes that it is not much good to an investor to receive compensation in the form of a currency that cannot be exchanged into one that is functionally valuable in terms of its capacity to be used in commercial transactions. This could occur for example if the expropriating state uses its own currency which may be undergoing a period of gross devaluation and which is consequently not recognized by banks around the world. Providing clarity with respect to this aspect of the Hull Formula, the investment chapter of the New Zealand–Taiwan Economic Cooperation Agreement of 2013 elaborates that compensation paid in the event of expropriation must be 'fully realisable and freely transferable'.[13] This phrase is defined in the following way:

> freely usable currency means 'freely usable currency' as determined by the International Monetary Fund under its Articles of Agreement and amendments thereto, or any currency that is used to make international payments and is widely traded in the international principal exchange markets.[14]

---

[12] ICSID Case No. ARB/96/1 (17 Feb 2000) at [78].   [13] Art 13(2)(d) (10 July 2013).
[14] Art 2 definitions.

This definition would cover the world's chief currencies, such as the US dollar, the euro, the British pound and now likely even the Chinese renminbi. In practice most investment arbitration awards tend to be denominated in US dollars, or in some cases euros.

7.2.2 The Calvo Doctrine

The standard of prompt, adequate and effective compensation is the methodology adopted by the developed world and accords investors generous protection against breaches of IIAs and in particular against expropriation. This view of appropriate compensation must be contrasted with one of the dominant ideologies from the developing world as well as countries that do not have as strong a tradition of protecting private property against state interference. Gauging the standard of compensation is another sphere of international investment law in which the tensions between the rights of individuals and the rights of states are played out, much as was described in the previous chapter. With this debate in mind, the Calvo Doctrine of compensation, grounded in the principle of sovereign equality of all states regardless of economic size, emerged as something of an alternative methodology. This measure of compensation was named after the Argentinian jurist Carlos Calvo, whose writings reflected a reluctance to embrace international law in favour of a more nationalistic approach. It should be noted that the Calvo Doctrine can refer to any system of policies towards foreign investment which are grounded in national law rather than by reference to an international standard. For example, it may compel a foreign investor to pursue local remedies before seeking to bring a claim in investor–state arbitration, as will be discussed below.[15] It is an approach that is thought to embody the repudiation of investor–state dispute settlement exhibited by some Latin American countries and is essentially characterized by a general rejection of international law. Under the Calvo method of ascertaining appropriate compensation, the law of the host state decides the measure of compensation for actions such as expropriation.

Put simply, foreigners operating within the state should be treated no differently from residents in terms of receiving compensation for the actions undertaken by governments that impair the value of their assets,

---

[15] As discussed in *CMS Gas Transmission* v. *Argentina*, ICSID Case No. ARB/01/8, Decision on Jurisdiction (17 July 2003).

such as an expropriation. This approach is grounded in the view that there must be equality of treatment between foreigners and nationals; or more specifically, foreign investors should not get better treatment than locals simply because they may originate from an industrialized capital-exporting state. In setting the appropriate level of compensation under the Calvo Doctrine, tribunals must therefore take into account relevant national laws of the expropriating state in addition to all of the other circumstances considered by it to be relevant. International law, including the customary principle of an international minimum standard of treatment for aliens, is effectively sidelined.[16] Perhaps most controversially, this method can also require tribunals to consider the extent of the profits already made by the investor as well as contributions that they have made to the host state economy. In other words, compensation may be diminished if the host state feels that the investor has already made sufficient profits from their activities given the benefits they have brought. It is not difficult to see how notions of 'having made enough money' could be offensive to firms from states with a tradition of free enterprise.

It must be noted that the Calvo approach to compensation does not take the form of specific provisions on compensation in IIAs. There are no known IIAs which specify that compensation will be determined by the national law of the host state. Rather, this method of compensation is imposed through the requirement to exhaust local remedies before using investor–state dispute settlement or when parties exercise the option of using local remedies as an alternative to international arbitration. When allegations of mistreatment by host state governments claims are pursued under host state courts pursuant to these provisions, national legislation governing compensation will be applicable, rather than the internationally minded Hull Formula. Exhaustion of local remedies or fork-in-the-road (choice between domestic and foreign) provisions are common in a number of Latin American IIAs.[17]

Similar to the Calvo approach, some treaties link the level of compensation to that which may be paid to citizens of third countries. In Art 7.1 of the BIT between Australia and the Czech Republic, the following language is used:

---

[16] J. Salacuse, *The Law of Investment Treaties* (Oxford University Press, 2009), at 51.

[17] Argentina–US BIT, 1991. See further W. Shan, 'From North-South Divide to Public Private Partnership: Revival of the Calvo Doctrine and the Changing Landscape in International Investment Law' 27:3 *Northwestern Journal of International Law and Business* 631 (2007).

> When a Contracting Party adopts any measures relating to losses in respect of investments in its territory by citizens or companies of any other country owing to armed conflict, a state of national emergency, civil disturbance or other similar events, the treatment accorded to investors of the other Contracting Party as regards restitution, indemnification, compensation or other settlement shall be no less favourable than that which the first Contracting Party accords to citizens or companies of any third country.[18]

This assurance, which uses MFN language, appears to contemplate breach of the FPS standard and possibly also assertions of the Doctrine of Necessity, which will be explored further in Chapter 10. Other treaties include National Treatment as well as MFN in these provisions.[19] Like Calvo, such clauses contemplate a relative rather than an absolute standard of compensation such as envisioned by the Hull Formula. In that sense they may be seen as somewhat less concrete.

7.3 Illegal Takings and other Treaty Breaches

As noted in the introduction, there are many varieties of obligations which are placed upon host states in international investment law as embodied by IIAs, of which expropriation is but one. Each of these is deserving of compensation. Unlike expropriation, however, compensation for these breaches is not an inherent aspect of the legitimacy of these behaviours – breaching these other obligations is itself illegal. Put simply, these are what might be termed normal treaty breaches or breaches of international law.

The famous *Chorzow Factory* expropriation case of the PCIJ in 1928 (forerunner of the modern ICJ) is often cited as the classic statement on compensation for wrongful acts by states under international law:

> The essential principle contained in the actual notion of an illegal act – a principle which seems to be established by international practice and in particular by the decisions of arbitral tribunals – is that reparation must, as far as possible, wipe out all the consequences of an illegal act and re-establish the situation which would, in all probability, have existed if that act had not been committed. Restitution in kind, or if this is not possible, payment of a sum corresponding to the value which a restitution in kind

---

[18] 30 Sept 1993.   [19] China–Netherlands BIT Art 6 (26 Nov 2001).

> would bear; the award, if need be, of damages for loss sustained which
> would not be covered by restitution in kind or compensation for an act
> contrary to international law.[20]

This statement, including the rather grandiose phrase 'wipe out all the consequences' provides the foundational principles on which many other international courts and tribunals have based their assessment of compensation. This theory is now articulated, somewhat less dramatically, in the Articles on State Responsibility, which are often thought to codify customary international law: 'The responsible State is under an obligation to make full reparation for the injury caused by the internationally wrongful act.'[21] The Articles go on to explain that the state which is responsible for an internationally wrongful act is 'under an obligation to compensate for the damage caused... in so far as damage is not made good by restitution' and crucially: 'compensation shall cover any financially assessable damage including loss of profits.'[22]

It is essential to recognize, however, that the *Chorzow Factory* edict concerned unlawful expropriations, meaning one which did not satisfy the requirements of due process, non-discrimination, public purpose and compensation itself. It was not meant to capture the amount of compensation owing upon a lawful expropriation or whether compensation is specified by reference to the Hull Formula. The consequences of an illegal expropriation, meaning one that did not fulfil the four requirements noted above, has never been definitively resolved. Often the host state has taken property without compensating the investor so it falls to the tribunal to assess the consequences of that illegal action and to remedy it through a tribunal-imposed payment to make the injured investor whole. It is often suggested that when this happens, the measure of compensation for an illegal expropriation is no different from compensation for a lawful one. As alluded to above, this leads to the frustrating and intuitively unsatisfying conclusion that international law does not draw a distinction between lawful and unlawful actions, at least in terms of remedies. Of course there are also other types of IIA violation than expropriation. Breaches of the FET standard, National Treatment and so on also engage the obligation to pay compensation. Indeed one of the largest awards in investment

---

[20] *Factory at Chorzow (Germany v. Poland)*, PCIJ Rep (1928) Series A, No. 13 at 47.
[21] Art 31(1).   [22] Art 36.

arbitration levied against Argentina was based on the successful claim of breach of FET, with no finding of indirect expropriation.[23]

It is far from clear that the *Chorzow Factory* remedy is equivalent to that of the compensation requirement contained within the requirement of lawful expropriation, in other words, the Hull Formula. It may be more appropriate to conclude that the remedy for an illegal expropriation and indeed other types of treaty violation will be determined by the general rules of state responsibility under international law. Compensation for unlawful expropriation and other types of IIA breaches may be better termed as 'damages' in order to clarify the difference between these pecuniary awards and those associated with lawful expropriation.

Monetary awards which are distinct from compensation are acknowledged in some IIAs by use of the phrase 'restitution', which may be intended as an allusion to the *Chorzow Factory* understanding of reparation for wrongdoings (including unlawful expropriation) rather than merely compensation for an asset that was lawfully expropriated. For example, the US Model BIT states as follows:

> if an investor of a Party, in the situations referred to in paragraph 4, suffers a loss in the territory of the other Party resulting from:
>
> (a) requisitioning of its covered investment or part thereof by the latter's forces or authorities; or
>
> (b) destruction of its covered investment or part thereof by the latter's forces or authorities, which was not required by the necessity of the situation,
>
> the latter Party shall provide the investor restitution, compensation, or both, as appropriate, for such loss. Any compensation shall be prompt, adequate, and effective.[24]

By establishing that certain situations will require both restitution *and* compensation, this treaty implies first that there is a difference between these two concepts and more practically, when both are awarded the total should be higher (more money) than when either is awarded individually. Presumably such situations will not include 'normal' compensation payable upon lawful expropriation.

The tribunal in the NAFTA dispute *SD Myers* helped illustrate the difference between compensation for lawful takings and damages (or

---

[23] *Enron* v. *Argentina*, ICSID Case No. ARB/01/3, Award (22 May 2007).   [24] Art 5.4.

reparation) for unlawful ones, noting that the former may not include amounts linked to future profits.[25] In that case, the investor was awarded compensation based on a denial of National Treatment, not an expropriation. Factoring in lost future earnings in rendering the award as this tribunal did seems to be an eminently sensible approach, as including the lost profit stream into an assessment of compensation will in most cases result in a higher overall quantum than simply repaying the value of the investment itself. Surely receiving what the investment would be worth in the market will not cover lost income streams in the future. Under this logic, breaches of international investment law as contained in IIAs will tend to be compensated by the payment to the investor by the host state of some combination of future profits and the value of the investment project which was either damaged or seized. In most cases damages (or restitution) will amount to more money because they are intended to redress behaviour that was fundamentally unlawful in a way that taking property is not. Recall that states are deemed to have the sovereign right to expropriate property belonging to private individuals.

Interestingly and probably not coincidentally, lost profits, sometimes described in international law cases as *lucrum cessans*, also denote the normal standard of compensation for breach of contract in the common law where they are known as the expectation measure. Parties in breach of contract are required to put the injured party in the position it would have been had the contract been fulfilled – which in most cases should lead to increased wealth. In contrast, the value of the investment itself (which is the measure of compensation for a lawful expropriation) is sometimes labelled in international law as *damnum emergens*. This measure of compensation resembles that of the so-called reliance measure of damages in the common law.[26] This is the amount of money that will put the injured party in the position it would have been in, had the contract never been entered into at all. This measure of damages is rarely used in contract law because by nature the process of contracting envisions a profit-making activity. Contracting parties seek to be in better positions following their contracts so awarding them the value of their pre-contractual expenses is usually unhelpful, although it may make sense when future profits were

---

[25] UNCITRAL, Second Partial Award (21 Oct 2002).

[26] D. Collins, 'Reliance Remedies at the International Centre for the Settlement of Investment Disputes' 29 *Northwestern Journal of International Law and Business* (2009) 101–22.

too speculative.[27] This is why the reliance measure tends to be awarded in tort cases, where the aim is to restore injured parties to their pre-injured status, in other words, to make them whole.

A useful way of understanding the differences between remedies for lawful (expropriation satisfying the four criteria) versus unlawful behaviour (expropriation which does not satisfy the four criteria as well by implication of all other kinds of treaty breach) in international investment law was articulated by one legal scholar based on his views of *Chorzow Factory* as well as some of the key oil nationalization cases brought under the Iran–US Claims Tribunal:

> What is important is that for lawful taking only damnum emergens is payable as compensation, i.e. the value of the property, however, established lucrum cessans (lost future profits) and other consequential damage not being taken into account. For an unlawful taking it is damages and not merely compensation that are payable – this includes damnum emergens (value of the property), lucrum cessans (lost profits), and any other consequential damage that may be found and is directly connected with the taking of the property.[28]

This is a satisfyingly elegant if simplistic statement of the law of remedies in international investment law. It also appears to echo the statement of the Articles on State Responsibility noted above, and in that sense it is not without legal merit. Unfortunately it has not always been borne out in the actual disputes which tend to treat the issue of compensation, as with most matters in international investment law, on a case-by-case basis where compensation based on future projections such as lost profits are not always practical.

7.4 Special Compensation Provisions

Some IIAs contain specialized compensation provisions for certain types of conduct, apart from expropriation, as discussed above. The most common of these are for treatment suffered as a consequence of armed conflict

---

[27] E.g. *McRae* v. *Commonwealth Disposals* [1951] HCA 79 (Australia High Court).
[28] C. F. Amerasinghe, 'Assessment of Compensation for Expropriated Foreign Property: Three Critical Problems' in R. St John Macdonald (ed.), *Essays in Honour of Wang Tieya* (Martinus Nijhoff, 1994), at 55.

or civil strife, which appears to contemplate situations covered by the FPS standard. For example, the TPP states under this provision:

1. ...each Party shall accord to investors of another Party and to covered investments non-discriminatory treatment with respect to measures it adopts or maintains relating to losses suffered by investments in its territory owing to armed conflict or civil strife.
2. Notwithstanding paragraph 1, if an investor of a Party, in a situation referred to in paragraph 1, suffers a loss in the territory of another Party resulting from: (a) requisitioning of its covered investment or part thereof by the latter's forces or authorities; or (b) destruction of its covered investment or part thereof by the latter's forces or authorities, which was not required by the necessity of the situation, the latter Party shall provide the investor restitution, compensation or both, as appropriate, for that loss.

This provision is interesting not only because it sets out a dedicated regime for compensation for certain types of exceptional circumstances which may harm investors, but it also specifies remedies including restitution as well as compensation. This may indicate that non-pecuniary remedies may be appropriate, such as returning the lost assets or repair of the damaged ones. The availability of non-pecuniary remedies will be discussed below. This provision of the TPP expressly does not include actions taken pursuant to the doctrine of necessity, which will be explored further in Chapter 10.

7.5 Valuation of Investment

The valuation of the investment is a separate issue that occurs after the measure of compensation is determined. In this analysis the tribunal must assess how much the investment was actually worth to the investor so that a correct level of compensation can be awarded. This can be difficult given that actions of host states which result in harms to investors, such as outright expropriations, can render market-based approaches to valuation impossible. Highly regulated spheres of activity where assets such as licences are not readily available are also problematic, as are businesses operating as monopolies. The valuation of assets that have been lost as a consequence of regulatory action will involve close analysis of various different forms of evidence, often in collaboration with experts such as accountants who regularly appear as expert witnesses in arbitrations. Unfortunately, despite its importance there is limited consistency in this practice. Most IIAs provide for the review of decisions made by tribunals with respect to valuations, as in this provision in the ECT:

> The Investor affected shall have a right to prompt review, under the law of the Contracting Party making the Expropriation, by a judicial or other competent and independent authority of that Contracting Party, of its case, of the valuation of its Investment, and of the payment of compensation, in accordance with the principles [of prompt, adequate and effective compensation].[29]

In contrast, some earlier Chinese BITs provided that disputes relating to the assessment of the quantum of compensation would be the only type of dispute that could be referred to international arbitration, with questions regarding the existence or not of an expropriation to be resolved exclusively by domestic courts.[30] Surely the latter variety of legal question is the more fundamental in terms of its challenge to the state's sovereignty.

Many different methods can be used to ascertain the value of an investment, all of which attempt in one way or another to approximate the full market value of the investment, as envisioned by the Hull Formula. The most commonly used methods include the following:

7.5.1 Book Value

Among the most straightforward methods of valuation, book value represents the difference between the investor's assets and liabilities as stated in its accounts books. In that sense it captures the taxable value of an asset. The value is based on the original cost of the asset less any depreciation, meaning reductions based on the asset's natural deterioration over time. This type of valuation does not capture any lost profits, at least not directly, and as such it has a higher degree of certainty than some other methods. It is thought to be more useful also for investments which are healthy and profitable. Book value is probably the method of valuation most used in assessing the value of property by investment tribunals. It was applied for example in the *LIAMCO* v. *Libya* oil nationalization case

---

[29] Art 13(2).   [30] E.g. China–Thailand (12 March 1985).

to assess the level of compensation needed for various physical assets such as the oil wells themselves as well as ships and other supplies. The tribunal simply added up the stated values of the various assets drawn from the financial records of the company.[31] Performing such arithmetic is hardly a legal exercise, but there can often be debates regarding the validity or admissibility of the evidence used, such as dates of appraisal or depreciation rates. Such issues may be less contentious where the financial statements have been prepared by a reputable firm, as in *Siemens* v. *Argentina*, where the tribunal relied on materials prepared by the investor and audited by KPMG.[32]

One of the problems with the book value method is that, unlike other valuation methods, it does not reflect the added value that the management could bring to a business, nor the value of goodwill, reputation, know-how or other intangible features of the investment which tend not to be recorded in the financial statements. These soft assets can represent a significant aspect of the overall worth of an investment. It should be noted that some tribunals have used the book value method without expressly referring to it as such.[33]

7.5.2 Replacement Value

Replacement value is in theory the simplest of all forms of compensation at it is probably the one that is most closely aligned with the criterion of 'adequacy' seen in the Hull Formula. Replacement value is another way of expressing market value – the amount which the property should exchange between a willing buyer and a willing seller in an arm's length transaction where the parties acted knowledgably and without compulsion. Unlike strict market value, which cannot be fully appraised because the actual market often no longer exists as a consequence of the expropriation, replacement value considers the amount of money that would be necessary for the investor to buy the equivalent assets that it lost on the open market, as if such replacement assets hypothetically exist. Replacement accommodates various categories of assets, including hard assets (tangibles such as buildings, equipment and land) and soft assets

---

[31] *LIAMCO* v. *Libya*, ad hoc, Award (12 April 1977) 20 ILM 1 (1981).

[32] *Siemens* v. *Argentina*, ICSID Case No. ARB/02/8 (6 Feb 2007) at [358]–[360].

[33] E.g. *Asian Agricultural Products Ltd* v. *Sri Lanka*, ICSID Case No. ARB/87/3 (27 June 1990) at [100].

(intangibles such as costs associated with training personnel as well as research and development). Taken together, money equal to these costs should 'adequately' compensate the investor – it will be able to get back an asset equivalent to the one it lost. Despite the fact that the replacement value method has been rarely used in investment arbitration, it has been endorsed by a wide variety of courts and tribunals, including the ICJ,[34] the Iran–US Claims Tribunal[35] and various ICSID tribunals[36] (although there is no recorded case of an ICSID tribunal ever actually using it).

Using the replacement value method requires the investor to prove what similar assets or equipment would have cost at the time of the host state's interference, for example through expropriation. Replacement value should in theory take future profitability into account because part of what makes something valuable is the profit stream that it can generate in the future. However, replacement value was expressly challenged by the tribunal in *Amoco* v. *Iran* for this reason. The tribunal noted that in some instances the cost of replacing a lost asset will not adequately capture the earning power of that asset.[37] As with other forms of evaluation, assessing the validity of a replacement value claim will depend on the credibility of each party's expert witnesses. Tribunals will normally not supplant the expert's judgement of asset costs with their own, but they can and will often consider the factual sufficiency of any assumptions which underlie expert appraisals.

7.5.3 Discounted Cash Flow

This is a relatively new basis of valuation, introduced to address opposition to the market value method often voiced by countries that are less wedded to the ideals of the free market. It is focused on the income stream anticipated from the affected investment. Discounted cash flow requires the projection of the future receipts expected by the investing business after deducting costs. In effect this method encompasses future net profits while recognizing that money that will be earned in the future is less valuable than money that is currently owned. Future cash flows are thus 'discounted' or slightly reduced in order to give their present

---

[34] 'The Corfu Channel Case (UK v Albania) Merits', *ICJ Reports* 1949.

[35] *Oil Fields of Texas* v. *Iran*, 12 Iran–US Claims Tribunal (1986) 308 at [44].

[36] *Vivendi* v. *Argentina*, ICSID Case No. ARB/97/3 (20 Aug 2007) at [8.3.15].

[37] Iran–US Claims Tribunal, Award (16 June 1990) at [257].

values. The precise rate of discount is often quite controversial because at a very fundamental level it captures the extent to which humans are willing to defer gratification, which is often a highly subjective concept. The World Bank guidelines state that this is the method that should be used where the company that is expropriated is a 'going concern', meaning a healthy, active business. When implementing this method, tribunals should consider the investment's track record, any agreements secured by the investors and their timeframes, the business plan of the investors and finally, the economic conditions of the host country.[38]

Discounted cash flow has been used or endorsed by a number of investment arbitration tribunals over the years. One of the early uses of it was in *Amoco* v. *Iran*, an early oil nationalization case. Here the Iran–US Claims Tribunal noted that arbitration tribunals often resort to many methods of valuation in order to arrive at an appropriate level of compensation. It turned to discounted cash flow on the understanding that lost profits would have been too speculative because of fluctuations in profits each year common to the petroleum sector. It observed:

> the speculative element rapidly increases with the number of years to which a projection relates...Such projections can be useful indications by a prospective investor, who understands how far it can rely on them and accepts the risks associated with them; they certainly cannot be used by a tribunal as the measure of a fair compensation.[39]

In contrast, discounted cash flow was helpful in cases where a large investment had been made up front and the investor is seeking to recoup money based on the likely level of return. Still, the discounted cash flow method is not without its own controversy as it relies on projections and necessitates the establishment of a specific rate of discount, which will often be a source of much debate among parties. The tribunal in *CME* v. *Czech Republic* observed the need to have a clear track record of past operations in order to make use of the discounted cash flow method in conjunction with other valuation methods over a five-year period.[40]

The tribunal in *Quiborax* v. *Bolivia*[41] found Bolivia liable for breaches of its BIT with Chile, awarding compensation to the Chilean investor for

---

[38] I. Marboe, *Calculation of Compensation and Damages in International Investment Law* (Oxford University Press, 2009), at 242–3.

[39] Iran–US Claims Tribunal, Award (16 June 1990) at [239].

[40] UNCITRAL, Partial Award (13 Sept 2001) at [124].

[41] ICSID Case No. ARB/06/2 (16 Sept 2015).

breach of the FET standard as well as for expropriation. Bolivia had challenged the applicability of the discounted cash flow valuation approach, arguing that the investment had no track record in the state. It argued that there was too much uncertainty over the mineral reserves as well as future market prices. Unlike the *Amoco* tribunal which was willing to employ discounted cash flow, the *Quiborax* tribunal ultimately found that the claimants' two years of operation of the mine did not provide sufficient history to justify even the discounted cash flow approach, preferring instead to look at the cost of the assets to the investor.

7.5.4 Liquidation Value

The liquidation value method contemplates the value of an investment according to the estimated proceeds which would result from the sale, during liquidation proceedings and not in the ordinary course of business of the individual assets comprising the investment, after all liabilities are paid. It looks at the value of assets being sold on a piecemeal basis on the understanding that these assets will have a smaller secondary market than they would if they were sold together. This method also considers costs associated with the liquidation process itself which would be deducted from the value of the assets for the purpose of obtaining the final liquidation value. The liquidation value is premised on the notion of a forced sale or distressed liquidation, meaning one in which the potential seller has been compelled to sell because of the particular circumstances, such as undergoing a bankruptcy. In that sense it captures an unusual situation and conveys valuations that are likely to result from depressed sales prices due to associated pressures. This method of valuation has been rarely used in investment arbitration for the simple reason that there are very few factual circumstances that have occurred to which it can be appropriately applied. Tribunals appear to have been quite willing to consider this approach, as in *Vivendi* v. *Argentina*, which expressly endorsed it as a suitable method of valuation.[42] It has been used frequently by the Iran–US Claims Tribunal[43] and may be most appropriate in situations where there has been an indirect expropriation or a partial expropriation. The liquidation method, which focuses on the value of individual assets rather than an entire enterprise, allows tribunals to assess the value of the

---

[42] ICSID Case No. ARB/97/3 (20 Sept 2007) at [8.3.15].
[43] *Sedco* v. *IMICO*, Iran–US Claims Tribunal, Award (30 March 1989) at [58].

expropriated part of the investment, again recognizing that such assets will often have a smaller market than the overall enterprise. It was used in this way by the tribunal in *CME* v. *Czech Republic*[44] (along with other methodologies).

7.5.5 Cost of the Investment

The cost of the investment method, also known as the sunk costs method, recognizes that one of the problems in establishing an appropriate level of compensation tied to future earnings or lost profits is that such amounts are highly speculative. Tribunals have shown an unwillingness to award lost profits or earnings for precisely this reason.[45] To the extent that future profits are difficult to predict for various reasons such as extraordinary market conditions or lack of sufficient track record, investment tribunals in these instances have been prepared to award damages calculated on the costs of the investment already incurred. This cost of the investment method therefore refers to the amount of money spent by the investor in establishing the business up to the point that it is affected by the host state's actions.[46] This requires a calculation of how much the investor spent setting up their business – it does not call for an analysis of future sales or other projections. An investor may be more likely to claim compensation based on their net investment rather than on market value of discounted cash flow if they are in a position where they were losing money. Clearly those methods of valuation could and perhaps should result in situations where the investor would not receive any money from the host state. This compensation will comprise costs to the investor to establish the investment, such as buying machinery, equipment, advertising and possibly hiring personnel. The invested costs method, however, does not capture goodwill, market position and other intangibles that often play into future profit streams.

The cost of the investment method of asset valuation can be traced back to the *Chorzow Factory* case which speaks of the re-establishment of

---

[44] *CME* v. *Czech Republic*, UNCITRAL Final Award (14 March 2003) at [416].

[45] *Metalclad Corporation* v. *Mexico*, Case No. ARB(AF)/97/1 (30 Aug 2000); *Wena Hotels Ltd.* v. *Egypt*, ICSID Case No. ARB/98/4, Award (8 Dec 2000).

[46] As in *Metalclad* (ibid.) and *Wena Hotels* (ibid.). The terms 'sunk costs', 'wasted costs' or 'out of pocket expenses' are also used to describe these expenses. See further, Collins, 'Reliance Remedies at the International Centre'.

the investor's position prior to the illegal act occurring.[47] This valuation logic recalls that of the so-called 'reliance' measure of the common law system which is predicated on the notion of restoring the injured party to the position they were in before the harm occurred, not elevating them to a higher position, meaning the one they would have been in had the project unfolded as planned. Such valuation is not unlike that of *damnum emergens*, as mentioned above. This is often used where the investment was seized before any profits were received so compensation based on lost profits would be speculative.

For example, in *Mobil* v. *Venezuela*,[48] which concerned the interruption of petroleum projects during the Hugo Chavez presidency, the tribunal elected to award compensation to the investor by reference to the value of the assets comprising the investment rather than projecting lost profits, because the oil project was in the developmental stage. The tribunal was cautious that to do otherwise could lead to an award of compensation fraught with errors. Likewise, in *Metalclad* v. *Mexico* the tribunal awarded compensation for expropriation on the basis of the value of the investment because the business had barely begun operations at the time the expropriation took place. The tribunal reasoned: 'where the enterprise has not operated for a sufficiently long time to establish a performance record or where it has failed to make a profit, future profits cannot be used to determine going concern or fair market value.'[49] The *Metalclad* tribunal proceeded to consider the documentation tendered by the investor indicating the expenses incurred for each asset that was taken.

It is important to recognize that the cost of the investment methodology does not capture the suggestion, noted above, that reparation or damages for unlawful behaviour (as distinct from compensation for lawful expropriation) may in some cases necessitate payments of both lost profits and cost of the investment. If future profits are too speculative such that only cost can be awarded, then there may be an invidious situation in which an unlawful act is compensated at the same level as a lawful one.

Cost of the investment valuation may be appropriate for breaches of pre-establishment National Treatment given that an unestablished investment is by definition one which does not have a history of profit-making.

---

[47] *Factory at Chorzow (Germany v. Poland)*, PCIJ Rep (1928) Series A, No. 13 at 47.

[48] *Mobil Corporation v. Venezuela*, ICSID Case No. ARB/07/27 (9 Oct 2014).

[49] ICSID Case No. ARB(AF)/97/1 (30 Aug 2000) at 120.

If a host state refused to allow a foreign investor to set up an otherwise lawful investment in its territory pursuant to such an obligation, no demonstrable injury may have been sustained at all, particularly if the investor had not engaged in any pre-investment expenditure. Awarding lost profits to a foreign investor that had been denied establishment would be unfair because this could lead to a sizable award against a host state where no effort had been exerted by the foreign investor, other than the mere declaration that they had intended to commence business in a sector where restrictions on foreign ownership were unlawfully imposed. The tribunal could gauge the extent of genuine pre-investment expenditures that had been incurred by the investor in the good faith assumption that a National Treatment obligation would be upheld. State-to-state dispute settlement between two treaty parties may be the most appropriate way to resolve such situations with a remedy sought that would compel the host state to remove any restrictions that violated the pre-establishment National Treatment promise.

7.6 Moral Damages

As suggested above, compensation aims to make the injured party whole and in that sense it is restorative. It does not aim to punish the wrongdoer nor is it intended to make an example of them in order to deter future wrongdoing. However, in some instances there can be types of behaviour that are egregiously harmful, often in a less perceptible way such that the mere recovery of the value of the damaged business in pure financial terms is insufficient. Such situations may be appropriate for an award of moral damages. While there is no universal definition of moral damages, it is understood to encompass monetary compensation for civil wrongs that are accompanied by torts or other harms that are intangible or otherwise difficult to quantify. They are often associated with physical injuries or harassment but may also encompass loss of business reputation. To be sure, moral damages are meant to be compensatory; they should not be viewed as punitive or exemplary, although these motivations can be discerned from the language of the tribunals which have made such awards. They are also available to legal persons (meaning investing companies) in addition to natural ones (people). Under international law, reparation for moral harms is provided for expressly in the Articles on State Responsibility.[50]

The first ICSID case to award compensation for moral damages was *Desert Line* v. *Yemen*,[51] a dispute in which the foreign investor had been coerced by the host state into an unfavourable settlement of a prior arbitral award. The investor's employees had also been physically threatened, arrested and detained. The tribunal in *Lemire* v. *Ukraine*[52] established that moral damages should only be awarded when the actions of the host state involve physical duress, have a grave effect and result in mental suffering or loss of reputation.

An award of moral damages has been rejected in many investment cases. For example, in *Stati* v. *Kazakhstan*[53] the tribunal ruled that Kazakhstan had breached its obligations under the ECT by engaging in coordinated harassment of the investors. The claim was rejected despite the fact that one of the investor's employees had been detained, arrested and incarcerated for a period of several months under a criminal charge that had no basis under domestic law. Somewhat surprisingly, this behaviour did not amount to the 'very exceptional circumstances' which are required for an award of moral damages to be made.

Moral damages were considered in *OI European Group B.V.* v. *Bolivarian Republic of Venezuela*,[54] a claim based on the nationalizations of bottle-making plants during Chavez's administration. Venezuela seized the plants under its expropriation law and a newly state-owned company took over production. In addition to various claims under the BIT, the investor also claimed relief for moral damages amounting to almost US $1 billion based on the host state's conduct during the nationalizations. Denying the moral damages claim, the tribunal held that the investor did not appropriately describe the relevant facts in their statements of claim and other materials. In particular, it ruled that the investor could not demonstrate that Venezuela's officials harassed or threatened the employees to continue working in the plants, nor that they were physically aggressive or threatening when dealing with the companies.

---

[50] Art 30.2.   [51] ICSID Case No. ARB/05/17 (26 Feb 2008).
[52] ICSID Case No. ARB/06/18 (28 March 2011).
[53] SCC Arbitration V (116/2010) (4 Feb 2014).
[54] ICSID Case No. ARB/11/25 (2 March 2015).

In *Quiborax* v. *Bolivia*[55] the tribunal considered the possibility of awarding moral damages because of the host government's behaviour when it falsely accused the investors of fraud and corruption in a cross-claim. It felt that these allegations were unsubstantiated, although the tribunal stopped short of making a ruling to that effect. The tribunal did decline to award compensation for moral damages on the basis of these baseless allegations, noting that there was no evidence of damage to the claimant's reputation as a consequence of the allegations.

One recent instance of a case in which moral damages were awarded by an investment tribunal is *Al-Karafi* v. *Libya*,[56] a claim based on the premature and unjustified cancellation of an oil project. Here US $30 million in compensation for moral damages was granted because of damage caused to the investor's worldwide professional reputation. This included harm suffered to the investor's stock market valuation as well as their reputation in global construction markets. The persuasive value of this decision in the future may be limited, however, given that the tribunal reached this decision based on Libyan domestic law on moral damages.

Moral damages have also been the subject of cross-claims by respondent states. *Levi* v. *Peru*[57] was a dispute brought by a French finance company on the basis of the Peruvian government's intervention in the company's liquidation, exacerbating the claimant's collapse to the detriment of its shareholders. Rejecting the investor's claims of expropriation, the tribunal ruled that Peru's regulation of the bank was a legitimate exercise of authority over the banking sector and that much of the damage suffered by the investor was the consequence of their own directors' negligence. The tribunal denied Peru's cross-claim for moral damages against the investor, partially because some of the harms suffered to both parties were the consequence of the Peruvian financial crisis, clearly beyond the control of the parties. Moreover the mere fact that the shareholders of the investor made repeated complaints to the Peruvian courts and as well as derogatory comments to the media regarding the Peruvian government were not sufficient to warrant compensation via moral damages. There is no known example of an arbitration decision in which a respondent state has been awarded moral damages based on the behaviour of

---

[55] ICSID Case No. ARB/06/2 (16 Sept 2015).
[56] Ad hoc tribunal, Final Award (22 March 2013).
[57] ICSID Case No. ARB/10/17 (9 Jan 2015).

the investor, but clearly tribunals have been at least willing to consider such arguments. Given the predominately one-sided nature of IIAs (which place obligations on states and not on investors), such awards may be a way of levelling the playing field between parties in investor–state arbitration. Frivolous claims may be one such area in which moral damages claims could be made by states against investors.[58]

It is clear from the investment arbitration case law that the behaviour of a party must be particularly egregious in order for moral damages to be appropriate. Rather than award moral damages, many tribunals appear to be more inclined to use costs to address inappropriate conduct by parties. Parties that have demonstrated bad faith or engaged in other types of unseemly behaviour have been compelled to bear the costs of both parties during the arbitration proceedings. As it is essentially a matter of process, the issue of costs will be considered in more depth in the next chapter.

7.7 Non-Pecuniary Remedies

Monetary compensation is the primary objective of most investors when seeking a remedy against a host state. In this respect international investment law is more closely analogous to private contract law which prioritizes damages for breach of contractually incurred obligations than to public law which typically mandates a certain form of conduct as remedy. The preference for monetary awards is despite the fact that many other forms of remedy are available under customary international law as a consequence of a wrongful act of a state. The International Law Commission Articles on State Responsibility include cessation, reparation and restitution as remedies for wrongful acts by states.[59] Likewise, the Dispute Settlement Understanding of the WTO adopts a chief remedy of removal of the unlawful measure[60] – indeed there is no provision for monetary remedies at all in WTO law. In situations where foreign investors undertake long-term operations in host states, non-pecuniary remedies such as the cessation of interference or the modification of intrusive regulations might be entirely well received as an alternative to money. Such non-pecuniary remedies are known as 'specific performance' in the common

---

[58] See e.g. M. Parish, A. Newlson and C. Rosenberg, 'Awarding Moral Damages to Respondent States in Investment Arbitration' 29:1 *Berkeley Journal of International Law* 224 (2011).
[59] Art 37.   [60] Art 19(1).

law of contract because they effectively require the party in breach to follow through with what it said it would do.

Non-monetary remedies are not unheard of in international investment law. The Iran–US Claims Tribunal was prepared to order non-pecuniary relief in the *TOPCO* v. *Libya* nationalization claim, holding that restitution, not monetary damages, should be the primary remedy. Monetary remedies were more common simply because restitution was impractical or impossible. The tribunal stated that 'any possible award of damages should necessarily be subsidiary to the principal remedy of performance itself'.[61] It consequently ordered Libya to fulfil its various breached contracts undertaken with the investor.

The ICSID Convention states that parties must enforce the *pecuniary* obligations within awards as if they were final judgments of courts,[62] with no express provision for extraordinary or injunctive relief. Still, ICSID tribunals can and often do require that losing states take a particular course of action or refrain from doing so. One of the reasons that they have generally not done so is simply because investors seek monetary relief as a matter of course. Such non-pecuniary orders often contemplate the cessation of legal proceedings rather than a modification of legislation or a fundamental restructuring of governance. The tribunal in *Antoine Goetz* v. *Burundi* demonstrated a willingness to award a non-monetary remedy when it offered the losing respondent the option of revoking a measure (its withdrawal of a certificate of tax-free exemption which it would therefore have to reinstate) or paying compensation to the investor for their losses associated with the revocation of the certificate which was held to amount to an indirect expropriation. Rather than force the specific performance, the tribunal emphasized that 'the choice lies within the sovereign discretion of the Burundian government'.[63] The parties ultimately reached a settlement, part of which required that Burundi reinstate the tax-free zone regime, so in that sense this case is not truly an example of a non-pecuniary award. The non-pecuniary measure contemplated here was clearly intended to displace compensation for a lawful expropriation, not damages for an illegal one.[64]

---

[61] 17 ILM 1 (1978) at 508.   [62] Art 54(1).

[63] ICSID Case No. ARB/01/2 (21 June 2012) at 516.

[64] See C. Schreuer, 'Non-Pecuniary Remedies in ICSID Arbitration' 20:4 *Arbitration International* 325 (2004) at 329–30.

The tribunal in *Enron* v. *Argentina*[65] examined the issue of whether or not ICSID tribunals were empowered to grant non-pecuniary remedies. Here the claimant investor had argued that stamp taxes imposed by the government of Argentina constituted indirect expropriation, requesting that the taxes be declared unlawful and that their collection be permanently prohibited. Argentina argued that the tribunal did not have the power to award such a remedy, but the tribunal held otherwise. Considering the powers accorded to other international tribunals such as the ICJ, which had demonstrated its capacity to award non-pecuniary remedies, the tribunal established that it was able to award a remedy of specific performance as an inherent aspect of its jurisdiction.

While not strictly speaking a remedy, procedural orders compelling parties to behave in a certain manner are within the purview of investment tribunals. There are many examples of these types of orders. One tribunal required that all domestic legal proceedings against the investor must be terminated because of the investor's decision to pursue its claim through international arbitration.[66] Similarly, the restoration of the right to proceed to arbitration was granted by the tribunal in *ATA* v. *Jordan*.[67] That tribunal ruled that although the award barred any further judicial proceedings regarding the substance of the dispute, the Jordanian courts could be invoked at the enforcement stage as well as other procedural matters.

Of course the power of investment tribunals to make non-pecuniary awards as an alternative to monetary compensation can be restricted in the text of the IIA which gives the tribunal its jurisdiction over the claim. For example, the US–Singapore FTA states:

> Where a tribunal makes a final award against a respondent, the tribunal may award, separately or in combination, only: (a) monetary damages and any applicable interest; and (b) restitution of property, in which case the award shall provide that the respondent may pay monetary damages and any applicable interest in lieu of restitution.[68]

Preserving the exclusivity of monetary remedies in this fashion ensures that host states will not be compelled to make legislative or other administrative changes in a manner which may be politically onerous or seen

---

[65] ICSID Case No. ARB/01/3, Decision on Jurisdiction (14 Jan 2000).

[66] *ATA Construction, Industrial and Trading Company* v. *Jordan*, ICSID Case No. ARB/08/2 (18 May 2010).

[67] ICSID Case No. ARB/08/2 (11 July 2011).   [68] Art 15.25(1) (6 May 2003).

as an affront to the country's sovereignty. On the other hand, in some circumstances non-pecuniary remedies would probably be quite welcome among many developing states with insufficient resources to fulfil monetary awards issued by investment tribunals, or where doing so would place their economy in jeopardy.

7.8 Conclusion

International investment law has established a reasonably detailed set of rules governing compensation for breaches of IIAs and investment contracts. Chief among these is the requirement that host states pay compensation for expropriation by reference to the market value of the affected assets at the time they were taken. Refinements of this principle have developed over time, in particular in relation to the application of methodology for precisely quantifying the value of assets in order to set an appropriate payout. Still, tying the degree of compensation to expropriation has in some respects muddled the understanding of compensation in international investment law, the modern iteration of which is characterized by IIAs which impose many other kinds of obligations on host states, each of which also engages the obligation to pay compensation.

Distinguishing between what would appear at first glance to be two kinds of compensation – that payable on a lawful expropriation and all other kinds of illegal action – has provided a welcome degree of clarity and cohesion. The latter kind of compensation may be usefully termed damages and tends to embody a higher quantum because it includes lost profits, whereas the former retains the label 'compensation' and captures the restoration of the value of initial assets only. Appropriate modifications of this simple (and somewhat artificial) edict are formulated through applications of various methodologies of valuation which may or may not incorporate a forward-looking profit stream depending on the circumstances including the availability of adequate evidence. Additional remedies may be available depending on the parties' behaviour, and the availability and suitability of enforced obligations as an alternative to cash.

With these rules in mind, clearly one of the primary reasons that foreign investors seek international arbitration rather than pursuing remedies in domestic courts is that there is thought to be a greater chance of receiving higher amounts of compensation from international tribunals. This prospect, along with high-profile mega-awards such as those in the *Yukos* cases, has obviously played a role in encouraging foreign investors to engage in commercial operations in high-risk countries. This has in turn, one would hope, brought economic advantages to those regions that would otherwise have been foregone. Still, there remains a worrying perception that compensation awards in international investment law are excessive and that forcing countries, many of which are in an early developmental stage, to pay out millions of dollars to large multinationals is economically damaging and fundamentally unfair.

Rules on compensation in international investment law have addressed these pressing issues to a degree. As we have seen, tribunals strive to apportion monetary awards in a manner that captures the true value of the investments which have been adversely affected by the host state's behaviour. In other respects, however, these fundamental issues on the function and effectiveness of dispute resolution between investors and states in international law are more squarely faced by the rules on the investor–state arbitration procedure itself. The features of this vitally important process of investment arbitration under IIAs will be dealt with in the next chapter.

8 Dispute Settlement

8.1 Introduction

The protections in IIAs that have been considered so far in this book would be immaterial if there was no way for investors to enforce them in order to receive remedies such as monetary compensation. This is why, in addition to substantive obligations, IIAs also contain procedural guarantees for access to dispute settlement. Through one of these mechanisms, investor-state arbitration, investors can seek direct redress against host states if the other substantive features of the IIA or investment contract are not honoured. It is no overstatement to claim that the greatest advantage in international investment law to investors is access to neutral international dispute settlement. This procedure offsets one of the most significant risks involved in investing abroad – ineffective access to justice through the legal system of the host state.

This chapter will explore dispute settlement in international investment law, evaluating the criticisms that it is undemocratic and non-transparent and at the same time seen as a major advantage to foreign firms because it ensures fairness and confidentiality. It will outline perhaps the most popular system of investor–state dispute settlement in the world today, the ICSID, exploring some of its key procedural features and trends. It will also consider UNCITRAL Arbitration Rules as well as the pressing procedural matters in these fora such as costs. State-to-state and alternative systems of dispute resolution will also be considered, along with the important procedural issue of cost allocation.

Some form of investor–state dispute settlement is provided for in almost every IIA. Indeed, it is the single most important feature associated with the IIA phenomenon because almost everything else (for example FET, guarantees against expropriation without compensation, transparency) was arguably already captured by customary international law. Yet the international adjudication of investment disputes is seen as a major threat to national sovereignty as it often bypasses local courts, giving foreigners greater procedural rights than are available to local investors. While there are many lively issues in international investment law, this is without question the most controversial aspect of IIAs. There is growing scepticism across many segments of society towards investor–state arbitration, often tied to the perception that the process undermines national sovereignty at the behest of profit-driven multinational enterprises. Indeed investor–state dispute settlement has in recent times become synonymous with the global back-room deal-making between avaricious corporations and corrupt governments. Consultations instigated by the European Union in 2015 over the inclusion of investor–state dispute settlement in the TTIP, of which further will be made below, sparked an unprecedented furore among civil society groups and public observers. Many of these stakeholders failed to appreciate that these mechanisms have a well-established pedigree and, contrary to popular belief, host states tend to win the disputes more often than they lose.[1]

The multiplicity of claims brought by investors in numerous fora, massive damages awards against states, lack of consistency among decisions and confidentiality (or as many say, secrecy) of the arbitration process underlie this overarching concern. International investment arbitration provisions in IIAs overstep the jurisdiction of empowering tribunals to act as a kind of judicial review of governmental decisions. Host state sovereignty is infringed, so the argument typically goes, because international investment tribunals often render decisions on issues that are inherently of public concern, such as the natural environment, national security and the control over the domestic economy. This is viewed with derision because investor–state arbitration is essentially patterned from private commercial arbitration, which occurs without public participation in private offices and is adjudicated by party-selected arbitrators who often lack an appreciation of public international law rather than by appointed or elected judges with a deeper awareness of the impact of their decisions on the lives of citizens in host states.

One of the main criticisms of investor–state dispute settlement is that it is contained in IIAs between two developed countries, such as the

---

[1] A recent study reported that states win 36 per cent of cases while investors win 27 per cent, with the remainder either discontinued, settled or resulted in awards with no damages payable: UNCTAD, 'Recent Policy Developments and Key Issues', in *World Investment Report 2015* (2015), at 102–18; http://unctad.org/en/PublicationChapters/wir2015ch3_en .pdf.

much-maligned TTIP, where the above concerns of impartiality and incompetence should in theory not apply. Of course, the judicial systems of developed countries are often poorly administered with excessive delay; the USA and Italy are notorious examples.[2] Another plausible explanation for this phenomenon is that domestic courts are ill-suited to hearing matters of international law and that, on the principle of sovereign equality and in the interests of diplomatic harmony, it would be invidious to defer to the courts of one state while mistrusting those of another. Whatever the reason, it is clear that investors want these mechanisms, and for states to forego them could cause them to lose out on FDI to their more internationally minded neighbours.

Although there is no formal system of precedent in international arbitration, arbitrators consist of a relatively small number of specialists in international investment law who are aware of the published decisions made by earlier tribunals. The observed tendency of tribunals to refer to earlier decisions is both the cause as well as the effect of the increasing publication of decisions which has allowed these materials to become studied and interpreted as a distinct field of law. Published decisions typically contain numerous cross-references to other decisions. As such, it could be said that there is already a de facto system of persuasive precedent in international investment law as arbitrators attempt to render decisions that are justifiable through their consistency.[3]

8.2 International Arbitration as an Alternative to Domestic Courts

The first issue to come to terms with when evaluating investment arbitration is the nature of the procedural advantage that it accords to investors as distinct from the alternative, namely pursuing claims in the courts of the host state like normal litigants. If there is no clause in an investment

[2] C. Congyan, 'China–US BIT Negotiations and the Future of Investment Treaty Regime: A Grand Bilateral Bargain With Multilateral Implications' 12 *Journal of International Economic Law* 457 (2009) at 483.

[3] A. Bjorklund, 'Investment Treaty Arbitral Decisions as *Jurisprudence Constante*' in C. Picker, I. Bunn and D. Arne (eds.), *International Economic Law: The State and Future of the Discipline* (Hart, 2008).

contract or an IIA which specifies a particular forum for the resolution of disputes, the default route is that differences will be resolved in the domestic courts as the courts with the closest connection to the matter. This is probably not an ideal solution for the investor who may fear that the host state will lack impartiality. Whether or not that is true in every instance will often be unknown to the investor but the perception of impartiality may be enough to make the investor nervous about entering a foreign state, particularly one where there is no tradition of judicial independence. Moreover, investors will often have the serious concern that the courts of the host state may lack the expertise to deal with technical issues which often arise in international investment law. Clearly IIAs contain highly specialized provisions, the interpretation of which may be beyond the understanding of conventional judges.

From the host state's point of view, the courts of the investor's home state, which will also have a reasonably close connection to the dispute through the nationality of the claimant, will be unsuitable fora. As respondent, the host state will often mistrust the courts of the home state for similar reasons as those articulated above. It could fear that the home state will be biased in favour of the investor, or lack an understanding either of IIAs or of the particular legal environment in which the challenged laws have been enacted.

Domestic courts will be disfavoured as fora for the resolution of investment claims also because of jurisdictional issues. The courts of the home state may lack jurisdiction over events that have occurred in the territory over an investment in another state even if they are connected through the nationality of the claimant. Furthermore, the Doctrine of State Immunity, recognized in many national legal systems[4] and arguably a general principle of international law, will operate to prevent a domestic court from taking jurisdiction over a matter where a country was acting in the exercise of its sovereign powers rather than in a purely commercial capacity. Actions of government regularly form the basis of claims brought under IIAs. Lawsuits relating to an investment matter against a host state will therefore typically be inadmissible in any civil court. Furthermore, the related Act of State Doctrine prevents courts from questioning the legality of official acts of foreign states within their own territory. For example, a

---

[4] E.g. US Foreign Sovereign Immunities Act 1976.

UK court recently declined to take jurisdiction over a claim which required it to assess the legality of rendition by US officials of a prisoner to Libya.[5] Unwilling or unable to use domestic courts, investors and host states seek international arbitration as a means of settling their disputes.

Arbitration is a procedure whereby both sides to a dispute agree to let a designated third party, the arbitrator or the arbitral tribunal, decide the outcome of a legal dispute. The decision will be legally binding and as such it is quite different from mediation or diplomatic dispute resolution, both of which are commonly used in the international context. Arbitration is based on the consent of the parties and in that sense it may be seen as a kind of contract. Consent to international investment arbitration can be obtained in one of three ways: in an investment contract between the state and the investor, in a treaty between two states or in a piece of domestic legislation such as an investment code.

The advantages of arbitration over conventional litigation are numerous. First, as alluded to above, arbitrators are usually experts in the field of investment law, and it can be expected that they will render thoughtful and informed decisions reflecting an understanding of the commercial and ideally the public matters involved in the dispute. Second, arbitration is often cheaper and faster than normal litigation which can take many years to resolve. This aspect of investment arbitration is perhaps somewhat less evident than its speed. Modern investor–state arbitration can be very expensive, with legal fees and other costs regularly amounting to several million dollars. Third, arbitration is said to be less adversarial than court hearings, helping preserve the relationship between parties who wish to continue to do business with each other. This can be very important in the case of international investment as one of the criteria for satisfying the definition of investment, as indicated earlier, is that it has a long-term dimension. Finally, arbitration is normally confidential, meaning that it is not open to the public, and pleadings as well as judgments are not automatically made public. This can be advantageous if commercially sensitive information is being discussed. While this aspect of investment arbitration tends to be cited as an advantage for investors, it can clearly also be attractive to states which seek to avoid the negative publicity associated with claims of expropriation and other kinds of adverse

---

[5] *Belhaj and another* v. *Straw and Others* [2013] EWHC 4111 (QB) (20 Dec 2013).

behaviour, which can unquestionably affect their chances of attracting more FDI.

8.3 Alternative Dispute Resolution Provisions

Most IIAs now contain provisions regarding alternative dispute settlement before formal arbitration proceedings can be instigated. The trend towards informal resolution of conflict before pursuing formal dispute settlement is well entrenched in most national legal systems as it is seen as less expensive and conducive to conserving amity between parties. This is often presented in voluntary terms, with parties being expected to engage with these methods to the extent possible. For example, Egypt's Model BIT of 2012 states:

> Disputes between a Contracting Party and an investor of the other Contracting Party relating to an investment of the latter in the territory of the former, which concern an alleged breach of this Agreement (hereinafter referred to as 'investment dispute') shall, without prejudice to Article 12 of this Agreement (Disputes between the Contracting Parties), to the extent possible, be settled through consultation, negotiation or mediation (hereinafter referred to 'procedure of amicable settlement').[6]

Other treaties treat arbitration and alternative means of settlement as options which are equally available to parties, meaning that informal negotiation, in this case conciliation, is not required. This approach can be seen, for example, in the 2003 Israel Model BIT:

> If a dispute under paragraph 1 of this Article cannot be settled within six (6) months of a written notification of this dispute, it shall be on the request of the investor settled as follows:
>
> (a) by a competent court of the Host Contracting Party; or
> (b) by conciliation; or
> (c) by arbitration by the International Center for the Settlement of Investment Disputes (ICSID).[7]

The idea behind these alternative dispute settlement methods, such as conciliation (essentially discussions with a view to reaching a compromise)

[6] Art 11.   [7] Art 8.1.

and mediation (similar to arbitration but non-binding) is that these procedures are believed to save time and costs, and that they will preserve the integrity of the relationship between the parties. They can be seen as a form of structured diplomacy in order to prevent the escalation of conflict. It is worth recalling that historically, disputes between two countries were often resolved through military conflict or the threat of it.

The extent to which informal dispute settlement actually works is unclear, although ICSID reports that 36 per cent of the total disputes brought before its tribunals since its inception were settled.[8] The lack of information on the effectiveness of alternative dispute resolution in international investment law generally is at least in part because of the confidentiality of the dispute settlement process itself. Like arbitration, informal dispute settlement procedures are also confidential and it is difficult to know whether the informal procedures have played a role in settlements. Tribunals take the obligation to pursue conciliation contained in IIAs seriously. In *Murphy Exploration* v. *Ecuador*,[9] the tribunal emphasized that reference to consultation in the IIA was not a mere formality but an essential mechanism to reduce costs and delays in the resolution of disputes between parties in a long-term commercial relationship.

It should be recognized that some home states maintain informal dispute resolution mechanisms to address problems that may arise when their own companies engage in investment activities abroad. Canada has a special system in place which offers mediation services for stakeholders who may have been adversely affected by the activities of Canadian extractive sector companies operating within their territories.[10]

8.4 State-to-State Dispute Settlement Provisions

Most IIAs provide mechanisms for the resolution of disputes between the two Contracting Parties although these provisions are rarely used and far less important than investor–state dispute settlement provisions that will be discussed below. IIAs tend to refer to the establishment of an arbitration tribunal for this purpose, often following a period of attempted settlement

---

[8] ICSID Case Load Statistics, 2015 at 13.   [9] ICSID Case No. ARB/08/4 (15 Dec 2010).

[10] D. Collins, 'Alternative Dispute Settlement for Stakeholders in International Investment Law' 15:3 *Journal of International Economic Law* 673 (2012).

through negotiations or other alternative dispute settlement methods. For example, Art 8 of the Algeria–Serbia BIT of 2012 provides:

1. Disputes arising between the Contracting Parties concerning the interpretation or application of this Agreement shall be settled, as far as possible, by consultations and negotiations.
2. If a dispute between the Contracting Parties cannot thus be settled within six months from the date of the commencement of negotiations, it shall, upon the request of either Contracting Party be referred to an arbitration tribunal.[11]

This IIA, like many, goes on to specify how the arbitral tribunal will be appointed, that the law of the treaty itself (supplemented by the rules of international law) will govern the dispute, that the decision shall be binding on both parties, and that the tribunal shall select its own procedure.[12] There have been very few, if any, state-to-state arbitrations which have taken place pursuant to these provisions in IIAs.

The ICJ has played a limited role in international investment law despite its long history and the obvious potential for the treatment of foreign investment to be a source of tension among states. IIAs do not reference the ICJ as a forum for the resolution of state-to-state claims. Of course the ICJ contributes to the creation of international law, and this jurisprudence often plays a role in investment arbitrations, as for example the famous *Chorzow Factory* dispute discussed in the previous chapter.

Some mention should be made, however, of how the WTO has featured in the settling of investment-orientated disputes. The WTO Dispute Settlement System is the most active international court in the world, having heard several hundred total disputes since its establishment in 1995, considerably more than the ICJ. The WTO Dispute Settlement System consists of first level tribunals (panels) and a standing Appellate Body. The WTO panels and Appellate Body hear complaints brought by Member States against other Member States regarding the thirty or so WTO agreements, some of which have investment-orientated elements, as noted in Chapter 2. The WTO Dispute Settlement System has resolved a number of legal disagreements regarding Members' commitments under the GATS, the TRIPS and the TRIMS, which have had implications on foreign

---

[11] 13 Feb 2012.   [12] Art 8(3)–(6).

investment.[13] WTO tribunals have no jurisdiction over claims brought pursuant to IIA provisions – they can only hear claims based on the WTO agreements. Investors (or traders for that matter) have no standing before the WTO panels or Appellate Body – only Member States may use the WTO Dispute Settlement System.

8.5 Investor–State Dispute Settlement Provisions

8.5.1 Scope

Investor–state arbitration is the most important procedural feature in IIAs and the source of the controversy described above. Such provisions are, for now, found in most IIAs. Treaties usually specify the matters which are eligible for adjudication through investor–state arbitration. It is quite common for the treaty to refer broadly to 'any dispute between either Contracting Party and a national or person of the other Contracting Party concerning an investment of that national or person in the territory of the former Contracting Party'.[14] These clauses effectively operate as a waiver of sovereign immunity, meaning a state's right not to have its sovereign acts challenged by a tribunal outside its own jurisdiction.

Some treaties choose to list the matters to which the investor-state dispute settlement provisions apply. This somewhat more cautious approach can be seen for example in the US Model BIT:

> a) the claimant, on its own behalf, may submit to arbitration under this Section a claim
>   (i) that the respondent has breached
>   (A) an obligation under Articles 3 through 10 [FET, FPS, guarantee against expropriation],
>   (B) an investment authorization, or
>   (C) an investment agreement;[15]

Alternatively, an IIA may expressly exclude certain provisions from the scope of investor–state dispute settlement, meaning that all other provisions of the treaty can be settled through this mechanism. In this regard,

---

[13] E.g. India – Measures Affecting the Automotive Sector, WT/DS146/AB/R (19 March 2002) (regarding the application of performance requirements as violations of the TRIMS Agreement).

[14] Netherlands–Oman BIT (2009).   [15] Art 24.

the Malaysia–Pakistan Comprehensive Economic Cooperation Agreement of 2007 states:

> This Article [on investor–state dispute settlement] shall not apply to any dispute arising between a Party and an investor of the other Party on any right or privileges conferred or created by Article 89 [National Treatment] and 92 [Performance Requirements].

The excluded provisions are presumably too sensitive to be evaluated by an international tribunal, and accordingly any such disputes must be resolved by domestic courts. Some IIAs exclude particular policy areas or certain sectors from the reach of the investor–state dispute settlement provision, in some cases through an annex to the agreement. The Canada–Colombia FTA of 2008 specifies:

> A decision by Canada following a review under the Investment Canada Act...with respect to whether or not to permit an acquisition that is subject to review, shall not be subject to the dispute settlement provisions of Section B of this Chapter [on investor–state dispute settlement] or of Chapter Twenty-One (Dispute Settlement).[16]

Investor–state dispute settlement may be excluded for certain policy matters, in some cases through a Denial of Benefits clause. In what has been seen as a revolutionary development, the TPP states that tobacco control measures cannot be challenged under the treaty's investor–state dispute settlement mechanism if the signatory party makes such an election.[17] Denial of Benefits clauses will be explored further in the next chapter.

Related to the scope of investor–state dispute settlement provisions, states can also structure the extent of their commitment to that procedure by framing their consent to it in different ways. Recall that arbitration must be based on the consent of parties, and that such consent can be express or implied. An example of express consent in an IIA can be seen in the Mexico–Singapore BIT of 2009: 'Each Contracting Party hereby gives its unconditional consent to the submission of a dispute to international arbitration in accordance with this Section.' The Italian Model BIT contains an implied consent clause tied to the failure of alternative dispute settlement: 'If within six months the investment dispute cannot

---

[16] Annex 837.

[17] Art 29.5 (the benefits of the investor–state dispute settlement feature will be denied if a tobacco control measure is challenged).

be settled [through alternative dispute settlement] and the investor is not satisfied with the outcome of the domestic administrative procedure, the investor may submit the dispute either to:...'[18]

Some states place conditions on their granting of consent, as in the Australia–Lithuania BIT of 1998, which promises the following: 'if an investor of one Party refers a claim to arbitration before ICSID, the other Party shall consent in writing to the submission of the dispute to the Centre within thirty days of receiving such a request from the investor.'[19] The strategic purpose of these provisions is clear – host states will only agree to submit to investor–state dispute settlement under the circumstances in which they perceive it to be to their advantage.

8.5.2 Prior Exhaustion of Local Remedies

Under traditional international law, the investor must seek to achieve a remedy through domestic law before it can put forth a claim at an international tribunal. This is called the exhaustion of local remedies and in a sense embodies a sense of deference to each country's sovereignty. In IIAs, some host states require the exhaustion of local remedies before they will accept the jurisdiction of an arbitral tribunal, while others frame this as an option to the investor to use local remedies or international ones. A good example of the former style is that of the Argentina–Spain BIT of 1991:

> 2. If the dispute cannot thus be settled within six months following the date on which the dispute has been raised by either party [consultations], it shall be submitted to the competent tribunal of the Contracting Party in whose territory the investment was made.
> 3. The dispute may be submitted to international arbitration in any of the following circumstances:
>   a) at the request of one of the parties to the dispute, if no decision has been rendered on the merits of the claim after the expiration of a period of eighteen months from the date on which the proceedings referred to in paragraph 2 of this Article have been initiated, or if such decision has been rendered, but the dispute between the parties continues;
>   b) if both parties to the dispute agree thereto.[20]

---

[18] Art IX.2.   [19] Art 13.3 (24 Nov 1998).   [20] Art IX.2 (translated from Spanish).

Under this Agreement, the investor must at least try to use the local courts to have the matter resolved before international arbitration can be pursued. An optional local remedy clause can be seen in the 2006 Ethiopia–Spain BIT:

> If the disputes referred to in paragraph (1) of this Article cannot be thus settled amicably within six months from the date of the written notification, the investor shall be entitled to submit, at his choice, for resolution to:
>
> a) The competent court of the Contracting Party in whose territory the investment was made; or [investor–state dispute settlement under UNCITRAL or ICSID] . . . [21]

Exhaustion of local remedy clauses have been a source of much debate in arbitration decisions, with tribunals grappling with the issue of whether or not they can take jurisdiction over the claim based on the observation of these requirements by investors. Generally speaking it is the responsibility of the host state to make the exhaustion of local remedies a condition of consent to arbitration, with claimants otherwise entitled to institute claims directly before international tribunals.[22] Such provisions tend to be quite rare in modern IIAs.

8.5.3 Choice of Specific Fora

Investor–state dispute settlement provisions in IIAs usually refer to a specific format for arbitration, with ICSID and UNCITRAL rules as the most popular. NAFTA, for example, grants investors an option of using either of these fora. Other treaties give parties the power to agree on other, unspecified arbitration rules.[23]

A number of IIAs list more than one dispute resolution forum that an investor may use. This raises the issue of whether the same dispute can be submitted to several fora, such as domestic and international ones simultaneously, a situation sometimes referred to as parallel proceedings. Equally, this can raise the problem that the same dispute could be submitted to two different fora, one after the other. These circumstances are

---

[21] Art 11(2) (17 March 2006).
[22] As in *CME* v. *Czech Republic*, UNCITRAL, Partial Award (13 Sept 2001).
[23] E.g. Mexico–Singapore BIT (2009).

arguably unfair in that they compel the state to defend itself twice, raising costs and potentially pressuring settlement. Some treaties deal with
this by what is known as the 'fork-in-the-road' clause, meaning a provision which requires the investor to choose between the domestic courts or
international arbitration from the beginning. Once the choice is made by
starting a proceeding, it cannot be rescinded and the investor is stuck with
the forum it has chosen. This can be seen for example in the Indonesia–
Chile BIT: 'Once an investor has submitted the dispute to the competent
tribunal of the Contracting Party in whose territory the investment was
made or to international arbitration, that election shall be final.'[24] Fork-
in-the-road clauses can be controversial because certain aspects of the
dispute may be properly heard brought before a local court, and certain
other aspects may quite legitimately be resolved at the international level.
It also is often difficult to segregate the various claims each tribunal will
be willing to hear. A fork-in-the-road clause was evaluated in *Pantechniki*
v. *Albania*, where the investor brought the claim in the domestic forum,
then having lost tried again in international arbitration. Finding that the
two claims were essentially of the same substance, the ICSID arbitrator
declined to take jurisdiction.[25]

In contrast, some treaties expressly preserve an investor's right to use
arbitration after they have initiated domestic court proceedings but before
a judgment has been rendered by these courts. This approach can be seen
in Art 8 of the Israel Model BIT.

> Unless otherwise agreed, an investor who has submitted the dispute to
> national jurisdiction may have recourse to the arbitral tribunals mentioned
> in paragraph 2 of this Article so long as a judgment has not been delivered
> on the subject matter of the dispute by a national court.

Yet another variety of the forum selection clause gives priority to international remedies, capturing situations where the local courts have either
taken too long to issue a decision, or that decision did not result in a
complete resolution of all of the issues at hand. An example of this type
of clause can be seen in Art 8 of the Argentina–UK BIT of 1993:

> (2) disputes shall be submitted to international arbitration in the following
>   cases:

---

[24] Art IX.3 (7 April 1999).   [25] ICSID Case No. ARB/07/21 (30 July 2009).

(a) if one of the Parties so requests, in any of the following circumstances:

  (i) where, after a period of eighteen months has elapsed from the moment when the dispute was submitted to the competent tribunal of the Contracting Party in whose territory the investment was made, the said tribunal has not given its decision;

  (ii) where the final decision of the aforementioned tribunal has been made but the parties are still in dispute;

(b) where the Contracting Party and the investor of the other Contracting Party have so agreed.

Choice of forum clauses specifying use of domestic procedures are regularly challenged before arbitration tribunals. Key to the assessment is whether or not the two claims are in substance the same. In *CMS* v. *Argentina*, for example, the tribunal held that the subsequent procedure in international arbitration (after failure in the domestic court) was dissimilar because the domestic claim dealt with contractual rights whereas the international arbitration claim involved treaty-based ones.[26]

8.5.4 Transparency and Access

One of the major criticisms of investor–state dispute settlement is that it is characterized by an unacceptable lack of transparency given its clear public dimension. Since the decisions issued by investment tribunals determine whether the actions of governments are legal or not, they impact the rights of citizens and other stakeholders. If these groups' rights can be affected by the investment arbitration process, it is thought that they should be able to know what goes on during the hearings and possibly also participate in them. But of course this would defeat the principle of confidentiality that is central to arbitration as a system of dispute resolution.

Transparency in investor–state dispute settlement is poor because key documents such as the notice of arbitration and more importantly the award are not publicly available. While the number of cases for which documents are publicly disclosed is clearly increasing (as evinced by the growing databases of cases online), many remain completely confidential.

---

[26] ICSID Case No. ARB/01/8 (17 July 2003).

Some IIAs, such as the US Model BIT of 2012 have attempted to redress this problem:

> 1. Subject to paragraphs 2 and 4, the respondent shall, after receiving the following documents, promptly transmit them to the non-disputing Party and make them available to the public: (a) the notice of intent; (b) the notice of arbitration; (c) pleadings, memorials, and briefs submitted to the tribunal by a disputing party and any written submissions submitted pursuant to Article 28(2) [Non-Disputing Party submissions] and (3) [Amicus Submissions] and Article 33 [Consolidation]; (d) minutes or transcripts of hearings of the tribunal, where available; and (e) orders, awards, and decisions of the tribunal.[27]

During the heated TTIP negotiations that captivated the public, the media regularly made reference to the 'secret courts' in which governmental decisions could be challenged. Yet a number of recent IIAs have specifically provided for greater public access to the arbitration tribunal proceedings. The same article of US Model BIT of 2012 goes on to state:

> 2. The tribunal shall conduct hearings open to the public and shall determine, in consultation with the disputing parties, the appropriate logistical arrangements. However, any disputing party that intends to use information designated as protected information in a hearing shall so advise the tribunal. The tribunal shall make appropriate arrangements to protect the information from disclosure.

These provisions are subject to editing and other protection for sensitive information. While civil society groups may demand the right to attend investor–state dispute settlement hearings, the reality is that very few citizens who have this opportunity will choose to exercise it, for the simple reason that investment disputes can be quite technical and uninteresting. Moreover, stakeholders are unlikely to travel overseas to a hearing taking place in another country. This is one of the reasons that online streaming of investment arbitration hearings has been attempted in cases with a significant public interest element.[28] UNCITRAL Transparency Rules, discussed further below, have helped address some of the perceived concerns of this feature of investor–state dispute settlement.

---

[27] Art 29.

[28] As in *Commerce Group and San Sebastian Gold Mines* v. *El Salvador*, ICSID Case No. ARB/09/17 (14 March 2011).

There have also been calls for investment arbitration tribunals to accept or consider submission from third parties which are not involved directly in the dispute but may have an interest in the outcome. Such submissions, known as amicus curiae (friends of the court), would allow various stakeholders such as NGOs and community organizations to participate in the proceedings. In this respect, the Norway Model BIT of 2007 Art 18 reads:

> 3. The Tribunal shall have the authority to accept and consider written amicus curiae submissions from a person or entity that is not a disputing Party, provided that the Tribunal has determined that they are directly relevant to the factual and legal issues under consideration. The Tribunal shall ensure an opportunity for the parties to the dispute, and to the other Party, to submit comments on the written amicus curiae observations.

Very few IIAs allow for this type of participation and there is a legitimate debate to be had as to whether amicus curiae submission could end up frustrating the arbitration process by adding to time and costs. Investment tribunals have begun to consider amicus curiae submissions and it is expected that this will become a more common feature of investor–state dispute settlement in future.

8.5.5 Applicable Law

Investor–state arbitration tribunals, like any other adjudicatory body, must render their decision by reference to a system of law. In the case of disputes arising under investment contracts, the system of law that will govern disputes is normally specified in the contract's choice of law clause. Such clauses normally point to the law of the host state, but in some cases the law of the home state may be stipulated where the investment activities are closely related to the host state's legal system.[29] Quite often other well-regarded systems of law are specified, such as that of England and Wales or New York State. IIAs usually specify the law applicable to investor–state disputes by reference to the law of the relevant treaty itself, often supplemented by the rules of international law. For example, the ECT states: 'A Tribunal established under paragraph (4) shall decide the issues in dispute in accordance with this Treaty and applicable rules

---

[29] *Colt Industries* v. *The Republic of Korea*, ICSID Case No. ARB/84/2 (3 Aug 1990).

and principles of international law.'[30] Somewhat more elaborate choice of law provision can be found in some Latin American IIAs, such as the Argentina–Netherlands BIT of 1992 which specifies:

> The Arbitration Tribunal addressed in accordance with paragraph (5) of this Article shall decide on the basis of the law of the Contracting Party which is a party to the dispute (including its rules on the conflict of law), the provisions of the present Agreement, special Agreements concluded in relation to the investment concerned as well as such rules of international law as may be applicable.[31]

This points to a mix of host state law, any systems of law specified in contractual commitments and international law. International law is often taken into account by tribunals even when it is not expressly referred to in an IIA or in an investment contract, reflecting a reluctance on the part of tribunals to forego international law entirely in case the relevant domestic law is arbitrary or results in manifest unfairness.[32]

Merely identifying the substantive law by which the tribunal must render its decision is often not enough as many treaty parties will have established specific interpretations of features of their treaties which they wish to be binding on tribunals. Some IIAs accordingly authorize the issuing of joint interpretations by the parties regarding certain features of the treaty which will bind the arbitral tribunal. This can be seen for example in the Japan–Mexico FTA of 2004 which specifies that:

> 2. An interpretation of a provision of this Agreement adopted by the Joint Committee shall be binding on a Tribunal established under this Section. Such interpretation shall be made publicly available through the means that each Party considers appropriate.[33]

This treaty goes on to provide that the Joint Committee shall interpret certain provisions and then issue a binding interpretation on the tribunal:

> Where a disputing Party asserts as a defense that the measure alleged to be a breach is within the scope of a reservation or exception set out in Annex 6, Annex 7, Annex 8 or Annex 9, on request of the disputing Party, the Tribunal shall request the Joint Committee to adopt an interpretation on

---

[30] Art 26(6).   [31] Art 10(7).
[32] As in *SPP* v. *Egypt*, 20 May 1992, 3 ICSID Reports 189.
[33] Art 84(2) (17 Sept 2004).

the issue. The Joint Committee, within 60 days of delivery of the request, shall adopt an interpretation and submit in writing its interpretation to the Tribunal.[34]

One interesting innovation in some recent IIAs are clauses empowering the state party which is not the respondent in the ongoing dispute settlement (i.e. the home state of the investor) to make submissions relating to the interpretation of particular elements of the treaty. Such a provision can be seen for example in the Japan–Peru BIT of 2008.[35] This helps establish a system through which ambiguities in the treaty can be resolved by the parties themselves rather than by recourse to the appointed tribunal.

8.5.6 Other Common Features of Investor–State Dispute Settlement Provisions

There are several other common features of IIAs regarding the investor-state dispute mechanism that are worth mentioning in brief. First, in some cases, limitation periods are applied to exclude claims that are submitted to arbitration too long after the dispute arose. Such rules guard against problems caused by delay such as changes in government or decay of evidence. This is done by reference to a refinement of the consent to arbitration tendered by treaty parties. Canada's Model BIT of 2004 specifies that claims cannot be submitted if more than three years have elapsed from the date at which the investor knew (or should have known) about the alleged breach.[36] Limitation periods are common in all spheres of law.

The ability of the tribunal to award interim or provisional measures before the ultimate disposition of the award occurs can be quite important to parties which risk being adversely affected because of the length of proceedings. Accordingly, some tribunals specifically provide for this power, as in the Japan–Peru BIT of 2008, which makes express mention of the capacity of tribunals to issue orders to preserve evidence.[37] These powers are regularly exercised by arbitration tribunals and are also a feature of specific institutional rules, such as those of ICSID.

The ability of tribunals to consolidate claims has become virtually essential given that one measure imposed by a government has the potential to affect more than one investor. This could lead to a situation where

---

[34] Art 89.   [35] Art 18 (22 Nov 2008).   [36] Art 22.2.   [37] Art 18 (22 Nov 2008).

multiple investors bring effectively the same claim against the host state, which can place undue pressure on the respondent as well as raise costs. Some IIAs address this kind of parallel proceedings by allowing for these claims to be brought together. Article 32 of the Canada Model BIT offers a specimen of such a provision:

> 2. Where a Tribunal established under this Article is satisfied that claims submitted to arbitration under Article 27 (Submission of a Claim to Arbitration) have a question of law or fact in common, the Tribunal may, in the interests of fair and efficient resolution of the claims, and after hearing the disputing parties, by order: (a) assume jurisdiction over, and hear and determine together, all or part of the claims; or (b) assume jurisdiction over, and hear and determine one or more of the claims, the determination of which it believes would assist in the resolution of the others.

Claims may be consolidated if they have common questions of law or fact and joining them serves the interests of fairness and efficiency.

Some IIAs contain enforcement provisions which ensure that decisions of investment arbitration tribunals will have effect in the domestic courts of the party states. Such provisions, which are not required in the case of ICSID arbitrations (of which more will be discussed below), recognize the reality that a binding decision of an arbitration tribunal is useless if the losing party cannot be compelled to follow through with the order by paying compensation. Awards of most ordinary commercial arbitration tribunals are enforceable (and recognized, essentially meaning that they cannot be reheard by another court) under the New York Convention on the Recognition and Enforcement of Foreign Arbitral Awards,[38] but this regime is not required if the IIA itself provides for recognition and enforcement. An enforcement (and recognition) provision may be found in the ECT: 'The awards of arbitration ... shall be final and binding upon the parties to the dispute ... Each Contracting Party shall carry out without delay any such award and shall make provision for the effective enforcement in its Area of such awards.'[39]

Lastly, as noted in the previous chapter, some IIAs specify the nature of the remedies that a tribunal may award. Such provisions tend to limit

---

[38] Convention on the Recognition and Enforcement of Foreign Arbitral Awards, 330 UNTS 38 (10 June 1958).
[39] Art 26(8).

remedies to monetary compensation or restitution of property, as in the same section of the ECT noted above: 'An award of arbitration concerning a measure ... of the disputing Contracting Party shall provide that the Contracting Party may pay monetary damages in lieu of any other remedy granted.' Most IIAs evince a preference for monetary remedies.

8.6 Arbitration Systems

A large portion of investment arbitration is ad hoc, which means that the tribunal is constituted for that particular dispute at hand outside an institutional framework. Adjudicators are selected and assembled by the parties for the purpose of deciding upon that particular matter, often by reference to a specific set of procedural rules; the most well-known for the purposes of international investment law are those developed by UNCI-TRAL (the United Nations Commission on International Trade Law). As an alternative to ad hoc arbitration for the settlement of investment disputes there is also institutional arbitration, in which a specific system of procedural rules will be used which will govern the arbitration along with its own administrative structure to assist in the process. Some common arbitration institutions are the LCIA and the ICC. The most popular institutional arbitration forum in international investment law is ICSID. The key procedural features of ICSID and other systems will now be examined. This section will also provide some background to the Iran–US Claims Tribunal, which has rendered a number of significant investor–state dispute settlement awards.

8.6.1 ICSID

The Convention on the Settlement of Investment Disputes Between States and the Nationals of Other States (the ICSID Convention, also known as the Washington Convention) entered into force on 14 October 1966. ICSID provides for the settlement of disputes between host states and foreign investors from other states through arbitration as well as conciliation, addressing a gap that had existed in international law where private parties could not bring claims against states for breach of international obligations. ICSID was created by the World Bank as a tool of international economic development with the rationale that the availability of neutral dispute settlement for investment disputes would help make developing states more attractive to foreign firms. As a consequence of ICSID's popularity in the last few decades it is now regularly used as a forum for the resolution of disputes involving developed states, so much so in fact that ICSID has become a household name, certainly among lawyers. The seat of ICSID is in Washington DC at the offices of the World Bank, although the seat does not necessarily determine the place of proceedings. The parties may decide on another place for it and frequently do so. ICSID enjoys wide membership among developed and emerging economies and is specified as the procedural mechanism to resolve investor–state disputes arising under many IIAs and investment contracts worldwide. Its dominant status can be attributed to its flexible rules that enable parties to structure the arbitration process to fit their needs combined with the degree of certainty for consistency and predictability. Many of the accusations that have been levied against ICSID as a forum, including its alleged bias against developing states in favour of investors, have been dispelled following recent empirical studies.[40] Over the years, Argentina has been the dominant respondent state in ICSID arbitrations. Most disputes have been brought under BITs, and the most common sector for disputes is oil and gas.[41]

Some of the key features of ICSID are as follows. First, under Art 25 of the ICSID Convention, the jurisdiction of ICSID extends to any legal dispute arising directly out of an investment between a Contracting State (a signatory of the ICSID Convention) and a national of another Contracting State. With respect to the parties, ICSID's jurisdiction over contracting states and nationals of other contracting states has been extended through its Additional Facility rules, which allow claims to be brought where only one party has a connection to ICSID (either the host state has ratified ICSID or the investor comes from a state which has done so). The relevance of the Additional Facility rules has diminished somewhat, given that ICSID Convention membership is near universal (151 states as of late 2015). Persistent hold-outs include some of the large emerging markets such as India and Russia. Secondly, with regards to subject matter, the existence of an 'investment' remains a highly contentious matter, engaging the debates

---

[40] S. Franck, 'The ICSID Effect? Considering Potential Variations in Arbitration Awards' 51:4 *Virginia Journal of International Law* 977 (2011).

[41] *ICSID Annual Report, 2015* (4 Sept 2015).

that were discussed in Chapter 3. But the ICSID Convention itself does not define 'investment', leaving it up to parties to set their own definition of this concept in their IIAs or investment contracts. ICSID tribunals normally defer to definitions contained in these instruments. Lastly, ICSID will only concern itself with a genuine legal dispute, not diplomatic or political ones. Simple differences of views on certain issues that do not have a bearing on enforceable legal rights are outside ICSID's purview. Investors must therefore frame their complaint against host states in concrete legal terms, referencing breach of legal entitlements.

As all arbitration is based on consent, Art 25 of the ICSID Convention specifies that the parties to the dispute must consent in writing to submit the dispute to the Centre. Mere ratification of the Convention does not satisfy this requirement. When the parties have given their consent, no party may withdraw its consent unilaterally. Whether or not formal consent has been tendered is often itself the subject of a dispute, with ICSID tribunals maintaining the power to determine their own jurisdiction in this matter. For example, in the recent dispute *PNG* v. *Papua New Guinea*[42] the tribunal evaluated whether the host state had granted consent in domestic legislation governing investment. Looking at the statute closely, the tribunal held that the provision's natural and ordinary meaning was a declaration that the terms of the investment statute applied to foreign investments but did not specifically grant consent to ICSID. Rather, the statute merely contemplated that future consent was required for submission of claims to ICSID. The tribunal accordingly dismissed the case for lack of jurisdiction.

It must be acknowledged that consent as tendered by parties will be valid according to its own terms. ICSID tribunals will take jurisdiction only over disputes that are covered by the parameters of the consent. In this regard, Art 26 of the Convention further establishes that consent to arbitration through ICSID shall be deemed to be consent to such arbitration to the exclusion of any other remedy, unless otherwise stated. In other words, the exhaustion of local remedies is excluded unless otherwise stated. So once the parties have given consent to ICSID arbitration, they have lost their right to seek relief in another forum, such as a national court. This feature captures the 'self-contained' nature of ICSID proceedings that give it much of its appeal as a forum for dispute settlement. ICSID

---

[42] ICSID Case No. ARB/13/33 (5 May 2015).

arbitrations do not need the support of local courts, and all other proceedings are foreclosed, preventing vexatious litigation on multiple fronts. Of course, states may insist in advance on the use of the domestic court system first through an exhaustion of local remedies clause if they wish, and this should be seen as a condition on its consent to ICSID arbitration. As a further manifestation of the self-contained nature of ICSID arbitration, Art 27 of the Convention provides that the arbitration process is insulated from inter-state claims through the exclusion of diplomatic protection. In other words, once the arbitration has begun, investors cannot attempt to use diplomatic channels to place pressure on the respondent state. The home state of the investor would be precluded by this provision from taking any diplomatic measures in this regard. It is often said that this feature of the Convention 'de-politicizes' the dispute.

Regarding the identity of the adjudicators of disputes, ICSID maintains a Panel of Conciliators and a Panel of Arbitrators. These are effectively lists of persons who may act as conciliators (informal alternative dispute settlement) or arbitrators (the formal binding adjudication procedure). In theory the lists are intended to help the parties to the proceedings find appropriate individuals who can resolve disputes. To be clear, an individual does not have to be on the list to be chosen as an arbitrator – parties are free to choose whomever they wish to act as an arbitrator, although such choices may be challenged by opposing parties as is customary in arbitration. There are, however, a set of qualifications that all individuals must possess in order to act as arbitrators. Under Art 14 of the Convention these qualifications include high moral character, recognized competence in the fields of law, commerce, industry or finance and the ability to exercise independent judgement. Qualification as a lawyer is not required. In practice there is a very small pool of individuals who have appeared as ICSID arbitrators, a fact which has not gone unnoticed by commentators. A core group of twenty-five arbitrators, of whom almost half hold European nationality, has been shown to exist, with very few originating from developing countries.[43] Once selected, the tribunal will consist of a sole arbitrator (which is quite rare) or any uneven number of arbitrators as the parties shall agree with the default option being three people, one appointed by each party and the third appointed by the designated

[43] S. Puig, 'Social Capital in the Arbitration Market' 25:2 *European Journal of International Law* 387 (2014).

president among the two who have been chosen. The appointment process is often quite lengthy and represents one of the crucial strategic decisions of the arbitration process. The tribunal will decide questions by a majority of the votes of all its members. Members of the tribunal may attach individual opinions to the award, although this is uncommon. Recently there has been a trend for tribunal members to issue dissent judgments although the purpose of this practice is questionable given that, as will be mentioned in a moment, there is no appeal available under ICSID rules. One obvious explanation for this practice is that arbitrators seek to ensure that their reputation as pro-investor or pro-state is not tarnished in order to facilitate further appointments.

The ICSID Convention does not provide substantial rules for the relationship between host states and foreign investors. It is merely designed to establish a procedural framework for the settlement of investment disputes based on laws found in other agreements, such as IIAs or investment contracts. Under Art 42, the tribunal is empowered to render its decision on the dispute in accordance with the rules of law as may be agreed by the parties. In the absence of such agreement (which may appear in the IIA as noted above), the tribunal shall apply the law of the Contracting State Party to the dispute, and such rules of international law as may be applicable. Art 42 is intended to provide both flexibility and certainty to parties. There is flexibility in that the parties have the autonomy to choose the legal rules that they want, and certainty in that the host state law will otherwise govern. The default reference to the host state's law is intuitively appealing because one would presume that the legal environment of the host state should naturally be assumed to govern events which occur in that state's territory. Moreover, a state's legal system is presumably a key feature of what facilitates its economic advantage in terms of low cost labour or market dynamism.

Under Art 43 the ICSID tribunal may, unless the parties say otherwise, at any stage of the proceedings call upon the parties to produce documents or other evidence and to visit the scene connected with the dispute, and conduct such inquiries as it may deem appropriate. This power was exercised for example in the decision *Tidewater* v. *Venezuela*[44] which involved a procedural order regarding the production of documents in relation to an alleged expropriation. The tribunal ruled that the claimant must produce

---

[44] ICSID Case No. ARB/10/5 (29 March 2011).

various charter agreements relating to the company's corporate structure. The host state was ordered to conduct a new investigation into any documents which it might require from the claimant. While ICSID tribunals have broad evidentiary powers in terms of the production of documents and expert witnesses, the tribunal has no power to summon witnesses although witnesses, particularly experts, often do give evidence at the behest of the parties.

Access to ICSID arbitration hearings remains limited. The deliberations of ICSID tribunals tend to take place in private and remain confidential. Recall that this feature is one of the key advantages of arbitration where there is often negative publicity associated with conventional litigation which can affect a company's value or a state's international reputation. This is why all attendance at hearings is subject to both parties' consent. As suggested above, there have been increasing demands for transparency in investor–state dispute settlement because of the public interest matters engaged in many disputes. It is important to note that the ICSID Convention itself says nothing about confidentiality. Confidentiality must be requested by parties, most of whom regularly do so. Still, while the hearings themselves tend to be inaccessible, many ICSID awards and other procedural decisions are now publicly reported and made available on ICSID's website (subject to both parties' consent). This feature undermines some of the assertions made by the media and other public interest groups that ICSID is a secret business persons' court. In terms of participation in the proceedings, amicus curiae briefs may now be permitted by the tribunal regarding a matter within the scope of the dispute. This determination will depend on whether this would assist the tribunal in making its decision and whether the non-party has a significant interest in the proceedings.

Under Art 50 if there is a dispute between the parties as to the meaning or scope of an award, either party may request interpretation of the award by an application in writing to the Secretary General of ICSID. The purpose of interpretation is to clarify points which had been settled. It must not address new issues that go beyond the limits of the award. Either party may also request revision of an award if some fact of such a nature that would decisively affect the award has become known to them. The new element must be one of fact and not of law, and again the fact must be capable of affecting the award decisively, either on jurisdiction (whether or not the tribunal could hear the matter) or merits (the substance of the claim). New facts regarding the quantification of damages would not count for the purposes of revision.

As noted above, there is no appeal from the decision of an ICSID tribunal. The lack of an appellate mechanism is thought to be a major procedural advantage of the ICSID system because it achieves finality, and as such shortens the timeframes and lowers the costs associated with protracted claims going through several layers of adjudication. Controlling costs is vital considering most obviously lawyers' fees but also the costs of ICSID itself, which is currently US $3000 per day. Still, the lack of an appeals mechanism within ICSID has been cited by a number of commentators as indicative of the ICSID system's illegitimacy as a forum for the administration of justice.[45] The capacity to appeal a legal interpretation to a higher authority is often seen as an essential component of a fair and properly functional legal system. More practically speaking, the lack of an appellate system was believed to be one of the reasons that some Latin American countries withdrew from the ICSID Convention. An appeals system for first-level tribunal decisions has been expressly contemplated by the proposed investment chapter of the TTIP and the EU–Vietnam FTA (of which more below). It is difficult to envisage precisely what form an appellate court from which ICSID decisions could be heard would take. Since there are thousands of IIAs, it would be impossible to establish an authoritative court which had specialized expertise in each of these instruments.

While there is no appeal from an ICSID decision, an award may be annulled under the procedure outlined in Art 52. But the grounds of annulment are very narrow. Either party can request that an award be annulled if the tribunal was not properly constituted; if the tribunal manifestly exceeded its powers; if there was corruption on the part of a member of the tribunal; if there has been a serious departure from a fundamental rule or procedure; or if the award failed to state the reasons on which it was based. An ad hoc committee of arbitrators will then be selected to assess the award and annul it if the allegation turns out to be accurate. Commentators have noted that the selection of the annulment committee itself places too much power in the hands of the Chairman of ICSID (who is also the President of the World Bank), removing control from the

---

[45] E.g. D. Collins, *The BRIC States and Outward Foreign Direct Investment* (Oxford University Press, 2013).

parties.[46] While the consistency of annulment decisions has been criticized, generally speaking most annulment committees have taken a very conservative approach with respect to their own authority, deferring to the decision of the tribunal. An annulment committee recently denied the application for annulment in *El Paso Energy International Company* v. *Argentina*[47] on the basis that Argentina had been given ample opportunity to present its case and that the tribunal had properly established its jurisdiction under the IIA. Similarly, in *Alapli Elektrik* v. *Turkey*[48] the annulment committee dismissed the investor's application for annulment in its entirety, noting that the original arbitrator had applied the law correctly when ruling that the investor's corporate restructuring was for the sole purpose of gaining access to international arbitration. The ad hoc committee reiterated that it cannot review the original tribunal's decision, as the investor appeared to want it to do, but only verify whether the tribunal identified and applied the proper law to the dispute, which it did in this instance. The annulment committee may stay the enforcement of the award pending its decision, and an annulled award can be subsequently submitted to a new tribunal. The consequence of an annulment is a total invalidation of the original decision. Compared to the overall number of cases, there have been very few requests of annulment since the establishment of ICSID.

Crucially, there is no power of review of an ICSID award by a domestic court, as there are in other types of arbitration. This insulation from interference is perhaps the greatest procedural advantage of an ICSID arbitration compared to other dispute settlement systems in international investment law. Under Art 53 an award shall be binding on the parties and shall not be subject to any appeal other than the request for revision or annulment mentioned above. Each party shall abide by and comply with the terms of the award, except for any stay of enforcement pending revision or annulment. This also means that the place of arbitration in ICSID proceedings is irrelevant for the award's validity and enforcement, which is automatic. ICSID arbitration is de-localized and independent of judicial interference in the country where the proceedings take place and the award it rendered. Moreover, a party to ICSID proceedings may not

---

[46] D. Collins, 'ICSID Annulment Committee: Too Much Discretion to the Chairman?' 30:4 *Journal of International Arbitration* 333–44 (2013).

[47] ICSID Case No. ARB/03/15 (31 Oct 2011).   [48] ICSID Case No. ARB/08/13 (10 July 2014).

initiate action before a domestic court to seek annulment or other types of review of an ICSID award.

Finally, with respect to the ultimate enforcement of an award, under Art 54 courts of all contracting states of the ICSID Convention must treat ICSID awards as the equivalent to final judgments of their highest courts. Many other arbitration systems require domestic laws to be enforced, although enforcement provisions in IIAs tend to ensure that this will occur, as discussed above. Whether or not host states actually comply with awards in terms of paying out compensation claims to winning investors is another matter. It is often suggested that ICSID's affiliation with the World Bank acts as an incentive to comply. If a state party refuses to pay the compensation as awarded, they may not be able to secure a loan from the World Bank in the future, which can be a significant incentive for a developing country. The compliance record of ICSID awards is generally quite good, although Argentina, for example, has failed to fulfil all of its compensation obligations pursuant to ICSID decisions. Practically speaking, compliance tends to be secured on the basis of a host state's reputation to the international business community. If it does not pay its obligations then future investors will be reluctant to invest within its territory. It should be noted also that should a state fail to comply with an award issued by an ICSID tribunal, the investor's right of diplomatic protection is re-engaged and its home state can take action to demand the losing state pay the compensation and or damages.

In addition to its rules on formal arbitration, the ICSID Convention also provides for conciliation. Conciliation is not based on an adversarial procedure resulting in a binding third-party decision but aims to reach an agreed settlement. It is an informal process that is particularly appropriate where the parties are prepared to continue their cooperation in relation to the investment, and is often thought to be less costly than arbitration. Article 34 of the Convention provides for the establishment of a Conciliation Commission to clarify the issues in a dispute between the parties and endeavour to bring about agreement between them on mutually acceptable terms. Parties are required to cooperate in good faith with the Commission in order to enable it to carry out its functions. The Convention also includes rules relating to the constitution of the Commission which are substantially similar to those relating to the establishment of an arbitration panel. Conciliation Commissions maintain their own system of procedural rules which are more flexible and informal than those relating to arbitration. There has been limited application of the ICSID conciliation rules, possibly because parties have chosen not to make their requests for conciliation known.

8.6.2 Non-ICSID Systems

Chief among the non-ICSID procedural rules for the settlement of disputes between investors and host states are those of UNCITRAL, the United Nations Commission on International Trade Law. UNCITRAL itself was established by the United Nations in 1964 to harmonize international trade laws with a view to promoting economic development. Importantly for the resolution of investment disputes, UNCITRAL established a model system of procedural rules for international arbitration, originally drafted in 1985 but revised most recently in 2013. UNCITRAL does not establish an institutional setting for an arbitration: the parties must arrange this themselves. As noted above, reference to UNCITRAL rules can be found in a number of IIAs. UNCITRAL rules are comprehensive, covering all aspects of an arbitration from the appointment of arbitrators, jurisdiction, interim measures to awards and enforcement. The rules have some limited differences from other systems such as those of ICSID. One of the distinctive features of the UNCITRAL rules is that they tend to require very specific statements of claim as well as a clear indication of the relief that is sought. Unlike ICSID, under UNCITRAL rules the parties have the option of seeking provisional measures, such as injunctions, directly from domestic courts which results in a considerable time-saving. UNCITRAL-based hearings, initially designed for commercial arbitration, were seen as less transparent than those of ICSID. UNCITRAL recently created its Rules on Transparency in Treaty-Based Investor–state Arbitration in an effort to address some of the concerns about the openness of its procedures. These rules, which were mentioned in Chapter 2, will apply automatically to all UNCITRAL arbitrations, unless the state parties to the relevant IIA agree otherwise.[49] UNCITRAL's transparency rules aim at enhancing public accessibility as well as participation in dispute settlement, including notably a default rule that hearings will be publicly held.[50] Most importantly, arbitrations constituted under UNCITRAL rules are not automatically enforceable. Unless the relevant IIA itself provides that the arbitration decisions issued under

---

[49] Art 1.   [50] Art 6(1).

the terms of the treaty will be enforceable, this means that enforcement will rely on the New York Convention, which provides that arbitration decisions may be reviewed on various grounds for procedural irregularity by domestic courts. There is no official data as to how often UNCITRAL rules are used, but they are probably used somewhat less than ICSID which normally handles roughly half of all recorded investor–state disputes. While it is not self-enforcing like ICSID, UNCITRAL is linked to the UN, a body which by virtue of its composition and voting structure is more representative of developing countries. This may be one reason why it has become a popular system of rules for disputes involving these countries.

The Iran–US Claims Tribunal, located in The Hague, Netherlands, has been one of the leading fora for dispute settlement in international investment law. This specialized tribunal was created during a particular historical circumstance during the aftermath of the Islamic Revolution in 1979 when a number of expropriations of US firms, particularly in the petroleum sector, took place. While the Iran–US Claims Tribunal was also able to resolve state-to-state claims between the USA and Iran, its primary function was investor–state dispute settlement. More than 4000 private claims from US investors against Iran (and Iranian investors against the US) have been heard by the tribunal which was created in 1981. It was closed to new claims after 1982 and issued its final judgment (on investor-state matters) in the early 2000s. When the tribunal was first constituted, US \$1 billion of Iranian money held by Iranian banks in the USA was placed in an account in the Netherlands out of which claims against Iran recognized by the tribunal would be satisfied, with a provision that whenever the balance in the security account fell below US \$500 million, the Iranian government would have to top it up. Panels composed under the Iran–US Claims Tribunal consisted of nine members, three of whom were appointed by the US, three by Iran and three by agreement of the two parties. UNCITRAL rules applied to the proceedings although the Tribunal modified these rules to some extent. Extensive case law was generated by the tribunal and although there was no principle of precedent, there was an effort by the variously constituted tribunals to achieve consistency. Some may question the value of jurisprudence from the Iran–US Claims Tribunal in terms of establishing broadly applicable rules of international investment law because of the tribunal's particular historical and factual context. It is generally regarded as a landmark contributor in the development of international investment law, establishing key principles of expropriation and compensation.

The LCIA is one of the world's leading arbitration institutions. It has operated since 1986 as a successor to the London Chamber of Arbitration, which itself dates from the nineteenth century. The LCIA maintains its own set of procedural rules for arbitrations and provides facilities for the conduct of arbitrations as well as a roster of panellists to assist parties in the selection of arbitrators. The rules are comprehensive and flexible, allowing parties to maximize their control of the arbitral procedure as needed. While it was originally designed for commercial arbitrations, it can and has been used to resolve investor–state disputes brought under IIAs and investment contracts, although use of LCIA rules for these types of disputes is uncommon. The LCIA rules operate under a principle of confidentiality, although this can be waived upon consent of both parties. The LCIA offers mediation services and holds events of interest to arbitrators, practitioners and students.

The ICC is an international organization dedicated to the promotion of international business. Its arbitration facilities are perhaps the most well-known in the world, having been established at the ICC's headquarters in Paris in 1923. Since its creation, the ICC has administered more than 20,000 cases from more than 180 countries. In addition to those of the provision of administrative assistance to arbitrating parties, the ICC has its own system of procedural rules governing international arbitration which came into effect in 2012 as well as a roster of approved arbitrators from which the ICC itself can select arbitrators for the parties if they empower it to do so. Awards issued by tribunals pursuant to ICC rules are flexible and efficient as well as binding and susceptible to enforcement anywhere in the world. The ICC itself does not render judgments or awards but the ICC Court supervises all arbitrations conducted under its rules from beginning to end, including a review of any issued awards for accuracy or administrative errors and assistance in enforcement. As with many other arbitration institutions, the ICC also offers mediation services.

Lastly, the Permanent Court of Arbitration (PCA) continues to play a key role in the settlement of investment disputes between investors and state governments. Also located in The Hague, the PCA was established in 1899 by The Hague Peace Conference. It is not truly an adjudicatory body but rather a forum which facilitates arbitration and conciliation, as well as fact-finding missions. Investor–state disputes are among the many varieties of claims which it administers between states and private parties. In addition to providing administrative support for the settlement of disputes, the PCA has its own rules of procedure or can adopt other ones, such as those of UNCITRAL upon which the PCA's own rules are largely based. It can also act as an appointing authority for the tribunal on behalf of parties should the parties choose to empower it to do so, and for this purpose it maintains a list of suitable arbitrators. If the parties consent, the PCA will publish documents relating to disputes on its website, such as final awards and other orders of the arbitration tribunal.

8.7 Enhanced Investor–State Dispute Settlement: New Regimes

Given the extensive controversy surrounding investor–state dispute settlement, in particular its lack of transparency and its perceived affront to the sovereignty of national courts, a new model of investor–state dispute settlement was proposed for the investment chapter of the TTIP in 2015.[51] This was conceived largely in response to the backlash against the existing system which resulted from the public consultation undertaken by the European Commission during the TTIP negotiations. The unique system of dispute settlement contained in the investment chapter of the TTIP (the negotiations of which are still ongoing at the time of writing) is no longer purely theoretical – it has been adopted in the EU–Vietnam FTA as well as the CETA, and is expected to form the basis of future European IIAs. Briefly, this new regime for investor–state dispute settlement consists of a roster of state-appointed arbitrators from which parties may select tribunal members. As these individuals are appointed by states rather than by the parties, they have the appearance of judges rather than arbitrators, lending a degree of public legitimacy to the process that many believed was lacking in conventional investor–state dispute settlement arbitration. There is also a code of conduct specified for all adjudicators, which has never been seen in another instrument and which again reflects concern that previous processes lacked integrity in this regard. Most remarkably, the new system establishes an appeal process from tribunal decisions to a standing body of full-time judges who are also designated by state

---

[51] http://trade.ec.europa.eu/doclib/docs/2015/september/tradoc_153807.pdf.

parties.[52] This is a truly revolutionary feature as investor–state dispute settlement decisions under all other systems had been final. The new 'investment court' model may be seen as something of a compromise between those who advocated for a complete removal of investor–state dispute settlement from IIAs and those who wished it to remain untouched. It is unclear whether this new system of investor–state dispute settlement will be adopted by other countries in addition to those of the EU, but if it is then it is poised to fundamentally change the landscape of dispute settlement in international investment law. Investor–state dispute settlement through international arbitration as contained in most IIAs has been challenged most vigorously in the context of treaties between two developed states where there is a strong rule of law and independent courts. In the case of the TTIP, for example, why would American investors not trust the ability and impartiality of EU courts, and vice versa? Still, the fact that many European states chose to include investor–state arbitration provisions in their pre-Lisbon BITs with other EU Member States suggests that there is some mistrust with respect to European Member States' courts' capacity to resolve these types of disputes effectively.[53]

8.8 Costs

Costs in investor–state dispute settlement can in many instances amount to several million dollars for large and complex matters. The concept of costs includes the fees of the lawyers hired to represent the parties (normally the most expensive element), the arbitrators' fees, and charges incurred in using an arbitration institution's facilities, which can amount to several thousand dollars per day. Few IIAs make express reference to the costs in arbitration proceedings, although this is not unheard of. The Japan–Oman BIT provides that each party will bear its own costs, but that provision refers to the state-to-state dispute settlement, not investor–state dispute settlement.[54] Australia's 2015 FTA with China provides somewhat more clarity in the matter, focusing on preliminary objections to the tribunal's jurisdiction and any related objections:

---

[52] EU–Vietnam FTA, Trade in Services, Investment and E-Commerce, Chapter II, Section 3.
[53] E.g. Germany–Poland (16 Sept 1989).   [54] Art 14(5).

> the tribunal may, if warranted, award to the prevailing disputing party rea-
> sonable costs and attorney's fees incurred in submitting or opposing [a pre-
> liminary objection to the tribunal's jurisdiction]. In determining whether
> such an award is warranted, the tribunal shall consider whether either the
> claimant's claim or the respondent's objection was frivolous, and shall
> provide the disputing parties a reasonable opportunity to comment.[55]

Canada's BIT with Mali of 2014 specifies that each party will bear its own
costs generally, but adds: 'the arbitral panel may, however, award that a
higher portion of costs be borne by one of the two Parties.'[56] The ICSID
Convention provides that the tribunal has the discretion to award costs,
unless the parties agree otherwise.[57] UNCITRAL rules state that arbitration
costs shall in principle be borne by the losing party,[58] although in many
cases both parties may succeed on some aspect of the dispute and fail on
others.

Tribunals tend to allocate costs depending on their view of the ret-
rospective assessment of the merits of the allegations and the defences,
often awarding costs where investors brought claims frivolously or where
the behaviour of the host state was particularly egregious. For example,
in *LETCO* v. *Liberia*, the tribunal awarded the full costs of the arbitration
to the claimants, forcing the respondents to pay the winner's expenses
because of Liberia's bad faith in pursuing domestic judicial proceedings in
order to nullify the arbitration.[59] In *ADC* v. *Hungary* the tribunal awarded
costs to the winning investor, observing that if claimants are not reim-
bursed for their costs, 'it could not be said that they were being made
whole'[60] because of the magnitude of the costs relative to the value of
the claim. ICSID tribunals have demonstrated a willingness to shift costs
onto the losing party in a number of recent cases based on the conduct of
parties during the proceedings.[61]

Commentators have observed that the traditional approach of investment tribunals has been to order that each party pays its own costs. This
is believed to encourage the use of arbitration by reducing the overall

---

[55] Art 9.16(7) (17 June 2015).   [56] Art 37(8) (28 Nov 2014).   [57] Art 61(2).
[58] Art 42(1).   [59] ICSID Case No. ARB/83/2, Award (31 March 1986), at 378.
[60] Award, 2 Oct 2006 at 533.
[61] E.g. *Renée Rose Levy and Gremcitel* v. *Peru*, ICSID Case No. ARB/11/17 (9 Jan 2015) and
Hassan Awdi v. *Romania*, ICSID Case No. ARB/10/13 (2 March 2015).

exposure of claimants, whereas placing one side's costs onto the other party (the 'loser pays' principle) can act as a deterrent to arbitration. This type of cost allocation increases the overall risk in the proceedings, even if the rewards of arbitration are enhanced by the prospect of having one's own costs paid by one's opponent in addition to the award itself.[62] A cost-shifting regime, rather than one in which each side pays its own expenses, may be less relevant in terms of motivation when claims are large relative to the anticipated costs of bringing them. This is often the case in modern investment arbitration where awards in the hundreds of millions of dollars are not uncommon. A 'loser pays' rule, however, could deter potential claimants in cases in which claimants are not confident in their claims and the claims are small relative to the anticipated costs.[63]

8.9 Conclusion

Investor–state dispute settlement through neutral and confidential arbitration is one of the pillars of international investment law. It is provided for in almost every IIA and recognized by every major capital importing and exporting nation in the world. The near universal adoption of the ICSID Convention means that awards issued by investor–state arbitrations through ICSID procedures are automatically recognized and enforceable in most countries, precluding the requirement of a second expensive and often time-consuming domestic procedure. An established investment treaty arbitration jurisprudence has emerged, partly as a consequence of the preference among parties for a small group of arbitrators, enhancing the consistency and predictability of the dispute settlement process. This has contributed to the legitimization of international investment law as a coherent discipline that straddles public and private international law, a factor which may be responsible for some of the observed growth in FDI of the last few decades. While provisions on investor–state dispute settlement in IIAs tend to be brief, reference to a specific system of procedural rules (such as ICSID or UNCITRAL) combined with a clear choice of law provides sufficient certainty for firms and governments that the substantive

---

[62] B S. Vasani and A. Ugale, 'Cost Allocation in Investment Arbitration: Back toward Diversification,' *Columbia FDI Perspectives*, No. 100 (29 July 2013).

[63] J. Nicholson and J. Gaffney, 'Cost Allocation in Investment Arbitration: Forward towards Incentivization', *Columbia FDI Perspectives*, No. 123 (9 June 2014).

features of these treaties can be adjudicated in an effective, impartial and typically confidential manner.

Yet despite the wide acceptance of investor–state dispute settlement as a mechanism for the resolution of claims under IIAs and investment contracts, much controversy surrounds this feature of international investment law and will likely do so for some time. Calls for increased transparency and access, a roster of approved arbitrators as well as the inclusion of appellate mechanisms continue to be issued by commentators and governments alike. Whether or not such features, particularly the ground-breaking addition of a dedicated appellate court for all claims, will ever become standard is highly questionable, particularly since this type of modification will most likely undermine the speed, cost-effectiveness and confidentiality that makes arbitration the attractive process that commercial parties and governments have come to expect. Undue emphasis on the procedural improvements to investor–state dispute settlement such as these runs the risk of obscuring more fundamental debates about the nature of dispute settlement in international investment law, including the important role of public interest as a justification for a state's conduct and the associated need for investors to bear responsibility for adverse consequences of their commercial pursuits. These issues are the subject of the next chapter.

9 Public Interest Issues: The Environment, Human Rights and Culture

9.1 Introduction

The activities of international firms can place stress on the environments in which they locate. This can take the form of normal competitive pressures, but it can also constitute hardships which are often secondary to the business activities themselves. Economists call these adverse effects 'externalities' which, because of their unintended nature, tend to go unnoticed by host states seeking to attract FDI. Chief among these is environmental harm itself. As companies, especially in the extractive sectors, pursue lower cost resources they may unintentionally damage the natural ecosystem. Foreign investment may also have negative impacts on labour: as again firms seek to lower their expenses, they may end up underpaying their employees or in the worst cases, exposing them to unsafe working conditions. FDI can also pose challenges to public health, particularly where the products or services in which the foreign investors trade are in some way dangerous to consumers. Lastly, the cultures of many host states are vulnerable to the influence of foreign firms, sometimes in ways that are hard to capture or assess empirically. The challenge to international investment law is to recognize these situations and to make allowances for host states who seek to mitigate these harms by enacting regulations which may transgress the protections they have offered to foreign firms in treaties. Since such measures may in some cases represent disguised protectionism, this exercise can require a delicate balancing of the policy goals, the ways in which they are facilitated and the expectations of foreign investors as generated by IIAs and customary international law.

This chapter will consider the extent to which host states are able to circumvent the substantive obligations they have made in investment treaties for various public policy purposes, such as the protection of the environment, culture, labour and by extension human rights. These justifications may be asserted on the basis of exceptions contained in investment treaties or based on general carve-outs affording states the right to regulate on a wide range of matters. Where bright line rules are not always available under international law, guidelines created by groups like the OECD and the World Bank have been established in an effort to control the harmful effects of FDI. These will be examined near the end of this chapter.

The possibility that modern IIAs would expressly allow for certain types of regulation taken in what might generally be described as 'the public interest' to defeat treaty obligations is somewhat ironic, given that the very purpose of IIAs adopted in the twentieth century was to constrain the policy space of newly independent countries and to curtail regulations enacted for these purposes, particularly those which culminated in the expropriation of foreign investments. Clearly the host state needs to protect the welfare of its citizens by maintaining a set of regulations which cannot be challenged under international law. At the same time, the host state must not be given carte blanche to enact whatever laws it wishes which might harm investments simply by referring to such actions as matters of public interest. To allow otherwise would be to defeat the very purpose of international investment law in the first place.

In many respects the struggle to achieve a balance between these competing interests represents perhaps the most fundamental tension of international investment law. The extent to which FDI impacts on the capacity of host states to enact laws which preserve public interest issues is a matter of much debate. It is often suggested that international investment law, developed at the behest of the investors by their home states and the host states ardently seeking to attract it, has been insufficiently sensitive to this topic.[1] This is in large part because the concept of 'public interest' as a justifying norm is notoriously difficult to define. The debate over the limits of a state's regulatory capacity in pursuit of these goals which might interfere with a foreign investor's legitimate expectations enshrined in other provisions of IIAs is particularly acute in the context of expropriation, where public interest is one of the requirements for an expropriation to be viewed as lawful. The relevance of public interest-orientated exceptions to IIAs is also linked to the debate surrounding access to and participation in international investment arbitration. Non-parties such as indigenous groups or NGOs are often the organizations that are most likely

---

[1] See generally M. Sornarajah, *The International Law on Foreign Investment* (Cambridge University Press, 2010).

to raise these types of concerns because the host states may have a vested interest in not challenging the actions of their investors. The extent to which IIAs expressly consider the public interest will now be examined.

9.2 Categories of Public Interest

9.2.1 General Public Interest and Sustainable Development

IIAs tend not to specify the scope of a host state's discretion to regulate in the public interest in favour of broad statements regarding policy objectives or, in some cases, expansive concepts like sustainable development. Such indeterminate justifications for regulatory interference with foreign investors are often covered in the preamble. While preambular language is generally not binding on treaty parties, it provides context for the interpretation of other concrete obligations found elsewhere in the instrument; indeed this is one of the interpretive aids specified in the VCLT.[2] In that sense the preamble can be said to constitute the soul or spirit of the treaty.

With this in mind, some IIAs have included positive language in their preambles to reinforce the commitments of the Contracting Parties to safeguard public interest. For example, the preamble of the New Zealand–Taiwan FTA of 2013 recognizes the Contracting Parties' 'right to regulate, and to introduce new regulations on the supply of goods, services and investment in order to meet government policy objectives'.[3] This phrase is a concession to public interest at perhaps its most general level. It is doubtful whether, given its vagueness, this provision could functionally work as a defence to a claim for violation of an obligation such as FET or, even less so, expropriation without compensation.

Acknowledging a developmental purpose expressly, the India–Singapore Comprehensive Economic Cooperation Agreement of 2005 specifies in its preamble that parties reaffirm 'their right to pursue economic philosophies suited to their development goals and their right to regulate activities to realise their national policy objectives'.[4] Again, this language is so broadly conceived that it could potentially extend to any measure which had a developmental aim, such as would characterize, for example, infant industry protections that would otherwise be discriminatory against foreign firms.

---

[2] Art 31(2).   [3] 10 July 2013.   [4] 29 June 2005.

An equally generous example of preambular language addressing public policy can be seen in Canada's 2013 FTA with Honduras, which speaks of state parties 'Preserv[ing] their flexibility to safeguard the public welfare'. Public welfare is of course left undefined, allowing space for vast fields of regulation which could have adverse effects on international investors.

In a more concrete fashion, the US Model BIT refers to several distinct public policy goals in its preamble: 'Desiring to achieve [economic cooperation] in a manner consistent with the protection of health, safety, and the environment, and the promotion of internationally recognized labor rights.' Yet, again, this is only the preamble and as such it is unclear whether laws which have their basis in these objectives could allow host states to escape liability for breaches of the substantive obligations found elsewhere in the treaty.

In addition to generally worded references to public interest, sustainable development is a non-specific concept that is increasingly referenced in treaties and policy documents concerning the regulatory objectives of governments at all levels. The essence of the principle of sustainable development is that economic growth strategies should be pursued which are mindful of their long-term feasibility. In other words, resources should be used in such a way that future generations may be able to benefit from them. While it may initially have been associated with the conservation of natural resources and the protection of the environment, today it arguably captures a wide range of policy goals which can affect foreign investors, including not only the environment but also health and safe working conditions. The Albania–Azerbaijan BIT of 2012 addresses this objective in its preamble: 'Desiring to achieve these objectives in a manner consistent with the protection of health, safety and the environment and the promotion of sustainable development.' The Canada Model BIT of 2004 specifies the objective of sustainable development in its preamble. The New Zealand–Malaysia FTA does the same in this manner:

> Aware that economic development, social development and environmental protection are components of sustainable development and that free trade agreements can play an important role in promoting sustainable development.[5]

---

[5] 26 Oct 2009.

As suggested above, by including this phrase in the preamble of the treaty, state parties are able to emphasize that interpretations which are favourable to these concerns should be those which are taken by arbitration tribunals. A study carried out in 2008 showed that there has been relatively limited reference to the language of the preamble of IIAs as indicative of the treaty's object and purpose by ICSID tribunals in particular.[6] Still, although the use of the preamble in this way has legal effects that are different from those of general exceptions, it does send the political signal that Contracting Parties do not place investment protection above other important public policy objectives, and this is not without its benefits in terms of structuring inward FDI.

Some IIAs speak of a general right to regulate without mentioning any particular goals or purpose. For example, the EU–Iraq BIT of 2012 states the following: 'Consistent with the provisions of this Section, each Party retains the right to regulate and to introduce new regulations to meet legitimate policy objectives.'[7] This would seem to confer considerable authority to host states to deviate from treaty guarantees.

In contrast, many of the public interest-based exceptions contained in IIAs are founded upon those which were specifically enumerated in the general exceptions of the treaties of the WTO. Contained in Art XX, the GATT's general exceptions which are of most relevance to international investment law are as follows:

(a) [measures] necessary to protect public morals;
(b) [measures] necessary to protect human, animal or plant life or health;...
(d) [measures] necessary to secure compliance with laws or regulations...including those relating to customs enforcement, the enforcement of monopolies...the protection of patents, trademarks and copyrights, and the prevention of deceptive practices;...
(g) [measures] relating to the conservation of exhaustible natural resources;

---

[6] O. Fauchauld, 'The Legal Reasoning of ICSID Tribunals – An Empirical Analysis' 19:2 *European Journal of International Law* 301 (2008) (only thirteen of ninety-eight decisions examined made reference to the preamble).

[7] Art 23.5 (11 May 2012).

Similarly, GATS Art XIV allows the following:

(a) [measures] necessary to protect public morals or to maintain public order;

(b) [measures] necessary to protect human, animal or plant life or health;

(c) [measures] necessary to secure compliance with laws or regulations... including those relating to: (i) the prevention of deceptive and fraudulent practices... (ii) the protection of the privacy of individuals... (iii) safety.

Both sets of exceptions, some of which will be referred to under specific public interest headings below, are subject to the overarching requirement that:

such measures are not applied in a manner which would constitute a means of arbitrary or unjustifiable discrimination between countries where the same conditions prevail, or a disguised restriction on international trade.[8]

This so-called 'chapeau' essentially governs the manner in which the exception is applied, and is often thought to contemplate a requirement of good faith. Language clearly inspired by these public policy exceptions is incorporated by reference into the investment chapters of the new CETA between Canada and the EU,[9] the TTIP[10] and the China–New Zealand Free Trade Agreement of 2008, which incorporates both GATT XX and GATS XIV.[11] The ACIA repeats the general exceptions from GATS almost verbatim[12] and the MERCOSUR–India Preferential Trade Agreement expressly incorporates GATT Art XX.[13] Although only a handful of BITs have included general exceptions modelled on those of the GATT/GATS, the Canadian Model BIT borrows some language from the GATT and GATS, including categories for 'human, animal, plant life or health' and 'the conservation of living or non-living resources', both with the qualifier 'necessary'.[14] The use of these specific terms drawn from the WTO instruments suggests that states wish to acknowledge existing legal

---

[8] GATT Art XX, GATS Art XIV.   [9] Chapter 32 Art X.02.

[10] *Public Consultation on Modalities for Investment Protection and ISDS in TTIP*, http://trade.ec.europa.eu/doclib/docs/2014/march/tradoc_152280.pdf at 19–20.

[11] Art 200 (signed April 2008).   [12] Art 17.1 (signed 26 Feb 2009).

[13] Art 9 (signed 25 Jan 2004).

[14] Art 10.1(a) and (c) (2004). Canada includes general exceptions in eighteen of its BITs.

commitments made in other contexts when crafting investment commitments, rather than risk breaking new ground with phrasing that has not
been tested through decades of jurisprudence, as many of the GATT/GATS
exceptions have been by the WTO panels and Appellate Body.

Likewise, the negotiated draft of the investment chapter of the TTIP contains a provision which specifies a number of key policy areas which may
operate as justifications for breaches of the treaty's investor protections:

> The provisions of this section shall not affect the right of the Parties to reg-
> ulate within their territories through measures necessary to achieve legit-
> imate policy objectives, such as the protection of public health, safety,
> environment or public morals, social or consumer protection or promotion
> and protection of cultural diversity.[15]

This statement can also be found in the investment chapter of the innovative EU–Vietnam FTA of 2015.[16] The categories of environment, health,
safety (especially for workers) as well as cultural preservation alluded to
here represent the dominant categories of public interest protection found
in most IIAs. Each will be discussed in turn.

9.2.2 The Environment

Protection of the environment has been the purpose behind much domestic legislation as well as a number of international treaties. While there has
been much difficulty in achieving international regulatory consensus on
climate change, there are several environmental treaties controlling harmful emissions in geographically distinct areas. These, along with similarly
themed domestic legislation, often capture the 'polluter pays' principle
in which the party that was responsible for the environmental harm is
required to bear the costs of compensating those who are injured by it.
Given the existence of international obligations referencing environmental protection, a host state's implementation of regulations for this purpose
may arguably be viewed as legitimate under customary international law,
even if they have a detrimental impact on foreign investors and appear to
breach obligations enshrined in IIAs.

Still, criticisms that international investment law has been insensitive
to environmental issues fail to appreciate the reality that it is the primary

---

[15] Art 2(1).   [16] Art 13.1 bis.

responsibility of the host state to consider the potential effects on the environment, as indeed all other matters, when signing investment contracts or when setting conditions on investment in IIAs. Pre-existing environmental standards under national laws should in turn dictate the legitimate expectations of the investor which are protected in the treaty, as under FET, for example. Changes of policy which are inconsistent with these laws may, however, support claims for compensation. National laws enacted for the purpose of protecting the environment will of course bind foreign investors just as they do local ones. Compliance with such measures may involve additional costs for firms, making host states with the strictest environmental standards less appealing. It is therefore in the economic interest of host states to keep their environmental standards low in order to remain attractive to foreign investors. This 'pollution haven' theory, mentioned in Chapter 1, is most closely associated with the extractive industries. As suggested earlier, there is actually little evidence that polluting industries relocate to jurisdictions with lower environmental standards in order to reduce compliance costs.[17]

Despite its obvious importance to society, specific provision for environmental protection is not common in IIAs. Still, a number of IIAs recognize the rights of states to adopt measures designed to ensure that investment activity is undertaken in a manner sensitive to environmental concerns. The OECD reported in 2011 that approximately 8 per cent of all IIAs contain some reference to environmental protection. The study showed that such provisions are more common in the more recent treaties, suggesting that recognition of environmental protection has become more entrenched in the regulatory mind set of many countries. Indeed, half of all IIAs signed since 2005 have them. They are more common in FTAs with investment chapters than in BITs.[18] There are a wide variety of means for addressing environmental protection in IIAs, including a thematic respect for the environment in the preamble, general exceptions as in GATT, statements that environmental protection cannot constitute regulatory expropriation, or general provisions about strengthening cooperation with respect to environmental protection.

---

[17] See e.g. A. Harrison, 'Do Polluters Head Overseas: Testing the Pollution Haven Hypothesis' *ARE Update* (University of California Giannini Foundation of Agricultural Economics, 1 Dec 2002).

[18] K. Gordon and J. Pohl, 'Environmental Concerns in International Investment Agreements: A Survey' *OECD Working Papers on International Investment* (2011/01).

With respect to preamble, the India–Singapore Comprehensive Economic Agreement states that 'economic and trade liberalisation should allow for the optimal use of natural resources in accordance with the objective of sustainable development, seeking both to protect and preserve the environment'.[19] As noted above, such a statement should guide interpreting tribunals towards understandings of legal obligations that accord recognition to environmental protection.

In some treaties states are bound not to weaken their environmental standards for the purposes of attracting FDI, evidently dealing with the 'pollution haven' problem head-on. For example, NAFTA also contains a requirement that host states must not lower their environmental laws for this purpose.[20] The Norway Model BIT also specifically provides that host states may not weaken environmental regulations to attract investments.[21] With such an injunction in place, governmental officials in contracting states may not collude with investors in damaging their environment. This is an ingenious method of placing the burden of protecting the environment on the host state rather than the investors, which cannot be directly bound by treaties between two states. One of the problems with these types of provisions in treaties is that it is difficult to see how such an allegation could ever be proven. While the lowering of a standard could be empirically measured, the purpose behind this action would be virtually impossible to demonstrate.

A number of IIAs concluded by the USA and Canada and third countries specifically empower host states to regulate to protect the environment, possibly allowing them to escape liability for expropriations or other types of regulatory interference, such as violation of the FET standard or guarantees against discrimination. The US Model BIT, for example, recognizes the right of state parties to enact environmental laws, despite the possible infringement on the rights of investors.[22]

In a similar fashion, Art 17 of the Canada–Latvia BIT states:

> Nothing in this Agreement shall be construed to prevent a Contracting Party from adopting, maintaining or enforcing any measure otherwise consistent with this Agreement that it considers appropriate to ensure that investment activity in its territory is undertaken in a manner sensitive to environmental concerns.

---

[19] 26 June 2005.   [20] Art 1114.   [21] Arts 11 and 12 respectively.   [22] Art 8.3(c).

This is quite broadly phrased language, covering 'any measure' and conduct which only needs to be 'sensitive to' environmental concerns, not the more probably stringent 'related to' or 'necessary for' as developed in WTO jurisprudence.

As explained above, the GATT/GATS general exception includes a category which allows measures enacted for purposes of protecting human, animal or plant life or health and another one for measures necessary to conserve living and non-living resources.[23] As this language appears to embrace harm to all sorts of wildlife, they may be seen to be equivalent to environmental protection, such as it was understood in the 1940s when the GATT was drafted before the terms 'environment' or 'climate change' had entered the lexicon. These exceptions are repeated verbatim in the Canada Model BIT, the Egypt Model BIT and the ACIA.[24]

Perhaps according among the widest latitude to host states in terms of environmental justifications, the Taiwan–Panama FTA contains the following exception:

> Nothing in this Chapter shall be construed to prevent a Party from adopting, maintaining or enforcing any measure otherwise consistent with this Chapter that it considers appropriate to ensure that investment activity in its territory is undertaken under its ecological or environmental laws.[25]

This provision, which also occurs in NAFTA,[26] is noteworthy because it is framed in self-judging language. It is up to the host state itself to determine whether or not an environmental issue has been raised which justifies its departure from a commitment made elsewhere in the investment chapter. This effectively places the assessment of these decisions beyond the discretion of an arbitration tribunal. It is up to the state to make its own determination on the matter. Self-judging exceptions will be considered further in the next chapter.

There have been relatively few investment arbitration decisions which have considered the environmental justifications for measures which may have transgressed investors' rights under an IIA or an investment contract. Many of these have arisen under NAFTA, which, as noted above, contains

---

[23] GATT Art XX, GATS Art XIV(b).

[24] Art 10.1(a) and (c) of the Canadian Model BIT and Art 17.1 of the ASEAN Comprehensive Investment Agreement (signed 26 Feb 2009).

[25] Art 10.15 (21 Aug 2008).   [26] Art 1114.1.

exceptions for regulations enacted with the objective of environmental protection. Generally speaking, in those cases where such questions have come before tribunals, arbitrators have supported the approach of finding that an environmental purpose can operate to negate a host state's commitment to foreign investors. For example, the NAFTA tribunal in *Methanex* v. *USA* held that a US state ban on the manufacturing and sale of a gasoline additive did not amount to an indirect expropriation, nor was any compensation owed to the foreign investor. This result was based in part on the tribunal's finding that the measure had been adopted for a public purpose, namely protection of the environment from a hazardous chemical.[27] In another NAFTA-based arbitration, environmental justifications did not excuse the state's regulatory expropriation of an investment relating to a hazardous waste disposal site, although this was due to the uneven manner in which the measure was imposed rather than its substantive environmental aim.[28] In *Pac Rim* v. *El Salvador*,[29] which is still pending, a tribunal was called upon to consider whether the host state's refusal to allow mining activities based on environmental testing constituted a breach of FET and indirect expropriation. In the multi-million dollar *Chevron* v. *Ecuador*[30] dispute decided in favour of the investor, an UNCITRAL tribunal addressed allegations of environmental damage perpetrated by an oil company during its extraction activities which also had a severely detrimental impact upon local populations. In another high-profile investment arbitration case which raised environmental issues, Costa Rica was able to defend itself against claims of expropriation as well as breach of FET in relation to a series of measures imposed on a tourist resort project situated near to an ecological reserve.[31] Given the potential for environmental matters to encroach on a wide range of activities, as well as the propensity for governments to change their policies on these matters frequently, there will unquestionably be more such claims in the future.

---

[27] *Methanex* v. *United States*, 44 ILM 1345 (2005). Another environmental dispute brought under NAFTA was later settled after the Canadian government conceded that there was no scientific basis for a ban on a chemical manufactured by an American investor: *Ethyl Corporation* v. *Canada*, 38 ILM 708 (1998).

[28] E.g. *Metalclad* v. *Mexico*, ICSID case No. ARB(AF)/97/1 (30 Aug 2000).

[29] ICSID Case No. ARB/09/12 (1 June 2012).

[30] UNCITRAL, 2009, Claimant's Notice of Arbitration.

[31] *Santa Elena* v. *Costa Rica*, ICSID Case No. ARB/12/12 (17 Feb 2000).

9.2.3 Health

Closely related to that of environmental protection are issues relating to public health. Host states may wish to assert that their measures should not be challenged under international investment law because they are aimed at safeguarding the health of their citizens. Such issues may arise where a foreign investor engages in commercial activity that makes use of chemicals or deals in products which are known to be harmful to human health, perhaps most controversially of which are tobacco products.

Explicit reference to measures taken in pursuit of public health can be found in a number of IIAs, often alongside reference to the environment. For instance, the negotiated draft of the investment chapter of the TPP reads:

> Nothing in this Chapter shall be construed to prevent a Party from adopting, maintaining or enforcing any measure otherwise consistent with this Chapter that it considers appropriate to ensure that investment activity in its territory is undertaken in a manner sensitive to environmental, health or other regulatory objectives.[32]

Again, broad linking language referring to 'sensitivity' is used here, suggesting a very wide, possibly even tenuous, connection between the goal and the means by which it is achieved. Somewhat more narrowly yet lacking in connective language, the Romania–Mauritius BIT of 2000 specifies: 'this Agreement shall not prevent a Contracting Party from applying restrictions of any kind or taking any other action to protect its . . . public health or to prevent diseases or pests in animals or plants.'[33]

The preamble of the Japan–Kuwait BIT of 2012 states that the treaty is concluded '[r]ecognising that [its main objectives of promoting foreign investment] can be achieved without relaxing health, safety and environmental measures of general application'. This approach is similar to that described above, in which host states undertake not to lower their standards in order to attract foreign investment, helping to ensure that governments do not collude with foreign investors in a manner that is adverse to the health of their own people.

Echoing the language of the general exceptions of the GATT/GATS, the Argentina–New Zealand BIT of 1999 provides:

[32] Art 9.15.   [33] Art 2(1) (20 Jan 2000).

> The provisions of this Agreement shall in no way limit the right of either Contracting Party to take any measures (including the destruction of plants and animals, confiscation of property or the imposition of restrictions on stock movement) necessary for the protection of natural and physical resources or human health, provided such measures are not applied in a manner which would constitute a means of arbitrary or unjustified discrimination.[34]

Under this treaty, measures aimed at protecting human health must be necessary (given GATT jurisprudence, this probably means that there was no less investment-restrictive way possible to achieve the aim) and should be applied in an even-handed manner (probably meaning that the same types of risks should be handled the same way).

Health-based issues have arisen in a number of investment arbitration disputes, typically in conjunction with environmental concerns, reflecting the obvious linkage between activities that are harmful to ecosystems at large and the humans who inhabit them. The NAFTA disputes *Methanex* and *Metaclad*, noted above, dealt with chemical substances that posed harm to human health. Several disputes were brought against Canada under NAFTA in relation to its regulation of products which represented various risks to public health.[35] Among the most recent high profile disputes which engaged public health issues is *Vattenfall* v. *Germany*,[36] regarding a Swedish nuclear power plant manufacturer which initiated a claim based on the host state's decision to discontinue the construction of nuclear power plants because of the risk of radiation emission in the event of a catastrophe. Perhaps most notorious of all is *Philip Morris* v. *Australia*,[37] in which a tobacco company alleged that the host state's plain-packaging requirement for cigarettes aimed at reducing the instance of smoking amounted to an indirect expropriation of the investor's IP rights. As noted earlier, this claim was ultimately rejected due to jurisdictional reasons. Unfortunately there has been relatively little by way

---

[34] Art 5(3) (27 Aug 1999).

[35] *Dow Agrosciences* v. *Canada*, (UNCITRAL, 2011) (pesticide); *Chemtura* v. *Canada* (UNCITRAL, 2010) (food product ban); *SD Myers* v. *Canada* (UNCITRAL, 2000) (industrial waste transport prohibition); and *Ethyl Corp* v. *Canada* (UNCITRAL, 1998) (unleaded gasoline mixture ban).

[36] ICSID Case No. ARB/12/12 (2 July 2013) (which eventually settled).

[37] UNCITRAL, 2012 (PCA Case No. 2012–12) (which was eventually rejected based on jurisdiction).

of arbitral reasoning in terms of the precise application of health-based justifications in IIAs. As with environmental matters, the regulation of public health is likely to continue to be a source of much tension between investors and host states in the coming years.

9.2.4 Labour

As suggested in Chapter 1, maintaining poor labour standards, such as denying workers the ability to bargain collectively or more fundamentally to have a safe workplace, is one way in which corporations can lower their costs when conducting business overseas. It is often thought that capital-importing states may be tempted to weaken labour standards or human rights protections in order to attract foreign investors pursuing such strategies, another classic 'race to the bottom' situation. Whether this 'sweat shop' model of firm behaviour actually occurs is a matter of debate, although studies have indicated that multinational enterprises tend to offer superior rather than inferior working conditions than their local counterparts, possibly because they often have greater resources to do so.[38]

The International Labour Organization maintains a number of conventions aimed at safeguarding workers' rights which bind state governments. Such 'core' labour rights include the freedom to bargain collectively, freedom of association, elimination of discrimination in the workplace, elimination of workplace abuses such as forced labour, adequate wages and safe working conditions. These rights are reflected to a degree in the OECD Guidelines for Multinational Enterprises, which will be considered below. Despite these assurances under international law, attempts by host states to impose regulations designed to protect and promote core labour rights may have a detrimental effect on foreign investors, and as such an investor may seek to claim that these are violations of an IIA. This is why some IIAs now recognize labour rights in various ways. The 2013 Canada–Honduras FTA mentions labour issues in its preamble that parties should resolve to '[p]rotect, enhance, and enforce basic workers' rights', although precisely what rights this entails is not explained. Similarly, the preamble to the Austria–Georgia BIT of 2004 contains the phrase 'REAFFIRMING

---

[38] H. Gorg, E. Strobl, and F. Walsh, 'Why Do Foreign-Owned Firms Pay More? The Role of On-the-Job Training' *IZA Discussion Paper* No. 590 (22 Oct 2004).

their commitment to the observance of internationally recognized labour standards', presumably capturing those promulgated by the International Labour Organization.

As with environmental and health matters, one of the ways in which countries assert their ability to impose labour-based measures is through the promise not to lower these standards as a means of attracting foreign investors eager to reduce their labour costs. The Norway Model BIT contains such a clause,[39] as does the US Model BIT.[40] Article 13 of the Rwanda–USA BIT of 2008 contains a more detailed provision of this nature:

> 1. The Parties recognize that it is inappropriate to encourage investment by weakening or reducing the protections afforded in domestic labor laws. Accordingly, each Party shall strive to ensure that it does not waive or otherwise derogate from, or offer to waive or otherwise derogate from, such laws in a manner that weakens or reduces adherence to the internationally recognized labor rights... as an encouragement for the establishment, acquisition, expansion, or retention of an investment in its territory. If a Party considers that the other Party has offered such an encouragement, it may request consultations with the other Party and the two Parties shall consult with a view to avoiding any such encouragement.
> 2. For purposes of this Article, 'labor laws' means each Party's statutes or regulations, or provisions thereof, that are directly related to the following internationally recognized labor rights:
>   (a) the right of association;
>   (b) the right to organize and bargain collectively;
>   (c) a prohibition on the use of any form of forced or compulsory labor;
>   (d) labor protections for children and young people, including a minimum age for the employment of children and the prohibition and elimination of the worst forms of child labor; and
>   (e) acceptable conditions of work with respect to minimum wages, hours of work, and occupational safety and health.[41]

This statement is interesting because, unlike some of the other 'non-lowering' provisions found in IIAs, it specifies a mechanism through which such allegations can be made, strengthening the efficacy of this obligation, which as suggested above could be difficult to prove. This section

---

[39] Arts 11 and 12 respectively.   [40] Art 13.   [41] 19 Feb 2008.

is also interesting because it outlines precisely the nature of the rights contemplated by 'labor laws' which under normal circumstances could be viewed as somewhat insubstantial.

Some US BITs make reference to the desire to promote respect for workers' rights, but they do not contain substantive obligations in this regard.[42] China included a Memorandum of Understanding on Labour Cooperation as part of its FTA with New Zealand, acknowledging the need to maintain a safe working environment for employees although the enforceability of these provisions is uncertain.[43] While it does not contain a reference to labour or human rights, the GATS establishes a general exception for reasons of 'safety',[44] echoed or incorporated directly in a number of IIAs.[45] This could indicate a recognition of the need for minimum standards in working conditions if not the right to bargain collectively, surely the most important of the core labour rights. Perhaps most noteworthy, the TPP contains a chapter on labour in which signatory states reaffirm their commitment to uphold the International Labour Organization's core labour rights.[46] To be clear, these are not framed as exceptions to the protections found in the investment chapter, but as obligations in their own right.

There are no known investment arbitration cases which have addressed labour-based exceptions contained in IIAs, although such cases may be forthcoming given the increasing prevalence of these terms in treaties such as those indicated above. The absence of such cases may further be explained by the willingness of aggrieved workers to pursue remedies for these harms at the domestic level through national labour or tort regimes. The national courts of some industrialized home states have been willing to hold foreign companies accountable to harms done to employees in the territories of the states in which their investors have located. The US Alien Tort Claims Act,[47] which allows US courts to take jurisdiction over torts committed abroad involving either US claimants or defendants, has been a key facilitator of such lawsuits against multinationals. The British courts have also been prepared to take jurisdiction over the activities of British

---

[42] E.g. Preamble to US–Bolivia BIT (signed 17 April 1998) and US–Argentina BIT (signed 14 Nov 1994).

[43] *New Zealand–China Free Trade Agreement: Summary of Outcomes* at www.bellgully.com/resources/pdfs/NZ_China_FTA.pdf (Sept 2011).

[44] Art XIV(c)(iii).   [45] E.g. EU–Singapore FTA Art 9.3(d)(iii).

[46] Art 19.2.   [47] 28 U.S.C. § 1350.

corporations and their subsidiaries abroad that injure workers.[48] Curiously, labour rights may be seen as one sphere of international investment law where, for the time being at least, domestic dispute settlement may be superior to that available at the international level.

In addition to challenging laws aimed at protecting the labour rights of workers, there may be scope for foreign investors to seek compensation for human rights-inspired regulatory measures taken by host states. One clear example of this type of measure are those related to indigenization policies. These types of laws which have the purpose of redressing historic injustices suffered by certain groups of people within a given society could grant preferential status to companies on the basis of their race or ethnic background. Such a measure imposed by the government of South Africa was challenged when three Italian mining companies instigated an arbitration dispute on the basis that the host state's racially discriminatory requirements for businesses violated IIA protections. These aspects of the dispute were settled between the parties during the proceedings.[49]

When considering the application of human rights laws to foreign investors it must be remembered that states have an obligation to safeguard human rights under various international treaties as well as under customary international law. As with core labour rights, these obligations could potentially be used to defend regulatory decisions that have an adverse effect on foreign investment projects.

9.2.5 Culture

One of the problems associated with FDI is that foreign investors can create tensions in local communities within a host state because of cultural differences between the home state from which the investor originates and that of the state in which it chooses to do business. While it is unquestionably an indeterminate concept, 'culture' could be defined as a body of objects, knowledge and skills of a community which provides a sense of identity. Cultural protections are not unknown to international law.[50]

---

[48] *Lubbe* v. *Cape* [2000] UKHL 41.

[49] *Foresti* v. *South Africa*, ICSID Case No. ARB(AF)/07/01 (4 Aug 2010).

[50] T. Voon, *Cultural Products and the World Trade Organization* (Cambridge University Press, 2011), Chapter 1.

The UN's Educational Scientific and Cultural Organization (UNESCO) administers a number of instruments that have the objective of preserving culture. For example, the World Heritage Convention officially recognizes the importance of cultural heritage,[51] and the International Covenant on Civil and Political Rights also protects the right of individuals to enjoy their culture.[52]

In situations where there is a significant number of employees at the foreign enterprise who are host state nationals, cultural tensions could manifest via different management models, as is sometimes suggested in the case of Asian firms operating in Europe or North America. Perhaps more intrusively is the presence of goods and services in the host state that, while produced locally, represent manifestations which are unfamiliar or which challenge convention. This problem is often conceived in terms of American 'cultural imperialism'. Throughout the latter part of the twentieth century, many US companies successfully expanded internationally, in some cases displacing local firms and with them indigenous habits of consumption. While this might be viewed in a positive light by some consumers eager for choice and low price, the degradation of culturally specific products like books, cinema and music may in some instances have caused a significant erosion of the host state's self-identity. Today many capital-importing states are sensitive to the fragile nature of their cultural industries and may consequently take steps to protect them, possibly through discriminatory practices, such as a mandatory component of local ownership. This could be viewed as a hostile action by a foreign investor, who could allege violation of an IIA, for example under a National Treatment clause.

Cultural exemptions are not common in IIAs. Still, reference to the preservation of 'public order' found in many treaties[53] could be construed to cover culture. This connection is predicated on the rationale that the stability of society is tied to a state's capacity to preserve its cultural identity. Such an exception may be found in the China–Finland BIT:

---

[51] Convention Concerning the Protection of the World Cultural and Natural Heritage, 1037 UNTS 151 (entered into force 15 Dec 1975).

[52] International Covenant on Civil and Political Rights Art 1, opened for signature 16 Dec 1966, S. Exec. Doc. E, 95-2, at 31 (1978), 999 UNTS 171, 179 (entered into force 23 March 1976) Art 27.

[53] E.g. Russia–Sweden BIT, Art 3(3) (19 April 1994).

> Provided that such measures are not applied in a manner which would
> constitute a means of arbitrary or unjustifiable discrimination by a Con-
> tracting Party, or a disguised investment restriction, nothing in this Agree-
> ment shall be construed as preventing the Contracting Parties from taking
> any measure necessary for the maintenance of public order.[54]

The concept of public order may also be found in the GATS where the
phrase 'public morals' can also be seen, another potential shorthand for
culture, capturing understood ethical standards of a society. Safeguarding
public morals was argued as a defence to a measure imposed by China
restricting the distribution of various magazines and sound recordings by
non-SOEs in a WTO dispute brought under GATS. In that case China failed
to demonstrate that the restrictions, which effectively prevented foreign
firms from dealing in various forms of media, were necessary to safeguard
public morals, which it equated with culture. Ruling in favour of the USA,
the WTO panel was careful to state that it was not evaluating China's
capacity to protect its culture, but rather the way the Chinese government
had chosen to do so in this instance.[55] It should be noted that cultural
restrictions on foreign investment are also reflected in a number of WTO
Members' GATS specific commitments, allowing host states to dictate the
degree of foreign intervention in various services sectors which may have
a link to the state's sense of self-identity.

Explicit reference to cultural protection can be found in some modern
IIAs. For example, the France–Uganda BIT reads:

> Nothing in this agreement shall be construed to prevent any contracting
> party from taking any measure to regulate investment of foreign com-
> panies and the conditions of activities of these companies in the frame-
> work of policies designed to preserve and promote cultural and linguistic
> diversity.[56]

The use of the term 'diversity' here is curious because it appears to suggest that a wide range of cultural influences are welcome, whereas it is
probably intended to safeguard French culture and language in a world
dominated by English-language-based culture. It is no surprise that France

---

[54] Art 3 (15 Nov 2004).
[55] *China – Publications and Audiovisual Products*, WT/DS363/AB/R (21 Dec 2009).
[56] Art 6 (3 Jan 2003).

had insisted upon a cultural exception in the negotiations for the Multilateral Agreement on Investment in the late 1990s, as did Canada, urged in no small part by its influential French-speaking constituents. Canada omitted cultural industries entirely from any obligations in its Model BIT,[57] as did France.[58] Canada also requires that foreign investments in 'cultural businesses' must undergo a special assessment under its domestic review procedure.[59]

There have been several investment arbitrations which have addressed the subject of cultural protection directly. In one dispute the sanctity of the ancient Giza pyramid site near Cairo was threatened by the construction of a foreign hotel.[60] The hotel builders were a Hong Kong-based company which had entered into a joint venture with Egypt. After they began construction of the complex, the Egyptian public complained that the project could harm undiscovered archaeological artefacts in the area. The Egyptian government consequently halted all construction on the basis of its need to protect its cultural heritage. The matter was also framed as one of world heritage because the Giza Pyramids had been designated a UNESCO World Heritage Site. While the tribunal stated that the protection of antiquities is unquestionably an attribute of sovereignty, it declined to accept Egypt's justification because Egypt only nominated the pyramid site to become a Heritage Site well after the project had already been approved. Perhaps most crucially, the tribunal ruled that the site's archaeological status did not preclude the requirement to compensate the investor. Had there been a cultural exception in the relevant IIA, the result might have been different.

In *Parkerings* v. *Lithuania*[61] an investment tribunal was called upon to assess whether cultural preservation could operate as a justification for the breach of contract between the local government of the city of Vilnius and the Norwegian investor which had won a concession to operate a car park in the town's historic town centre. The local government terminated the contract because of public opposition to the development, leading to claims of expropriation and failure to assure the investor's legitimate expectations in a secure legal environment. The tribunal rejected

---

[57] Art 10.6.   [58] France Model BIT Art 1.6.   [59] Investment Canada Act, Art 24(2).
[60] *SPP* v. *Egypt*, ICSID Case no ARB/84/3 (20 May 1992).
[61] ICSID Case No. ARB/05/8 (9 Aug 2007).

the investor's claims, holding that governments retain the right to change laws under various circumstances and that investors must anticipate this. Despite the fact that there was no express cultural exception in the Lithuania–Norway BIT, the tribunal felt that the refusal of the project was justified on the basis of historical and archaeological conservation, a finding which was supported by the site's status as a UNESCO culturally protected area.

The tribunal in *Lemire* v. *Ukraine* considered whether cultural protection could justify breach of a host state's commitments to foreign investors. The issue in that case concerned restrictions placed on the sale of radio and television licences to a foreign company. The tribunal ruled in favour of the host state, holding that it would not second-guess the regulation of cultural industries by the Ukraine. The tribunal stated that the right to regulate 'extends to promulgating regulations which define the State's own cultural policy' and that this right is 'reinforced in cases where the purpose of the legislation affects deeply felt cultural or linguistic traits of the community'.[62] These concepts can be difficult to establish but the suggestion here appears to be that the tribunal will tend to defer to the assertions made by host states in this regard. Clearly the state itself will be in the best position to define the contours of its own cultural traits.

The heritage of indigenous people is often seen as being especially susceptible to harm from foreign investment, both because of the importance placed upon culture within these communities and these groups' inherent vulnerability.[63] Many capital-importing states are concerned that their indigenous people's cultural practices, such as hunting and fishing, may be threatened by the presence of multinational enterprises which engage in these activities on a commercial scale. While the protection of unique and fragile communities is obviously a laudable goal of which international investment law must be mindful, as with other spheres of public interest there is a genuine concern that unchecked claims of cultural preservation could amount to disguised protectionism undermining commitments negotiated in good faith under international law.

---

[62] Ibid., at [505].

[63] V. Vadi, 'When Cultures Collide: Foreign Direct Investment, Natural Resources and Indigenous Heritage in International Investment Law' 42 *Columbia Human Rights Law Review* 797 (2011).

9.3 Public Interest and Expropriation

As noted in Chapter 7, the distinction between legitimate and illegitimate measures which amount to indirect expropriations is predicated in part on whether or not the measure served the public interest. Public interest as specified in these sections of IIAs should not be viewed in a different light from that which comprises general exceptions in IIAs or under customary international law. Still, it is worth noting that IIAs often contain expropriation-specific elaborations of public interest, most likely because public interest will most often be argued as a defence to this particular form of regulatory interference with investors' interests. To re-emphasize a point made in Chapter 7, satisfying the definition of public interest found in an IIA's guarantee against expropriation does not preclude the payment of compensation. Rather, it enables the characterization of the expropriation as one that was done lawfully which, as suggested earlier, may indicate that a lower quantum is payable.

Focusing on one particular form of public interest regulation, the Colombian Model BIT provides that measures taken for the purposes of environmental protection cannot be considered indirect expropriation.[64] The Canadian Model BIT of 2004 takes a broader approach, specifying several categories of public interest which may defeat claims of indirect expropriation:

> Except in rare circumstances, such as when a measure or series of measures are so severe in the light of their purpose that they cannot be reasonably viewed as having been adopted and applied in good faith, non-discriminatory measures of a Party that are designed and applied to protect legitimate public welfare objectives, such as health, safety and the environment, do not constitute indirect expropriation.[65]

As suggested above, the phrase 'legitimate public welfare objectives' is a particularly broad one, potentially capturing all sorts of laws, of which health, safety and the environment are specific examples. This language might therefore be said to capture the notion of 'police powers' discussed in Chapter 6. Similar provisions can be found in expropriation clauses in the China–New Zealand FTA of 2008 and in the Expropriation Annex to the draft TTIP. As the VCLT informs that provisions of treaties should be

[64] Art VI.2.c.   [65] Art B.13(1)(c).

interpreted according to their context and in light of the overall purpose of the instrument,[66] then the appearance of exceptions for various public interest matters for the purpose of defining indirect expropriation provision could, by extension, be reasonably construed to apply as derogations from other commitments found in the same treaty, such as FET or non-discrimination. Alternatively, as these public interest exceptions expressly define the lawfulness of indirect expropriation and only indirect expropriation, they could be confined to that provision, meaning that they in no way operate to diminish obligations found elsewhere in the instrument.

9.4 Corporate Social Responsibility (CSR)

An increasing expectation has been placed on multinational enterprises to acknowledge certain minimal standards of behaviour when engaging in their commercial activities overseas. These standards are often described as CSR and essentially consist of voluntary codes of conduct, embodying openness, fair dealing and a commitment not to harm the society in which they operate. Adhering to such standards may be seen as both a moral obligation as well as an indication of good business strategy – the extent to which firms obey these guidelines often dictates their capacity to attract discerning consumers. Put more bluntly, along with being a badge of good behaviour, CSR is a sensible marketing tool. Still, as IIAs cannot place obligations directly on investors, there is limited capacity for these instruments to compel foreign investors to adhere to CSR principles where they do not wish to.

This does not mean that IIAs are silent on this issue. CSR is expressly addressed, for instance, in this article of the Canada–Peru FTA:

> Each Party should encourage enterprises operating within its territory or subject to its jurisdiction to voluntarily incorporate internationally recognized standards of corporate social responsibility in their internal policies, such as statements of principle that have been endorsed or are supported by the Parties. These principles address issues such as labour, the environment, human rights, community relations and anti-corruption. The Parties therefore remind those enterprises of the importance of incorporating such corporate social responsibility standards in their internal policies.[67]

---

[66] Art 31(1) (7 April 2008).   [67] Art 810 (21 Nov 2008).

The obligation described herein, which alludes to some of the public interest issues discussed above, rests on the home and host states to encourage firms to adhere to CSR principles, but it is only an obligation of 'best efforts', meaning that it would be difficult to initiate a claim on this basis. A similar commitment can be found in the investment chapter of the TPP.[68]

The Singapore–USA FTA of 2008 speaks of 'principles of corporate stewardship' with the following:

> Recognizing the substantial benefits brought by international trade and investment as well as the opportunity for enterprises to implement policies for sustainable development that seek to ensure coherence between social, economic and environmental objectives, each Party should encourage enterprises operating within its territory or subject to its jurisdiction to voluntarily incorporate sound principles of corporate stewardship in their internal policies, such as those principles or agreements that have been endorsed by both Parties.[69]

It is worth noting the appearance of the catch-all phrase 'sustainable development' in this provision, rather than reference to explicit policy goals such as environmental protection or human rights. Again, as this provision does not command state parties but rather encourages them, its enforceability is questionable. It is probably best to view these provisions as ones of good faith – treaty parties will make all reasonable efforts to ensure that firms operating within their territories (or coming from territory in the case of home states) observe CSR principles as they are understood by the international community. This understanding is now reflected in several well-recognized guidelines.

9.5 Voluntary Guidelines Encompassing Public Interest

Regardless of whether there is an effective public interest-based exception in an IIA which may operate to control a host state's liability and ultimately its obligation to pay compensation, there is limited capacity within international investment law to proactively dictate the conduct of an investor in terms of its support of recognized public interest / sustainability norms. As private actors, foreign investors themselves are not

---

[68] Art 9.16.   [69] Art 18.9.

obliged to uphold international law including IIA commitments, because they are not truly subjects of international law,[70] just as they are not signatories of IIAs. This is one reason why numerous organizations have created voluntary codes of conduct for multinational enterprises to oblige them to respect matters such as human rights, environmental protection and core labour standards. Such guidelines are regarded sceptically because of their non-binding nature, but integrating them into IIAs by placing obligations on state parties to encourage investors to uphold them could provide some indirect assurance that their aims will be fulfilled. Some of the most influential of these guidelines are detailed below.

9.5.1 OECD Guidelines for Multinational Enterprises

The OECD's Guidelines on Multinational Enterprises[71] are probably the most influential of the voluntary CSR guidelines. Revised most recently in 2011, they attempt to encourage positive contributions that multinational enterprises can make to economic and social progress, and to minimize any problems that their activities can cause through their operations, particularly in the developed world which is often lacking sufficient public interest-based laws or the capacity to enforce them. The guidelines were created in the 1970s because of increased demands from the OECD countries for greater control over multinational enterprises. Essentially the guidelines consist of business ethics-type recommendations regarding conditions of employment of workers; human rights; environmental protection; information disclosure and transparency; and the prevention of bribery. Similar to the Guidelines for Multinational Enterprises, the OECD's General Policies[72] contain what may be described as an emerging consensus on the social obligations of multinational enterprises. The policies include statements that enterprises should contribute to economic, social and environmental progress; respect human rights of those affected by their activities; encourage local capacity building through close cooperation with local communities; encourage capital formation, in particular by creating employment and training opportunities; refrain from seeking or accepting exemptions from regulations, especially in relation to health,

---

[70] I. Brownlie, *Principles of Public International Law* (Oxford University Press, 2008), at 65.
[71] www.oecd.org/daf/inv/mne/48004323.pdf.
[72] https://mneguidelines.oecd.org/2011GeneralPolicies.pdf.

safety and tax; develop and apply good corporate governance practice and abstain from involvement in local political activities.

9.5.2 UN Global Compact

The UN's Global Compact,[73] established in 1999, calls upon companies with international activities to observe the principles of sustainable development, including respect for human rights, labour, the environment and anti-corruption, and also to take positive actions to advance the social objectives enshrined in the UN's Sustainable Development Goals with an emphasis on collaboration and innovation. The Global Compact is distilled into ten principles covering these aims, many of which are themselves derived from other UN instruments such as the Universal Declaration on Human Rights and the Rio Declaration on the Environment and Development. The Global Compact requirements are reasonably specific but they are neither binding nor is there a formal auditing or certification process. This is one reason why some NGOs have been critical of them. Some major multinational enterprises have signed up to the Global Compact, including the financial services firms Deutsche Bank, HSBC and Morgan Stanley.

9.5.3 The Collevecchio Declaration on Financial Services

The Collevecchio Declaration on Financial Services[74] was created by a coalition of NGOs in 2003 in an effort to achieve 'sustainable finance', meaning access to capital from ethical sources. The various NGOs which launched the scheme had been critical of some of the business-friendly codes of conduct of the time which had not been sufficiently protective of public interests, notably environmental matters. The Collevecchio Declaration comprises six principles that stress sustainability, accountability, transparency and stakeholder rights in the financing of investment projects. One of its key objectives is that financial institutions sponsoring foreign investments will 'do no harm'. Since it was prepared by people outside the financial sector, the Collevecchio Declaration presents itself as among the more credible CSR guidelines. Approximately a hundred NGOs

---

[73] https://www.unglobalcompact.org/.
[74] www.banktrack.org/download/collevechio_declaration/030401_collevecchio_ declaration_with_signatories.pdf.

have endorsed the Declaration which is now administered by BankTrack, a global network of NGOs cooperating in the field of private banking.

9.5.4 The Equator Principles

Formally launched in 2003, the Equator Principles[75] are a prominent set of CSR policies of relevance to the project finance market. They provide lenders with a framework to manage their social and environmental impacts and were formulated primarily by the banking industry under the auspices of the World Bank's IFC. The Equator Principles were designed to govern private commercial lending in developing countries and emerging economies where environmental regulation may be weak. NGOs such as the World Wildlife Fund and the Friends of the Earth were instrumental in the creation of these principles, gaining them significant respect internationally. Almost eighty financial institutions worldwide, accounting for over 85 per cent of the global project financing market, have signed the Equator Principles, most of which are located in North America or Western Europe. Among notable signatories are Barclays and HSBC, which promise to implement the Equator Principles when extending funding to investment projects. There are some controversies associated with various projects that have allegedly violated these guidelines, including the Baku Oil pipeline project and the Uruguay Pulp Mills. The Equator Principles have also been criticized by some groups for lacking accountability mechanisms and being insufficiently responsive to climate change.

9.5.5 The Ceres Principles

Ceres stands for the Coalition for Environmentally Responsible Economies and it is a partnership of investors, foundations, trade unions and environmental, religious and other civil society groups that was established in 1989. This organization drafted the Ceres principles[76] which consists of a ten-point environmental code of conduct that commits signatories to goals of sustainable business including the protection of the environment, the conservation of natural resources and the reduction of waste.

---

[75] www.equator-principles.com/.
[76] www.ceres.org/about-us/our-history/ceres-principles.

Companies cannot unilaterally endorse the Ceres principles, they must ask Ceres for certification.

9.5.6 The Santiago Principles

The Santiago principles[77] are generally accepted principles and practices for use by Sovereign Wealth Funds, which as observed in Chapter 1, are growing in global importance as sources of FDI. They were proposed in 2008 through a joint effort by the IMF and the International Forum of Sovereign Wealth Funds (IFSWF). The Santiago principles aim to ensure that Sovereign Wealth Funds are properly transparent and accountable in their international investment activities and that they bring benefits to both home and host countries. The Santiago principles consist of twenty-four voluntary guidelines which include commitments that signatories will contribute to a stable global financial system and that they will adhere to the regulatory and disclosure requirements of the states in which they locate. Adequate risk management and sound governance are also key aspects of the Santiago principles. Twenty-five Sovereign Wealth Funds have signed onto the principles.

9.6 Public Interest in Development Bank Lending Guidelines

The observance of public interest objectives by foreign investors may be achieved through conditions placed on their financing, either by private banks following some of the CSR principles discussed above, or through development banks, where financing is obtained for the purpose of engaging in FDI in the developing world. Indeed the development banks are one of the chief sources of financial support for international investment. These organizations lend money to investors that might not be able to secure loans from ordinary commercial banks because of the risk involved in locating in developing states with unstable political systems and legal environments. In some cases loans are offered by development banks at below commercial rates because of the beneficial purpose of the investment project to the community in which it will be situated. Such financing is typically extended to cover infrastructure-related projects such as

---

[77] www.iwg-swf.org/pubs/eng/santiagoprinciples.pdf.

highways, dams and airports. Since these investments can have a significant impact on the environment or social conditions of the host state, the lending banks tend to apply conditions to their loans that borrowing firms must address the public interest implications of their activities in host states.[78] Some of these organizations were mentioned in Chapter 2.

9.6.1 The Multilateral Investment Guarantee Agency (MIGA)

MIGA, which will be examined more closely in the final chapter, provides guarantees against non-commercial risks for investment in developing countries. Importantly for the purpose of ensuring the adherence to public interest norms, MIGA maintains an Environmental Assessment Policy, which requires that all projects must engage in an environmental assessment before they receive funding. This includes a component of public participation. MIGA requires an environmental impact assessment of investment projects before offering coverage in some circumstances.[79] It is important to note that a number of IIAs also mandate environmental assessment as a requirement of a foreign investor's entry into host states, notably the ECT[80] and NAFTA.[81]

9.6.2 The International Finance Corporation (IFC)

The IFC provides loans to the private sector for the purpose of investment in the developing world. As a supporter of public interest matters in host states, the IFC imposes environmental assessment requirements on the projects that it funds. This assessment forms part of the various stages of a project from its inception to its conclusion. The IFC's detailed environmental guidelines also include the requirement of public and stakeholder consultation. The World Bank's Inspection Panel, which is an internal dispute settlement body, allows anyone affected by the IFC's decision to extend funding for a particular project to file a complaint. The complaints are based on the fact that the IFC failed to adhere to its own guidelines when

---

[78] D. Collins, 'Environmental Impact Statements and Public Participation in International Investment Law' 7:2 *Manchester Journal of International Economic Law* 4 (2010).

[79] *MIGA Performance Standards on Social and Environmental Sustainability* (1 Oct 2007), www.miga.org/documents/performance_standards_social_and_env_sustainability.pdf (May 2012).

[80] Art 19(1)(i).   [81] Art 1106(2).

it extended funding, for example if it loaned to a project that violated social or environmental concerns.

9.6.3 The Regional Development Banks

The European Bank for Reconstruction and Development, which provides project financing for private sector banks, industries and businesses from Europe to Central Asia, maintains its Environmental and Social Policy and Performance Requirements. These require that each project which receives financing must be appraised for its effect on the community in which it is located. This will include an assessment of environmental impacts as well as effects on culture, living standards and employment. The Asian Development Bank, located in Manila, The Philippines, has a similar agenda in Asia, but it also facilitates public–private partnerships for development projects. It maintains guidelines for environmental due diligence and environmental management accountability. Public participation of affected groups is included in this process. Likewise, the Inter-American Development Bank (targeting Latin America and the Caribbean) requires that borrowers prepare environmental and social impact assessments for projects that have the potential to impose substantial environmental or social harms, following a procedure outlined in its Environment and Safeguards Compliance Policy. These assessments are made available to affected populations before the bank delivers its support. The African Development Bank places similar obligations on its borrowers, in some cases also requiring an integrity and anti-corruption assessment along with an environmental and social one.

9.6.4 The New Development Bank (NDB)

The NDB is a multilateral development bank created in 2015 and operated by the consortium of Brazil, Russia, India, China and South Africa. It is unclear at this point from the bank's constituent documents whether it will require environmental or social impact assessments as a condition of its support, or whether it encourages CSR or sustainability practices on the part of borrowing states and private entities. It should be noted, however, that the NDB's foundational agreement expressly mentions in its preamble that the parties are 'desirous to contribute to an international financial system conducive to economic and social development respectful of the global environment'.[82] This suggests that projects applying for financing from the bank will be required to demonstrate that their activities have taken these objectives into account.

9.7 Balancing Public Interest against Treaty Protections

If an IIA contains an exception for a public interest concern, then it is conceivable that the host state may bear no liability whatsoever for enacting a regulation in pursuit of that goal. In instances of expropriation, a finding of public interest could enable a tribunal to rule that the expropriation was lawful, resulting in the obligation to pay compensation rather than damages, or in the case of extreme public interest falling within the understanding of police powers, there may be no expropriation at all. In order for tribunals to interpret public interest provisions in a way that eliminates or reduces compensation owed, there must be some link between the measure and the objective. In other words, the regulatory interference with the investor's rights under the treaty must bear some rational connection to the public interest that has been asserted. This requires a cautious balancing of competing norms. In the absence of WTO-inspired language referencing standards of 'necessary' and the avoidance of a 'disguised restriction' on international investment, there is little indication of precisely how an investment tribunal should conduct this exercise.

One way for investment tribunals to balance the public interest against the rights of the investor is the principle of proportionality which has been proposed by commentators as an effective method for the resolution of this type of normative conflict.[83] Proportionality analysis has also received support from tribunals in the form of 'counterbalancing' competing obligations found in the regimes of international investment law and international human rights law.[84] In *Tecmed* v. *Mexico*, for example, the tribunal used proportionality analysis to rule in favour of the investor, concluding that the environmental harms caused by the investor were not sufficient to warrant the non-renewal of the licence by the host state,

---

[82] Agreement on the New Development Bank (15 July 2014), http://ndbbrics.org/.

[83] S. Schill, 'Cross-Regime Harmonization through Proportionality Analysis: The Case of International Investment Law, the Law of State Immunity and Human Rights' 27 ICSID Review – FILJ (2012) 87 (focusing on human rights issues).

[84] *SAUR* v. *Argentina*, ICSID Case No. ARB/04/4 (6 June 2012) at [332].

precluding the obligation to pay compensation. The *Tecmed* tribunal's use of proportionality analysis has been cited with approval in subsequent awards relating to both guarantees against expropriation[85] and FET.[86]

Generally speaking, in conducting proportionality analysis the tribunal must first determine whether the measure giving effect to the interest is capable of achieving its objective. It must then be ascertained whether the measure is necessary to achieve its end, or whether a less restrictive but equally effective measure could be used instead. Finally the tribunal must consider if the effects of the measure imposed are excessive compared to the competing right or interest that has been infringed. In performing this three-step process, the arbitrator must assess the weight of each interest before a conclusion can be drawn regarding whether the means used achieve their ultimate goal. Of course one of the problems with this exercise is that for the balancing of values to work, the relative interests must be intrinsically comparable. If they are too diverse, then it is impossible to gauge them against each other in order to determine whether the measure is justified.[87] This can be difficult in the context of international investment law where the essential values being protected (the property rights of investors) are weighed against wider policy concerns such as human rights or environmental harms, support for which may in some cases be in the text of the treaty but may equally derive from broader public international law.

As public interest is increasingly argued as a justification for regulatory interference, investment tribunals must carefully consider the relationship between international investment law regimes and other spheres of international law, such as the environment and human rights. This is by no means an easy task and it is not clear that it can be done through the application of a formulaic proportionality 'test'. Among those few investment tribunals that have explicitly invoked the proportionality principle, very few have followed the step-by-step analytical procedure developed by various domestic and international courts. Still, arbitration tribunals are beginning to apply proportionality analysis in situations where the

---

85 *LG&E* v. *Argentina*, ICSID Case No. ARB/02/1 (3 Oct 2006) at [195].

86 *Occidental* v. *Ecuador*, ICSID Case No. ARB/06/11 (2 Nov 2015) at [404]–[409].

87 B. Kingsbury and S. Schill, 'Public Law Concepts to Balance Investors' Rights with State Regulatory Actions in the Public Interest – the Concept of Proportionality' in S. Schill (ed.), *International Investment Law and Comparative Public Law* (Oxford University Press, 2010), at 78.

regulatory interests of host states have to be balanced vis-à-vis guarantees provided to foreign investors in IIAs.[88]

In addition to some kind of balancing exercise, certain formal requirements could assist a tribunal in verifying whether or not public interest-orientated measures may be viewed as a legitimate exercise of a state's authority, potentially precluding the requirement to pay compensation for various regulatory interferences. For example, full transparency and timely notification of the measure could indicate its authenticity and also likely diminish the damaging effects on the investor's profitability. Effective judicial or administrative reviewability as well as involvement of high-level government officials in the event of restrictive investment policy measures could also support a claim by a host state that the measure was genuinely in the public interest rather than an attack against a foreign firm. The principle of due process, often thought to be enshrined in the guarantee of FET, may be an effective means of acknowledging public interest regulations within the framework of international investment law.

9.8 Conclusion

International investment law recognizes a country's capacity to enact regulations in support of various public policies. In severe cases, such measures may constitute the type of police powers which legitimize actions such as indirect takings, meaning that they are no longer compensable. If IIAs so specify, certain public interest justifications may preclude liability for other treaty breaches which have been explored throughout this book. Some recent IIAs have accordingly established exceptions for measures relating to environmental protection, health, core labour rights (possibly embracing human rights) and the preservation of culture. With the exception of environmental issues, there has been limited assessment of these features of treaties in arbitral case law. In yet other circumstances, there may be no provision for public interest in an IIA, but international law may be construed to dictate that support for certain policies are manifestations of a state's responsibility under international law, particularly

---

[88] See X. Han, 'The Application of the Principle of Proportionality in Tecmed v. Mexico' 6:3 *Chinese Journal of International Law* 635 (2007) at 636.

where a relevant treaty exists. In such situations, investment tribunals may be able to excuse governments from liability for measures imposed to achieve these objectives even where they harm investors' commercial interests.

When confronting public interest issues in international investment arbitration, it is necessary for tribunals to find a balance between the often conflicting principles of international law as well as, perhaps most fundamentally, the balance between economic and non-economic values. To this end, a new generation of IIAs has embraced a larger space for the regulation by host states in matters such as human health and safety, the environment, human and labour rights as well as the preservation of local cultures, giving tribunals clearer guidance as to a demarcation point between investors' and national interests. The inclusion of public interest exceptions into international investment law acknowledges some of the adverse consequences of economic globalization, such as environmental degradation and social instability. The capacity of IIAs to preserve enlarged regulatory policy space may further be viewed as the consequence of the observed rebalancing of global FDI flows. Developing states that were once exclusively host states are now also home states from which much FDI originates, just as developed states have reconsidered their IIAs from their perspective as capital importers. This has caused governments to approach publicly minded laws with less reservation.

The proliferation of soft law on CSR is indicative of a global mindset which has recast the role of the multinational enterprises as not only one of the chief forces of globalization but also, in some respects, subjects of international law which should be held to the standards of good governance expected of states. Transparency, accountability and sensitivity to public interest values like sustainability, while not themselves obligations contained in IIAs, are increasingly viewed as responsibilities which foreign investors must bear, ensuring that economic growth is provided in a manner that is not harmful to society.

10 Non-Precluded Measures: Essential Security, Economic Stability and the Defence of Necessity

10.1 Introduction

The public interest issues discussed in the previous chapter are without question important; they would not appear as express exceptions in IIAs were it not so. Clearly there are some issues which are, in certain circumstances, more important than the protection of foreign investors' commercial interests. But there are certain categories of exceptions that are so important and which are therefore deserving of special treatment by investment tribunals, as well as dedicated discussion in this book. This chapter will accordingly discuss two critical and related varieties of measures which appear as distinct exceptions in many IIAs: essential security and economic emergency, which are sometimes dealt with together under the heading of non-precluded measures. Non-precluded means simply that the obligations contained in the treaty should not be construed to derogate from the state's right to enact measures in these spheres. This chapter will also look at the related concept of necessity under public international law, discussing how this defence was used successfully and unsuccessfully in a series of investment disputes involving Argentina.

The substance of these two key areas of regulatory activity is captured simply by their seriousness in terms of their impact on the functioning of society. While conserving the environment and culture are certainly important, in a relative sense they are far less so than the need to preserve the integrity of society itself. This is not to say that an environmental emergency (or a cultural one for that matter) could never arise, but commonly speaking we would not normally view these issues as ones of urgency or where the failure to take adequate steps could be a matter of life or death. Essential security and economic emergency measures represent responses to an actual or potential crisis, which by definition are situations which arise only exceptionally and entail the gravest of consequences. Because of their severity these types of exceptions are handled somewhat differently in IIAs and under customary international law.

10.2 Essential Security

Perhaps the most serious of all risks to organized society are those relating to its security from attack by outsiders. The manner in which this is addressed by international investment law will be explored below.

10.2.1 FDI as a Risk to Essential Security

Essential security, or to put in more conventional language national security (also encompassing the more indeterminate international security), is a sphere of public policy that is considered to be especially important, enabling host states, under some circumstances, to abandon the promises that they have made under their IIAs without explanation. In that sense, national security is possibly the most important legitimate policy restriction on foreign investment. It informs many of the barriers to FDI seen in countries' national and international commitments. Studies have shown that the most restricted sectors for FDI are those that are sensitive to national security concerns, namely telecommunications, transport, finance and public utilities like water and electricity. Breakdown in these systems can pose a very real danger to life and health, not to mention the obvious risks to the normal functioning of society.

It is worth recalling that FDI is often viewed as a threat to national security because foreign ownership of a key infrastructure may compromise the ability of the state to withstand invasion from abroad or attacks from within.[1] The implication is that non-nationals will be more likely to pursue activities which are hostile to the state than would natives. Foreign ownership of telecommunications companies represents one of the most significant real threats to national security because of their potential to sabotage the country's vital communications network. Banking and transportation are other vital systems for which excessive foreign

---

[1] J. Alvarez, 'Political Protectionism and the United States' International Investment Obligations in Conflict: The Hazards of Exon-Florio' 30 *Virginia Journal of International Law* 1 (1989).

ownership could be dangerous. Probably the best-known example of national security-based opposition to FDI was the attempt by the Saudi Arabian Dubai Ports World to assume management of six major sea ports in the USA. The acquisition was blocked by the US government, leading to allegations of protectionism along with celebrations of nationalism. Clearly foreign ownership of key industries as well as natural resources is an emotive issue for many people. In some respects it captures some of the essential tensions, if not fears, which are associated with globalization.

Given its importance as well as its often elusive nature, national security can take many forms and can accordingly be asserted in a wide range of situations. International tribunals have been willing to take a broad view of what constitutes a risk to national security. For example, the ICJ has held that security interests extend beyond physical attacks and could include interruptions in the flow of international commerce.[2] Investment tribunals have also been prepared to construe risks to security quite liberally, considering severe economic crises to raise risks of national security.[3] National security could conceivably cover measures relating to the prevention of health epidemics. Indeed, once any type of concern reaches the level of crisis, even one which is occurring outside a state's own borders, there may be a risk that a state's essential security is under threat.

10.2.2 Essential Security Exceptions in IIAs

Essential security-based exceptions to IIA obligations are framed, as indicated above, through 'essential security' provisions, referencing the common wording which is used. IIAs tend not to define 'essential security', allowing for maximum flexibility in interpretation by implementing host states and potentially by arbitration tribunals. Clearly the word 'essential' is meant to convey that these types of claims should not be made lightly. These clauses are intended to capture situations of actual crisis or more likely, imminent and hopefully preventable crisis.

NAFTA contains an exception for essential security interests,[4] as does the ECT[5] and the GATS.[6] Essential security interest exceptions also appear

---

[2] *Nicaragua* v. *US*, 1986 ICJ 14 (27 June 1986) and *Iran* v. *US*, 2003 ICJ 161 (6 Nov 2003).
[3] *CMS* v. *Argentina*, ICSID Case No. ARB/01/8 (12 May 2005) at 360.
[4] Art 2102.   [5] Art 24.   [6] Art XIV bis.

in the Model BITs of India,[7] Canada[8] and the USA. The essential security exception of the US Model BIT reads:

> Nothing in this Treaty shall be construed:... 2. to preclude a Party from applying measures that it considers necessary for the fulfilment of its obligations with respect to the maintenance or restoration of international peace or security, or the protection of its own essential security interests.[9]

International peace and security are wide-ranging concepts, conceivably embracing all sorts of situations, including those which may be happening elsewhere in the world. An even more expansive but detailed example of an essential security provision can be found in the China–New Zealand FTA:

> 1. Nothing in this Agreement shall be construed:
>   (a) to require a Party to furnish or allow access to any information the disclosure of which it determines to be contrary to its essential security interests;
>   (b) to prevent a Party from taking any actions which it considers necessary for the protection of its essential security interests
>   (i) relating to the traffic in arms, ammunition and implements of war and to such traffic in other goods and materials or relating to the supply of services as carried on, directly or indirectly, for the purpose of supplying or provisioning a military establishment;
>   (ii) taken in time of war or other emergency in international relations;
>   (iii) relating to fissionable and fusionable materials or the materials from which they are derived; or
>   (c) to prevent a Party from taking any action in pursuance of its obligations under the United Nations Charter for the maintenance of international peace and security.[10]

This Article refers to 'other emergency in international relations' which appears to be somewhat narrower than 'other emergency', suggesting that there has to be a risk to states other than the host state itself. Reference to 'other emergency' could also illustrate the link between what might be termed conventional national security (as in the prevention of armed attacks) and other types of crisis, which may in the long run be equally

---

[7] Art 12.   [8] Art 10.   [9] Art 18.   [10] Art 201 (7 April 2008).

damaging to society even if no hostile forces are involved. Again, health epidemics may be one such crisis.

Unlike many of the other policy-orientated defences to breaches of international investment law that were discussed in the previous chapter, essential security-based defences in IIAs tend to be framed in 'self-judging' language: the host state is entitled to take any actions 'which it considers necessary'. Self-judging means that states have the capacity to make determinations as to the potential for a national security threat of their own accord and to assess whether they feel that this permits them to depart from other obligations in the treaty, precluding assessment by an international tribunal. This represents what is effectively an 'all bets off' approach to security risks and demonstrates why essential security is distinct from the other exceptions contained in IIAs, such as the environment or labour rights. This special status reflects the severity of the host state's national security relative to other policy issues, as well as the highly sensitive nature of the information that would need to be considered to make the determination as to whether it should be invoked or not. International tribunals cannot be granted access to sensitive information that is in the possession of national authorities as this would represent an excessive encroachment upon state sovereignty and could itself pose a risk to national security. They are accordingly unqualified to assess regulations made on this basis.

Still, commentators have viewed self-judging essential security clauses as tantamount to an evisceration of investor protections contained elsewhere in IIAs.[11] As they are immune from evaluation by international tribunals, these provisions are in a sense offensive to the very idea of international investment law, in which principles of international law are interpreted by neutral international arbitrators. Essential security can be asserted without proof, making it highly susceptible to abuse. Other commentators hold that as long as the self-judging essential security provision is open and notorious, then foreign investors' legitimate expectations should not be diminished as a consequence, indeed they probably would not have been very high in the first place. Self-judging essential security provisions in IIAs may merely be seen as a way of shifting the risk of injury arising from a denial of protection to the investor and away from the state and its citizens, who would be required to pay compensation

---

[11] Alvarez, 'Political Protectionism', at 430.

for breach if the exception was not in place. Companies engaging in investments which have the potential to pose a risk to national security must raise the cost of their goods and services or obtain insurance accordingly.[12]

Put another way, self-judging essential security exceptions can be seen as a reasonable limitation on foreign investment given the high level of global political instability which exists today. Furthermore, permitting an essential security exception to be implemented at the discretion of the host state may be regarded as a counterpoint to the host state's duty to provide FPS to foreign investors in times of war or civil unrest.[13] Given that states are liable to ensure a reasonable level of protection to investors under most IIAs, it is perhaps fair that the state should be empowered to deliver that protection by retaining control over its vital systems, including transportation, energy and communications.

It should be recognized that the preservation of national (and international) security may also be achieved through a Denial of Benefits provision in an IIA, a variety of article first mentioned in Chapter 3 with respect to the definition of 'investor' for the purposes of jurisdiction. For example, CETA's investment chapter declares:

> A Party may deny the benefits of this Chapter to an investor of the other Party ... if investors of a non-Party own or control the enterprise; and the denying Party adopts or maintains measures with respect to the non-Party that: are related to maintenance of international peace and security;[14]

This means that a host state can refuse to extend various protections in the IIA if it turns out that the investor is owned by a company from a non-signatory state of the treaty (i.e. outside Europe and Canada) and the denial of the measures achieves the purpose of preserving international peace and security. International peace and security, which is undefined, presumably refer to matters affecting the security of other countries, not just the states which have signed the CETA.

---

[12] W. Burke-White and A. von Staden, 'Investment Protection in Extraordinary Times: The Interpretation and Application of Non-Precluded Measures Provisions in Bilateral Investment Treaties' 48 *Virginia Journal of International Law* 307 (2008).
[13] D. Collins, 'Applying the FPS Standard of International Investment Law to Digital Assets' 12:2 *Journal of World Investment and Trade* 225 (2011).
[14] Art X.15.

10.2.3 Domestic Screening Laws and National Security

Essential security interests tend to be found in most country's national laws with respect to foreign investment, engaged by IIA language which specifies that investors are only admitted if they are in accordance with host state law. Many countries adopt review procedures for foreign investments which contemplate potential threats to the host state's national security. It must be recalled, as illustrated in Chapter 3, that along with IIAs, most host states operate domestic foreign investment legislation which will apply to foreign investors seeking entry into their territory. This is why obtaining a complete picture of the nature of the legal obligations facing foreign investors usually requires some assessment of national law.

Among the most well-known domestic procedures for the screening of foreign investment for matters including national security is that of the Committee on Foreign Investment in the United States (CFIUS). CFIUS is a government board that is empowered by statute to review any 'covered transaction', which is defined as any merger, acquisition or takeover by or with a foreign person which could result in foreign control of a business in the USA, for its possible impact upon national security. 'Control' essentially means a direct role in the management of the enterprise, distinguishing it from mere portfolio investment where the foreign elements contribute resources but have a negligible role in decision-making. Several factors are to be considered by CFIUS in determining the impact upon national security, which is undefined. These include domestic production needed for projected national defence requirements, the capability and capacity of domestic industries to meet national defence requirements, the control of domestic industries and commercial activity by foreign citizens as it affects the capability and capacity of the USA to meet the requirements of national security, including its critical infrastructure. The committee must also consider the potential effects of the proposed investment on the USA's international technological leadership in areas affecting the country's national security. Notifying CFIUS is entirely voluntary but the committee may initiate its own review in certain circumstances. If the acquiring foreign party is an SOE, CFIUS will conduct an investigation of the transaction as a national security investigation, as has happened with a number of Chinese companies in recent years.[15] It is interesting to

---

[15] 50 USC App. §2170.

note that this purview does not appear to cover greenfield FDI, the implication being that this type of investment does not normally pose a risk to national security.

Australia's Foreign Investment Review Board places special requirements on FDI in certain 'sensitive' businesses which it defines non-exhaustively as 'media; telecommunications; transport; defence and military related industries and activities; encryption and securities technologies and communications systems; and the extraction of uranium or plutonium; or the operation of nuclear facilities'.[16] Each of these contemplates national security risks, with the possible exception of media, which may be controlled because of cultural sensitivities.

Canada's domestic review procedure of foreign investment contained in the Investment Canada Act, discussed earlier in Chapter 3, contains a special procedure for foreign investments which may raise issues of national security. National security is not defined in the Act and there is no guidance as to the type of issues that such investigations will encompass, meaning that it is essentially up to the relevant government minister and his or her advisors to assess this on a case-by-case basis.[17] Unlike CFIUS, the national security review procedure in the Investment Canada Act also applies to greenfield investments, most likely reflecting the vital importance of natural resources to the Canadian economy. A number of mergers and acquisitions of Canadian businesses by foreign companies have been refused on the basis of national security concerns through this process, notably a contemplated sale of the BlackBerry technology company to the Chinese firm Lenovo in 2013. The procedure under the Investment Canada Act is perhaps equally well-known for some of its decisions not to deny acquisitions by foreign companies, such as the purchase of various oil sands projects by the Chinese SOE CNOOC in 2014.

While most countries, such as the USA, Australia and Canada, attempt to make their review procedures as transparent and even-handed as feasible, there is obviously the potential that the highly discretionary nature of the national security review procedures may be motivated by covert protectionism, or at least the perception of it. Equally likely is that anti-investor decisions of these government bodies may be welcomed by citizens who fear that ownership of key businesses or resources may be economically harmful as well as a threat to public safety.

---

[16] Foreign Acquisitions and Takeovers Act, 1975, Division 2, s 26.   [17] Part IV.

10.2.4 Essential Security and Economic Sanctions

Many states impose economic sanctions against other states as a consequence of their own national security interests as well as their obligations as members of the UN and other international organizations such as the North Atlantic Treaty Organization (NATO). Such sanctions, such as asset freezes and travel bans, could conflict with rights conferred under international investment law. For example, in 2014 several countries including those of the EU as well as Japan, the USA and Canada implemented sanctions against Russia for its annexation of the Crimea region of the Ukraine. Sanctions were also recently imposed by many countries against Iran for its refusal (until recently) to discontinue its nuclear weapons programme. Russian and Iranian citizens whose bank accounts were frozen under these sanctions could potentially bring claims of expropriation or FET through IIAs or under customary international law. If such claims were successful, then the states imposing the sanctions could be compelled to pay compensation to the injured investors, undermining the effectiveness of the sanctions in the first place. Of course the commercial activity undertaken would have to satisfy the relevant IIA's definition of investment. It is unclear whether a bank account itself could count as such, although the targeting of specific firms could arguably strengthen this claim. A long-term asset freeze would more likely constitute an indirect expropriation depriving the owner of effective use, even if legal title remained.

Such sanctions may be defended, however, on the basis of the essential security provisions found in some modern IIAs which, as observed above, often speak of the maintenance or restoration of international peace and security. Such concepts would most likely justify the imposition of sanctions, particularly those which were authorized by international organizations like the UN which is tasked with the maintenance and development of international law. In situations where the relevant IIA does not contain such a clause, customary international law may yet defend a host state's decision to impose a sanction which affects the commercial interests of a foreign firm.

The principle of international law most suited to this situation would be that of countermeasures. In this regard, the International Law Commission's Articles on State Responsibility specify that injured states are permitted to take measures to react to that injury[18] and furthermore, that

---

[18] Arts 42, 49.

non-injured states may take measures to fulfil obligations owed to the international community as a whole.[19] The Russian and Iranian sanctions brought by countries not directly involved in the relevant conflict, such as the USA and the EU, would probably not constitute a reaction to injury. The lack of authorization by the UN (as was the case with the sanctions against Russia which did not receive approval by the UN's Security Council) could undermine the imposition of sanctions by non-injured countries under the latter category as the response of the UN may be seen as a barometer of the global community. Accordingly many of the recent countermeasures imposed by European and other states in the form of sanctions against Russia and possibly also Iran (which were supported by the UN Security Council) could violate the customary international law of countermeasures. Clearly the involvement of the UN adds a layer of legitimacy to a measure that is allegedly pursued in the interests of international peace. If countermeasures in the form of sanctions by non-injured states were permitted under customary international law because of their link to the security of the international community, they would still need to respect fundamental human rights principles.[20] The interplay of these issues is poised to become a contentious issue as international investment arbitration continues to flourish, much as non-military responses to conflict are regarded as the most acceptable response to international conflicts.

10.3 Economic Stability Objectives

The global financial crisis of 2008–09 and its aftermath raised concerns that the interrelatedness of the global economy, while a source of wealth generation, is also fraught with the risk that recession in one country can pass very easily across international borders. States are eager to preserve their capacity to respond to such situations.

10.3.1 FDI and Economic Crises

The economic sovereignty of states is one of the basic principles of international law. A state which does not have the capacity to control its

---

[19] Art 48.

[20] A. van Aaken, 'International Investment Law and Decentralized Targeted Sanctions: An Uneasy Relationship' *Columbia FDI Perspectives* No. 164 (4 Jan 2015).

economy will soon cease to function at other, more fundamental levels, a situation seen all too well in some of the recent sovereign debt crises in countries such as Greece and Venezuela. As mentioned at the beginning of this book, nations are now recognized to have permanent sovereignty over their natural resources as well as the right to economic self-determination, meaning the right to develop at their own pace. This means that countries should not be pressured into accepting too much foreign capital if they are unprepared for it in terms of its effect on their social conditions. Economic sovereignty and the right of economic self-determination of states are so important that they are often considered *jus cogens*, meaning that they override all other rules whether treaty-based or part of customary international law. As these principles are non-derogable, it is far from certain that the obligations contained in IIAs or investment contracts could ever undermine them, meaning that exceptions intending to prevent economic emergencies could in a sense be viewed as redundant. With this principle in mind, host states can accordingly claim that they have instigated certain regulatory action in order to protect the integrity of their economic systems, and in theory this should not amount to a breach of an IIA. On the other hand, IIAs must be seen as binding commitments under international law which create very real obligations on states and which, if transgressed, can engender liability and the obligation to pay compensation.

Measures that aim to prevent or mitigate severe economic crises are among the most important counter-balances to an IIA's investor protections, allowing for a wide range of measures that preserve state's economic sovereignty in emergency situations. It is through this category that government stimulus and bailout programmes, common throughout the world following the 2008–09 financial crisis, would likely be permitted had they been challenged as discriminatory. While not strictly speaking a public policy exception in the manner of environmental protection or cultural preservation because it deals squarely with measures aimed at safeguarding the economy, such regulations could have fundamental repercussions on the overall welfare of society, including avoiding mass unemployment, homelessness or worse. These unpleasant realities demonstrate the link between economic emergency exceptions and national security.

Response to economic crisis can inflict severe financial damage to foreign firms. For example, some developing countries that suffer from chronic indebtedness need to conserve foreign currency to pay for essential goods and services. States such as Mexico and Venezuela have limited foreign investors' capacity to make unrestricted money transfers in case this leads to sudden widespread capital exodus, as occurred in the East Asian financial crisis of the late 1990s. Many developing countries have exchange control laws to regulate the conversion and transfer of currency abroad. Some countries, such as China and India, also maintain restrictions on the amount of domestic capital that can be removed from the home country by their own domestic investors' internationalization. Although some of these policies could transgress IMF rules on free transfer of currency as well as IIA capital transfer obligations discussed earlier in this book, IIAs can permit states to enact these types of restrictions in times of economic crisis or to avert an impending crisis.

Rapid exit of FDI, the so-called 'capital flight', can lead to severe economic harms including massive unemployment and the inability of governments to pay for basic services. China implemented a number of capital controls in 2015 in order to prevent an outflow of foreign investment. Such policies could transgress IMF rules on free transfer of currency, although in recent years the IMF has softened its stance against currency transfer for precisely this reason. It is thought that India and China were able to escape the effects of the Asian economic crisis in the 1990s in part because they had not liberalized their financial sectors in terms of their openness to FDI to the same extent as other Asian countries.[21] As there were fewer foreign firms active in this sector, there was a reduced likelihood that capital would be removed from the jurisdiction.

10.3.2 Economic Stability and Prudential Measures

In light of the above mentioned concerns, exceptions that specifically reference economic crisis management are found in many IIAs. For example, the Canadian Model BIT contains a broad exception for measures needed to protect the integrity of the financial system.[22] The EU–Korea FTA speaks of parties' restrictive measures being lawful when parties are in 'external financial difficulties' or suffering balance-of-payments problems.[23] The treaty further specifies that:

---

[21] W. Jiangyu, 'Financial Liberalization and Regulation in East Asia: Lessons of the Financial Crisis and the Chinese Experience of Controlled Liberalization' 4:1 *Journal of World Trade* 211 (2007).
[22] Art 10.2(b).   [23] Art 15.8 (14 Nov 2010).

> Any restrictive measures adopted or maintained under this Article shall be non-discriminatory, of limited duration, not go beyond what is necessary to remedy the balance-of-payments and external financial situation.

In other words, measures taken to deal with economic crises must be applied in a balanced fashion with a view to their legitimate purpose – they should not be used as a form of protectionism against foreign firms. GATS also establishes that WTO Members may adopt or maintain restrictions to trade in services in the event of serious balance-of-payments or financial difficulties.[24]

A number of IIAs concluded by the USA allow state parties to take any measures relating to financial services for 'prudential reasons'. For example, Art 20.1 of the US–Rwanda BIT of 2008[25] (concluded ironically a few months before the onset of the global financial crisis) states:

> A Party shall not be prevented from adopting or maintaining measures relating to financial services for prudential reasons, including for the protection of investors, depositors, policy holders, or persons to whom a fiduciary duty is owed by a financial services supplier, or to ensure the integrity and stability of the financial system.

A footnote to this Article explains:

> it is understood that the term 'prudential reasons' includes the maintenance of the safety, soundness, integrity, or financial responsibility of individual financial institutions, as well as the maintenance of the safety and financial and operational integrity of payment and clearing systems.

This appears to suggest that measures aimed at dealing with economic emergencies are only those which affect investors in financial services, not foreign investors generally, meaning that it has a relatively restricted scope. In near identical language, the GATS Annex on Financial Services, which commits WTO Members to liberalizing their financial services sectors including allowing for the entry of foreign suppliers, establishes that WTO Members should not be prevented from taking prudential measures to ensure the integrity of their respective financial systems. This exception

---

[24] Art XII. GATS does not yet provide for an emergency safeguard regime, although Art X provides that there shall be negotiations for such a regime.
[25] 19 Feb 2008.

is tempered by the somewhat obvious requirement that it must not be used as a means of avoiding commitments under the GATS.[26]

As noted above, some IIAs contain exceptions relating to measures aimed at addressing problems in the host state's balance-of-payments status, meaning the relationship between all of the country's inward and outward transactions. Clearly if there is a significant removal of capital by foreign firms, countries may need to impose capital controls to ensure the integrity of the country's economy. Such actions may often conform with the state's IMF obligations, as the IMF requires that its Members remain solvent at all times. Like GATS and the EU–Korea FTA, many BITs establish that parties may adopt or maintain restrictions on foreign investors, notably in relation to currency transfer, in the event of serious balance-of-payments or financial difficulties, even if they have not yet arisen. For instance, the Cambodia–Japan BIT elaborates:

> A Contracting Party may adopt or maintain measures not conforming with its obligations... relating to cross-border capital transactions...
>
> (a) in the event of serious balance-of-payments and external financial difficulties or threat thereof; or
> (b) in cases where, in exceptional circumstances, movements of capital cause or threaten to cause serious difficulties for macroeconomic management, in particular, monetary and exchange rate policies.[27]

The fact that even the threat of financial difficulties is enough to justify these measures is interesting, perhaps reflecting Japan's apprehension about economic stability in light of its recent experience with recession. This Article goes on to establish that such measures must be consistent with IMF obligations and that they must be no more onerous than necessary,[28] intending to prevent covert protectionism. Identifying the relevance of these concepts to emerging as well as developed economies, the India–Mexico BIT allows parties to maintain restrictions on currency transfer, provided that they are in accordance with IMF obligations.[29]

The prevention of economic emergencies could fall within the sphere of maintaining public order, a phrase which is common to many IIAs,[30] as

---

[26] GATS Annex on Financial Services, 2.a.   [27] Art 19(1) (14 June 2007).
[28] Art 19(2).   [29] Art 4(a) (21 May 2007).
[30] Russia–Sweden BIT, Art 3(3) (19 April 1995).

explored in the previous chapter. A functioning economy in which citizens have access to money to buy goods and services is a vital aspect of an orderly society. The lack of availability of cash seen in the Greek sovereign debt crisis and the ensuing social and political unrest is evidence of the harm that can befall a country when the integrity of the money supply is undermined.

10.4 The Doctrine of Necessity

In addition to express exceptions found in the text of IIAs governing economic matters such as general prudential measures or balance-of-payments obligations, there may be room for a host state to breach its commitments to investors during times of economic or other crises through customary international law.

10.4.1 The Scope of the Doctrine

The public interest in the overall stability of the economy of the host state found in some IIAs is linked to the defence of necessity that exists in customary international law. This is a justification for behaviour that is available to host states, under certain narrow circumstances, regardless of what the text of the relevant IIA states. Put simply, necessity means that the state is excused for its actions because it had no other option as a consequence of a very severe situation that has arisen which the state did not cause. The threshold for satisfying the test of necessity is a high one but it could include situations of severe economic crisis, particularly where lives are at stake, meaning that the crisis takes on a social dimension. This defence may be especially important for developing countries because they may not have as ready access to resources to respond adequately to such emergencies. If the claim of necessity is accepted by an international investment tribunal, the state may not be required to pay compensation for any adverse consequences faced by foreign investors.

The nature of the doctrine of necessity, including what is needed to succeed in asserting it, is outlined in Art 25 of the Articles on State Responsibility, which is framed in negative terms:

1. Necessity may not be invoked by a State as a ground for precluding the wrongfulness of an act not in conformity with an international obligation of that State unless the act: (a) is the only way for the State to safeguard an essential interest against a grave and imminent peril; and (b) does not seriously impair an essential interest of the State or States towards which the obligation exists, or of the international community as a whole.

2. In any case, necessity may not be invoked by a State as a ground for precluding wrongfulness if: (a) the international obligation in question excludes the possibility of invoking necessity; or (b) the State has contributed to the situation of necessity.

A number of key points must be discerned from this Article. First, necessity is an affirmative defence – meaning that the burden of its proof is on the state asserting the defence. Second, it will only operate in extreme circumstances, so it will not cover normal periods of economic recession. In terms of the link between the measure and the desired goal (i.e. the avoidance of the monumental harm) there must be no other less intrusive way to achieve the measure's objective taking into consideration its impact on the rights of another state. Even where this is the case, meaning that where the measure was effectively the only way to avoid the horrendous harm, the measure still cannot undermine a very important right belonging to another state or the international community. Put more simply, the doctrine of necessity will only work in the most exceptional of cases.

It should be observed that the Articles on State Responsibility also contain provision for the related *force majeure* as a way of escaping international law obligations in times of crisis. This principle of law means that unforeseeable and extraordinary events may allow a state to terminate its obligations under treaty or contract, much as the related doctrine of frustration works in the common law of contract.[31] Article 23 states that for *force majeure* to function to relieve a party of its obligations, the situation should not only be extraordinary and unforeseeable but it should also be as a result of an occurrence of an irresistible force, beyond the control of the state, which makes it materially impossible in the circumstances to perform the obligation. Impossible in this sense is entirely different from

[31] E.g. *Krell v. Henry* [1903] 2 KB 740.

very difficult, which appears to be a somewhat closer approximation to the doctrine of necessity which does not contemplate such extreme language. *Force majeure* does not include circumstances in which the performance of the obligation has become more difficult but is still feasible, such as would arise during a political or economic crisis.[32] In other words, there was no way that the contract or treaty could possibly have been fulfilled given what has happened.

10.4.2 The Argentina Cases

Economic emergency measures and the doctrine of necessity have been the subject of a number of investment arbitrations, including several relating to the Argentine financial crisis of 2001. In the final weeks of that year, Argentina suffered a catastrophic financial collapse. Desperate to control the disaster, Argentina adopted a series of measures intended to stabilize the economy and restore political confidence. This included most notably a massive devaluation of its currency, the peso, which inflicted devastation on a number of companies including foreign investors. In the aftermath, Argentina was sued in forty-three ICSID arbitrations brought by investors who claimed that they had been injured as a consequence of Argentina's response to the economic crisis. Many of the investments had related to projects connected to the mass privatization of the country's utilities undertaken during the 1990s. Argentina faced (and still faces) a total liability of more than US $8 billion, more than the entire financial reserves of the country at the time the crisis had begun to abate in 2002. Argentina remains the most common respondent state in ICSID arbitration by a significant margin because of these events which contemplated both exceptions for economic crises contained in various IIAs and the doctrine of necessity in customary international law. Understanding the degree to which host states such as Argentina can implement emergency measures in violation of IIA obligations has been problematic from an interpretive standpoint because of the interplay between the exceptions contained in the text of many treaties and that available under the customary international law of necessity. A discussion of some of the key decisions arising out of the Argentine financial crisis follows.

---

[32] J. Crawford (ed.), *The International Law Commission's Articles on State Responsibility: Introduction, Text and Commentaries* (Cambridge University Press, 2002), at 171.

In *LG&E Energy Corp*, the tribunal recognized that the state's ability to protect public order as specified in Argentina's BIT with the USA and under customary international law entitled it to violate investment treaty obligations, including guarantees against expropriation and FET through the drastic measures which it had taken.[33] Specifically, as noted above, Argentina had passed a law which had eliminated the conversion of tariffs from US dollars to pesos, seriously harming the value of foreign investors' assets in the country. The tribunal stated:

> to conclude that such a severe economic crisis could not constitute an essential security interest is to diminish the havoc that the economy can wreak on the lives of an entire population and the ability of the Government to lead. When a State's economic foundation is under siege, the severity of the problem can equal that of any military invasion.[34]

This somewhat dramatic statement is significant because it equates economic turmoil with national security. When an economic crisis becomes so severe, it reaches a level at which the functioning of society itself is under threat. These are precisely the types of situations which are also envisioned by the doctrine of necessity. The *LG&E* tribunal ultimately ruled that the measures enacted by the Argentine government were the only means available to deal with the catastrophe, which had not substantially been of the government's own making.

A year before *LG&E*, the *CMS Gas Transmission Co v. Argentina* tribunal rejected the plea of necessity to excuse measures undertaken during the crisis. The tribunal reached this decision by focusing on the fact that the measures employed were not 'the only way' to cope with the situation and equally importantly, Argentina had itself contributed to the situation. The tribunal felt that the crisis had been caused by flawed government policies that had been in place for some time. Furthermore, the tribunal held that the emergency provision found in the Argentina–USA BIT was not applicable because such a provision should not be interpreted in a manner that places the investor in a less favourable situation than accorded under customary international law. In other words, the customary international law standard embodies the maximum level of discretion to which a state should be entitled. The protections in an IIA (as diminished by various exceptions such as economic emergency) cannot take

---

[33] *LG&E v. Argentina*, ICSID Case No. ARB/02/1 (3 Oct 2006).   [34] Ibid., at [238].

away from the investor's rights any more than the doctrine of necessity does already. An ICSID annulment committee upheld the tribunal's determination that the necessity defence, either as contained in the relevant IIA or under customary international law, was inapplicable to the situation at hand. The annulment committee further clarified that this decision was reached in part because the state of necessity did not satisfy the requirement of being temporary.[35] Still, the committee criticized the reasoning of the original tribunal on its treatment of the doctrine of necessity, suggesting that on the facts the defence should have been available to the host state, as it had been in other cases dealing with the same crisis. This criticism seems at least somewhat valid, as it is not clear why a state would bother including an emergency provision in an IIA if it did not grant them any greater capacity to enact measures than already exist under customary international law. To be sure, despite the annulment committee's criticisms, *CMS* v. *Argentina*'s narrow view of necessity remains valid law, as it were.

Sempra Energy International v. *Argentina* was another ICSID decision dealing with the Argentine crisis which also came before an annulment committee. Here the committee elected to annul the original award, holding that a state's failure to satisfy the requirements of necessity under customary international law does not preclude a successful plea of necessity under the relevant BIT. There are indeed two different standards. Argentina was therefore able to use the essential security exception in the treaty to justify its actions against foreign investors taken during the crisis, even if its necessity argument was unsubstantiated. The annulment committee found that the first arbitration tribunal had manifestly exceeded its powers by referring only to customary international law, rather than economic emergency under the BIT.[36] This is one of the rare occasions where an annulment committee, acting under its very limited powers, has found against the decision of the lower tribunal.

In *Enron Corporation and Ponderosa LP* v. *Argentina* the tribunal was unwilling to accept the host state's defence which was based on the doctrine of necessity even though the situation (Argentina's economic crisis)

---

[35] *CMS Gas Transmission Co.* v. *Argentina*, ICSID Case No. ARB/01/8, Annulment Proceeding (12 May 2005) at [137].

[36] *Sempra Energy International* v. *Argentina*, ICSID Case No. ARB/02/16, Annulment Proceeding (29 June 2010) at [280].

was similar to previous cases where various other tribunals had done so. The *Enron* tribunal acknowledged that there was a crisis but concluded that the unfortunate events did not in themselves amount to a legal excuse. The tribunal explained:

> the argument that such a situation compromised the very existence of the State and its independence so as to qualify as involving an essential interest of the State is not convincing. Questions of public order and social unrest could be handled as they in fact were, just as questions of political stabilization were handled under the constitutional arrangements in force.[37]

This decision confirms that the doctrine of necessity under customary international law will not be an easy claim to make – it will not be satisfied unless the state's very existence is under threat. Perhaps more problematically, it also reveals the highly discretionary nature of arbitrators' decision-making processes. A virtually identical factual situation can lead to two radically different takes on the same principle of law.

One of the key issues which arises when considering the application of necessity and essential security provisions in IIAs is their effect on the compensation which is owed to investors when such situations are lawfully engaged. The *LG&E* tribunal held that measures enacted pursuant to the doctrine of necessity did not trigger an obligation to pay compensation to the investor. This view has received support from other tribunals which have examined the Argentine crisis.[38] In contrast, the *CMS* tribunal clarified that as soon as the circumstances which gave rise to the claim of necessity end, then the state's duties to the investor under the IIA would re-emerge, requiring an assessment of compensation for any harm sustained during that period when the state necessity applied. This appears to suggest that a finding of necessity merely works to delay the owing of compensation, not to extinguish it, similar to the doctrine of promissory estoppel under English contract law.[39] In another decision relating to the Argentine crisis, *El Paso* v. *Argentina*, the tribunal (which ultimately rejected the host state's claim of necessity) considered the issue of compensation during a state of necessity, holding:

---

[37] ICSID Case No. ARB/01/3 (14 Jan 2004).
[38] *Continental Casualty* v. *Argentina*, ICSID Case No. ARB/03/9 (23 Oct 2009).
[39] *D & C Builders* v. *Rees* [1965] 2 QB 617.

> No compensation must be awarded for damage suffered during the period
> of emergency, as the BIT does not apply in such a period, except if the state
> has substantially contributed to create it, while damages might be awarded
> for measures taken during the state of emergency and not cancelled when
> the state of emergency has ceased to exist.[40]

This statement seems to suggest that as long as the customary international law doctrine of necessity applies then no compensation is payable,
but as soon as the state which gives rise to the necessity ends, the potential for compensation will exist if the relevant measures are not removed.
It does not appear that any 'back payment' is then due for actions taken
during the emergency.

Commentators seeking to explain some of the confusion surrounding the availability of the defence of necessity for economic crises have
emphasized the slightly differing factual situations in the various Argentine disputes which occurred at different stages of the same economic
crisis and in different parts of the country.[41] This logic could possibly
apply by difficult extension to the issues surrounding compensation as
well. Conflicting interpretations can be seen as the inevitable result of
flexible, often highly fact-dependent dispute settlement, coupled with the
lack of precedent in international arbitration. Other commentators have
seized upon the inconsistency in the Argentine crisis cases to point to the
fragmentation of international investment law.[42] It may also be taken as
an illustration of the 'illegitimacy' of investor–state dispute settlement in
contrast to, for example, the more coherent jurisprudence found in the
law of the WTO or even more so, domestic legal systems operating under
strict doctrines of precedent.

10.5 Conclusion

Essential security and other emergency exceptions are found in almost
all IIAs, disclosing the paramount importance of preserving a basic level

---

[40] ICSID Case No. ARB/03/15 (31 Oct 2012) at [612].

[41] See e.g. A. Reinisch, 'Necessity in International Investment Arbitration: An Unnecessary
Split of Opinions in Recent ICSID Cases?' 8 *Journal of World Investment & Trade* 191
(2007).

[42] J. Alvarez, *The Public International Law Regime Governing International Investment*
(The Hague Academy of International Law, 2011), at 284.

of order in society relative to the purpose of these instruments, namely increasing FDI flows between party states for the purpose of economic development and growth. Taken together these provisions are often referred to as non-precluded measures and are among the most controversial features of international investment law because they pit investor protection against the host state's most fundamental needs. Although the situations in which they may be asserted are by their nature rare occurrences, the far-reaching implications of these provisions and the manner in which they are interpreted by tribunals in many respects subvert the purpose of international investment law as a system of rules for protecting and enforcing investors' rights vis-à-vis host states.

Such articles in treaties allow states to take actions otherwise inconsistent with the treaty when it is necessary for the maintenance of public safety or to respond to an emergency such as an economic crisis. As some economic emergencies (and potentially other types such as health-orientated ones) can become so catastrophic that they threaten the public safety, then in a sense they may be viewed as equivalent to national or essential security concerns. Taken together, such justifications effectively permit host states to interfere with the commercial activities of foreign investors, clearly weakening the IIA as a regime of investor protection. As long as the host state's actions are taken in pursuit of one of these exceptional concerns, measures otherwise prohibited by the treaty will not constitute breaches and states should accordingly face no liability and therefore may be excused from the payment of compensation.

While seemingly clear-cut, essential security and emergency justifications in IIAs can be problematic because they are often framed using self-judging language. This removes them from the scrutiny of international tribunals, allowing such decisions to be taken unilaterally by host states. Although this may be said to uphold state sovereignty over critical matters (surely national security is more important than FDI), it does raise the spectre of unbridled protectionism masquerading as public concern. In this sense, non-precluded measures are quite different from the other public interest exceptions discussed in the previous chapter, most of which can be tested by tribunals for their rationale and effects. Precluding liability for emergency measures is further complicated by the interplay between express justifications for essential security and other emergencies in IIAs and the doctrine of necessity under customary international law, which exists regardless of what is specified in the treaty. While a plea of necessity on the part of a host state is very difficult to establish in part because of the severity which is required, if successful the host state may be precluded from the payment of compensation entirely. The application of this doctrine in international investment law has a chequered history because of numerous seemingly inconsistent decisions associated with the Argentine financial crisis. This situation is probably responsible for a good deal of the negative association with international investment law within the media and probably also the broader academic and legal community for two reasons. One, inconsistent rulings in similar situations undermines the predictability and by extension the legitimacy of a legal system. And two, compelling an impoverished country recovering from an economic meltdown to pay billions of dollars in compensation to wealthy multinational enterprises conveys a sense of injustice and immorality. It perhaps comes as no surprise that Argentina has failed to pay a number of the awards brought against it, just as several states from Latin America have removed themselves from the ICSID regime in the aftermath of these events.

11.1 Introduction

Foreign investment can generate significant wealth for multinational enterprises, just as it can offer major economic benefits for the states which receive it. However, as this book has demonstrated, there are many dangers involved with placing investments overseas. Decisions on how and, equally importantly, where to invest are among the most important choices made by managers. A recent study among several leading multinational enterprises identified strong 'rule of law' as among the most important factors when firms make these decisions, along with the 'ease of doing business' and a 'stable political environment'. Likewise, the three greatest risks in host states as identified by multinational investors are the prevalence of corruption, political or social instability and a lack of transparency in rulemaking.[1]

With these strategic considerations in mind, IIAs are clearly important to multinational enterprises as a source of legal protection, but interestingly, they rank below national laws in terms of their perceived importance. The studies revealed that just under half of surveyed multinationals indicated that the absence of an IIA between home and host governments deterred an investment which the company was considering, with an additional third of respondents stating that the absence of an investment treaty would cause them to reduce the size of an existing or planned investment.[2]

Beyond protections offered by legal instruments such as IIAs or national laws enshrining contract and property rights, foreign investors also appear to value adherence by their host country business partners to voluntary corporate codes of conduct, such as those governing human rights,

---

[1] *Risk and Return: Foreign Direct Investment and the Rule of Law* (Hogan Lovells, Bingham Centre for Rule of Law, British Institute of International and Comparative Law, 2014) at 6–7. The survey was conducted among 301 'senior decision-makers' at Forbes 2000 companies with global annual revenues of at least US $1bn annually.
[2] Ibid.

employee rights and environmental protection, with four-fifths of surveyed firms indicating that such regimes were either essential or very important.[3] Some of these codes, such as most notably the OECD Guidelines for Multinational Enterprises, were explored in Chapters 2 and 9. These results suggest that many of these initiatives have been quite successful, and are testimony to the value of multinational organizations.

This chapter will investigate the chief alternative strategy to pursuing protection under IIAs: Political Risk Insurance (PRI) as offered variously by private banks, states and development organizations. It will examine the extent to which PRI has been used by foreign investors and will address some of its drawbacks, further considering strategies for attracting FDI by host states beyond an investment treaty regime. These include improvements to the local regulatory environment and the offering of incentive packages. This chapter will conclude by exploring some of the overarching criticisms of international investment law, including its apparent tendency towards fragmentation, imbalance in terms of preferring investors over states, its extension into inappropriate spheres of regulation, as well as its role as an agent of re-constitutionalization of host states around the world.

11.2 Risk Mitigation

The main objective of international investment law, at least from the perspective of investors, is to provide protection against non-commercial risks that may be faced by foreign investors in other countries. In that sense, the entire body of law may be seen as a risk-mitigation strategy. Investors have incurred significant up-front costs by placing their assets within the control of often unfamiliar and untrusted governments. FDI can be dangerous in part because of the long-term nature of the investor's activities in the host state. It may be several years after an initial investment has been made before the investor ultimately sees any profit. As this time passes, there is a greater likelihood that the host state's behaviour will change, potentially reducing or eliminating entirely the investor's gains. By simple law of averages, the risk that something will go wrong increases the longer the investor stays. These problems are exacerbated in unstable countries where there is a greater chance that the government will alter its laws or cease to offer a stable legal environment that is conducive to

---

[3] Ibid., at 7.

the investor's business. Legal security can act as a vital reassurance that these interests will not be taken or otherwise interfered with excessively.

Ordinary commercial risks, such as could arise when a product or service provided by a foreign firm is unpopular among local consumers, or when an extracted resource turns out to be unviable, are not of interest to international investment law. A business's non-profitability is not a matter that should be brought before international investment tribunals – courts do not help with poor business decisions. In contrast, when the investor suffers through no fault of its own, international investment law may offer recourse. We have seen that IIAs offer the possibility of compensation for violations of guarantees such as those relating to National Treatment, FET and indirect expropriation. The rationale behind this remedy is that monetary compensation should be sufficient to make investors whole in these circumstances. In other words, with properly calibrated compensation, the investor should in theory be indifferent about whether an IIA is obeyed or whether it is violated.

Despite the security of the protections contained in an IIA, there may be situations where the investor suffers as a consequence of events beyond the host state's control, such as civil disturbances, war, revolution or in some cases, severe economic crises. These situations are sometimes known as 'political risks' because they relate to political decisions that the government has taken (or failed to take). It may be possible for actions taken by the state in response to these events not to be answerable under international law for the reasons discussed in the previous chapter. The defence of necessity may apply (as it did in some cases for Argentina) or else the IIA may exempt measures taken during a time of emergency or in the interests of public order.

Moreover, if a host state loses a claim in international investment arbitration after having been found liable for breaching an IIA and it cannot pay the award (again, as happened with Argentina), the result will be unhelpful to the foreign investor which has seen its business falter without bearing any fault. Compensation cannot be extracted from a government that is insolvent, and countries experiencing severe economic crises will most likely be entitled under international law to deal with the most pressing concerns of their citizens before paying out obligations to foreign firms from investment arbitration decisions they have lost. Any amounts that can be paid by the host state may be insufficient to offset losses, making the whole process of bringing a claim under an IIA largely futile, particularly given the legal costs associated with these procedures. This is one of the reasons that FDI, while potentially very lucrative, remains a decidedly risky business.

11.3 Political Risk Insurance (PRI)

International investment law, as embodied by a home state signing and an investor later relying on an IIA, is not the only risk-mitigation strategy available to apprehensive firms seeking overseas opportunities. The other method, which can also address situations such as those described above where winning an investment dispute is futile, is one which has been used to offset risk in many spheres of activity: investors can obtain insurance to cover any losses they may suffer from political risks they may face abroad.

PRI is a financial product like any other kind of insurance. In exchange for the payment of regular but relatively small premiums based on the level of perceived danger, the insured party will be covered by the insurer for losses suffered in the event that something goes wrong, sometimes in conjunction with the contribution of a deductible to spread the risk. The insurer hopes that the premiums will over time amount to more than any loss claimed, whereas the insured gains the comfort that if an unfortunate event does occur, they will not bear the loss. By paying out the amount of an investor's loss resulting from various kinds of losses inflicted by host states, PRI can lessen the likelihood that the investor will suffer from a situation in the host country that is either beyond the control of the host government, or which the investor is unwilling to tolerate over a period of months or years as its profits shrink. Of course, investors will have to satisfy the conditions specified in the various PRI packages' terms and conditions. They will also likely need to pay for the PRI through regular premiums, as is common with most traditional forms of insurance. Indeed this is what makes the industry commercially viable.

There are four main categories of PRI: national or bilateral guarantee programmes offered by home states; multilateral investment guarantee programmes provided by international organizations; regional development bank programmes aimed at augmenting FDI to geographical areas; and lastly, private insurance packages whose essential motivation is profit.

11.3.1 National Providers

National providers of PRI are government-owned and operated pro-grammes offering insurance to national investors, meaning ones origi-nating from their own territory, which are located or planning to locate in eligible host countries. A number of developed states offer national PRI programmes in order to encourage their investors to internationalize to places of high risk because of the profits that may ultimately be gener-ated. These can be operated commercially in which there is an intention to secure a profit for the government, or in some case the insurance is subsidized by the government itself, meaning that it may not necessar-ily be profitable but can help the firm establish itself in the longer term. This is particularly the case where the national programme only offers insurance where the investor cannot secure it privately, as a lender of last resort. While there may be a developmental objective for host states, most national PRI is directed at increasing domestic firms' competitiveness in global markets. National providers of PRI tend to offer longer coverage periods than other types of programmes, sometimes up to twenty years. The long-term nature of the coverage may demonstrate an emphasis on building beneficial relationships with the host state, reflecting the devel-opmental focus of many of these schemes.[4]

Home countries supporting their investors will usually include a sub-rogation provision in their IIAs in order to ensure that it will be able to substitute itself for the foreign investor when bringing claims against the host state. The home state, having guaranteed the losses of the investor, is then able to exercise all claims and rights that would have been available to the investor towards the host country under the IIA. Such a provision may be found in the Afghanistan–Germany BIT:

> If either Contracting State makes a payment to any of its Investors under a guarantee it has assumed in respect of an investment in the territory of the other Contracting State, the latter Contracting State shall, without prejudice to the rights of the former Contracting State under Article 10 [dispute settlement], recognize the assignment, whether under a law or pursuant to a legal transaction, of any right or claim of such investor to the former Contracting State.[5]

---

[4] K. Nadakavukaren Schefer, *International Investment Law* (Edward Elgar, 2013), at 517.
[5] Art 6 (20 April 2005).

This ensures that any compensation which is payable to the investor pursuant to an award of an investment tribunal must be transferred to the home state which has acted as guarantor, for example under a PRI policy.

Perhaps the most well-known example of a national provider of PRI is the US Overseas Private Investment Corporation (OPIC).[6] OPIC was established in 1971 to encourage US businesses to invest in countries that were seen as too risky for investors. It is an important part of the US foreign aid regime, and its efforts with PRI are based on the idea that through FDI US investors can contribute to the development of host states. The objectives of OPIC are economic development as well as assisting countries in the transition from non-market to market economies. OPIC coverage is therefore limited to projects that contribute to the development of host states, especially least developed ones. It also has an objective of sustainable development, and particularly encourages lending to small businesses. The political risks covered by OPIC include currency restrictions; expropriation due to confiscation; loss of business due to war; and revolution or civil strife.

11.3.2 Multilateral Providers

Although many developed states have their own internal system of investment guarantee for those investing in developing countries, there has been a need for an international system of PRI provision to safeguard investors against certain types of unusual, non-commercial risks. This is because of the developmental component of FDI in situations where long-term profitability and competitiveness may be uncertain. The most important of the multilateral providers is the MIGA of the World Bank, which was mentioned in Chapter 2. MIGA was created as a member of the World Bank Group in 1988 by Convention as a means of providing guarantees for non-commercial risks associated with foreign investment projects in developing countries.

Article 11 of the MIGA Convention outlines the types of situations that may be covered by the guarantee of the Agency, many of which form the basis for protections found in IIAs. These include: restrictions on currency transfers; expropriation; breaches or repudiations of a contract when there are no effective judicial processes available for redress; and war and civil

---

[6] www.opic.gov/.

disturbances in the host country. Coverage for these various risks may be purchased by investors individually or in combination. Certain risks are not covered by the guarantee, such as losses as a consequence of devaluation or depreciation and acts of the host government which have been consented to by the investor.

In order for the investment to be eligible for protection under MIGA's PRI scheme, the foreign investment must be new (not an existing investment); commercially sound; contribute to the development of the host country; and be in conformity with the host country's laws, development objectives and investment conditions. Applicant projects will be reviewed by MIGA to ensure that these conditions are satisfied. The investors eligible for the protection of the MIGA's PRI guarantees generally comprise natural or juridical persons, who are nationals of another member country of MIGA (most countries in the world), other than the host state. As per the World Bank's mandate, the eligible host country must be a developing one. In the contract between the investor and MIGA, the investor promises to operate on a commercial basis and the investor is required to pay premiums for the benefit of the guarantee. Any disputes which arise in connection with the guarantee are to be resolved through arbitration. One of MIGA's strengths compared to national and private providers of PRI is its membership of the World Bank, which allows it to intervene with host governments to resolve claims before they are filed.

As of the time of writing, it is unclear whether the multilateral NDB operated by the BRICS consortium of states will offer PRI as an aid to development along the lines of MIGA, although it is likely that this will be the case given the NDB's stated objectives and its broadly similar focus to the World Bank. Whether any PRI schemes available through this new multilateral organization will differ substantially from those of MIGA is probably less likely, but its smaller membership will mean that, at least for now, any NDB PRI products will be available for projects in fewer countries.

11.3.3 Regional Development Bank Providers

There are a number of regional development banks which offer insurance policies to investors for the purposes of offsetting political risks for investors in eligible countries. These PRI products are similar to MIGA except that they are targeted at particular regions and have an institutional structure that has expertise in that particular region. This is one reason why such organizations often claim to be preferable to those of the World Bank, which does not purport to have regional expertise. The regional development banks tend to insure the same types of projects as MIGA; those with a development purpose and which are focused on risks like expropriation or currency restriction.

To take a few examples of regional providers, the Asian Development Bank's PRI policies cover the standard kind of political risks: expropriation; political violence; and contractual disputes including the denial of justice in judicial or administrative proceedings. Policies are normally extended in financial services investment or infrastructure investments. Its PRI policies may cover a maximum of 40 per cent of the project or US $400 million, whichever is less.[7] The African Development Bank does not offer PRI itself, but it financially supports the activities of the African Trade Insurance Agency, which does so.[8] The Inter-American Development Bank's PRI packages cover risks such as breach of contract guarantees; expropriation; and restrictions on currency convertibility. The available coverage extends up to 50 per cent of project costs or $150 million, whichever is less.[9]

11.3.4 Private Providers

PRI is also available from private financial institutions, such as ordinary insurance companies which offer insurance to a range of investors (and individual consumers) for many types of investments at commercial rates. These products are costed, typically along with a deductible, which reflects the level of perceived political risk associated with the project. As these providers aim to secure a profit rather than necessarily to assist in the development of host states or in augmenting the competitiveness of the covered firm, they tend to be less willing to tolerate risks. These companies screen their clients on the basis of assessments as to whether the claims payouts in the event of a risk crystallizing will be less than the premiums collected.

Given that private providers are motivated by profit rather than national policy interests, there are normally no special conditions on an investor's

---

[7] www.adb.org/.   [8] www.afdb.org/en/.
[9] www.iadb.org/en/inter-american-development-bank,2837.html.

eligibility to obtain the coverage. Private providers' policies and their prices can be individually tailored to the particular investor's project and the location they are locating in. However, somewhat paradoxically, since the projects insured by private providers tend to be of lower risk than those of public providers, the policies are often less expensive to the investors than those from public agents such as OPIC or MIGA. Private providers tend also to offer insurance for shorter periods than public ones, often for only a few years at a time, again a reflection of their risk aversion.[10] Some of the leading private providers of PRI include the major insurance companies such as Lloyd's of London, AIG and Zurich.

11.3.5 Effectiveness of PRI

The PRI provider and policy chosen by the investor depends on the investor's individual needs and circumstances. Investors who seek quick access to coverage and do not wish to be monitored for compliance with social and environmental standards, such as those discussed in Chapter 9, would likely prefer a PRI policy offered by a private company. On the other hand, a foreign investor who values the deterrent effect on interfering states represented by the World Bank's institutional backing may choose to be insured by MIGA. Investors can also potentially lower the cost of their PRI payments or deductibles by engaging strategically with host communities and host governments to reduce the probability of an investment loss.[11]

Irrespective of whether there are suitable PRI schemes available for investors, there remains much debate regarding its effectiveness in terms of encouraging FDI in high-risk places. Recent studies have shown that despite its apparent advantages to investors in terms of mitigating risk, PRI does not appear to be widely used by multinational enterprises. It is especially unpopular among investors from the developing world,[12] which, as was mentioned earlier, is becoming an increasing source of FDI, now accounting for more than a third of global FDI flows. The lack of uptake

---

[10] Nadakavukaren Schefer, *International Investment Law*, at 525.

[11] J. Water, 'A Comparative Analysis of Public and Private Political Risk Insurance Policies with Strategic Implications for Risk Mitigation' 25 *Duke Journal of International and Comparative Law* 361 (2015).

[12] P. M. Satyanand, 'How BRIC MNEs Deal with International Political Risk' *Columbia Perspectives on FDI* No. 22 (5 May 2010).

by these kinds of investors may be explained by the fact that investors from these countries are already accustomed to high levels of political risk within their own home states. It may also be because some emerging market companies are uncomfortable with the sustainability and other social policy goals associated with coverage from public providers such as MIGA and the regional development banks. A 2008 study showed that 30 per cent of FDI to the developing world is insured, whereas less than 5 per cent of global FDI is believed to be insured. This stark difference suggests that PRI does have a significant positive effect on the encouragement of FDI – investors are quite willing to use PRI when investing in high-risk areas.[13]

In addition to its uneven usage by foreign investors, there is a concern that PRI causes foreign investors to be less careful in terms of managing their operations abroad because they know that the insurance company is going to cover their losses. This could lead to a situation where the investor does not press the host state to fulfil their obligations under IIAs or investment contracts. This 'moral hazard', which is associated with all kinds of insurance, could in turn reduce the likelihood that the foreign investor's presence will help improve the host state's own internal governance practices. Disregarding political risks because of PRI backing could indirectly harm the international community's interest in accountable, rule-of-law abiding states. Expensive deductibles for PRI policies help in risk-sharing between the insured and the insurer, potentially offsetting this problem. This is a classic risk-sharing strategy that is intended to offset moral hazard. It should be noted that the existence of an IIA between the host state and the investor's home state may reduce the cost of PRI premiums as well as deductibles. This is because of the perception that such states are less likely to engage in harmful behaviour because they are exposed to claims in international arbitration.

11.4 Improvements in Domestic Governance

Certain host states may be more attractive as destinations of FDI as a consequence not only of their natural resources, low cost labour or untapped markets, but also because of their legal stability. Foreign investors may

---

[13] Nadakavukaren Shefer, *International Investment Law*, at 531.

be less inclined to feel there is a need for an IIA between their home country and the host state in which they are considering locating if that host state has a strong rule of law, particularly in the sphere of contract and property rights, along with robust institutions such as an independent judiciary and a democratically elected government that is accountable to its citizens. The study of multinational enterprises' major factors influencing locational decisions alluded to above found that 95 per cent of firms surveyed claimed that the quality of national laws is essential.[14] This is why improvements in domestic governance, as it is often generically termed, can operate as an alternative (or certainly as a complement) to international investment law. Generally speaking, stable liberal democracies represent lower risks to investors because, as these systems emphasize the primacy of the individual against unwarranted demands by the state, there is a decreased likelihood that the investor's property will be taken arbitrarily or that the investor will suffer targeted discrimination or other undue interferences with their commercial activities. Of course, the relative safety of states with a secure domestic legal environment is belied by the reality that many such states, such as the EU or the USA, continue to sign IIAs with each other, as evinced by the recent CETA and TPP.

While the quality of the domestic governance of most developed countries is reasonably well established and trusted by multinational enterprises around the world, developing and transitional economies often do not enjoy this reputation. Many developing countries, even liberal democratic ones, are probably perceived as being less secure than they actually are, possibly due to the legacies of civil unrest and in some cases meddling with foreign investors which may have happened decades earlier under a different regime. Signing an IIA is one way of remedying this situation. Another way is to earn the approval of an international organization which collects and disseminates data on the strength of individual countries' legal landscape from the perspective of a commercial entity considering overseas business opportunities. There are a number of influential studies which have been developed for this purpose, sending a crucial signal to potential investors.

Among the most well-known and respected of these is the World Bank's annual Doing Business report.[15] The Doing Business project, which was launched in 2002, gathers data on a wide range of metrics concerning

---

[14] *Risk and Return*, at 7.   [15] www.doingbusiness.org/reports.

the establishment and running of a business in each of the World Bank's 189 member countries, along with additional material on the regulations issued by sub-central governments and municipalities. The data now covers eleven objective indicators, including the state's laws on registering a business; obtaining permits and utilities; bringing a claim in a local court; securing credit; paying taxes; and dealing with insolvency. Together these are compiled into an 'ease of doing business' score, which then yields a global ranking. Singapore has ranked first overall in this objective metric for the last several years. It is perhaps unsurprising that the top rankings are almost always held by developed countries. The Doing Business report also indicates which countries have made the greatest improvements, which could act as a significant catalyst for foreign investment. India's recent jump of twelve places in the rankings was heavily promoted by the country's Prime Minister in efforts to augment inward FDI flows.

Another important report on the riskiness of host states to foreign investors is the World Justice Project's Rule of Law Index.[16] The World Justice Project was founded in 2006 as an initiative of the America Bar Association and has partners throughout the world. Based on forty-four factors, their now highly regarded Rule of Law Index considers the extent to which 102 countries in the world can be said to offer to individuals (including businesses) a system of governance that is accountable and transparent as well as fair and effective. The assessment includes data on the process through which laws are made and administered as well as how they are enforced through courts. The absence of corruption is one of the key components of a high score on the Rule of Law Index. In the most recent report, Denmark and Norway ranked first in the index, with Venezuela in last place.

11.5 Incentives

As highly mobile multinational enterprises can pick and choose among various states in which they wish to locate, there is often an intense competition among host states to entice foreign firms. Many countries eager to attract foreign capital offer incentives to foreign firms to win this battle.

---

[16] http://worldjusticeproject.org/rule-of-law-index.

Maintaining a stable legal environment and signing IIAs may be one way, but given that many countries around the world have succeeded in employing both these strategies, direct financial inducements may be necessary. The most common incentive to draw in foreign investment is probably relief on taxation. There can also be grants for research and development as well as access to tariff-free zones or use of subsidized infrastructure. The signing of an IIA is itself sometimes considered to be an incentive in that it guarantees that the host state will avoid certain types of harmful behaviour and also grants access to specialized dispute settlement which is not available to local firms.

In many instances, such incentives can be harmful to the host state as the government ends up surrendering more to the investor than it gains in FDI and associated benefits. Indeed, many commentators agree that the offering of incentives is a dangerous 'prisoner's dilemma' in which foreign investors compel countries to compete against each other to furnish ever higher incentives, without any measurable advancement. Successfully outbidding a competing host state may be seen as somewhat of a winner's curse, in which the host state overspends to attract a firm that may have invested within their territory anyway. Despite these very real risks to host states, investment incentives are barely regulated under international law. Some treaties, such as NAFTA, require that state parties cannot weaken certain laws in order to attract foreign investments,[17] but these provisions are quite limited and say nothing about financial incentives such as tax breaks or tariff exemptions. The WTO Agreement on Subsidies and Countervailing Measures controls the use of subsidies on traded goods, but its primary aim is to restrict assistance to domestic firms, not foreign ones. A few countries have experimented with prohibitions on incentives, with the EU's regulation of state aid the most comprehensive and arguably most successful.[18]

From the perspective of host governments, one of the most dangerous aspects of investment incentives is the consequences of their removal and the ensuing effect on an investor's expectations. In the recent *Micula* v. *Romania* investment arbitration,[19] a tribunal found that the removal of a

---

[17] Art 1114.

[18] D. Collins, *Performance Requirements and Investment Incentives under International Economic Law* (Edward Elgar, 2015).

[19] ICSID Case No. ARB/05/20 (11 Dec 2013).

tax-based incentive that had been offered to a foreign investor operating a soft drink company amounted to the breach of the FET guarantee under the Romania–Sweden BIT. This was despite the fact that the incentive was terminated pursuant to the EU's framework prohibiting certain types of state aid. Somewhat bizarrely, in 2015 the European Commission stated that Romania's paying the arbitration award was itself a violation of EU state aid rules. While the impact of this decision may be narrower than realized because of the fact that the incentives were removed in a manner that was more harmful than it needed to be (there was delay and a lack of sufficient notice), the *Micula* case illustrates the danger of host states offering incentives which they may not be able to sustain in the long term. A number of investment arbitrations brought under IIAs are pending in both Europe and Canada regarding the removal of environmental incentives such as subsidies for renewable energy companies. If future tribunals decide these disputes in favour of the investors, it will surely cause many countries to think twice about any incentive packages they may wish to offer foreign firms.

11.6 Concluding Criticisms of International Investment Law

Having considered some of the alternatives to international investment law as tools for augmenting FDI, it is illustrative now to reflect upon some of the principal criticisms of international investment law. On the understanding that the above mentioned strategies do not always work, or do not work in isolation, the value of international investment law, as embodied primarily by IIAs, should be re-examined in light of its aims and shortcomings. In a sense the term 'criticism' is perhaps too strong. The themes below can be more accurately described as narratives or frameworks through which international investment law has been construed.

11.6.1 Fragmentation

There remains strident criticism that international investment law is unduly fragmented – that is, it is not internally coherent or sufficiently predictable as a distinct body of law or jurisprudence.[20] This is problematic

---

[20] J. Alvarez, *The Public International Law Regime Governing International Investment* (The Hague Academy of International Law, 2011), at 284.

for governments and investors seeking economic gain from FDI, and, as ever, for law students who tend to seek coherent and holistic solutions to the complex issues with which they are presented. For their part, lawyers who may complain about the law's incoherence are just as likely to reap the rewards of its uncertainty through the provision of advice in what has become an increasingly convoluted area of practice. Much of the debate regarding international investment law's congruity (or lack thereof) turns on the issue of whether international investment law should be viewed as a *lex specialis*, meaning a self-contained legal regime that exists in isolation of public international law, or if it should be understood in light of the broader corpus of international law, including contributions from fields such as human rights and environmental law. This tension is crystallized for example in the ongoing discussion of whether certain standards of protection common to IIAs (such as FET) are so well entrenched in practice that they have themselves attained the status of customary international law, obviating the need for their specific inclusion in treaties. It may also be seen in the suggestion that adherence to an international obligation enshrined in another treaty, such as one concerning environmental protection, should colour the commitments made by states in IIAs.

It would seem that the international investment law, embodied in many thousands of broadly consistent IIAs including the new mega-regionals like the TPP, is drifting away from customary international law in favour of a more literal existence tied to the wording found in specific instruments. This is problematic in light of the VCLT's pronouncement that treaties should be interpreted according to 'any relevant rules of international law applicable to the relations between the parties'. Indeed it is not unheard of for an investment arbitration tribunal to ignore customary international law or other international law regimes when rendering their decisions. It could legitimately be asked by an arbitrator or lawyer – why bother resorting to vague principles where there are bright line standards available? It is not clear that modern investment arbitrators see themselves as adjudicators of international law at all, despite the ICJ Statute's reference to international courts and tribunals as a subsidiary source of international law.

The lack of a doctrine of precedent along with the narrow ICSID annulment process, in which annulment committees are able to severely criticize a tribunal's decision without actually having the authority to reverse it, are seen as some of the contributing factors to the destabilized or fragmented nature of international investment law. It is not clear where exactly international investment law comes from if there is no central authority through which it is applied and thousands of treaties from which substantive legal principles are derived. The need for the security and congruity of an additional layer of legal scrutiny imbued with a higher interpretive authority can be seen in the new investment court systems in the EU–Vietnam FTA and in the proposed TTIP, alluded to in Chapter 7. The hierarchy of an appellate court of international investment may offer a partial solution to issues such as the inconsistent rulings in the Argentine as well as other perennial controversies such as the scope of an MFN provision and the nature of public interest for the purpose of legitimizing an indirect expropriation. Differences in interpretation among varying tribunals, for example as to the effect of an umbrella clause, have led to a dangerous discontinuity that has stirred discontent among investors and states, both of which had hoped that IIAs would instead provide the predictable legal rules which are essential for long-term relationships.

11.6.2 Imbalance

Much attention has been devoted to the need for so-called 'balance' in international investment law, meaning that there should be a more even weighting of obligations in IIAs placed on host states and on investors. To be otherwise, so the argument often goes, deprives international investment law of much of its legitimacy as any sphere of international law should purport to achieve a degree of fairness among parties. It is easy to find evidence to support the assertion of imbalance. This book has outlined the features of IIA which place obligations on host states including non-discrimination, FET, FPS, and guarantees against expropriation without compensation. Yet there are remarkably few, arguably none, which assign responsibilities to the investors. For many this is hypocritical, particularly given that these instruments are concluded precisely for the benefit of states. In order to legitimize IIAs it might seem just that these treaties allocated at least some duties to the foreign firms which benefit from them.

Attempts to 'rebalance' international investment law, as embodied by IIAs, have taken many forms. A focus on the preamble of treaties has led to suggestions that there is a duty on the part of investors to contribute to the development of host states. Ascribing this duty as a component of the definition of investment is one way of indirectly placing this obligation on firms – those which do not do so are not to be considered as investments at all and therefore they do not gain the protections afforded in the treaty. Broader Denial of Benefits provisions seen in some modern IIAs, typically referencing a certain level of connection to the host state, are another way of achieving this aim. Other methods of establishing duties on investors in IIAs include obliging state parties to recognize and enforce recognized CSR guidelines. In this way, home states may be able to use their national laws to curtail their investors' harmful behaviour towards host states. Of course, incorporating clear public interest exceptions in IIAs indirectly encourages foreign investors to take heed of these interests when conducting their activities.

Another more fundamental way of looking at this debate is to consider that, while unbalanced, IIAs do represent voluntary commitments of sovereign nations which should be respected regardless of their content, whether equitable or not. This claim is weakened by the counterpoint that there is also an imbalance in the bargaining power of the parties to many IIAs. Traditionally these treaties were concluded between wealthy capital-exporting industrial states and comparatively impoverished, developing ones. In other words, the rich states were never truly bearing any obligations under the treaty. Rather they were foisting them on the poorer states which have always been on the receiving end of FDI. In light of the fact that global trends in FDI flows appear to be drifting towards equilibrium, this criticism is less convincing. With a large portion of global FDI now coming from within the developing world, the states that had once been host states are now home states. Having signed many IIAs with other industrialized states, the USA and the Member States of the EU are now also very much host states. While the treaties themselves remain one-sided in favour of investors, their practical effects on global capital flows are therefore much more egalitarian than is often appreciated.[21]

It is also worth questioning the premise on which the allegation of lack of balance is based, namely that IIAs were never meant to apportion rights and obligations evenly.[22] These instruments were designed to foster

---

[21] See generally, D. Collins, *The BRIC States and Outward Foreign Direct Investment* (Oxford University Press, 2013).

[22] E.g. M. Paparinskis, 'International Investment Law and the European Union: A Reply to Catherine Titi' 26:3 *European Journal of International Law* 663 (2015).

international investment, not to dispense justice or serve some abstract notion of equality, if such a concept were even possible when the entities being compared are sovereign states and private firms. With the original purpose of IIAs carefully in mind, observers should perhaps be cautious of criticizing investment tribunals for failing to interpret their provisions through the lens of fairness or balance. These instruments are unbalanced for a reason and this should not be dismissed by appealing to indefinite, philosophical norms.

11.6.3 Extension

International investment law is certainly open to the allegation that it has encroached on matters that are beyond its originally intended purview. The undue extension of international investment law is of course a matter of interpretation, but it is not easy to see how laws aimed at protecting the environment should face challenge under instruments which have as their purpose the increase of FDI flows and the promotion of economic cooperation between party states. Surely international investment law, as applied by investor–state dispute settlement tribunals, was never intended to make pronouncements about environmental protection, or a range of other social concerns such as culture or human rights. This debate becomes somewhat more muddled when one considers the crossover between international investment issues and other international economic matters, such as trade, competition, IP or taxation.

Considering for a moment the potential intrusion of international investment law into the scope of international trade, a number of trade-based disputes have been framed as investment ones by claimants in order to access the investor–state dispute settlement regime found in IIAs, rather than forcing parties to rely on state-to-state mechanisms such as that of the WTO.[23] Unlike dispute settlement under IIAs, the WTO Dispute Settlement System does not provide direct access to private firms, nor does it offer the possibility of monetary compensation. As such it is not difficult to see why aggrieved traders focus on the investment-orientated elements of their disputes when seeking relief under international law. Investment

---

[23] Such as the series of cases brought under NAFTA regarding corn syrup producers: e.g. *Tate & Lyle* v. *Mexico*, ICSID Case No. ARB(AF)/04/05 (21 Nov 2007).

tribunals so constituted must consider their own jurisdiction over these matters judiciously.

One wonders also whether the competition-based tests for discrimination contained in the National Treatment standard do not also represent an overly ambitious widening of international investment law. Many National Treatment cases brought under NAFTA rely heavily on assessments of equality of competitive conditions and other economic tests to ground determinations of likeness between domestic and foreign firms. When performed by investment tribunals this analysis is often superficial and vague, often weakly pointing to WTO case law as a justification.[24] Perhaps these types of assessments should be made by national competition tribunals applying domestic law rather than by international tribunals composed of arbitrators who may or may not grasp the economic nuances of competition principles in each jurisdiction. This may be particularly advisable where the states involved are highly developed and have sophisticated internal machinery for dealing with specialized claims.

One of the most commonly asserted inappropriate extensions of international investment law relates to taxation issues. Most IIAs exclude taxation from their scope of coverage, suggesting that this sphere of activity was never intended to form part of the discipline. However this has not prevented investors from bringing tax-orientated claims against host states under these treaties' investor–state dispute settlement mechanisms. Clearly the imposition of taxes can constitute a form of indirect expropriation as well as a breach of the FET standard. For example, in *Vodafone* v. *India*,[25] the investor brought a claim against the Indian government on the basis that its tax demands constituted indirect expropriation. Vodafone had been ordered to pay tax because it had structured its business using offshore companies, allowing it to escape capital gains tax in India. Likewise, a number of cases were brought by US agricultural companies against Mexico for its imposition of taxes on soft drinks which contained high fructose corn syrup.[26] The taxes had been imposed in order to help control Mexico's obesity epidemic, again raising the related issue of whether international investment law was ever meant to encroach on

---

[24] Collins, *Performance Requirements and Investment Incentives*, Chapter 2.
[25] UNCITRAL, 17 April 2014.
[26] E.g. *Cargill* v. *Mexico*, ICSID Case No. ARB(AF)/05/2 (18 Sept 2009).

a state's capacity to regulate in the interests of public health. The removal of tax-based incentives as breaches of the FET standard of IIAs, such as occurred in the *Micula* decision noted above, is poised to become an entirely new species of claim in international investment law, which calls into question the notion that taxation has indeed been carved out of many IIAs at all.

11.6.4 Re-Constitutionalization

One of the more compelling claims that have been levied against international investment law in recent times is the description of the network of IIAs as interpreted and applied by international arbitration tribunals as a kind of 're-constitutionalization' of host states. Put more bluntly, this theory suggests that investment treaties are being used by well-resourced multinational enterprises (as represented by the wealthy states from which they originate) effectively to rewrite the constitutions of capital-importing states. This theory is cast in negative terms – host states are being forced to restructure their own constitutions against their will, or else they will be left behind when it comes to attracting FDI, which is essential to their development. The sovereign powers which are manifest in the capacity to regulate the economy have been stripped away in favour of the narrow commercial interests of corporate actors. At a fundamental level, so the argument goes, IIAs were designed to function without the political involvement of either host or home governments but as standalone guarantees to be instigated at the behest of the investors at their will. In some respects, enlarging the defence of necessity as well as exceptions such as national security and economic emergency (as well as potentially the other ones such as culture and human rights) coupled with an attenuated view of indirect expropriation and of the effect of umbrella clauses, could be depicted as a backlash against this loss of state autonomy.

At the most general level, sovereign states possess the constitutional power to readjust the relationship between private interests and the public interest. Indeed this is what it means to be an autonomous nation. States have the constitutional duty to allocate costs and benefits across society in their perpetual quest to fulfil the public good, which may take the form of increased foreign investment but will also include regulations that are antithetical to it. In that sense, laws are always being created that benefit one section of the population at the expense of another. Investors may suffer for the public good when this is necessary. The legitimate power to harm constitutes a fundamental aspect of statehood, yet through a redefinition of the scope and limits of the rules under which states may face liability, IIAs appear to be creating a new body of law that surpasses domestic constitutional law within the state's own territory. Since IIAs delegate jurisdiction of a constitutional character to international arbitration tribunals, constitutional jurisdiction can no longer be found exclusively in domestic courts. The constitutions of host states no longer furnish a comprehensive regulatory framework for the state to implement of its own accord.

It is clear that a vast array of regulatory actions of countries around the world is now susceptible to direct challenge by investment arbitration tribunals. These include measures relating to taxation, the revocation of licences, environmental protection, economic emergency, and the termination of contracts and incentive regimes. Modern international investment law, some argue, has consequently supplanted domestic administrative law in its authority to evaluate the exercise of these vital governmental powers.[27] The effect of IIAs on the administrative powers of host states is so significant because, as has been demonstrated throughout this book, international investment law (including IIAs) does not always establish concrete rules. There are many highly indeterminate standards which suffer from multiple interpretations by arbitration tribunals. This process, which often takes place in private with limited public participation, effectively converts investor–state dispute settlement into what might be seen as a system of global governance.[28] Whether for good or ill, this may be seen as an illegitimate usurpation of power.

A plausible solution to the re-constitutionalization dilemma may then be to focus on the process of investment arbitration at the heart of the criticism rather than on the substantive contents of the IIAs which have, for better or worse, been lawfully consented to by sovereign states which are notionally equal under international law. Enhanced public participation, an appointed roster of judges rather than privately selected arbitrators and a possibility of appeal to a higher court, as recently proposed

---

[27] D. Kalderimis, 'Investment Treaty Arbitration as Global Administrative Law' in C. Brown and K. Miles (eds.), *Evolution in Investment Treaty Law and Arbitration* (Cambridge University Press, 2011).

[28] See generally, D. Schneiderman, *Constitutionalization Economic Globalization* (Cambridge University Press, 2008).

in new IIAs, could be seen as a step in the right direction. While such improvements would not shift the decision-making authority over foreign investment back to domestic constitutional courts where some might argue it should be given the broad impact of many of the decisions, it would add a layer of legitimacy to the inevitable re-constitutionalization process associated with international dispute settlement. If surrendering constitutional authority to the international sphere is an undeniable component of a system of law which safeguards international investors' rights across borders for the ultimate purpose of economic prosperity for all (or most), such a system may be the best that can be expected.

11.7 Conclusion

International investment law is not the only way in which investors can seek to mitigate the risks associated with their foreign projects, whether perceived or real. PRI policies, while still relatively unpopular among multinational firms, can be useful tools for offsetting the dangers of unrest in host states, providing guarantees for actions such as expropriations and breach of contract. For their part, host states may make themselves more attractive to foreign investors by improving their own domestic governance, especially as it relates to business activities. Moving up the rankings in respected metrics like the World Bank's Doing Business report can signal such achievements, much as IIAs do themselves. Host states can also offer investment incentives, such as tax relief, although this strategy has questionable effectiveness and may pose the risk of claims should these policies be terminated prematurely.

Having evaluated the alternatives to international investment law, it is perhaps appropriate to reconsider some of the underlying criticisms of the regime that has been the focus of this book. International investment law has been described as fragmented and by implication incoherent and unpredictable, undermining its effectiveness for countries and firms. Some have accused it of being unbalanced and unfair because it places obligations only on states and not investors, who enjoy all of the system's rights without shouldering any of its burdens. At times international investment law appears to have overextended itself, reaching beyond its designated purpose and encroaching on public interest concerns as well as into spheres of which it has little competence or role, such as competition and taxation. Finally and perhaps most overarching of all, international investment law has been equated with a system of illegitimate global governance which has, through its far-reaching investor–state dispute settlement procedure, usurped the constitutional function of sovereign states and their courts. Each of these criticisms is intriguing and certainly contains elements of validity as well as thoughtful, if artful, overstatement. It is difficult to resist the suggestion, however, that many of these allegations are rooted in an anti-capitalistic ideology. One of the main purposes of any system of law is to control the excesses of government in order to safeguard the interests of individuals, a role which critics of international investment law appear to ignore once the individual in question has a commercial character, as if the upholding of liberty against tyranny is somehow inapplicable whenever profit-making is involved. As far back as the Phoenicians, business people have also been vulnerable to the whims of the rulers. What is more obviously true is that international investment law remains one of the most vibrant and exciting fields of international law, and is poised to become even more so in the decades to come.

Bibliography

Adlung, R. and M. Roy, 'Turning Hills Into Mountains? Current Commitments Under the General Agreement on Trade in Services and Prospects for Change' 39:6 *Journal of World Trade* 1161 (2005).

Aharoni, Y., 'Reflections on Multinational Enterprises in a Globally Interdependent World Economy' in K. Sauvant et al. (eds.), *Foreign Direct Investment from Emerging Markets* (Palgrave MacMillan, 2010).

Alvik, I., *Contracting With Sovereignty: State Contracts and International Arbitration* (Hart, 2011).

Alvarez, J., 'Political Protectionism and the United States' International Investment Obligations in Conflict: The Hazards of Exon-Florio' 30 *Virginia Journal of International Law* 1 (1989).

  The Public International Law Regime Governing International Investment (The Hague Academy of International Law, 2011).

Amerasinghe, C. F., 'Assessment of Compensation for Expropriated Foreign Property: Three Critical Problems' in R. St John Macdonald (ed.), *Essays in Honour of Wang Tieya* (Martinus Nijhoff, 1994).

Berger, A., *Developing Countries and the Future of the International Investment Regime* (German Federal Ministry of Economic Cooperation and Development, December 2015).

Beugelsdijk, S. et al., *International Economics and Business* (2nd edn, Cambridge University Press, 2013).

Borchard, E., 'Minimum Standard of Treatment of Aliens' 38:4 *Michigan Law Review* 445 (1940).

Kapossy, B. and R. Whitmore (eds.), *The Law of Nations or the Principles of Natural Law* (Indianapolis Liberty Fund, 2008).

Brahm, L., 'A New Global Financial Architecture Emerges' *Institutional Investor* (22 December 2015).

Brown, D. et al., 'The Effects of Multinational Production on Wages and Working Conditions in Developing Countries' *National Bureau of Economic Research*, Working Paper no. 9669 (May 2003).

Brownlie, I., *Principles of Public International Law* (Oxford University Press, 2008).

Brunnee, J. and J. Toope, 'A Hesitant Embrace: The Application of International Law by Canadian Courts' *Canadian Yearbook of International Law* (Volume 40) (2002).

Burgstaller, M., 'Sovereign Wealth Funds and International Investment Law' in C. Brown and K. Miles (eds.), *Evolution in Investment Treaty Law and Arbitration* (Cambridge University Press, 2011).

Burke-White, W. and A. von Staden, 'Investment Protection in Extraordinary Times: The Interpretation and Application of Non-Precluded Measures Provisions in Bilateral Investment Treaties' 48 *Virginia Journal of International Law* 307 (2008).

Christie, G., 'What Constitutes a Taking of Property under International Law?' 38 *The British Year Book of International Law* 338 (1962).

Collins, D., 'Applying the Full Protection and Security Standard of International Investment Law to Digital Assets' 12:2 *Journal of World Investment and Trade* 225 (2011).

The BRIC States and Outward Foreign Direct Investment (Oxford University Press, 2013).

'Environmental Impact Statements and Public Participation in International Investment Law' 7:2 *Manchester Journal of International Economic Law* 4 (2010).

'ICSID Annulment Committee: Too Much Discretion to the Chairman?' 30:4 *Journal of International Arbitration* 333–44 (2013).

'National Treatment in Emerging Market Investment Treaties' in A. Kamperman Sanders (ed.), *The National Treatment Principle in a EU and International Context* (Edward Elgar, 2014).

Performance Requirements and Investment Incentives under International Economic Law (Edward Elgar, 2015).

'Reliance Remedies at the International Centre for the Settlement of Investment Disputes' 29 *Northwestern Journal of International Law and Business* 101 (2009).

Coyle, J. F., 'The Treaty of Friendship, Commerce and Navigation in the Modern Era' 51 *Columbia Journal of Transnational Law* 302 (2013).

Crawford, J. (ed.), *The International Law Commission's Articles on State Responsibility: Introduction, Text and Commentaries* (Cambridge University Press, 2002).

Delimatsis, P., *International Trade in Services and Domestic Regulations* (Oxford University Press, 2007).

Desierto, D., 'Development as an International Right: Investment in the New Trade-Based IIAs' 3:2 *Trade Law and Development* (2011).

DiMascio, N. and J. Pauwelyn, 'Nondiscrimination in Trade and Investment Treaties: Worlds Apart or Two Sides of the Same Coin?' 102 *American Journal of International Law* 48 (2008).

Dolzer, R. and C. Schreuer, *Principles of International Investment Law* (Oxford University Press, 2012).

Dreher, A. and M. Gassebner, 'Do IMF and World Bank Programs Induce Government Crises? An Empirical Analysis' 66:2 *International Organization* 329 (2012).

Fauchauld, O., 'The Legal Reasoning of ICSID Tribunals – An Empirical Analysis' 19:2 *European Journal of International Law* 301 (2008).

Franck, S., 'The Legitimacy Crisis in Investment Treaty Arbitration: Privatizing Public International Law through Inconsistent Decisions' 73 *Fordham Law Review* (2004/05).

Friedman, M., *Capitalism and Freedom* (University of Chicago Press, 1962).

Gordon, K. and J. Pohl, 'Environmental Concerns in International Investment Agreements: A Survey' *OECD Working Papers on International Investment* (2011/01).

Gorg, H., E. Strobl, and F. Walsh, 'Why Do Foreign Owned Firms Pay More? The Role of On the Job Training' *IZA Discussion Paper* No. 590 (22 October 2004).

Grabowski, A., 'The Definition of Investment Under the ICSID Convention: A Defense of *Salini*' 15:1 *Chicago Journal of International Law* 287 (2014).

Graham, E., 'Will Emerging Markets Change Their Attitude Toward an International Investment Regime?' in K. Sauvant (ed.), *The Rise of Transnational Corporations from Emerging Markets* (Edward Elgar, 2008).

Grey, J., 'Ottawa's National Security Review a Warning to Foreign Investors' *The Globe and Mail* (Canada) 2 July 2015.

Grierson-Weiler, T. and I. Laird, 'Standards of Treatment' in P. Muchlinski and F. Ortino (eds.), *Oxford Handbook of International Investment Law* (Oxford University Press, 2008).

Griffiths, A. and S. Wall, *Applied Economics* (11th edn, Prentice Hall, 2007).

Grotius, H., *The Freedom of the Seas* (1608), Carnegie Endowment For International Peace, J. B. Scott (ed.) (Oxford University Press, 1916).

Han, X., 'The Application of the Principle of Proportionality in Tecmed v. Mexico' 6:3 *Chinese Journal of International Law* 635 (2007).

Harrison, A., 'Do Polluters Head Overseas? Testing the Pollution Haven Hypothesis' *ARE Update* (University of California Giannini Foundation of Agricultural Economics, 1 December 2002).

Henkels, C., 'Indirect Expropriation and the Right to Regulate' 15:1 *Journal of International Economic Law* 223 (2012).

Higgins, R., *The Path to Law* (Oxford University Press, 1994).

Howse R. and E. Chalamish, 'The Use and Abuse of WTO Law in Investor–state Arbitration: A Reply to Jürgen Kurtz' 20:4 *European Journal of International Law* 1087 (2010).

Jiangyu, W., 'Financial Liberalization and Regulation in East Asia: Lessons of the Financial Crisis and the Chinese Experience of Controlled Liberalization' 4:1 *Journal of World Trade* 211 (2007).

Kalderimis, D., 'Investment Treaty Arbitration as Global Administrative Law' in C. Brown and K. Miles (eds.), *Evolution in Investment Treaty Law and Arbitration* (Cambridge University Press, 2011).

Kingsbury, B. and S. Schill, 'Public Law Concepts to Balance Investors' Rights with State Regulatory Actions in the Public Interest – the Concept of Proportionality' in S. Schill (ed.), *International Investment Law and Comparative Public Law* (Oxford University Press, 2010).

Kurtz, J., 'The Merits and Limits of Comparativism: National Treatment in International Investment Law and the WTO' in S. Schill (ed.), *International Investment Law and Comparative Public Law* (Oxford University Press, 2010).

Lipstein, K., 'The Place of the Calvo Clause in International Law' 25 *British Yearbook of International Law* 130 (1945).

Locke, J., *Two Treaties of Government* (1690) (Yale University Press, 2003).

Lopez Escarcena, S., *Indirect Expropriation in International Law* (Edward Elgar, 2014).

McLachlan, C., L. Shore, and M. Weiniger, *International Investment Arbitration: Substantive Principles* (Oxford University Press, 2007).

Marboe, I., *Calculation of Compensation and Damages in International Investment Law* (Oxford University Press, 2009).

Montt, S., *State Liability in Investment Treaty Arbitration* (Hart, 2009).

Mosoti, V., 'Bilateral Investment Treaties and the Possibility of a Multilateral Framework on Investment at the WTO' 26 *Northwestern Journal of International Law and Business* 95 at 201 (2005–06).

Moss, C., 'Full Protection and Security' in A. Reinisch (ed.), *Standards of Investment Protection* (Oxford University Press, 2008).

Nadakavukaren Schefer, K., *International Investment Law* (Edward Elgar, 2013).

Neumayer, E. and L. Spess, 'Do Bilateral Investment Treaties Increase Foreign Direct Investment to Developing Countries?' in K. Sauvant and L. Sachs, *The Effect of Treaties on Foreign Direct Investment: Bilateral Investment Treaties, Double Taxation Treaties and Investment Flows* (Oxford University Press, 2009).

Newcombe, A. and L. Paradell, *The Law and Practice of Investment Treaties: Standards of Treatment* (Kluwer, 2009).

Paparinskis, M., 'International Investment Law and the European Union: A Reply to Catherine Titi' 26:3 *European Journal of International Law* 663 (2015).

The International Minimum Standard of Fair and Equitable Treatment (Oxford University Press, 2013).

Parish, M., A. Newlson, and C. Rosenberg, 'Awarding Moral Damages to Respondent States in Investment Arbitration' 29:1 *Berkeley Journal of International Law* 224 (2011).

Pilling, D., 'The "Anyone but China" Club Needs a Gatecrasher' *The Financial Times* (London) 7 October 2015.

Porterfield, M., 'An International Common Law of Investor Rights?' 27 *University of Pennsylvania Journal of International Economic Law* 79 (2006).

Poulsen, L., *Bounded Rationality and Economic Diplomacy: The Politics of Investment Treaties in Developing Countries* (Cambridge University Press, 2015).

Reinisch, A., 'Necessity in International Investment Arbitration: An Unnecessary Split of Opinions in Recent ICSID Cases?' 8 *Journal of World Investment & Trade* 191 (2007).

Sabahi, B., *Compensation and Restitution in Investor–State Arbitration: Principles and Practice* (Oxford University Press, 2011).

Salacuse, J., *The Law of Investment Treaties* (Oxford University Press, 2015).

Satyanand, P. M., 'How BRIC MNEs Deal with International Political Risk' *Columbia Perspectives on FDI* No. 22 (5 May 2010).

Sauvant, K. and L. Sachs, *The Effect of Treaties on Foreign Direct Investment: Bilateral Investment Treaties, Double Taxation Treaties and Investment Flows* (Oxford University Press, 2009).

Schill, S., 'Cross-Regime Harmonization through Proportionality Analysis: The Case of International Investment Law, the Law of State Immunity and Human Rights' 27 *ICSID Review* (2012).

   The Multilateralization of International Investment Law (Cambridge University Press, 2014).

Schneiderman, D., *Constitutionalizing Economic Globalization* (Cambridge University Press, 2008).

Schreuer, C., *The ICSID Convention: A Commentary* (Cambridge University Press, 2001).

   'Non-Pecuniary Remedies in ICSID Arbitration' 20:4 *Arbitration International* 325 (2004).

Shan, W., 'From North-South Divide to Public Private Partnership: Revival of the Calvo Doctrine and the Changing Landscape in International Investment Law' 27:3 *Northwestern Journal of International Law and Business* 631 (2007).

Shima, Y., 'The Policy Landscape for International Investment by Government-controlled Investors: A Fact Finding Survey' *OECD Working Papers on International Investment* (OECD Publishing, 2015/01), http://dx.doi.org/10.1787/5js7svp0jkns-en.

Sornarajah, M., *The International Law on Foreign Investment* (Cambridge University Press, 2010).

Subedi, S., *International Investment Law: Reconciling Policy and Principle* (Hart, 2008).

Titi, C., 'International Investment Law and the European Union: Towards a New Generation of International Investment Agreements' 26:3 *European Journal of International Law* (2015).

Tudor, I., *The Fair and Equitable Treatment Standard in the International Law of Foreign Investment* (Oxford University Press, 2008).

Vadi, V., 'When Cultures Collide: Foreign Direct Investment, Natural Resources and Indigenous Heritage in International Investment Law' 42 *Columbia Human Rights Law Review* 797 (2011).

Van Aaken, A., 'International Investment Law and Decentralized Targeted Sanctions: An Uneasy Relationship' *Columbia FDI Perspectives* No. 164 (4 January 2015).

Van den Bossche, P. and W. Zdouc, *The Law and Policy of the World Trade Organization* (Cambridge University Press, 2013).

Van Harten, G. and P. Malysheuski, 'Who Has Benefited Financially from Investment Treaty Arbitration? An Evaluation of the Size and Wealth of Claimants' *Osgoode Hall Law School Legal Studies Research Paper Series*, Research Paper no. 14, Vol 12:3 (2016).

Voon, T., *Cultural Products and the World Trade Organization* (Cambridge University Press, 2011).

Water, J., 'A Comparative Analysis of Public and Private Political Risk Insurance Policies with Strategic Implications for Risk Mitigation' 25 *Duke Journal of International and Comparative Law* 361 (2015).

Yackee, J. W., 'Bilateral Investment Treaties, Credible Commitment, and the Rule of (International) Law: Do BITs Promote Foreign Direct Investment?' 42:4 *Law and Society Review* 805 (2008).

Zampetti, A. B. and P. Sauve, 'International Investment' in A. Guzman and A. Sykes (eds.), *Research Handbook in International Economic Law* (Edward Elgar, 2007).

Index